iOS 15 Programming for Beginners

Sixth Edition

Kickstart your mobile app development journey
by building iOS apps with Swift 5.5 and Xcode 13

Ahmad Sahar

Craig Clayton

BIRMINGHAM—MUMBAI

iOS 15 Programming for Beginners
Sixth Edition

Group Product Manager: Rohit Rajkumar

Publishing Product Manager: Ashitosh Gupta

Senior Editor: Hayden Edwards

Content Development Editor: Aamir Ahmed

Technical Editor: Shubham Sharma

Copy Editor: Safis Editing

Project Coordinator: Kinjal Bari

Proofreader: Safis Editing

Indexer: Manju Arasan

Production Designer: Vijay Kamble

Marketing Coordinator: Elizabeth Varghese

First published: January 2017
Second Edition: January 2018
Third Edition: December 2018
Fourth Edition: January 2020
Fifth Edition: November 2020
Sixth Edition: December 2021

Production reference: 3090622

Published by Packt Publishing Ltd.
Livery Place
35 Livery Street
Birmingham
B3 2PB, UK.

ISBN 978-1-80181-124-8

www.packt.com

To my beloved wife, Oni.

– Ahmad Sahar

Contributors

About the authors

Ahmad Sahar is a trainer, presenter, and consultant at Tomafuwi Productions, specializing in conducting training courses for macOS and iOS, macOS Support Essentials certification courses, and iOS Development courses. He is a member of the DevCon iOS and MyCocoaHeads online communities in Malaysia, and has conducted presentations and talks for both groups. In his spare time, he likes building and programming LEGO Mindstorms robots.

Craig Clayton is a self-taught senior iOS engineer at Fan Reach, specializing in building mobile experiences for NBA, NHL, CHL, and NFL teams. He also volunteered as the organizer of the Suncoast iOS meetup group in the Tampa/St. Petersburg area for 3 years, preparing presentations and hands-on talks for this group and other groups in the community. He is launching a new site called Design To SwiftUI online, which specializes in teaching developers and designers how to build iOS apps from design to SwiftUI video courses.

About the reviewers

Ian Lockett is a skilled freelance mobile application developer based in the UK. With over 20 years' experience in the software industry, he has spent the last 12 years developing iOS and Android apps for a wide range of clients and industries from small startups to large enterprises. His major experience is in iOS development using both Swift and Objective-C and he has also created and maintained Android apps over the last two years using Kotlin. Ian prides himself on his attention to detail and delivering high-quality software. For the last three years, Ian has also been a volunteer co-organizer for the *Hacking with Swift Live* conference.

Juan Catalan is a software developer with more than 10 years of experience, having started learning iOS almost from the beginning. He has worked as a professional iOS developer in many industries including industrial automation, transportation, document management, fleet tracking, real estate, and financial services. Juan has contributed to more than 30 published apps, some of them with millions of users. He has a passion for software architecture, always looking for ways to write better code and optimize mobile apps.

Anoop Tomar has been in the tech industry for over 15 years with a demonstrated history of working in mobile, artificial intelligence, machine learning, computer visions, and full-stack engineering.

He is a co-founder of DevTechie.com with Neha Vishwakarma. DevTechie.com is an Ed-Tech company that promotes practical learning for anyone and everyone to learn to code and excel in a tech career. His combined published work includes 300+ videos on YouTube, 50+ video courses on Udemy, and 30+ articles on Medium with a focus on iOS, Swift, machine learning, and computer vision. In his free time, he enjoys reading about tech, building apps, traveling, and spending time with his family.

> *I thank my wife and daughter, who are my whole world. They are the loves of my life and a daily inspiration for me to do great things. I also thank my parents, who have always believed in me and helped me to pursue my passions. Special thanks to all the mentors, teachers, and friends who have stood by my side and supported me.*

Table of Contents

6

Functions and Closures

7

Classes, Structures, and Enumerations

8

Protocols, Extensions, and Error Handling

Part 2: Design

9

Setting Up the User Interface

10

Building Your User Interface

11

Finishing Up Your User Interface

12

Modifying and Configuring Cells

Part 3: Code

13

Getting Started with MVC and Collection Views

14

Getting Data into Collection Views

15

Getting Started with Table Views

16

Getting Started with MapKit

17

Getting Started with JSON Files

18

Displaying Data in a Static Table View

19

Getting Started with Custom UIControls

20

Getting Started with Cameras and Photo Libraries

21
Understanding Core Data

Part 4: Features

22
Getting Started with Mac Catalyst

23
Getting Started with SwiftUI

24

Getting Started with Swift Concurrency

25

Getting Started with SharePlay

26

Testing and Submitting Your App to the App Store

Index

Other Books You May Enjoy

Preface

Welcome to iOS 15 Programming for Beginners. This book is the sixth edition of the iOS Programming for Beginners series, and has been fully updated for iOS 15, macOS 12.0 Monterey, and Xcode 13.

In this book, you will build a restaurant reservation app called *Let's Eat*. You will start off by exploring Xcode, Apple's programming environment, also known as its **Integrated Development Environment (IDE)**. Next, you will start learning the foundations of Swift, the programming language used in iOS apps, and see how it is used to accomplish common programming tasks.

Once you have a solid foundation of using Swift, you will start creating the user interface of the *Let's Eat* app. During this process, you will work with storyboards and connect your app's scenes together using segues.

With your user interface complete, you will then add code to implement your app's functionality. To display your data in a grid, you will use collection views, and to display your data in a list, you will use table views. You will also look at how to add basic and custom annotations on to a map. You'll see how you can use JSON files to get actual restaurant data into your collection views, table views, and map. You'll enable users to add ratings, reviews and photos for a particular restaurant, which you'll save using Core Data.

You now have a complete app, but how about adding the latest iOS 15 features? You'll start by modifying your app to work on both iPhone and iPad, and make it work on Macs. Next, you will learn how to develop apps using SwiftUI, a great new way of developing apps for all Apple platforms. After that, you'll implement asynchronous and parallel programming using Swift Concurrency, and implement shared user experiences for your app using SharePlay.

Finally, you'll learn how to test your app with internal and external testers, and get it into the App Store.

Who this book is for

This book is for you if you are an experienced developer who is completely new to mobile application development for iOS and the Swift programming language. However, you'll also find this book useful if you're an iOS developer looking to explore the latest iOS 15 features.

What this book covers

Chapter 1, Getting Familiar with Xcode, takes you through a tour of Xcode and talks about all the different panes that you will use throughout the book.

Chapter 2, Simple Values and Types, deals with how values and types are implemented by the Swift language.

Chapter 3, Conditionals and Optionals, shows how `if` and `switch` statements are implemented, and how to implement variables that may or may not have a value.

Chapter 4, Range Operators and Loops, shows how to work with ranges and the different ways loops are implemented in Swift.

Chapter 5, Collection Types, covers the common collection types, which are arrays, dictionaries, and sets.

Chapter 6, Functions and Closures, covers how you can group instructions together using functions and closures.

Chapter 7, Classes, Structures, and Enumerations, talks about how complex objects containing state and behavior are represented in Swift.

Chapter 8, Protocols, Extensions, and Error Handling, talks about creating protocols complex data types can adopt, extending the capabilities of existing types, and how to handle errors in your code.

Chapter 9, Setting Up the User Interface, deals with creating the *Let's Eat* app, adding graphical assets, and setting up the initial screen the users will see.

Chapter 10, Building Your User Interface, covers setting up the main screen for the *Let's Eat* app.

Chapter 11, Finishing Up Your User Interface, covers setting up the remaining screens for the *Let's Eat* app.

Chapter 12, Modifying and Configuring Cells, is about customizing the table and collection view cells in a storyboard.

Chapter 13, Getting Started with MVC and Collection Views, concerns working with collection views and how you can use them to display a grid of items.

Chapter 14, Getting Data into Collection Views, concerns the incorporation of data into collection views.

Chapter 15, Getting Started with Table Views, teaches you how to work with table views and takes an in-depth look at dynamic table views.

Chapter 16, Getting Started with MapKit, deals with working with MapKit and adding annotations to a map. You will also create custom annotations for your map.

Chapter 17, Getting Started with JSON Files, involves learning how to use a data manager to read a JSON file and use the data inside your app.

Chapter 18, Displaying Data in a Static Table View, teaches you how to populate a static table view with data passed from one view controller to another using segues.

Chapter 19, Getting Started with Custom UIControls, takes a look at how to create your own custom views.

Chapter 20, Getting Started with the Cameras and Photo Libraries, talks about working with the device's camera and photo library.

Chapter 21, Understanding Core Data, covers the basics of using Core Data, and how to save reviews and restaurant photos.

Chapter 22, Getting Started with Mac Catalyst, deals with modifying your app to work well on the iPad's larger screen, and to make it work on a Mac.

Chapter 23, Getting Started with SwiftUI, is about building an app using Apple's new SwiftUI technology.

Chapter 24, Getting Started with Swift Concurrency, introduces you to the concepts of parallel and asynchronous programming, and shows you how you can implement it in your app.

Chapter 25, Getting Started with SharePlay, shows you how you can implement shared experiences for your users by using SharePlay and the Group Activities framework.

Chapter 26, Testing and Submitting Your App to the App Store, concerns how to test and submit your apps to the App Store.

To get the most out of this book

This book has been completely revised for iOS 15, macOS 12.0 Monterey, Xcode 13, and Swift 5.5. *Part 4* of this book also covers the latest technologies introduced by Apple during WWDC 2021, which are Mac Catalyst, SwiftUI, Swift Concurrency, and SharePlay.

To complete all the exercises in this book, you will need:

- A Mac computer running macOS 11 Big Sur or macOS 12.0 Monterey
- Xcode 13.0 or later

To check if your Mac supports macOS 12.0 Big Sur, see this link: `https://www.apple.com/macos/monterey/`. If your Mac is supported, you can update macOS using Software Update in System Preferences.

To get the latest version of Xcode, you can download it from the Mac App Store. Most of the exercises can be completed without an Apple Developer account and use the iOS Simulator. If you wish to test the app you are developing on an actual iOS device, you will need a free or paid Apple Developer account, and the following chapters require a paid Apple Developer account:

Chapter 25, Getting Started with SharePlay

Chapter 26, Testing and Submitting Your App to the App Store

Instructions on how to get a paid Apple Developer account are in *Chapter 26, Testing and Submitting Your App to the App Store.*

Download the example code files

You can download the example code files for this book from GitHub at `https://github.com/PacktPublishing/iOS-15-Programming-for-Beginners-Sixth-Edition`. If there's an update to the code, it will be updated in the GitHub repository.

We also have other code bundles from our rich catalog of books and videos available at `https://github.com/PacktPublishing/`. Check them out!

Code in Action

Visit the following link to check out videos of the code being run:

`https://bit.ly/3kdYBGc`

Download the color images

We also provide a PDF file that has color images of the screenshots/diagrams used in this book. You can download it here:

`https://static.packt-cdn.com/downloads/9781801811248_ColorImages.pdf`.

Conventions used

There are a number of text conventions used throughout this book.

`CodeInText`: Indicates code words in text, database table names, folder names, filenames, file extensions, pathnames, dummy URLs, user input, and Twitter handles. Here is an example: "So, this is a very simple function, named `serviceCharge()`."

A block of code is set as follows:

```
class ClassName {
    property1
    property2
    property3
    method1() {
        code
    }
    method2() {
        code
    }
}
```

When we wish to draw your attention to a particular part of a code block, the relevant lines or items are set in bold:

```
let cat = Animal()
cat.name = "Cat"
cat.sound = "Mew"
cat.numberOfLegs = 4
cat.breathesOxygen = true
print(cat.name)
```

Bold: Indicates a new term, an important word, or words that you see onscreen. For example, words in menus or dialog boxes appear in the text like this. Here is an example: "Launch **Xcode** and click **Create a new Xcode project**:"

> Tips or Important Notes
> appear like this.

Get in touch

Feedback from our readers is always welcome.

General feedback: If you have questions about any aspect of this book, mention the book title in the subject of your message and email us at customercare@packtpub.com.

Errata: Although we have taken every care to ensure the accuracy of our content, mistakes do happen. If you have found a mistake in this book, we would be grateful if you would report this to us. Please visit www.packtpub.com/support/errata, selecting your book, clicking on the Errata Submission Form link, and entering the details.

Piracy: If you come across any illegal copies of our works in any form on the Internet, we would be grateful if you would provide us with the location address or website name. Please contact us at copyright@packt.com with a link to the material.

If you are interested in becoming an author: If there is a topic that you have expertise in and you are interested in either writing or contributing to a book, please visit authors.packtpub.com.

Share Your Thoughts

Once you've read *iOS 15 Programming for Beginners Sixth Edition*, we'd love to hear your thoughts! Please click here to go straight to the Amazon review page for this book and share your feedback.

Your review is important to us and the tech community and will help us make sure we're delivering excellent quality content.

JOIN THE DISCUSSION!

The author of this book, Ahmad Sahar, will soon be hosting a Webinar for readers, and wants to hear from you.

We've set up a **Discord** server where you can get updates about the **Webinar**, as well as connect directly with Ahmad and meet other members of the iOS community.

Discuss this book, iOS development in general, and prepare for the conference!

Everyone is welcome to join, and we'd love for you to be a part of our new community.

To join, you can visit the below link or scan the QR code:

https://packt.link/iOSProgrammingforBeginners

www.packt.com

Part 1: Swift

Welcome to *Part 1* of this book. In this part, you will begin by exploring Xcode, Apple's programming environment, which is also known as the **Integrated Development Environment (IDE)**. After that, you will start learning the foundations of Swift 5, the programming language used in iOS apps, and see how it is used to accomplish common programming tasks.

This part comprises the following chapters:

- *Chapter 1, Getting Familiar with Xcode*
- *Chapter 2, Simple Values and Types*
- *Chapter 3, Conditionals and Optionals*
- *Chapter 4, Range Operators and Loops*
- *Chapter 5, Collection Types*
- *Chapter 6, Functions and Closures*
- *Chapter 7, Classes, Structures, and Enumerations*
- *Chapter 8, Protocols, Extensions, and Error Handling*

By the end of this part, you'll understand the process of creating an app and running it on a simulator or device, and you'll have a working knowledge of how to use the Swift programming language, in order to accomplish common programming tasks. This will prepare you for the next part and will also enable you to create your own Swift programs. Let's get started!

1
Getting Familiar with Xcode

Welcome to *iOS 15 Programming for Beginners*. I hope you will find this a useful introduction to creating and publishing iOS 15 apps on the App Store.

In this chapter, you'll learn how to download and install **Xcode** on your Mac. You'll familiarize yourself with the different parts of the Xcode user interface, and you'll create your first **iOS app** and run it in the **iOS simulator**. You will then learn how to connect an **iOS device** to Xcode via USB so that you can run the app on it, how to add an **Apple ID** to Xcode so the necessary digital certificates can be created and installed on your device, and how to trust the certificate on your device. Finally, you will learn how to connect to your device over Wi-Fi, so you no longer need to plug and unplug your device every time you want to run an app.

By the end of this chapter, you will know how to create and run apps on the iOS simulator or an iOS device, which you will need to do when you build your own apps.

The following topics will be covered:

- Downloading and installing Xcode from the App Store
- Understanding the Xcode user interface
- Running the app in the iOS simulator
- Using an iOS device for development

Technical requirements

To do the exercises for this chapter, you will need the following:

- An Apple Mac computer running macOS 11 Big Sur or macOS 12 Monterey
- An Apple ID (if you don't have one, you will create one in this chapter)
- Optionally, an iOS device running iOS 15

The Xcode project for this chapter is in the `Chapter01` folder of the code bundle for this book, which can be downloaded here:

`https://github.com/PacktPublishing/iOS-15-Programming-for-Beginners-Sixth-Edition`

Check out the following video to see the code in action:

`https://bit.ly/3wqcqpG`

You'll start by downloading Xcode, Apple's integrated development environment (IDE) for developing iOS apps from the App Store, in the next section.

> **Tip**
> The size of the download is very large (11.7 GB at the time of writing) so it may take a while to download. Ensure that you have enough disk space prior to downloading.

Downloading and installing Xcode from the App Store

Before you begin writing iOS apps, you need to download and install Xcode from the App Store. To do this, follow these steps:

1. Choose **App Store** from the **Apple** menu.
2. In the search field in the top-right corner, type `Xcode` and press the *Return* key.
3. You should see **Xcode** in the search results. Click **Get** and click **Install**.
4. If you have an Apple ID, type it in the **Apple ID** text box. If you don't have one, click the **Create Apple ID** button and follow the step-by-step instructions to create one:

Sign in to download from the App Store.

If you have an Apple ID, sign in with it here. If you have used the iTunes Store or iCloud, for example, you have an Apple ID. If you don't have an Apple ID, click Create Apple ID.

Apple ID: `example@icloud.com`

Forgot Apple ID or Password?

Create Apple ID   Cancel   Sign In

Figure 1.1: Apple ID creation dialog box

Important Information

You can see more information on how to create an Apple ID using this link: `https://support.apple.com/en-us/HT204316#appstore`.

---

5. Once Xcode has been installed, launch it. You should see the following **Welcome to Xcode** screen. Click **Create a new Xcode project** in the left-hand pane:

Figure 1.2: Welcome to Xcode screen

6. You will see the new project screen as follows. In the **Choose a template for your new project:** section, select **iOS**. Then choose **App** and click **Next**:

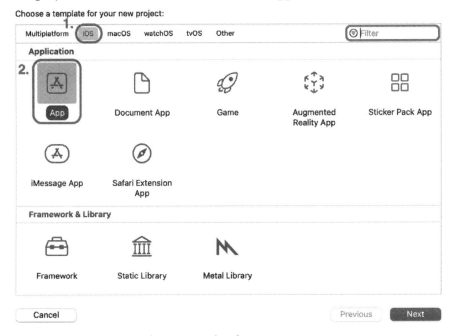

Figure 1.3: Choose a template for your new project screen

7. You will see the **Choose options for your new project:** screen:

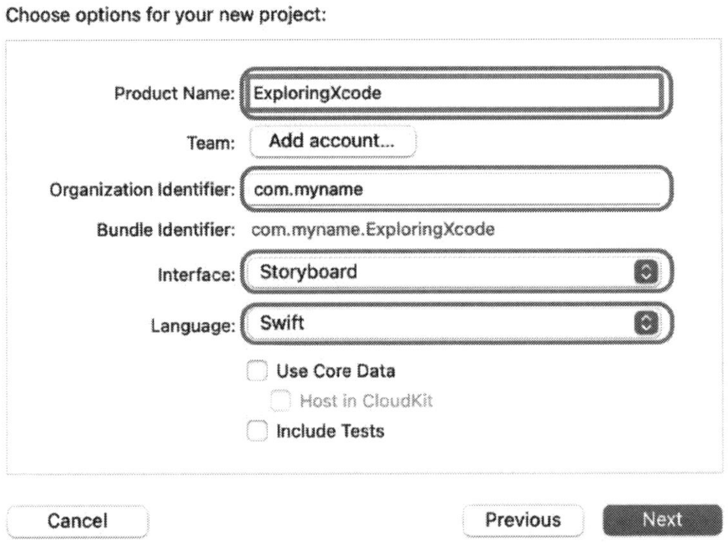

Figure 1.4: Choose options for your new project screen

Configure this options screen as follows:

- **Product Name**: The name of your app. Enter ExploringXcode in the text field.

- **Organization Identifier**: Used to create a unique identifier for your app on the App Store. Enter com.yourname for now. This is known as reverse domain name notation format, and is normally used here.

- **Interface**: The method used to create the user interface for your app. Set this to **Storyboard**.

- **Language**: The programming language to be used. Set this to **Swift**.

  Leave the other settings as their default values and make sure all the checkboxes are unticked. Click **Next** when done.

8. You'll see a **Save** dialog box. Choose a location to save your project, such as the **Desktop** or **Documents** folder, and click **Create**:

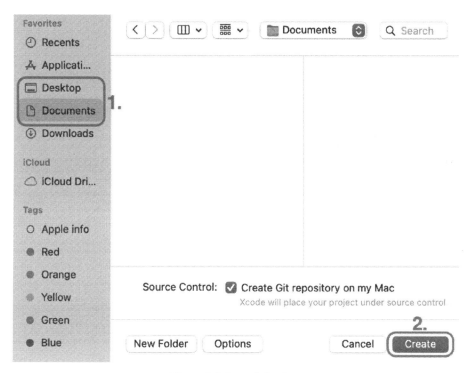

Figure 1.5: Save dialog box

9. If you see a dialog box saying **No author information was supplied by the version control system**, click **Fix**.

Important Information

The reason why you see this dialog box is because the **Source Control** checkbox is ticked. Apple recommends that Source Control be turned on. Source Control is outside the scope of this book but if you wish to learn more about version control and Git, see this link: `https://git-scm.com/video/what-is-version-control`.

10. You will see the **Source Control** preference screen as follows:

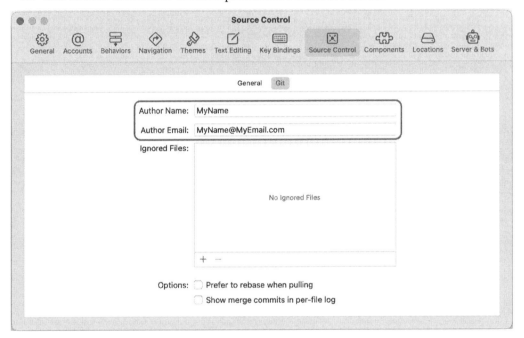

Figure 1.6: Source Control preference screen

Enter the following information:

- **Author Name:** – Your own name

- **Author Email:** – Your email address

Close the **Source Control** preference screen by clicking the red Close button in the top-left corner when done. The Xcode main window will appear.

Fantastic! You have now successfully downloaded and installed Xcode and created your first project. In the next section, you will learn about the Xcode user interface.

Understanding the Xcode user interface

You've just created your first Xcode project! As you can see, the Xcode user interface is divided into several distinct parts, as shown here:

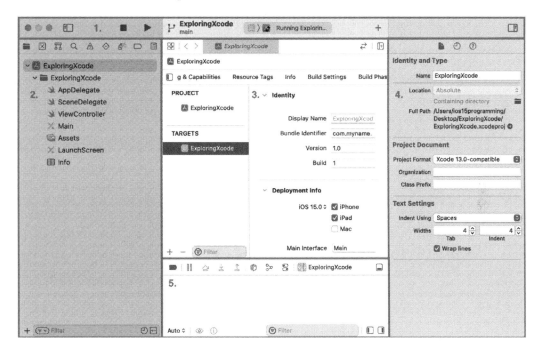

Figure 1.7: Xcode user interface

Let's look at each part in more detail. The following descriptions correspond to the numbers shown in the preceding screenshot:

- **Toolbar (1)** – Used to build and run your apps, and view the progress of running tasks.

- **Navigator area (2)** – Provides quick access to the various parts of your project. The **Project navigator** is displayed by default.

- **Editor area (3)** – Allows you to edit source code, user interfaces, and other resources.

- **Inspector area (4)** – Allows you to view and edit information about items selected in the Navigator area or Editor area.

- **Debug area (5)** – Contains the **debug bar**, the **variables view**, and the **Console**. The Debug area is toggled by typing *Shift + Command + Y*.

Next, let's examine the toolbar more closely. The left side of the toolbar is shown here:

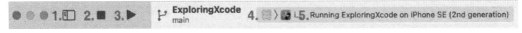

Figure 1.8: Xcode toolbar (left side)

Let's look at each part in more detail. The following description corresponds to the numbers shown in the preceding screenshot:

- **Navigator button (1)** – Toggles the Navigator area on and off.
- **Stop button (2)** – Only appears next to the **Play** button when the app is running. Stops the currently running app.
- **Play button (3)** – Used to build and run your app.
- **Scheme menu (4)** – Shows the specific scheme to build your project (**Exploring Xcode**) and the destination to run your app on (**iPhone SE (2nd generation)**).

  Schemes and destinations are distinct. Schemes specify the settings for building and running your project. Destinations specify installation locations for your app, and exist for physical devices and simulators.
- **Activity View (5)** - Displays the progress of running tasks.

The right side of the toolbar is shown here:

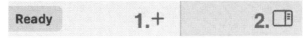

Figure 1.9: Xcode toolbar (right side)

Let's look at each part in more detail. The following description corresponds to the numbers shown in the preceding screenshot:

- **Library button (1)** – Displays user interface elements, code snippets, and other resources.
- **Inspector button (2)** – Toggles the Inspector area on and off.

Don't be overwhelmed by all the different parts, as you'll learn about them in more detail in later chapters. Now that you are familiar with the Xcode interface, you will run the app you just created in the iOS simulator, which displays a representation of your iOS device.

Running the app in the iOS simulator

The iOS simulator is installed when you install Xcode. It provides a simulated iOS device so that you can see what your app looks like and how it behaves, without needing a physical iOS device. It can model all the screen sizes and resolutions for both iPad and iPhone so you can test your app on multiple devices easily.

To run your app in the simulator, follow these steps:

1. Click the **Scheme** menu in the toolbar and you will see a list of simulators. Choose **iPhone SE (2nd generation)** from this menu:

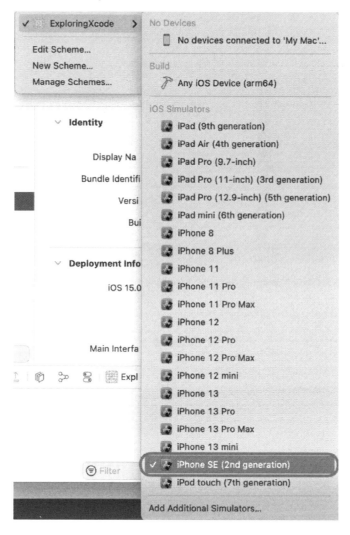

Figure 1.10: Xcode Scheme menu with iPhone SE (2nd generation) selected

2. Click the **Play** button to install and run your app on the currently selected simulator. You can also use the *Command + R* keyboard shortcut.

3. If you see the **Developer Tools Access** dialog box, enter the username and password of the Mac's administrator account, and click **Continue.**

4. The simulator will launch and show a representation of an iPhone SE (2nd generation). Your app displays a white screen, as you have not yet added anything to your project:

Figure 1.11: iOS Simulator

5. Switch back to Xcode and click on the **Stop** button (or press *Command + .*) to stop the currently running project.

You have just created and run your first iOS app in the simulator! Great job!

If you look at the **Scheme** menu, you may wonder what the **No Devices** and **Build** sections are for. Let's a look at them in the next section.

> **Important Information**
> If you are using an M1 Mac you will see **My Mac (Designed for iPad)** instead
> of **No Devices** in the **Scheme** menu.

Understanding the No Devices and Build sections

You learned how to choose a simulator in the **Scheme** menu to run your app in the
previous section. In addition to the list of simulators, the **Scheme** menu also has **No
Devices** and **Build** sections. These allow you to run apps on actual iOS devices, and
prepare apps for submission to the App Store.

Click the **Scheme** menu in the toolbar to see the **No Devices** and **Build** sections at the top
of the menu:

Figure 1.12: Xcode Scheme menu with Any iOS Device (arm64) selected

The **No Devices** section currently displays text stating **No devices connected to
'My Mac'...**, because you currently don't have any iOS devices connected to your
computer. If you were to plug in an iOS device, it would appear in this section, and you
would be able to run the apps you develop on it for testing. Running your apps on an
actual device is recommended as the simulator will not accurately reflect the performance
characteristics of an actual iOS device, and does not have some hardware features and
software APIs that actual devices have.

The **Build** section has only one menu item, **Any iOS Device (arm64)**. This is used when
you need to archive your app prior to submitting it to the App Store. You'll learn how to
do this in *Chapter 26, Testing and Submitting Your App to the App Store*.

Now let's see how to build and run your app on an actual iOS device. The vast majority of
the instructions in this book do not require you to have an iOS device though, so if you
don't have one, skip the next section and go straight to *Chapter 2, Simple Values and Types*.

Using an iOS device for development

Although you'll be able to go through most of the exercises in this book using the simulator, it is recommended to build and test your apps on an actual iOS device, as the simulator will not be able to simulate some hardware components and software APIs.

> **Important Information**
>
> For a comprehensive look at all the differences between the Simulator and an actual device, see this link: `https://help.apple.com/simulator/mac/current/#/devb0244142d`.

In addition to your device, you'll need an Apple ID or a paid Apple Developer account to build and run your app on your device. You'll use the same Apple ID that you used to download Xcode from the App Store for now. Follow these steps:

1. Use the cable that came with your iOS device to connect your device to your Mac, and make sure the iOS device is unlocked.

> **Tip**
>
> You can view connected devices by choosing **Window | Devices and Simulators** in the Xcode menu bar.

2. In the **Scheme** menu, choose your device (**iPhone** in this case) as the run destination:

Figure 1.13: Xcode Scheme menu with actual iOS device selected

3. Wait for Xcode to finish indexing and processing, which will take a while. Once complete, **Ready** will be displayed in the status window.

4. Run the project by clicking the **Play** button (or use *Command + R*). You will get the following error: **Signing for "Exploring Xcode" requires a development team.**:

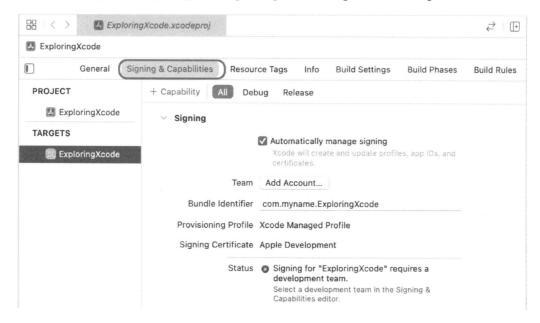

Figure 1.14: Xcode Signing & Capabilities pane

This is because a digital certificate is required to run the app on an iOS device, and you need to add an Apple ID or paid Apple Developer account to Xcode so the digital certificate can be generated.

> **Important Information**
>
> Using an Apple ID will allow you to test your app on an iOS device, but you will need a paid Apple Developer account to distribute apps on the App Store. You'll learn more about this in *Chapter 26, Testing and Submitting Your App to the App Store.*

> **Important Information**
>
> Certificates ensure that the only apps that run on your device are the ones you authorize. This helps to protect against malware. You can also learn more about them at this link: `https://help.apple.com/xcode/mac/current/#/dev60b6fbbc7`.

5.   Click the **Add Account...** button:

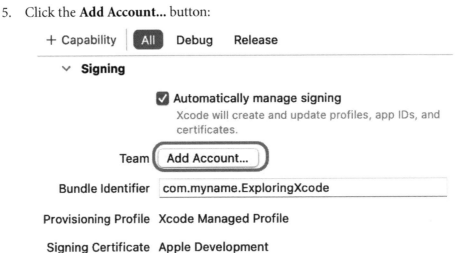

Figure 1.15: Xcode Signing & Capabilities pane with Add Account... button selected

6.   The Xcode **Preferences** window appears with the **Accounts** pane selected. Enter your **Apple ID** and click **Next**:

Figure 1.16: Apple ID sign in dialog box

> **Tip**
> You can also access Xcode preferences by choosing **Preferences** in the **Xcode** menu.

7.   Enter your password when prompted. After a few minutes, the **Accounts** pane will display your account settings:

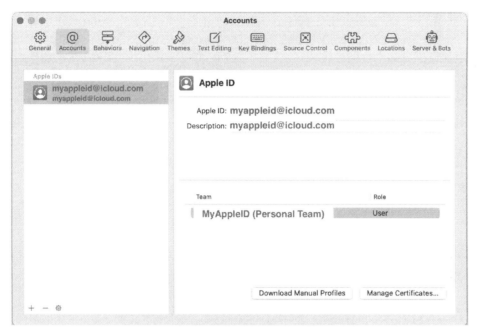

Figure 1.17: Accounts pane in Xcode preferences

8. Close the **Preferences** window when you're done by clicking the red Close button in the top-left corner.

9. In Xcode's Editor area, click **Signing & Capabilities**. Make sure **Automatically manage signing** is ticked and **Personal Team** is selected from the **Team** pop-up menu:

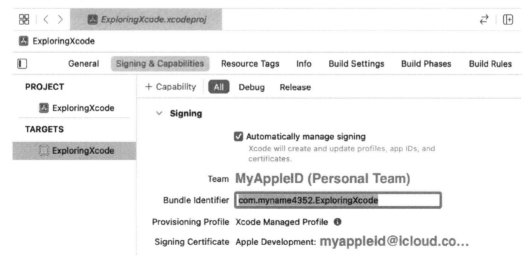

Figure 1.18: Xcode Signing & Capabilities pane with account set

10. If you still see errors in this screen, try changing your **Bundle Identifier** by typing some random characters into it, for example, com.myname4352. ExploringXcode.

11. Everything should work now when you build and run, and your app will be installed on your iOS device. However, it will not launch and you will see the following message:

Figure 1.19: Could not launch "ExploringXcode" dialog box

This means you need to trust the certificate that has been installed on your device. You'll learn how to do this in the next section.

Trusting the Developer App certificate on your iOS device

A **Developer App certificate** is a special file that gets installed on your iOS device along with your app. Before your app can run, you need to trust it. Follow these steps:

1. On your iOS device, tap **Settings** | **General** | **VPN & Device Management**:

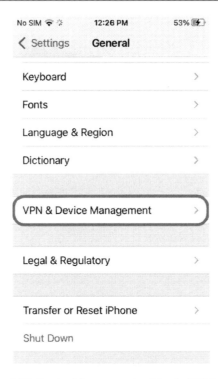

Figure 1.20: Device Management setting in iOS Settings

2. Tap **Apple Development**:

Figure 1.21: Apple Development section in Device Management settings

3. Tap **Trust "Apple Development: "**:

Trust "Apple Development: myapple...

Figure 1.22: Trust button

4.   Tap **Trust**:

Figure 1.23: Trust dialog box

5.   You should see the following text, which shows the app is now trusted:

Figure 1.24: Apple Development section with trusted certificate

6.   Click the **Play** button in Xcode to build and run again. You'll see your app launch and run on your iOS device.

Congratulations! Note that you have to connect your iOS device to your Mac using the cable to build and run your app. You'll learn how to connect to your device over Wi-Fi in the next section.

Connecting an iOS device wirelessly

Unplugging and replugging your iOS device to your Mac gets pretty cumbersome after a while, so you'll configure Xcode to connect to your iOS device over Wi-Fi now. Follow these steps:

1.   Make sure your iOS device is plugged into your Mac, and both the Mac and iOS device are on the same wireless network.

2. Choose **Window | Devices and Simulators** from the Xcode menu bar:

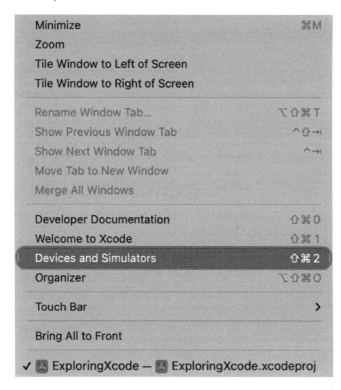

Figure 1.25: Xcode Window menu with Devices and Simulators selected

3. Click on the checkbox marked **Connect via network**:

Figure 1.26: Xcode Devices and Simulators Window with Connect via network checked

Awesome! Your iOS device is now connected wirelessly to Xcode, and you no longer need the USB cable to be connected to it.

Summary

In this chapter, you learned how to download and install Xcode on your Mac. You familiarized yourself with the different parts of the Xcode user interface. You created your first iOS app, selected a simulator, and built and ran the app. You learned what the **No Device** and **Generic iOS Device** menu items are for. This enables you to create and run iOS apps on your Mac without requiring an iOS device.

You learned how to connect an iOS device to Xcode via USB so that you can run the app on it. You added an Apple ID to Xcode so the necessary digital certificates can be created and installed on your device, and trusted the certificate on your device. This gives you the ability to run your apps on an actual device, so you can more accurately determine their performance, and make use of features not available in the iOS simulator.

Finally, you learned how to connect to your device over Wi-Fi, so you no longer need to plug and unplug your device every time you want to run an app. This makes it much more convenient to build and test your apps on an iOS device as any new builds can be transferred immediately over the air.

In the next chapter, you'll start exploring the Swift language using Swift Playgrounds, and learn how simple values and types are implemented in Swift.

Invitation to join us on Discord

Read this book alongside other iOS developers and the author Ahmad Sahar.

Ask questions, provide solutions to other readers, chat with the author via Ask Me Anything sessions and much more.

Scan the QR code or visit the link to join the community.

https://packt.link/iosdevelopment

2
Simple Values and Types

Now that you have had a short tour of Xcode, let's look at the Swift programming language.

First, you'll explore **Swift playgrounds**, an interactive environment where you can type in Swift code and have the results displayed immediately. Next, you'll study how Swift represents and stores various types of data. After that, you'll look at some cool Swift features such as **type inference** and **type safety**, which help you to write code more concisely and avoid common errors. Finally, you'll learn how to perform common operations on data and how to print messages to the Debug area to help you troubleshoot issues.

By the end of this chapter, you should be able to write simple programs that can store and process letters and numbers.

The following topics will be covered:

- Understanding Swift playgrounds
- Exploring data types
- Exploring constants and variables
- Understanding type inference and type safety
- Exploring operators
- Using the `print()` statement

> **Important Information**
>
> For more information about the latest version of the Swift language, visit `https://docs.swift.org/swift-book/`.

Technical requirements

To do the exercises for this chapter, you will need the following:

- An Apple Mac computer running macOS 11 Big Sur or macOS 12 Monterey
- Xcode 13 installed (refer to *Chapter 1*, *Getting Familiar with Xcode*, for instructions on how to install Xcode)

The Xcode playground for this chapter is in the `Chapter02` folder of the code bundle for this book, which can be downloaded here:

`https://github.com/PacktPublishing/iOS-15-Programming-for-Beginners-Sixth-Edition`

Check out the following video to see the code in action:

`https://bit.ly/3bTuizM`

In the next section, you'll create a new playground, where you can type in the code presented in this chapter.

Understanding Swift playgrounds

Playgrounds are interactive coding environments. You type code in the left-hand pane, and the results are displayed immediately in the right-hand pane. It's a great way to experiment with code and to explore system APIs.

> **Important Information**
>
> API is an acronym for Application Programming Interface. To learn more, visit this link: `https://en.wikipedia.org/wiki/API`.

Let's start by creating a new playground and examining its user interface. Follow these steps:

1. To create a playground, launch Xcode and choose **File** | **New** | **Playground...** from the Xcode menu bar:

Figure 2.1: Xcode menu bar with File | New | Playground... selected

2. The template screen appears. **iOS** should already be selected. Choose **Blank** and click **Next**:

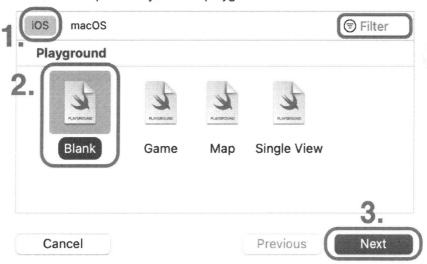

Figure 2.2: Choose a template for your new playground: screen

3. Name your playground `SimpleValues` and save it anywhere you like. Click **Create** when done:

Figure 2.3: Save dialog box

4. You should see the playground on the screen:

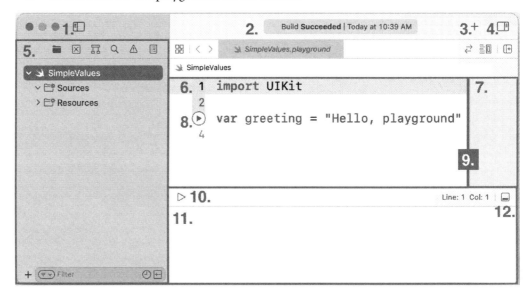

Figure 2.4: Xcode playground user interface

As you can see, it's much simpler than an Xcode project. Let's look at the interface in more detail:

- **Navigator button (1)** - Shows or hides the Navigator area.

- **Activity View (2)** - Shows the current operation or status.

- **Library button (3)** - Displays code snippets and other resources.

- **Inspector button (4)** - Shows or hides the **Inspector** area.

- **Navigator area (5)** - Provides quick access to various parts of your project. The Project navigator is displayed by default.

- **Editor area (6)** - You write code here.

- **Results area (7)** - Provides immediate feedback to the code you write.

- **Play button (8)** - Executes code from a selected line.

- **Border (9)** - This border separates the **Editor** and **Results** areas. If you find that the results displayed in the **Results** area are truncated, drag the border to the left to increase its size.

- **Play/Stop button (10)** - Executes or stops the execution of all code in the playground.

- **Debug area (11)** - Displays the results of the `print()` command.

- **Debug button (12)** - Shows and hides the **Debug** area.

You may find the code in the playground too small and hard to read. Let's see how to make it larger in the next section.

Customizing fonts and colors

Xcode has extensive customization options available. You can access them in the **Preferences...** menu. If you find that the text is small and hard to see, follow these steps:

1. Choose **Preferences...** from the **Xcode** menu to display the preferences window.

2. In the preferences window, click **Themes** and choose **Presentation (Light)** to make your code larger and easier to read:

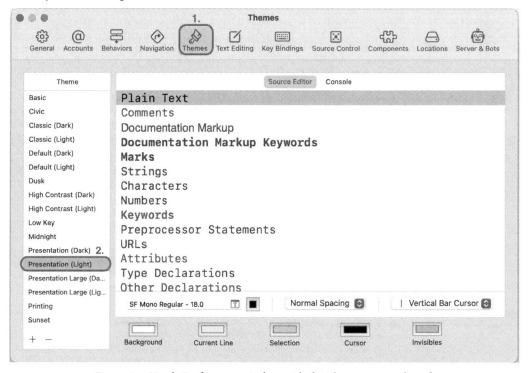

Figure 2.5: Xcode Preferences window with the Themes pane selected

3. Close the preferences window to return to the playground. Note that the text in the playground is larger than before. You can also try the other themes if you wish.

Now that you've customized the fonts and colors to your liking, let's see how to run code in a playground in the next section.

Running playground code

Your playground already has an instruction in it. To execute the instruction, follow these steps:

1. Click the **Play/Stop** button in the bottom-left corner of the playground. You may see the following dialog box:

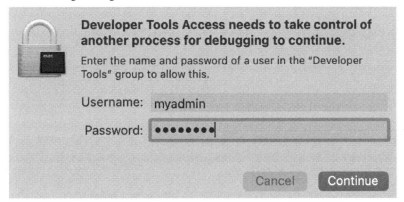

Figure 2.6: Developer Tools Access dialog box

2. Enter the **Username** and **Password** for your Mac's administrator account and click **Continue**. You will see "`Hello, playground`" displayed in the **Results** area:

Figure 2.7: Playground showing "Hello, playground" in the Results area

> **Tip**
> You can use the keyboard shortcut *Command + Shift + Return* to run the code in your Playground.

To prepare the playground for use in the remainder of this chapter, delete the `var greeting = "Hello, playground"` instruction from the playground. As you go along, type the code shown in this chapter into the playground, and if necessary, click the **Play/Stop** button to run it.

Let's dive into the simple data types used in Swift in the next section.

Exploring data types

All programming languages can store numbers, logic states, and words, and Swift is no different. Even if you're an experienced programmer, you may find that Swift represents these objects differently from other languages that you may be familiar with.

> **Important Information**
>
> For more information on data types, visit: `https://docs.swift.org/swift-book/LanguageGuide/TheBasics.html`.

Let's walk through the Swift versions of **integers**, **floating-point numbers**, **Booleans**, and **strings**, in the next sections.

Representing integers

Let's say you want to store the following:

- The number of restaurants in a city
- Passengers in an airplane
- Rooms in a hotel

You would use integers, which are numbers without a fractional component (including negative numbers).

Integers in Swift are represented by the `Int` type.

Representing floating-point numbers

Let's say you want to store the following:

- Pi (3.14159...)
- Absolute zero (-273.15 °C)

You would use floating-point numbers, which are numbers with a fractional component.

The default type for floating-point numbers in Swift is `Double`, which uses 64 bits, including negative numbers. You can also use `Float`, which uses 32 bits, but `Double` is preferred.

Representing Booleans

Let's say you want to store answers to simple yes/no questions, such as the following:

- Is it raining?

- Are there any available seats at the restaurant?

For this, you use Boolean values.

Swift provides a `Bool` type that can either be `true` or `false`.

Representing strings

Let's say you want to store the following:

- The name of a restaurant, such as "Bombay Palace"

- A job description, such as "Accountant" or "Programmer"

- A kind of fruit, such as "banana"

You would use Swift's `String` type, which represents a sequence of characters, and is fully Unicode-compliant. This makes it easy to represent different fonts and languages.

> **Important Information**
>
> To learn more about Unicode, visit this link: `https://home.unicode.org/basic-info/faq/`.

Now that you know how Swift represents these common data types, let's try them out in the playground you created earlier in the next section.

Using common data types in the playground

Anything that you type into a playground will be executed, and the results will appear in the **Results** area. Let's see what happens when you type in numbers, Boolean values, and strings into your playground and execute it. Follow these steps:

1. Type the following code into the **Editor** area of your playground:

```
// SimpleValues
42
-23

3.14159
```

```
0.1
-273.15

true
false

"hello, world"
"albatross"
```

Note that any word with // in front of it is a **comment**. Comments are a great way to create notes or reminders to yourself and will be ignored by Xcode.

2. Click the **Play/Stop** button to run your code.

3. Wait a few seconds. Xcode will evaluate your input and display results in the Results area, as follows:

```
42
-23

3.14159
0.1
-273.15

true
false

"hello, world"
"albatross"
```

Note that comments do not appear in the Results area.

Cool! You have just created and run your first playground. Let's look at how to store different data types in the next section.

Exploring constants and variables

Now that you know about the simple data types that Swift supports, let's look at how to store them, so you can perform operations on them later.

You can use **constants** or **variables** to store data. Both are containers that have a name, but a constant's value can only be set once and cannot be changed after it has been set, whereas a variable's value can be changed at any time.

You must declare constants and variables before you use them. Constants are declared with the `let` keyword whereas variables are declared with the `var` keyword.

Let's explore how constants and variables work by implementing them in your playground. Follow these steps:

1. Add the following code to your playground to declare three constants:

    ```
    let theAnswerToTheUltimateQuestion = 42
    let pi = 3.14159
    let myName = "Ahmad Sahar"
    ```

2. Click the **Play/Stop** button to run it.

    In each case, a container is created and named, and the assigned value stored.

    > **Tip**
    > You may have noticed that the names for constants and variables start with a lowercase letter, and if there is more than one word in the name, every subsequent word starts with a capital letter. This is known as **camel case**. You don't have to do this, but this is encouraged, as most experienced Swift programmers adhere to this convention.

    > **Important Information**
    > Note that a sequence of characters enclosed by double quotation marks, `"Ahmad Sahar"`, is used to assign the value for `myName`. These are known as **string literals**.

3. Add the following code after the constant declarations to declare three variables:

    ```
    var currentTemperatureInCelsius = 27
    var myAge = 50
    var myLocation = "home"
    ```

    Similar to constants, a container is created and named in each case, and the assigned value stored.

    > **Tip**
    > The stored values are displayed in the Results area.

4. The value of a constant can't be changed once it is set. To test this, add the following code after the variable declarations:

```
let isRaining = true
isRaining = false
```

As you're typing the second line of code, a pop-up menu will appear with suggestions:

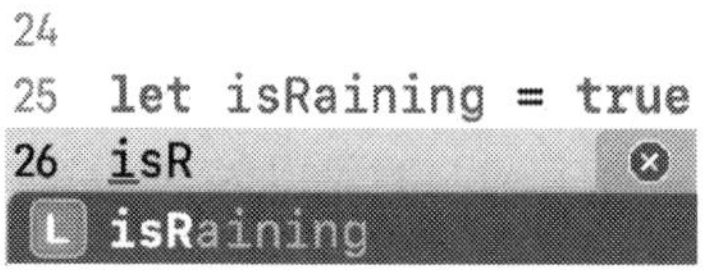

```
24
25  let isRaining = true
26  isR                        ⊗
    Ⓛ isRaining
```

Figure 2.8: Autocomplete pop-up menu

Use the up and down arrow keys to choose the isRaining constant and press the *Tab* key to select it. This feature is called **autocomplete** and helps to prevent typing mistakes when you're entering code.

5. When you have finished typing, wait a few seconds. On the second line, you should see a red circle with a white dot in the middle appear:

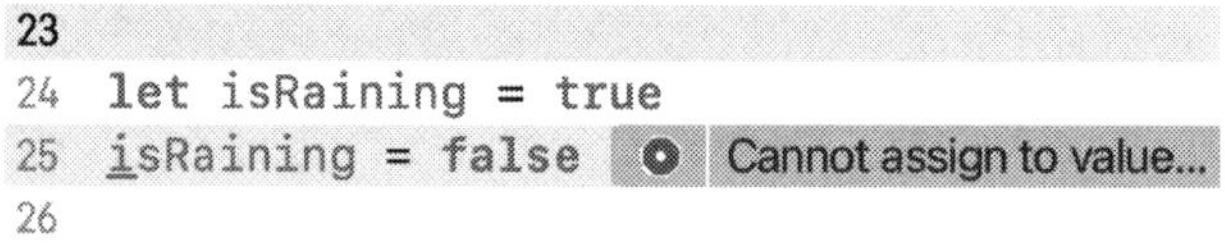

```
23
24  let isRaining = true
25  isRaining = false    ◉  Cannot assign to value...
26
```

Figure 2.9: Error notification

This means there is an error in your program, and Xcode thinks it can be fixed. The error appears because you are trying to assign a new value to a constant after its initial value has been set.

6. Click the red circle to expand the error message. You should see the following box with a **Fix** button:

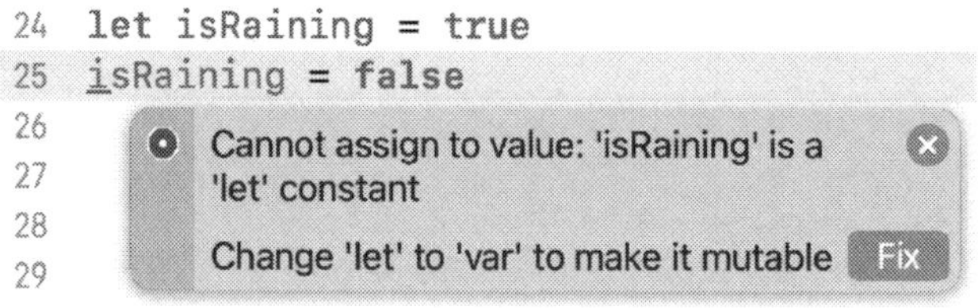

```
24  let isRaining = true
25  isRaining = false
26
27      ◉  Cannot assign to value: 'isRaining' is a    ⊗
28         'let' constant
29         Change 'let' to 'var' to make it mutable  [ Fix ]
```

Figure 2.10: Expanded error notification

Xcode tells you what the problem is (**Cannot assign to value: 'isRaining' is a 'let' constant**) and suggests a correction (**Change 'let' to 'var' to make it mutable**).

7. Click the **Fix** button.

8. You should see that the `isRaining` constant declaration has been changed to a variable declaration:

```
24
25  var isRaining = true
26  isRaining = false
27
```

Figure 2.11: Code with fix applied

Since a new value can be assigned to a variable after it has been created, the error is resolved. Do note, however, that the suggested correction might not be the best solution.

If you look at the code you typed in, you might be wondering how Xcode knows the type of data stored in a variable or constant. You'll learn about how that is done in the next section.

Understanding type inference and type safety

In the previous section, you declared constants and variables and assigned values to them. Swift automatically determines the constant or variable type based on the value you supplied. This is called **type inference**. You can see the type of a constant or variable by holding down the *Option* key and clicking its name. To see this in action, follow these steps:

1. Add the following code to your playground to declare a string:

```
let cuisine = "American"
```

2. Click the **Play/Stop** button to run it.

3. Hold down the *Option* key and click `cuisine` to reveal the constant type. You should see the following:

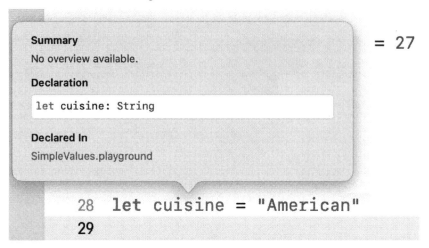

Figure 2.12: Type declaration pop-up

As you can see, `cuisine`'s type is `String`.

What if you want to set a specific type for a variable or constant? You'll see how to do that in the next section.

Using type annotation to specify a type

You've seen that Xcode tries to automatically determine the data type of a variable or constant based on the value provided. However, at times, you may wish to specify a type instead of letting Xcode do it for you. To do this, type a colon after a constant or variable name, followed by the desired type. This is known as **type annotation**.

Add the following code to your playground to declare a variable with a specific type, and click the **Play/Stop** button to run it:

```
var restaurantRating: Double = 3
```

Here, you specified `restaurantRating` has a specific type, `Double`. Even though you assigned an integer to `restaurantRating`, it will be stored as a floating-point number.

In the next section, you'll learn how Xcode helps you reduce the number of errors in your program by enforcing **type safety**.

Using type safety to check values

Swift is a type-safe language. It checks to see whether you're assigning values of the correct type to variables and flags mismatched types as errors. Let's see how this works by following these steps:

1. Add the following code to your playground to assign a string to
    `restaurantRating`:

    ```
    restaurantRating = "Good"
    ```

2. Click the **Play/Stop** button to run the code.

3. You should see a red circle with an **x** inside it. The exclamation mark means Xcode can't suggest a fix for this. Click on the red circle.

4. Since you are trying to assign a string to a variable of type `Double`, the following error message is displayed:

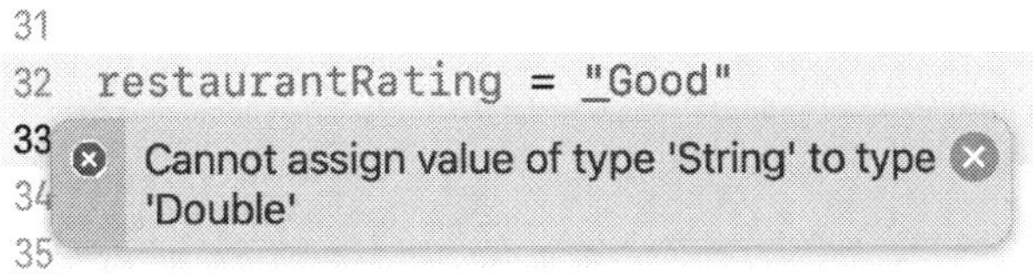

    ```
    31
    32  restaurantRating = "Good"
    33  ⊗  Cannot assign value of type 'String' to type  ⊗
    34       'Double'
    35
    ```

    Figure 2.13: Expanded error notification with no fix

5. Comment out the line by typing `//` before it as shown:

    ```
    // restaurantRating = "Good"
    ```

    The red circle disappears as there are no more errors in your program.

    > **Tip**
    > Selecting lines of code and typing *Command + /* will comment them out.

Now that you know how to store data in constants and variables, let's look at how to perform operations on them in the next section.

Exploring operators

You can perform arithmetic, comparison, and logical operations in Swift. **Arithmetic operators** are for common mathematical operations. **Comparison** and **logical operators** check an expression's value and return `true` or `false`.

> **Important Information**
>
> For more information on operators, visit `https://docs.swift.org/` `swift-book/LanguageGuide/BasicOperators.html`.

Let's look at each operator type in more detail. You'll start with arithmetic operators (addition, subtraction, multiplication, and division) in the next section.

Using arithmetic operators

You can perform mathematical operations on integer and floating-point numbers by using the standard arithmetic operators shown here:

+	Addition
-	Subtraction
*	Multiplication
/	Division

Figure 2.14: Arithmetic operators

Let's see how these operators are used. Follow these steps:

1. Add the following code to add arithmetic operations to your playground:

    ```
    let sum = 23 + 20
    let result = 32 - sum
    let total = result * 5
    let divide = total / 10
    ```

2. Click the **Play/Stop** button to run it.

    The results displayed in the Results area will be 43, -11, -55, and -5, respectively. Note that 55 divided by 10 returns 5 instead of 5.5, as both numbers are integers.

3. Operators can only work with operands of the same type. Enter the following code and run it to see what happens if the operands are of different types:

```
let a = 12
let b = 12.0
let c = a + b
```

You'll get an error message, **Binary operator '+' cannot be applied to operands of type 'Int' and 'Double'**. This is because a and b are different types. Note that Xcode can't fix this automatically, so it does not display any fix-it suggestions.

4. To fix the error, modify the program as follows:

```
let c = Double(a) + b
```

Double(a) gets the value stored in a and creates a floating-point number from it. Both operands are now of the same type, and now you can add the value in b to it. The value stored in c is 24.0, and 24 will be displayed in the Results area.

Now that you know how to use arithmetic operators, you'll look at compound assignment operators (+=, -=, *= and /=) in the next section.

Using compound assignment operators

You can perform an operation on a value and assign the result to a variable using compound assignment operators shown here:

+=	Adds a value and assigns the result to the variable
-=	Subtracts a value and assigns the result to the variable
*=	Multiplies with the value and assigns the result to the variable
/=	Divides with the value and assigns the result to the variable

Figure 2.15: Compound assignment operators

Let's see how these operators are used. Add the following code to your playground and click the **Play/Stop** button to run it:

```
var aa = 1
aa += 2
aa -= 1
```

The a += 2 expression is shorthand for a = a + 2, so the value in a is now 1 + 2, and 3 will be assigned to a. In the same way, a -= 1 is shorthand for a = a - 1, so the value in a is now 3 - 1, and 2 will be assigned to a.

Now that you are familiar with compound assignment operators, let's look at comparison operators (==, /=, >, <, >=, and <=) in the next section.

Using comparison operators

You can compare one value to another using comparison operators, and the result will be true or false. You can use the following comparison operators:

==	Equal to
!=	Not equal to
>	Greater than
<	Less than
>=	Greater than or equal to
<=	Less than or equal to

Figure 2.16: Comparison operators

Let's see how these operators are used. Add the following code to your playground and click the **Play/Stop** button to run it:

```
1 == 1
2 != 1
2 > 1
1 < 2
1 >= 1
2 <= 1
```

Let's see how this works:

- 1 == 1 returns true because 1 is equal to 1.

- 2 != 1 returns true because 2 is not equal to 1.

- 2 > 1 returns true because 2 is greater than 1.

- 1 < 2 returns true because 1 is less than 2.

- 1 >= 1 returns true because 1 is greater than or equal to 1.

- 2 <= 1 returns false because 2 is not less than or equal to 1.

The returned Boolean values will be displayed in the **Results** area.

What happens if you want to check more than one condition? That's where logical operators (**AND**, **OR** and **NOT**) come in. You'll study those in the next section.

Using logical operators

Logical operators are handy when you deal with two or more conditions. For example, if you are at a convenience store, you can pay for items if you have cash or a credit card. **OR** is the logical operator in this case.

You can use the following logical operators:

&&	Logical AND—returns `true` only if all conditions are true
||	Logical OR—returns `true` if any condition is true
!	Logical NOT—returns the opposite Boolean value

Figure 2.17: Logical operators

To see how these operators are used, add the following code to your playground and click the **Play/Stop** button to run it:

```
(1 == 1) && (2 == 2)
(1 == 1) && (2 != 2)
(1 == 1) || (2 == 2)
(1 == 1) || (2 != 2)
(1 != 1) || (2 != 2)
!(1 == 1)
```

Let's see how this works:

- `(1 == 1) && (2 == 2)` returns `true` as both operands are `true`, so `true` AND `true` returns `true`.

- `(1 == 1) && (2 != 2)` returns `false` as one operand is `false`, so `true` AND `false` returns `false`.

- `(1 == 1) || (2 == 2)` returns `true` as both operands are `true`, so `true` OR `true` returns `true`.

- `(1 == 1) || (2 != 2)` returns `true` as one operand is `true`, so `true` OR `false` returns `true`.

- (1 != 1) || (2 != 2) returns `false` as both operands are `false`, so `false` OR `false` returns `false`.

- !(1 == 1) returns `false` as `1==1` is `true`, so NOT `true` returns `false`.

The returned Boolean values will be displayed in the Results area.

So far, you've only worked with numbers. In the next section, you'll see how you can perform operations on words and sentences, which are stored as strings using Swift's `String` type.

Performing string operations

As you have seen earlier, a string is a series of characters. They are represented by the `String` type, and they are fully Unicode-compliant.

> **Important Information**
>
> For more information on strings, visit: `https://docs.swift.org/swift-book/LanguageGuide/StringsAndCharacters.html`.

Let's learn about some common string operations. Follow these steps:

1. You can join two strings together using the + operator. Add the following code to your playground and click the **Play/Stop** button to run it:

```
let greeting = "Good" + " Morning"
```

The values of the string literals `"Good"` and `" Morning"` are joined together and `"Good Morning"` is displayed in the Results area.

2. You can combine strings with constants and variables of other types by **casting** them as strings. Enter the following code and run it:

```
let rating = 3.5
var ratingResult = "The restaurant rating is " +
String(rating)
```

The `rating` constant contains `3.5`, a value of type `Double`. Putting `rating` in between the brackets of `String()` gets the value stored in `rating` and creates a new string based on it, `"3.5"`, which is combined with the string in the `ratingResult` variable, returning the string `"The restaurant rating is 3.5"`.

3. There is a simpler way of combining strings, called **string interpolation**. String interpolation is done by typing the name of a constant or variable between "\ (" and ") " in a string. Enter the following code and run it:

```
ratingResult = "The restaurant rating is \(rating)"
```

As in the previous example, the value in rating is used to create a new string, "3.5", returning the string "The restaurant rating is 3.5".

Thus far, you can see the results of your instructions in the Results area. However, when you're writing your app using Xcode, you won't have access to the Results area that you see in your playground. To display the contents of variables and constants while your program is running, you'll learn how to print them to the Debug area in the next section.

Using the print() statement

As you have seen in *Chapter 1, Getting Familiar with Xcode*, an Xcode project does not have a Results area that a playground has, but both project and playground have a Debug area. Using the print() statement will print anything between the brackets to the Debug area.

> **Important Information**
>
> The print() statement is a **function**. You'll learn more about functions in *Chapter 6, Functions and Closures*.

Add the following code to your playground and click the **Play/Stop** button to run it:

```
print(ratingResult)
```

You'll see the value of ratingResult appear in the Debug area:

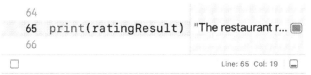

The restaurant rating is 3.5

Figure 2.18: Debug area showing result of print() statement

When you're just starting out, feel free to use as many print() statements as you like. It's a really good way to understand what is happening in your program.

Summary

In this lesson, you learned how to create and use playground files, which allow you to explore and experiment with Swift.

You saw how Swift represents different types of data, and how to use constants and variables. This enables you to store numbers, Boolean values, and strings in your program

You also learned about type inference, type annotation, and type safety, which help you to write code concisely and with fewer errors.

You looked at how to perform operations on numbers and strings, which lets you perform simple data processing tasks.

You learned how to fix errors, and how to print to the Debug area, which is useful when you're trying to find and fix errors in the programs that you write.

In the next chapter, you'll look at **conditionals** and **optionals**. Conditionals deal with making logical choices in your program, and optionals deal with cases where a variable may or may not have a value.

3
Conditionals and Optionals

In the last chapter, you looked at data types, constants, variables, and operations. At this point, you are able to write simple programs that process letters and numbers. However, programs don't always proceed in sequence. Oftentimes, you will need to execute different instructions based on a condition. Swift allows you to do this by using **conditionals**, and you will learn how to use them in this chapter.

Another thing you may have noticed is that, in the last chapter, each variable or constant was immediately assigned a value. What if you require a variable where the value may not be present initially? You will need a way to create a variable that may or may not have a value. Swift allows you to do this by using **optionals**, and you will also learn about them in this chapter.

By the end of this chapter, you should be able to write programs that do different things based on different conditions, and to handle variables that may or may not have a value.

The following topics will be covered:

- Introducing conditionals
- Introducing optionals and optional binding

> **Tip**
>
> Please spend some time understanding optionals. They can be daunting for the novice programmer.

Technical requirements

The Xcode playground for this chapter is in the `Chapter03` folder of the code bundle for this book, which can be downloaded here:

`https://github.com/PacktPublishing/iOS-15-Programming-for-Beginners-Sixth-Edition`

Check out the following video to see the code in action:

`https://bit.ly/3woRRKq`

Create a new playground and name it `ConditionalsAndOptionals`. You can type in and run all the code in this chapter as you go along. You'll start by learning about conditionals.

Introducing conditionals

At times, you'll want to execute different code blocks based on a specific condition, such as in the following scenarios:

- Choosing between different room types at a hotel. The price for bigger rooms would be higher.

- Switching between different payment methods at an online store. Different payment methods would have different procedures.

- Deciding what to order at a fast-food restaurant. Preparation procedures for each food item would be different.

To do this, you would use conditionals. In Swift, this is implemented using the `if` statement (for a single condition) and the `switch` statement (for multiple conditions).

> **Important information**
>
> For more information on conditionals, visit `https://docs.swift.org/swift-book/LanguageGuide/ControlFlow.html`.

Let's see how `if` statements are used to execute different tasks depending on a condition's value in the next section.

Using if statements

An `if` statement executes a block of code if a condition is `true`, and optionally another block of code if the condition is `false`. An `if` statement looks like this:

```
if condition {
    code1
} else {
    code2
}
```

Let's implement an `if` statement now to see this in action. Imagine that you're programming an app for a restaurant. The app would allow you to check if a restaurant is open, search for a restaurant, and check to see if a customer is over the drinking age limit.

Follow these steps:

1. To check if a restaurant is open, add the following code to your playground to create a constant and execute a statement if the constant's value is `true`. Click the **Play/ Stop** button to run it:

```
let isRestaurantOpen = true
if isRestaurantOpen {
    print("Restaurant is open.")
}
```

   First, you created a constant, `isRestaurantOpen`, and assigned `true` to it. Next, you have an `if` statement that checks the value stored in `isRestaurantOpen`. Since the value is `true`, the `print()` statement is executed and `Restaurant is open` is printed in the Debug area.

2. Try changing the value of `isRestaurantOpen` to `false` and run your code again. As the condition is now `false`, nothing will be printed to the Debug area.

3. You can also execute statements if a value is `false`. Let's say the customer has searched for a particular restaurant which is not in the app's database, so the app should display a message to say that the restaurant is not found. Type in the following code to create a constant and execute a statement if the constant's value is `false`:

```
let isRestaurantFound = false
if isRestaurantFound == false {
    print("Restaurant was not found")
}
```

The constant isRestaurantFound is set to false. Next, the if statement is checked. The isRestaurantFound == false condition returns true, and Restaurant was not found is printed in the Debug area.

4.   Try changing the value of isRestaurantFound to true. As the condition is now false, nothing will be printed to the Debug area.

5.   To execute one set of statements if a condition is true, and another set of statements if a condition is false, use the else keyword. Type in the following code, which checks if a customer at a bar is over the drinking age limit:

```
let drinkingAgeLimit = 21
let customerAge = 23
if customerAge < drinkingAgeLimit {
    print("Under age limit")
} else {
    print("Over age limit")
}
```

Here, drinkingAgeLimit is assigned the value 21 and customerAge is assigned the value 23. In the if statement, customerAge < drinkingAgeLimit is checked. Since 23 < 21 returns false, the else statement is executed and Over age limit is printed in the Debug area. If you change the value of customerAge to 19, customerAge < drinkingAgeLimit will return true, so Under age limit will be printed in the Debug area.

Up to now, you have only been dealing with single conditions. What if there are multiple conditions? That's where switch statements come in, and you will learn about them in the next section.

Using switch statements

To understand switch statements, let's start by implementing an if statement with multiple conditions first. Imagine that you're programming a traffic light. There are three possible conditions for the traffic light—red, yellow, or green—and you want something different to happen based on the color of the light. To do this, you can chain multiple if statements together. Follow these steps:

1.   Add the following code to your playground to implement a traffic light using multiple if statements and click the **Play/Stop** button to run it:

```
var trafficLightColor = "Yellow"
if trafficLightColor == "Red" {
```

```
    print("Stop")
} else if trafficLightColor == "Yellow" {
    print("Caution")
} else if trafficLightColor == "Green" {
    print("Go")
} else {
    print("Invalid color")
}
```

The first `if` condition, `trafficLightColor == "Red"`, returns `false`, so the `else` statement is executed. The second `if` condition, `trafficLightColor == "Yellow"`, returns `true`, so `Caution` is printed in the Debug area and no more `if` conditions are evaluated. Try changing the value of `trafficLightColor` to see different results.

The code used here works, but it's a little hard to read. In this case, a `switch` statement would be more concise and easier to comprehend. A `switch` statement looks like this:

```
switch value {
case firstValue:
    code1
case secondValue:
    code2
default:
    code3
}
```

The value is checked and matched to a case, and code for that case is executed. If none of the cases match, the code in the `default` case is executed.

2. Here's how to write the `if` statement shown earlier as a `switch` statement. Type in the following code:

```
trafficLightColor = "Yellow"
switch trafficLightColor {
case "Red":
    print("Stop")
case "Yellow":
    print("Caution")
case "Green":
```

```
        print("Go")
    default:
        print("Invalid color")
    }
```

The code here is much easier to read and understand when compared to the previous version. The value in trafficLightColor is "Yellow", so case "Yellow": is matched and Caution is printed in the Debug area. Try changing the value of trafficLightColor to see different results.

There are two things to remember about switch statements:

- switch statements in Swift do not fall through the bottom of each case and into the next one by default. In the example shown previously, once case "Red": is matched, case "Yellow":, case "Green":, and default: will not execute.

- switch statements must cover all possible cases. In the example shown previously, any trafficLightColor value other than "Red", "Yellow", or "Green" will be matched to default: and Invalid color will be printed in the Debug area.

This concludes the section on if and switch statements.

In the next section, you'll learn about optionals, which allow you to create variables without initial values, and **optional binding**, which allows instructions to be executed if an optional has a value.

Introducing optionals and optional binding

Up until now, every time you declared a variable or constant, you assigned a value to it immediately. But what if you want to declare a variable first and assign a value later? In this case, you would use optionals.

> **Important information**
>
> For more information on optionals, visit https://docs.swift.org/ swift-book/LanguageGuide/TheBasics.html.

Let's learn how to create and use optionals, and see how they are used in a program. Imagine you're writing a program where the user needs to enter the name of their spouse. Of course, if the user is not married, there would be no value for this. In this case, you can use an optional to represent the spouse's name.

An optional may have one of two possible states. It can either contain a value, or not contain a value. If an optional contains a value, you can access the value inside it. The process of accessing an optional's value is known as unwrapping the optional. Let's see how this works. Follow these steps:

1. Add the following code to your playground to create a variable and print its contents:

    ```
    var spouseName: String
    print(spouseName)
    ```

2. Click the Play/Stop button to run it. Since Swift is type-safe, it will display an error, **Variable 'spouseName' used before being initialized**.

3. To resolve this issue, you could assign an empty string to spouseName. Modify your code as shown:

    ```
    var spouseName: String = ""
    ```

    This makes the error go away, but an empty string is still a value, and spouseName should not have a value.

4. Since spouseName should not have a value initially, let's make it an optional. To do so, type a question mark after the type annotation and remove the empty string assignment:

    ```
    var spouseName: String?
    ```

    You'll see a warning because spouseName is now an optional string variable instead of a regular string variable, and the print() statement is expecting a regular string variable:

    ```
    44  var spouseName: String?
    45  print(spouseName)          ⚠  Expression implicitly coerced from 'String?' to 'Any'
    ```

    Figure 3.1: Warning notification

Click the Play/Stop button. Even though there is a warning, the program will execute. Ignore the warning for now. The value of spouseName is shown as "nil\n" in the Results area, and nil is printed in the Debug area. nil is a special keyword that means the optional variable spouseName has no value.

5. The warning appears because the `print` statement is treating `spouseName` as being of type `Any` instead of `String?`. Click the yellow triangle to display possible fixes, and choose the first fix:

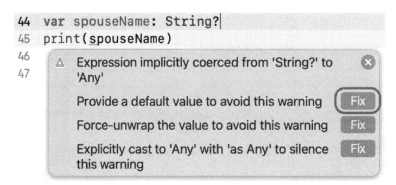

Figure 3.2: Expanded warning notification with the first fix selected

The statement will change to `print(spouseName ?? default value)`. Note the use of the `??` operator. This assigns `default value` to `spouseName` if it does not contain a value.

6. Replace the `default value` placeholder with `"No value in spouseName"` as shown. The warning will disappear. Run your program again and `"No value in spouseName"` will appear in the Results area:

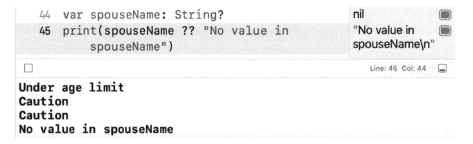

Figure 3.3: Results area showing default value

7. Let's assign a value to `spouseName`. Modify the code as shown:

```
var spouseName: String?
spouseName = "Nia"
print(spouseName ?? "No value in spouseName")
```

When your program runs, `Nia` appears in the Debug area.

8. Add one more line of code to join `spouseName` to another string as shown:

```
print(spouseName ?? "No value in spouseName")
let greeting = "Hello, " +  spouseName
```

You'll get an error, and the Debug area displays the error information and where the error occurred. This happened because you can't join a regular `String` variable to an optional using the + operator. To use the string inside the optional, you'll have to unwrap it first.

9. Click on the red circle to display possible fixes, and you'll see the following:

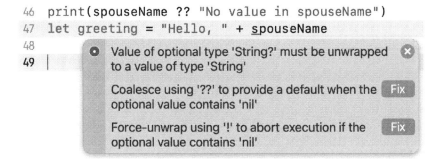

Figure 3.4: Expanded error notification

The second fix recommends **force-unwrapping** to resolve this issue. Force-unwrapping unwraps an optional whether it contains a value or not. It works fine if `spouseName` has a value, but if `spouseName` is `nil`, your program will crash.

10. Click the second fix, and you'll see an exclamation mark appear after `spouseName` in the last line of code, which indicates the optional is force-unwrapped:

```
let greeting = "Hello, " + spouseName!
```

11. When your program runs, `Hello, Nia` is assigned to `greeting`, as shown in the Results area. This means that `spouseName` has been successfully unwrapped.

12. To see the effect of force-unwrapping a variable containing `nil`, set `spouseName` to `nil`:

```
spouseName = nil
```

Your program crashes, and you can see what caused the crash in the Debug area:

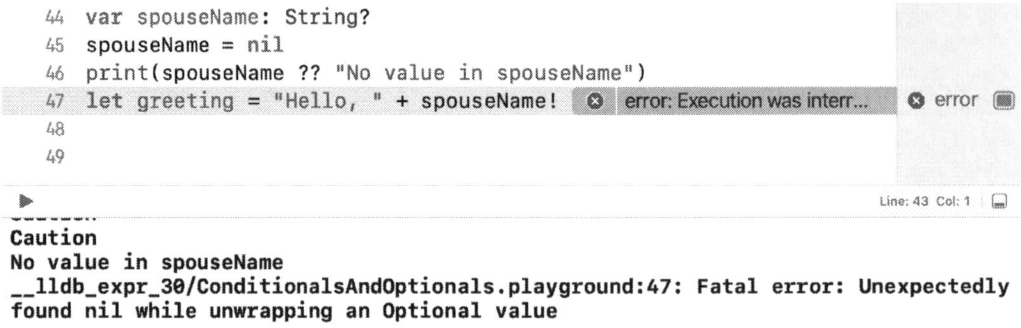

```
44  var spouseName: String?
45  spouseName = nil
46  print(spouseName ?? "No value in spouseName")
47  let greeting = "Hello, " + spouseName!    ⊗  error: Execution was interr...    ⊗ error  ▣
48
49
```

▶   Line: 43 Col: 1 ▣

```
Caution
No value in spouseName
__lldb_expr_30/ConditionalsAndOptionals.playground:47: Fatal error: Unexpectedly
found nil while unwrapping an Optional value
```

Figure 3.5: Crashed program with details in Debug area

Since spouseName is now nil, the program crashed while attempting to force-unwrap spouseName.

A better way of handling this is to use optional binding. In optional binding, you attempt to assign the value in an optional to a temporary variable (you can name it whatever you like). If the assignment is successful, a block of code is executed.

13. To see the effect of optional binding, modify your code as follows:

```
spouseName = "Nia"
print(spouseName ?? "No value in spouseName")
if let spouseTempVar = spouseName {
    let greeting = "Hello, " + spouseTempVar
    print(greeting)
}
```

Hello, Nia will appear in the Debug area. Here's how it works. If spouseName has a value, it will be unwrapped and assigned to a temporary variable, spouseTempVar, and the if statement will return true. The statements between the curly braces will be executed and the constant greeting will then be assigned the value Hello, Nia. Then, Hello, Nia will be printed in the Debug area. Note that the temporary variable spouseTempVar is not an optional.

If spouseName does not have a value, no value can be assigned to spouseTempVar and the if statement will return false. In this case, the statements in the curly braces will not be executed at all.

14. To see the effect of optional binding when an optional contains nil, assign nil once more to spouseName:

```
spouseName = nil
```

You'll notice that nothing appears in the Debug area, and your program no longer crashes even though spouseName is nil.

This concludes the section on optionals and optional binding, and you can now create and use optional variables. Awesome!

Summary

You're doing great! You learned how to use if and switch statements, which means you are now able to write your own programs that do different things based on different conditions.

You also learned about optionals and optional binding. This means you can now represent variables that may or may not have a value, and execute instructions only if a variable's value is present.

In the next chapter, you will study how to use a range of values instead of single values, and how to repeat program statements using loops.

4
Range Operators and Loops

In the previous chapter, you looked at conditionals, which allow you to do different things based on different conditions, and optionals, which enable you to create variables that may or may not have a value.

In this chapter, you will learn about **range operators** and **loops**. Range operators allow you to represent a range of values by specifying the start and end values for a range, and you'll learn about the different types of range operators. Loops allow you to repeat an instruction or a sequence of instructions over and over. You can repeat a sequence a fixed number of times, or repeat a sequence until a condition is met. You'll learn about the different types of loops used to accomplish this.

By the end of this chapter, you'll have learned how to use ranges, and how to create and use the different types of loops (`for-in`, `while`, and `repeat-while`).

The following topics will be covered:

- Exploring Range operators
- Exploring Loops

Technical requirements

The Xcode playground for this chapter is in the `Chapter04` folder of the code bundle for this book, which can be downloaded here:

`https://github.com/PacktPublishing/iOS-15-Programming-for-Beginners-Sixth-Edition`

Check out the following video to see the code in action:

`https://bit.ly/309pdRJ`

If you wish to start from scratch, create a new playground and name it `RangeOperatorsAndLoops`.

You can type in and run all the code in this chapter as you go along. Let's start with specifying a range of numbers using range operators.

Exploring Range operators

Range operators allow you to represent a range of values. Let's say you want to represent a sequence of numbers starting with `firstNumber` and ending with `lastNumber`. You don't need to specify every value; you can just specify the range in this way:

```
firstNumber...lastNumber
```

Imagine you need to write a program for a department store which automatically sends a discount voucher to customers between the ages of 18 and 30. It would be very cumbersome if you needed to set up an `if` or `switch` statement for each age. It's much more convenient to use a range operator in this case.

> **Important Information**
>
> For more information on range operators, visit: `https://docs.swift.org/swift-book/LanguageGuide/BasicOperators.html`.

Let's try this out in the playground. Follow these steps:

1. Add the following code to your playground and click the **Play/Stop** button to run it:

    ```
    let myRange = 10...20
    ```

This will assign a number sequence that starts with `10` and ends with `20`, including both numbers, to the `myRange` constant. This is known as a **closed range operator**.

2. The result displayed in the Results area may be truncated. Click the square icon to the right of the result. It will be displayed inline in the Editor area:

Figure 4.1: Editor area displaying inline result

You can now see the complete result in a box under the line of code. You can drag the right edge to make the box bigger if you wish.

> **Tip**
> Remember you can drag the border between the Results and Editor areas to increase the size of the Results area.

3. If you don't want to include the last number of the sequence in the range, use `. . <` in place of `. . . .`. Type in and run the following code:

```
let myRange2 = 10..<20
```

This will store the sequence starting with `10` and ending with `19` in the `myRange2` constant and is known as a **half-open range operator**.

There is one more type of range operator, the **one-sided range operator**, and you will learn about that in the next chapter.

Now that you know how to create and use ranges, you will learn about loops, the different loop types, and how to use them in the next section.

Exploring Loops

In programming, you frequently need to do the same thing over and over again. For example, each month, a company will need to generate payroll slips for each employee. If the company has 10,000 employees, it would be inefficient to write 10,000 instructions to create the payroll slips. Repeating a single instruction 10,000 times would be better, and loops are used for this.

There are three types of loop; the `for-in` loop, the `while` loop, and the `repeat-while` loop. The `for-in` loop will repeat for a known number of times, and the `while` and `repeat-while` loops will repeat as long as the loop condition is true.

> **Important Information**
>
> For more information on loops, visit: `https://docs.swift.org/swift-book/LanguageGuide/ControlFlow.html`.

Let's look at each type in turn, starting with the `for-in` loop, which is used when you know how many times a loop should be repeated.

Using the for-in loop

The `for-in` loop steps through every value in a sequence, and a set of statements in curly braces, known as the loop body, are executed each time. Each value is assigned to a temporary variable in turn, and the temporary variable can be used within the loop body. Here is what it looks like:

```
for item in sequence {
    code
}
```

The number of times the loop repeats is dictated by the number of items in the sequence. Let's begin by creating a `for-in` loop to display all the numbers in `myRange`. Follow these steps:

1. Add the following code to your playground and click the **Play/Stop** button to run it:

    ```
    for number in myRange {
        print(number)
    }
    ```

You should see each number in the sequence displayed in the Debug area. Note that the statements inside the loop are executed 11 times since myRange includes the last number in the range.

2. Let's try the same program, but this time with myRange2. Modify the code as follows and run it:

```
for number in myRange2 {
    print(number)
}
```

The statements inside the loop are executed 10 times, and the last value printed in the Debug area is 19.

3. You can even use a range operator directly after the in keyword. Type and run the following code:

```
for number in 0...5 {
    print(number)
}
```

Each number from 0 to 5 is displayed in the Debug area.

4. If you want the sequence to be reversed, use the reversed() function. Modify the code as follows and run it:

```
for number in (0...5).reversed() {
    print(number)
}
```

Each number from 5 to 0 is displayed in the Debug area.

Great job! Let's check out while loops in the next section, which are used when a loop sequence should be repeated as long as a condition is true.

Using the while loop

A while loop contains a condition and a set of statements in curly braces, known as the loop body. The condition is checked first; if true, the loop body is executed, and the loop repeats until the condition is false. Here is what it looks like:

```
while condition == true {
    code
}
```

Add the following code to create a variable, increment it by 5, and keep on doing it as long as the variable's value is less than 50. Click the **Play/Stop** button to run it:

```
var y = 0
while y < 50 {
    y += 5
    print("y is \(y)")
}
```

Let's step through the code. Initially, y is set to 0. The y < 50 condition is checked and returns true, so the loop body is executed. The value of y is incremented by 5, and y is 5 is printed in the Debug area. The loop repeats, and y < 50 is checked again. Since y is now 5 and 5 < 50 still returns true, the loop body is executed again. This is repeated until the value of y is 50, at which point y < 50 returns false and the loop stops.

If the while loop's condition is false to begin with, the loop body will never be executed. Try changing the value of y to 100 to see this.

In the next section, you'll study repeat-while loops. These will execute the statements in the loop body first before checking the loop condition.

The repeat-while loop

Like a while loop, a repeat-while loop also contains a condition and a loop body, but the loop body is executed first before the condition is checked. If the condition is true, the loop repeats until the condition returns false. Here is what it looks like:

```
repeat {
    code
} while condition == true
```

Add the following code to create a variable, increment it by 5, and keep on doing it as long as the variable's value is less than 50. Click the **Play/Stop** button to run it:

```
var x = 0
repeat {
    x += 5
    print("x is \(x)")
} while x < 50
```

Let's step through the code. Initially, x is set to 0. The loop body is executed. The value of x is incremented by 5, so now x contains 5, and x is 5 is printed to the Debug area. The x < 50 condition is checked, and since it returns true, the loop is repeated. The value of x is incremented by 5, so now x contains 10, and x is 10 is printed to the Debug area. The loop is repeated until x contains 50, at which point x < 50 returns false and the loop stops.

The loop body will be executed at least once, even if the condition is false to begin with. Try changing the value of x to 100 to see this.

You now know how to create and use different loop types. Awesome!

Summary

In this chapter, you looked at closed and half-open range operators, which allow you to specify a range of numbers rather than specifying every individual number discretely.

You also learned about the three different loop types, the for-in loop, the while loop, and the repeat-while loop. The for-in loop allows you to repeat a set of statements a fixed number of times, and the while and repeat-while loops allow you to repeat a set of statements as long as a condition is true. Great job!

In the next chapter, you will study collection types, which allow you to store a collection of data referenced by an index, a collection of key-value pairs, and an unstructured collection of data.

5
Collection Types

You've learned quite a lot at this point! You can now create a program that stores data in constants or variables and performs operations on them, and you can control the flow using conditionals and loops. But so far, you've mostly been storing single values.

In this chapter, you will learn ways to store collections of values. Swift has three collection types: **arrays**, which store an ordered list of values; **dictionaries**, which store an unordered list of key-value pairs; and **sets**, which store an unordered list of values.

By the end of this chapter, you'll have learned how to create arrays, dictionaries, and sets, and how to perform operations on them.

The following topics will be covered:

- Understanding arrays
- Understanding dictionaries
- Understanding sets

Technical requirements

The Xcode playground for this chapter is in the `Chapter05` folder of the code bundle for this book, which can be downloaded here:

`https://github.com/PacktPublishing/iOS-15-Programming-for-Beginners-Sixth-Edition`

Check out the following video to see the code in action:

`https://bit.ly/3H5blc2`

If you wish to start from scratch, create a new playground and name it `CollectionTypes`. You can type in and run all of the code in this chapter as you go along.

> **Important Information**
>
> To find out more about arrays, dictionaries, and sets, visit `https://docs.swift.org/swift-book/LanguageGuide/CollectionTypes.html`.

The first collection type you will learn about are arrays, which lets you store information in an ordered list.

Understanding arrays

Let's say you want to store the following:

- List of items to buy at a convenience store
- Chores that you have to do every month

Arrays would be suitable for this. An array stores values in an ordered list. Here's what it looks like:

Index	Value
0	value1
1	value2
2	value3

Figure 5.1: Array

Values must be of the same type. You can access any value in an array by using the array index, which starts with 0.

If you create an array using the `let` keyword, its contents can't be changed after it has been created. If you want to change an array's contents after creation, use the `var` keyword.

Let's see how to work with arrays. You'll create an array by assigning a value to it in the next section.

Creating an array

In previous chapters, you created a constant or variable by declaring it and assigning an initial value to it. You can create an array the same way.

Imagine that your spouse has asked you to get some items from a convenience store. Let's implement a shopping list using an array. Add the following code to your playground and click the **Play/Stop** button to run it:

```
var shoppingList = ["Eggs", "Milk"]
```

This instruction creates an array variable named `shoppingList`. The assigned value, `["Eggs", "Milk"]`, is an array **literal**. It represents an array with two elements of type `String`, with `"Eggs"` at index 0.

Using the `var` keyword here means that the array's contents can be modified. As Swift uses type inference, this array's elements will be of type `String`.

Imagine that you need to check how many items you need to get at the store. In the next section, you'll learn how to determine the number of elements in an array.

Checking the number of elements in an array

To find out how many elements there are in an array, use `count`. Type in and run the following code:

```
shoppingList.count
```

As the `shoppingList` array contains two elements, `2` is displayed in the Results area.

You can check to see if an array is empty by using `isEmpty`. Type in and run the following code:

```
shoppingList.isEmpty
```

As the `shoppingList` array contains two elements, `false` is displayed in the Results area.

> **Tip**
>
> It is also possible to see if an array is empty by using `shoppingList.count == 0`, but using `shoppingList.isEmpty` offers better performance.

Imagine that your spouse called, and asked you if you can get chicken and cooking oil while you're at the store. In the next section, you'll see how to add elements to the end of an array, and at a specified array index.

Adding a new element to an array

You can add a new element to the end of an array by using `append(_:)`. Type in and run the following code:

```
shoppingList.append("Cooking Oil")
```

`"Cooking Oil"` has been added to the end of the `shoppingList` array, which now contains three elements – `"Eggs"`, `"Milk"`, and `"Cooking Oil"`. This can be seen in the Results area.

> **Tip**
>
> You can also add a new element to an array with the + operator, using the following code: `shoppingList = shoppingList + ["Cooking Oil"]`.

You can add a new item at a specified index using `insert(_:at:)`. Type and run the following code:

```
shoppingList.insert("Chicken", at: 1)
```

This inserts `"Chicken"` at index 1, so now the `shoppingList` array contains `"Eggs"`, `"Chicken"`, `"Milk"`, and `"Cooking Oil"`. Note that `"Chicken"` is the second element in the array as the first element is at index 0. This can be seen in the Results area.

Imagine that you've got the first item on your shopping list, and now you need to know what's the next item in the list. In the next section, you'll see how to access a specific array element using the array index.

Accessing an array element

You can specify an array index to access a particular element. Type in and run the following code:

```
shoppingList[2]
```

This returns the array element stored at index 2, and `"Milk"` is displayed in the Results area.

Imagine that your spouse called and asked you to get soy milk instead of milk. As this array was declared using the `var` keyword, you can modify the values stored in it. You'll learn how in the next section.

Assigning a new value to a particular index

You can replace an existing array element by specifying the index and assigning a new value to it. Type in and run the following code:

```
shoppingList[2] = "Soy Milk"
shoppingList
```

This replaces the value stored at index 2, `"Milk"`, with `"Soy Milk"`. The `shoppingList` array now contains `"Eggs"`, `"Chicken"`, `"Soy Milk"`, and `"Cooking Oil"`, as shown in the Results area.

Note that the index used must be valid. For instance, you can't use index 4 as the only valid indexes here are 0, 1, 2, and 3. Doing so would cause the program to crash.

Imagine that your spouse called, and told you that there was chicken in the fridge, so you no longer have to get it. In the next section, you'll see two ways to remove elements from an array.

Removing an element from an array

You can remove an element from an array by using `remove(at:)`. Type in and run the following code:

```
shoppingList.remove(at: 1)
shoppingList
```

This removes the item at index 1, "Chicken", from the shoppingList array, so now it contains "Eggs", "Soy Milk", and "Cooking Oil". You can see this in the Results area.

If you're removing the last item from the array, you can use removeLast() instead.

Imagine that you've gotten every item in the list, and you would like to go through your list again to make sure. You'll need to access every array element in turn and perform operations on each element. You'll see how to do this in the next section.

Iterating over an array

Remember the for-in loop you studied in the previous chapter? You can use it to iterate over every element in an array. Type in and run the following code:

```
for shoppingListItem in shoppingList {
    print(shoppingListItem)
}
```

This prints out every element in the array to the Debug area.

You can also use **one-sided range operators**. These are range operators with only the starting value, for example, 1 . . . Type in and run the following code:

```
for shoppingListItem in shoppingList[1...] {
    print(shoppingListItem)
}
```

This prints out the elements of the array starting from the element at index 1 to the Debug area.

You now know how to use an array to create an ordered list, such as a shopping list, and how to perform array operations. In the next section, let's look at how to store an unordered list of key-value pairs using a dictionary.

Understanding dictionaries

Let's say you're writing an *Address Book* app. You would need to store a list of names and their corresponding contact numbers. A dictionary would be perfect for this.

A dictionary stores **key-value pairs** in an unordered list. Here's what it looks like:

Key	Value
Key 1	Value 1
Key 2	Value 2
Key 3	Value 3

Figure 5.2: Dictionary

All keys must be of the same type and must be unique. All values must be of the same type, but are not necessarily unique. Keys and values don't have to be of the same type as each other. You use the key to get the corresponding value.

If you create a dictionary using the `let` keyword, its contents can't be changed after it has been created. If you want to change the contents after creation, use the `var` keyword.

Let's look at how to work with dictionaries. You'll create a dictionary by assigning a value to it in the next section.

Creating a dictionary

Imagine that you're creating an *Address Book* app. For this app, you'll use a dictionary to store your contacts. Just like an array, you can create a new dictionary by declaring it and assigning an initial value to it. Add the following code to your playground and click the **Play/Stop** button to run it:

```
var contactList = ["Shah": "+60123456789", "Aamir":
"+0223456789"]
```

This instruction creates a dictionary variable named `contactList`. The assigned value, `["Shah": "+60123456789", "Aamir": "+0223456789" ]`, is a dictionary literal. It represents a dictionary with two elements. Each element is a key-value pair, with the contact name as the key and the contact number as the value. Note that since the contact name is the key field, it should be unique.

Since the `contactList` dictionary is a variable, you can change the contents of the dictionary after it has been created. Both key and value are of type `String` due to type inference.

Imagine that your app has to display the total number of contacts. In the next section, you'll learn how to determine the number of elements in a dictionary.

Checking the number of elements in a dictionary

To find out how many elements there are in a dictionary, use `count`. Type in and run the following code:

```
contactList.count
```

As there are two elements in the `contactList` dictionary, 2 is displayed in the Results area.

You can check whether a dictionary is empty by using `isEmpty`. Type in and run the following code:

```
contactList.isEmpty
```

Since the `contactList` dictionary has two elements, `false` is displayed in the Results area.

> **Tip**
> It is also possible to see if a dictionary is empty by using `contactlist.count == 0`, but using `contactList.isEmpty` offers better performance.

Imagine that you just finished a meeting, and want to add a new contact to your app. As this dictionary was declared using the `var` keyword, you can add key-value pairs to it. You'll learn how in the next section.

Adding a new element to a dictionary

To add a new element to a dictionary, provide a key and assign a value to it. Type in and run the following code:

```
contactList["Jane"] = "+0229876543"
contactList
```

This adds a new key-value pair with the key `"Jane"` and the value `"+0229876543"` to the `contactList` dictionary. It now consists of `"Shah": "+60126789345"`, `"Aamir": "+0223456789"`, and `"Jane": "+0229876543"`. You can see this in the Results area.

Imagine that you want to call one of your contacts, and you want the phone number for that contact. In the next section, you'll see how to access dictionary elements by specifying the key for the desired value.

Accessing a dictionary element

You can specify a dictionary key to access its corresponding value. Type in and run the following code:

```
contactList["Shah"]
```

This returns the value for the key "Shah", and +60123456789 is displayed in the Results area.

Imagine that one of your contacts has a new phone, so you have to update the phone number for that contact. You can modify the key-value pairs stored in a dictionary. You'll learn how in the next section.

Assigning a new value to an existing key

You can assign a new value to an existing key. Type and run the following code:

```
contactList["Shah"] = "+60126789345"
contactList
```

This assigns a new value to the key "Shah". The contactList dictionary now contains "Shah": "+60126789345", "Aamir": "+0223456789", and "Jane": "+0229876543". You can see this in the Results area.

Imagine that you have to remove a contact from your app. Let's see how you can remove elements from a dictionary in the next section.

Removing an element from a dictionary

To remove an element from a dictionary, assign nil to an existing key. Type in and run the following code:

```
contactList["Jane"] = nil
contactList
```

This removes the element with the key "Jane" from the contactList dictionary, and it now contains "Shah": "+60126789345" and "Aamir": "+0223456789". You can see this in the Results area.

If you want to retain the value you are removing, use `removeValue(for:Key)` instead. Type in and run the following code:

```
var oldDictValue = contactList.removeValue(forKey: "Aamir")
oldDictValue
contactList
```

This removes the element with the key `"Aamir"` from the `contactList` dictionary and assigns its value to `oldDictValue`. Now `oldDictValue` now contains `"+0223456789"` and the `contactList` dictionary contains `"Shah"`: `"+60126789345"`. You can see this in the Results area.

Imagine that you would like to call each contact to wish them a happy new year. You'll have to access every dictionary element in turn and perform operations on each element. You'll see how to do this in the next section.

Iterating over a dictionary

Just like arrays, you can use a `for-in` loop to iterate over every element in a dictionary. Type in and run the following code:

```
for (name, contactNumber) in contactList {
    print("\(name) : \(contactNumber)")
}
```

This prints every element in the dictionary to the Debug area. Since dictionaries are unordered, you may get the results in a different order when you run this code again.

You know now how to use a dictionary to create an unordered list of key-value pairs, such as a contact list, and how to perform dictionary operations. In the next section, let's see how to store an unordered list of values in a set.

Understanding sets

Let's say you're writing a *Movies* app and you want to store a list of movie genres. You could do this with a set.

A set stores values in an unordered list. Here's what it looks like:

Value
Value 1
Value 2
Value 3

Figure 5.3: Set

All values are of the same type.

If you create a set using the `let` keyword, its contents can't be changed after it has been created. If you want to change the contents after creation, use the `var` keyword.

Let's look at how to work with sets. You'll create a set by assigning a value to it in the next section.

Creating a set

Imagine that you are creating a *Movies* app and you would like to store movie genres in your app. As you have seen for arrays and dictionaries, you can create a set by declaring it and assigning a new value to it. Add the following code to your playground and click the **Play/Stop** button to run it:

```
var movieGenres: Set = ["Horror", "Action", "Romantic Comedy"]
```

This instruction creates a set variable named `movieGenres`. Note that the set literal assigned to it, `["Horror", "Action", "Romantic Comedy"]` has the same format as an array literal, so you use type annotation to set the type of `movieGenres` to `Set`. Otherwise, Swift's type inference will create an array variable and not a set variable.

Using the `var` keyword here means that the set's contents can be modified. This set's elements will be of type `String` due to type inference.

Imagine that you need to show the total number of genres in your app. Let's see how to find the number of elements there are in a set in the next section.

Checking the number of elements in a set

To find out how many elements there are in a set, use `count`. Type in and run the following code:

```
movieGenres.count
```

Since the `movieGenres` set contains three elements, 3 is displayed in the Results area.

You can check whether a set is empty by using `isEmpty`. Type in and run the following code:

```
movieGenres.isEmpty
```

As `movieGenres` contains three elements, `false` is displayed in the Results area.

> **Tip**
>
> It is also possible to see if a set is empty by using `movieGenres.count == 0`, but using `movieGenres.isEmpty` offers better performance.

Imagine that users of your app can add more genres to it. As this set was declared using the `var` keyword, you can add elements to it. You'll learn how in the next section.

Adding a new element to a set

You can add a new element to a set by using `insert(_:)`. Type in and run the following code:

```
movieGenres.insert("War")
movieGenres
```

This adds a new item, `"War"`, to the `movieGenres` set, which now contains `"Horror"`, `"Romantic Comedy"`, `"War"`, and `"Action"`. This is displayed in the Results area.

Imagine that a user would like to know if a certain genre is available in your app. In the next section, you'll learn how to check if an element is in a set.

Checking whether a set contains an element

To check whether a set contains an element, use `contains(_:)`. Type in and run the following code:

```
movieGenres.contains("War")
```

As "War" is one of the elements inside the movieGenres set, true is displayed in the Results area.

Imagine that a user wants to remove a genre from his list of genres. Let's see how to remove items from a set that are no longer needed in the next section.

Removing an item from a set

To remove an item from a set, use remove (_:). The value you are removing can be assigned to a variable or a constant. If the value doesn't exist in the set, nil will be returned. Type in and run the following code:

```
var oldSetValue = movieGenres.remove("Action")
oldSetValue
movieGenres
```

"Action" is removed from the movieGenres set and assigned to oldSetValue, and the movieGenres set now contains "Horror", "Romantic Comedy", and "War". You'll see this displayed in the Results area.

To remove all of the elements from a set, use removeAll().

Imagine that you would like to display all the genres your app has as recommendations for your app's users. You can iterate over and perform operations on each set element. Let's see how to do so in the next section.

Iterating over a set

As with arrays and dictionaries, you can use a for-in loop to iterate over every element in a set. Type in and run the following code:

```
for genre in movieGenres {
    print(genre)
}
```

You should see each set element in the Debug area. Since sets are unsorted, you may get the results in a different order when you run this code again.

Imagine that you want your app to perform operations on the genres you like with the genres that another person likes. In the next section, you will learn about the various operations that you can do with sets in Swift.

Exploring Set operations

It's easy to perform set operations such as **union**, **intersection**, **subtracting**, and **symmetric difference**. Type in and run the following code:

```
let movieGenres2: Set = ["Science Fiction", "War", "Fantasy"]
movieGenres.union(movieGenres2)
movieGenres.intersection(movieGenres2)
movieGenres.subtracting(movieGenres2)
movieGenres.symmetricDifference(movieGenres2)
```

Here, you are performing set operations on two sets, `movieGenres` and `movieGenres2`. Let's see the results of each set operation:

- `union(_:)` returns a new set containing all of the values in both sets, so `{"Horror", "Romantic Comedy", "War", "Science Fiction", "Fantasy"}` will be displayed in the Results area.

- `intersection(_:)` returns a new set containing only the values common to both sets, so `{"War"}` will be displayed in the Results area.

- `subtracting(_:)` returns a new set without the values in the specified set, so `{"Horror", "Romantic Comedy"}` will be displayed in the Results area.

- `symmetricDifference(_:)` returns a new set without the values common to both sets, so `{"Horror", "Romantic Comedy", "Science Fiction", "Fantasy"}` will be displayed in the Results area.

Imagine that you want your app to compare the genres you like with the genres that another person likes. In the next section, you'll learn how to check if a set is equal to another set, is part of another set, or has nothing in common with another set.

Exploring set membership and equality

It's easy to check if a set is equal to, a **subset**, a **superset**, or a **disjoint** of another set. Type in and run the following code:

```
let movieGenresSubset: Set = ["Horror", "Romantic Comedy"]
let movieGenresSuperset: Set = ["Horror", "Romantic Comedy",
"War", "Science Fiction", "Fantasy"]
let movieGenresDisjoint: Set = ["Bollywood"]
movieGenres == movieGenres2
movieGenresSubset.isSubset(of: movieGenres)
```

```
movieGenresSuperset.isSuperset(of: movieGenres)
movieGenresDisjoint.isDisjoint(with: movieGenres)
```

Let's see how this code works:

- The `isEqual` operator (`==`) checks whether all the members of one set are the same as those of another set. Since not all the members of the `movieGenres` set are the same as those in the `movieGenres2` set, `false` will be displayed in the Results area.

- `isSubset(of:)` checks whether a set is a subset of another set. Since all the members of the `movieGenresSubset` set is in the `movieGenres` set, `true` will be displayed in the Results area.

- `isSuperset(of:)` checks whether a set is a superset of another set. Since all the members of the `movieGenres` set are in the `movieGenresSuperset` set, `true` will be displayed in the Results area.

- `isDisjoint(with:)` checks whether a set has no values in common with another set. Since the `movieGenresDisjoint` set has no members in common with the `movieGenres` set, `true` will be displayed in the Results area.

You know now how to use a set to create an unordered list of values, such as a list of movie genres, and how to perform set operations. This concludes the chapter on collection types. Well done!

Summary

In this chapter, you looked at collection types in Swift. First you learned about arrays. This allows you to use an ordered list of values to represent an item like a shopping list, and perform operations on it.

Next, you learned about dictionaries. This allows you to use an unordered list of key-value pairs to represent an item like a contact list, and perform operations on it.

Finally, you learned about sets. This allows you to use an unordered list of values to represent an item like a movie genre list, and perform operations on it.

In the next chapter, you will study how to group a set of instructions together using functions. This is handy when you want to execute a set of instructions multiple times in your program.

6
Functions
and Closures

At this point, you can write reasonably complex programs that can make decisions and repeat instruction sequences. You can also store data for your programs using collection types. As the programs you write grow in size and complexity, it will become harder to comprehend what they do.

To make large programs easier to understand, Swift allows you to create **functions**, which lets you combine a number of instructions together and execute them by calling a single name. You can also create **closures**, which lets you combine a number of instructions together without a name and assign it to a constant or variable.

By the end of this chapter, you'll have learned about functions, nested functions, functions as return types, functions as arguments and the `guard` statement. You'll also have learned how to create and use closures.

The following topics will be covered:

- Understanding functions
- Understanding closures

Technical requirements

The Xcode playground for this chapter is in the `Chapter06` folder of the code bundle for this book, which can be downloaded here:

`https://github.com/PacktPublishing/iOS-15-Programming-for-Beginners-Sixth-Edition`

Check out the following video to see the code in action:

`https://bit.ly/3o2MYTs`

If you wish to start from scratch, create a new playground and name it `FunctionsAndClosures`.

You can type in and run all of the code in this chapter as you go along. Let's start by learning about functions.

Understanding functions

Functions are useful for encapsulating a number of instructions that collectively perform a specific task, for example:

- Calculating the 10% service charge for a meal at a restaurant.
- Calculating the monthly payment for a car that you wish to purchase.

Here's what a function looks like:

```
func functionName(parameter1: ParameterType, ...) -> ReturnType
{
    code
}
```

Every function has a descriptive name. You can define one or more values that the function takes as input, known as **parameters**. You can also define what the function will output when done, known as its **return type**. Both parameters and return types are optional.

You "call" a function's name to execute it. This is what a function call looks like:

```
functionName(parameter1: argument1, …)
```

You provide input values (known as **arguments**) that match the type of the function's parameters.

> **Important Information**
>
> To learn more about functions, visit `https://docs.swift.org/` `swift-book/LanguageGuide/Functions.html`.

Let's see how you can create a function to calculate a service charge in the next section.

Creating a function

In its simplest form, a function just executes some instructions, and does not have any parameters or return types. You'll see how this works by writing a function to calculate the service charge for a meal. The service charge should be 10% of the meal cost.

Add the following code to your playground to create and call this function and click the **Play/Stop** button to run it:

```
func serviceCharge() {
    let mealCost = 50
    let serviceCharge = mealCost / 10
    print("Service charge is \(serviceCharge)")
}
serviceCharge()
```

You've just created a very simple function named `serviceCharge()`. All it does is calculate the 10% service charge for a meal costing $50, which is `50 / 10`, returning 5. You then call this function using its name. You'll see `Service charge is 5` displayed in the Debug area.

This function is not very useful because `mealCost` is always `50` every time you call this function, and the result, 5, is only printed in the Debug area and can't be used elsewhere in your program. Let's add some parameters and a return type to this function to make it more useful.

Modify your code as shown:

```
func serviceCharge(mealCost: Int) -> Int {
    return mealCost / 10
}
let serviceChargeAmount = serviceCharge(mealCost: 50)
print(serviceChargeAmount)
```

This is much better. Now, you can set the meal cost when you call the `serviceCharge(mealCost:)` function, and the result can be assigned to a variable or constant. It looks a bit awkward, though. You should try to make function signatures in Swift read like an English sentence, as this is considered best practice. Let's see how to do that in the next section, where you'll use **custom labels** to make your function more English-like and easier to understand.

Using custom argument labels

Note that the `serviceCharge(mealCost:)` function is not very English-like. You can add a custom label to the parameter to make the function easier to understand.

Modify your code as shown:

```
func serviceCharge(forMealPrice mealCost: Int) -> Int {
    return mealCost / 10
}
let serviceChargeAmount = serviceCharge(forMealPrice: 50)
print(serviceChargeAmount)
```

The function works exactly the same as before, but to call it, you use `serviceCharge(forMealPrice:)`. This sounds more like English and makes it easier to figure out what the function does.

In the next section, you'll learn how to use several smaller functions within the bodies of other functions, and these are known as **nested functions**.

Using nested functions

It's possible to have a function within the body of another function, and these are called nested functions. A nested function can use the variables of the enclosing function. Let's see how nested functions work by writing a function to calculate monthly payments for a loan.

Type in and run the following code:

```
func calculateMonthlyPayments(carPrice: Double, downPayment:
Double, interestRate: Double, paymentTerm: Double) -> Double {
    func loanAmount() -> Double {
        return carPrice - downPayment
    }
    func totalInterest() -> Double {
```

```
        return interestRate * paymentTerm
    }
    func numberOfMonths() -> Double {
        return paymentTerm * 12
    }
    return ((loanAmount() + ( loanAmount() *
    totalInterest() / 100 )) / numberOfMonths())
}
calculateMonthlyPayments(carPrice: 50000, downPayment: 5000,
interestRate: 3.5, paymentTerm: 7.0)
```

Here, there are three functions within `calculateMonthlyPayments`
(`carPrice:downPayment:interestRate:paymentTerm:`).
Let's take a look at them:

- The first nested function, `loanAmount()`, calculates the total loan amount by subtracting `downPayment` from `carPrice`. It returns `50000 - 5000 = 45000`.

- The second nested function, `totalInterest()`, calculates the total interest amount incurred for the payment term by multiplying `interestRate` with `paymentTerm`. It returns `3.5 * 7 = 24.5`.

- The third nested function, `numberOfMonths()`, calculates the total number of months in the payment term by multiplying `paymentTerm` with `12`. It returns `7 * 12 = 84`.

Note that the three nested functions all use the variables of the enclosing function. The value returned is `( 45000 + ( 45000 * 24.5 / 100 ) ) / 84 = 666.96`, which is the amount you have to pay monthly for 7 years to buy this car.

As you have seen, functions in Swift are similar to functions in other languages, but they have a cool feature. Functions are **first-class types** in Swift, so they can be used as parameters and return types. Let's see how that is done in the next section.

Using functions as return types

A function can return another function as its return type. Type in and run the following code to create a function that generates a value for Pi:

```
func makePi() -> (() -> Double) {
    func generatePi() -> Double {
        return 22.0 / 7.0
```

```
        }
    return generatePi
}
let pi = makePi()
print(pi())
```

The `makePi()` function's return type is a function that has no parameters and the return type is `Double`. `generatePi()` is a function that has no parameters and the return type is `Double`, and will be the function that is returned. So, `pi` will be assigned `generatePi()` and will return `22.0/7.0` when called. `3.142857142857143` will be printed in the Debug area.

Let's see how a function can be used as a parameter for another function in the next section.

Using functions as parameters

A function can take a function as a parameter. Type in and run the following code to create a function that determines if a number meeting a certain condition exists within a list of numbers:

```
func isThereAMatch(listOfNumbers: [Int], condition: (Int) ->
Bool) -> Bool {
    for item in listOfNumbers {
        if condition(item) {
            return true
        }
    }
    return false
}
func oddNumber(number: Int) -> Bool {
    return (number % 2) > 0
}
var numbersList = [2, 4, 6, 7]
isThereAMatch(listOfNumbers: numbersList, condition: oddNumber)
```

`isThereAMatch(listOfNumbers:condition:)` has two parameters; an array of integers and a function. The function provided as an argument must take an integer value and return a Boolean value. `oddNumber(number:)` takes an integer and returns `true` if the number is an odd number, which means it can be an argument for the second parameter. `numbersList`, an array containing an odd number, is used as the argument for the first parameter. Since `numbersList` contains an odd number, `isThereAMatch(listOfNumbers:condition:)` will return `true` when called.

In the next section, you'll see how you can perform an early exit on a function if the arguments used are not suitable.

Using a guard statement to exit a function early

If there is something wrong with the input data, it is useful to be able to exit a function early. Let's say you need a function to be used in an online purchasing terminal. This function will calculate the remaining balance of a debit or credit card when you buy something. The price of the item that you want to buy is entered in a text field. The value in the text field is converted into an integer so that you can calculate the remaining card balance.

Type in and run the following code:

```
func buySomething(itemValueEntered itemValueField: String,
cardBalance: Int) -> Int {
    guard let itemValue = Int(itemValueField) else {
        print("error in item value")
        return cardBalance
    }
    let remainingBalance = cardBalance - itemValue
    return remainingBalance
}
print(buySomething(itemValueEntered: "10", cardBalance: 50))
print(buySomething(itemValueEntered: "blue", cardBalance: 50))
```

You should see this result in the Debug area:

```
40
error in item value
50
```

Let's see how this function works. The first line in the function body is a `guard` statement. This checks to see whether a condition is `true`; if not, it exits the function. Here, it is used to check and see whether the user entered a valid price in the online purchasing terminal. If so, the value can be converted successfully into an integer, and you can calculate the remaining card balance. Otherwise, the `else` clause in the `guard` statement is executed. An error message is printed to the Debug area and the unchanged card balance is returned.

For `print(buySomething(itemValueEntered: "10", cardBalance: 50))`, the item price is deducted successfully from the card balance, and `40` is returned.

For `print(buySomething(itemValueEntered: "blue", cardBalance: 50))`, the `guard` statement's condition fails and its `else` clause is executed, resulting in an error message being printed to the Debug area and `50` being returned.

You now know how to create and use functions. You have also seen how to use custom argument labels, nested functions, functions as parameters or return types, and the `guard` statement.

Now, let's look at closures. Like functions, closures allow you to combine a number of instructions together, but closures do not have names and can be assigned to a constant or a variable. You'll see how they work in the next section.

Understanding closures

A closure, like a function, contains a sequence of instructions and can take arguments and return values. However, closures don't have names. The sequence of instructions in a closure is surrounded by curly braces (`{ }`), and the `in` keyword separates the arguments and return type from the closure body.

Closures can be assigned to a constant or variable, so they're handy if you need to pass them around inside your program. For instance, let's say you have an app that downloads a file from the internet, and you need to do something to the file once it has finished downloading. You can put a list of instructions to process the file inside a closure and have your program execute it once the file finishes downloading. You'll see how closures are used in *Chapter 16, Getting Started with MapKit*.

> **Important Information**
>
> To learn more about closures, visit `https://docs.swift.org/swift-book/LanguageGuide/Closures.html`.

You'll now write a closure that applies a calculation on each element of an array of numbers. Add the following code to your playground and click the **Play/Stop** button to run it:

```
var numbersArray = [2, 4, 6, 7]
let myClosure = { (number: Int) -> Int in
    let result = number * number
    return result
}
let mappedNumbers = numbersArray.map(myClosure)
```

This assigns a closure that calculates a number's power of two to `myClosure`. The `map()` function then applies this closure to every element in `numbersArray`. Each element is multiplied by itself, and [4, 16, 36, 49] appears in the Results area.

It's possible to write closures in a more concise fashion, and you'll see how to do that in the next section.

Simplifying closures

One of the things that new developers have trouble with is the very concise way experienced Swift programmers use to write closures. Consider the code shown in the following example:

```
var testNumbers = [2, 4, 6, 7]
let mappedTestNumbers = testNumbers.map({ (number: Int)
    -> Int in
    let result = number * number
    return result
})
print(mappedTestNumbers)
```

Here, you have `testNumbers`, an array of numbers, and you use the `map(_:)` function to map a closure to each element of the array in turn. The code in the closure multiplies the number by itself, generating the square of that number. The result, [4, 16, 36, 49], is then printed to the Debug area. As you will see, the closure code can be written more concisely.

When a closure's type is already known, you can remove the parameter type, return type, or both. Single statement closures implicitly return the value of their only statement, which means you can remove the `return` statement as well. So, you can write the closure as follows:

```
let mappedTestNumbers = testNumbers.map({ number in
    number * number
})
```

When a closure is the only argument to a function, you can omit the parentheses enclosing the closure, as follows:

```
let mappedTestNumbers = testNumbers.map { number in
    number * number
}
```

You can refer to parameters by a number expressing their relative position in the list of arguments instead of by name, as follows:

```
let mappedTestNumbers = testNumbers.map { $0 * $0 }
```

So, the closure now is very concise indeed, but will be challenging for new developers to understand. Feel free to write closures in a way that you are comfortable with.

You now know how to create and use closures, and how to write them more concisely. Great!

Summary

In this chapter, you studied how to group statements together into functions. You learned how to use custom argument labels, functions inside other functions, functions as return types, and functions as parameters. This will be useful later when you need to accomplish the same task at different points in your program.

You also learned how to create closures. This will be useful when you need to pass around blocks of code within your program.

In the next chapter, you will study classes, structures, and enumerations. Classes and structures allow for the creation of complex objects that can store state and behavior, and enumerations can be used to limit the values that can be assigned to a variable or constant, reducing the chances for error.

7

Classes, Structures, and Enumerations

In the previous chapter, you've learned how to group instruction sequences together using functions and closures.

It's time to think about how to represent complex objects in your code. For example, think about a car. You could use a `String` constant to store a car name and a `Double` variable to store a car price, but they are not associated with one another. You've seen that you can group instructions together to make functions and closures. In this chapter, you'll learn how to group constants and variables together in a single entity using **classes** and **structures**, and how to manipulate them. You'll also learn how to use **enumerations** to group a set of related values together.

By the end of this chapter, you'll have learned how to create and initialize a class, create a subclass from an existing class, create and initialize a structure, differentiate between classes and structures, and create an enumeration.

The following topics will be covered in this chapter:

- Understanding classes
- Understanding structures
- Understanding enumerations

Technical requirements

The Xcode playground for this chapter is in the `Chapter07` folder of the code bundle for this book, which can be downloaded here:

`https://github.com/PacktPublishing/iOS-15-Programming-for-Beginners-Sixth-Edition`

Check out the following video to see the code in action:

`https://bit.ly/3HbRJTA`

If you wish to start from scratch, create a new playground and name it `Classes,StructuresAndEnumerations`. You can type in and run all of the code in this chapter as you go along. Let's start with learning what a class is, and how to declare and define it.

Understanding classes

Classes are useful for representing complex objects, for example:

- Individual employee information for a company
- Items for sale at an e-commerce site
- Items you have in your house for insurance purposes

Here's what a class declaration and definition looks like:

```
class ClassName {
    property1
    property2
    property3
    method1() {
        code
    }
    method2() {
        code
    }
}
```

Every class has a descriptive name, and it contains variables or constants used to represent an object. Variables or constants associated with a class are called **properties**.

A class can also contain functions that perform specific tasks. Functions associated with a class are called **methods**.

Once you have declared and defined a class, you can create **instances** of that class. Imagine you are creating an app for a zoo. If you have an `Animal` class, you can use instances of that class to represent different animal types at the zoo. Each of these instances will have different values for their properties.

> **Important information**
>
> To learn more about classes, visit: `https://docs.swift.org/` `swift-book/LanguageGuide/ClassesAndStructures.` `html`.

Let's look at how to work with classes. You'll learn how to declare and define classes, create instances based on the class declaration, and manipulate those instances. You'll start by creating a class declaration to represent animals in the next section.

Creating a class declaration

Let's declare and define a class that can store details about animals. Add the following code to your playground:

```swift
class Animal {
    var name: String = ""
    var sound: String = ""
    var numberOfLegs: Int = 0
    var breathesOxygen: Bool = true
    func makeSound() {
        print(self.sound)
    }
}
```

You've just declared a very simple class named `Animal`. Convention dictates that class names start with a capital letter. This class has properties to store the name of the animal, the sound it makes, the number of legs it has, and whether it breathes oxygen or not. This class also has a method, `makeSound()`, that prints the noise it makes to the Debug area.

Now that you have an `Animal` class, let's use it to create an instance of an animal in the next section.

Making an instance of the class

Once you have declared and defined a class, you can create instances of that class. You will now create an instance of the `Animal` class that represents a cat. Follow these steps:

1. To create an instance of the `Animal` class, list all its properties and call its `makeSound()` method, type the following after your class declaration and run it:

```
let cat = Animal()
print(cat.name)
print(cat.sound)
print(cat.numberOfLegs)
print(cat.breathesOxygen)
cat.makeSound()
```

   You access instance properties and methods by typing a dot after the instance name, followed by the property or method you want. You'll see the values for the instance properties and method calls listed in the Debug area. Since the values are the default values assigned when the class was created, `name` and `sound` contain empty strings, `numberOfLegs` contains 0, `breathesOxygen` contains `true`, and the `makeSound()` method prints an empty string.

2. Let's assign some values to this instance's properties. Modify your code as shown:

```
let cat = Animal()
cat.name = "Cat"
cat.sound = "Mew"
cat.numberOfLegs = 4
cat.breathesOxygen = true
print(cat.name)
```

   Now, when you run the program, the following is displayed in the Debug area:

```
Cat
Mew
4
true
Mew
```

The values for all the instance properties and the result of the `makeSound()` method are printed to the Debug area.

Note that here you create the instance first, and then assign values to that instance. It is also possible to assign the values when the instance is being created, and you do this by implementing an initializer in your class declaration.

3. An initializer is responsible for ensuring all of the instance properties have valid values when a class is created. Let's add an initializer for the `Animal` class. Modify your class definition as shown:

```
class Animal {
    var name: String
    var sound: String
    var numberOfLegs: Int
    var breathesOxygen: Bool
    init(name: String, sound: String, numberOfLegs:
    Int, breathesOxygen: Bool) {
        self.name = name
        self.sound = sound
        self.numberOfLegs = numberOfLegs
        self.breathesOxygen = breathesOxygen
    }
    func makeSound() {
        print(self.sound)
    }
}
```

As you can see, the initializer uses the `init` keyword and has a list of parameters that will be used to set the property values. Note that the `self` keyword distinguishes the property names from the parameters. For example, `self.name` refers to the property and `name` refers to the parameter. At the end of the initialization process, every property in the class should have a valid value.

4. You'll see some errors in your code at this point. You will need to update your function call to address this. Modify your code as shown and run it:

```
    func makeSound() {
        print(self.sound)
    }
}
let cat = Animal(name: "Cat", sound: "Mew",
```

```
    numberOfLegs: 4, breathesOxygen: true)
    print(cat.name)
```

The results are the same as those in *Step 2*, but you created the instance and set its properties in a single instruction. Excellent!

Now there are different types of animals, such as mammals, birds, reptiles, and fish. You could create a class for each type, but you could also create a **subclass** based on an existing class. Let's see how to do that in the next section.

Making a subclass

A subclass of a class inherits all of the methods and properties of an existing class. You can also add additional properties and methods to it if you wish. You'll now create `Mammal`, a subclass of the `Animal` class. Follow these steps:

1. To declare the `Mammal` class, type in the following code just after the `Animal` class declaration:

```
    class Mammal: Animal {
        let hasFurOrHair: Bool = true
    }
```

Typing : `Animal` after the class name makes the `Mammal` class a subclass of the `Animal` class. It has all the properties and methods declared in the `Animal` class, and one additional property, `hasFurOrHair`. Since the `Animal` class is the parent of the `Mammal` class, you can refer to it as the **superclass** of the `Mammal` class.

2. Modify your code that creates an instance of your class as shown, and run it:

```
    let cat = Mammal(name: "Cat", sound: "Mew",
    numberOfLegs: 4, breathesOxygen: true)
```

`cat` is now an instance of the `Mammal` class instead of the `Animal` class. As you can see, the results displayed in the Debug area are the same as before, and there are no errors. The value for `hasFurOrHair` has not been displayed though. Let's fix that.

3. Type in the following code after all other code in your playground to display the contents of the `hasFurOrHair` property and run it:

```
    print(cat.hasFurOrHair)
```

Since the initializer for the `Animal` class does not have a parameter to assign a value to `hasFurOrHair`, the default value is used, and `true` will be displayed in the Debug area.

You have seen that a subclass can have additional properties. A subclass can also have additional methods, and method implementation in a subclass can differ from the superclass implementation. Let's see how to do that in the next section.

Overriding a superclass method

So far, you've been using multiple `print()` statements to display the values of the class instance. You'll implement a `description()` method to display all of the instance properties in the Debug area, so multiple `print()` statements will no longer be required. Follow these steps:

1. Modify your `Animal` class declaration to implement a `description()` method, as shown:

```
class Animal {
    var name: String
    var sound: String
    var numberOfLegs: Int
    var breathesOxygen: Bool = true
    init(name: String, sound: String, numberOfLegs:
    Int, breathesOxygen: Bool) {
        self.name = name
        self.sound = sound
        self.numberOfLegs = numberOfLegs
        self.breathesOxygen = breathesOxygen
    }
    func makeSound() {
        print(self.sound)
    }
    func description() -> String {
        return "name: \(self.name)
        sound: \(self.sound)
        numberOfLegs: \(self.numberOfLegs)
        breathesOxygen: \(self.breathesOxygen)"
    }
}
```

2. Modify your code as shown to use the `description()` method in place of the multiple `print()` statements, and run the program:

```
let cat = Mammal(name: "Cat", sound: "Mew",
numberOfLegs: 4, breathesOxygen: true)
print(cat.description())
cat.makeSound()
```

You will see the following in the Debug area:

```
name: Cat sound: Mew numberOfLegs: 4 breathesOxygen: true
Mew
```

As you can see, even though the `description()` method is not implemented in the `Mammal` class, it is implemented in the `Animal` class. This means it will be inherited by the `Mammal` class, and the instance properties will be printed to the Debug area. Note that the value for the `hasFurOrHair` property is missing, and you can't put it in the `description()` method because the `hasFurOrHair` property does not exist for the `Animal` class.

3. You can change the implementation of the `description()` method in the `Mammal` class to display the `hasFurOrHair` property's value. Add the following code to your `Mammal` class definition and run it:

```
Mammal: Animal {
    let hasFurOrHair: Bool = true
    override func description() -> String {
        return super.description() + " hasFurOrHair:
        \(self.hasFurOrHair)"
    }
}
```

The `override` keyword is used here to specify that the `description()` method implemented here is to be used in place of the superclass implementation. The `super` keyword is used to call the superclass implementation of `description()`. The value in `hasFurOrHair` is then added to the string returned by `super.description()`.

You will see the following in the Debug area:

```
name: Cat sound: Mew numberOfLegs: 4 breathesOxygen: true
hasFurOrHair: true
Mew
```

The `hasFurOrHair` property's value is displayed in the Debug area, showing that you are using the `Mammal` subclass implementation of the `description()` method.

You've created class and subclass declarations and made instances of both. You've also added initializers and methods to both. Cool! Let's look at how to declare and use structures in the next section.

Understanding structures

Like classes, structures also group together properties and methods used to represent an object and do specific tasks. Remember the `Animal` class you created? You can also use a structure to accomplish the same thing. There are differences between classes and structures though, and you will learn more about those later.

Here's what a structure declaration and definition looks like:

```
struct StructName {
    property1
    property2
    property3
    method1() {
        code
    }
    method2() {
        code
    }
}
```

As you can see, a structure is very similar to a class. It also has a descriptive name, can contain properties and methods, and you can create instances.

> **Important information**
>
> To learn more about structures, visit: `https://docs.swift.org/swift-book/LanguageGuide/ClassesAndStructures.html`.

Let's look at how to work with structures. You'll learn how to declare and define structures, create instances based on the structure, and manipulate them. You'll start by creating a structure to represent reptiles in the next section.

Creating a structure declaration

Continuing with the animal theme, let's declare and define a structure that can store details of reptiles. Add the following code after all other code in your playground:

```
struct Reptile {
    var name: String
    var sound: String
    var numberOfLegs: Int
    var breathesOxygen: Bool
    let hasFurOrHair: Bool = false
    func makeSound() {
        print(sound)
    }
    func description() -> String {
        return "Structure: Reptile name: \(self.name)
        sound: \(self.sound)
        numberOfLegs: \(self.numberOfLegs)
        breathesOxygen: \(self.breathesOxygen)
        hasFurOrHair: \(self.hasFurOrHair)"
    }
}
```

As you can see, this is almost the same as the `Animal` class declaration you did earlier. Structure names also normally start with a capital letter, and this structure has properties to store the name of the animal, the sound it makes, how many legs it has, whether it breathes oxygen, and whether it has fur or hair. This structure also has a method, `makeSound()`, that prints the sound it makes to the Debug area.

Now that you have a `Reptile` structure declaration, let's use it to create an instance representing a snake in the next section.

Making an instance of the structure

As with classes, you can create instances from a structure declaration. You will now create an instance of the Reptile structure that represents a snake, print out the property values of that instance, and call the makeSound() method. Type the following after your structure declaration and run it:

```
var snake = Reptile(name: "Snake", sound: "Hiss",
numberOfLegs: 0, breathesOxygen: true)
print(snake.description())
snake.makeSound()
```

Note that you did not need to implement an initializer; structures automatically get an initializer for all of their properties, called the **memberwise** initializer. Neat! The following will be displayed in the Debug area:

```
Structure: Reptile name: Snake sound: Hiss numberOfLegs: 0
breathesOxygen: true hasFurOrHair: false
Hiss
```

Even though the structure declaration is very similar to the class declaration, there are two differences between a class and a structure:

- Structures cannot inherit from another structure.

- Classes are **reference types**, while structures are **value types**.

Let's look at the difference between value types and reference types in the next section.

Comparing value types and reference types

Classes are reference types. This means when you assign a class instance to a variable, you are actually storing the memory location of the original instance in the variable, instead of the instance itself.

Structures are value types. This means when you assign a structure instance to a variable, that instance is copied, and whatever changes you make to the original instance do not affect the copy.

Now, you will create an instance of a class and a structure and observe the differences between them. Follow these steps:

1. You'll start by creating a variable containing a structure instance and assigning it to a second variable, then change the value of a property in the second variable. Type in the following code and run it:

```
struct SampleValueType {
    var sampleProperty = 10
}
var a = SampleValueType()
var b = a
b.sampleProperty = 20
print(a.sampleProperty)
print(b.sampleProperty)
```

In this example, you declared a structure, SampleValueType, that contains one property, sampleProperty. Then, you created an instance of that structure and assigned it to a variable, a. After that, you assigned a to a new variable, b. Next, you changed the sampleProperty value of b to 20. When you print out the sampleProperty value of a, 10 is printed in the Debug area, showing that any changes made to the sampleProperty value of b do not affect the sampleProperty value of a. This is because when you assigned a to b, a copy of a was assigned to b, so they are completely separate instances that don't affect one another.

2. Next, you'll create a variable containing a class instance and assign it to a second variable, then change the value of a property in the second variable. Type in the following code and run it:

```
class SampleReferenceType {
    var sampleProperty = 10
}
var c = SampleReferenceType()
var d = c
c.sampleProperty = 20
print(c.sampleProperty)
print(d.sampleProperty)
```

In this example, you declared a class, `SampleReferenceType`, that contains one property, `sampleProperty`. Then, you created an instance of that class and assigned it to a variable, `c`. After that, you assigned `c` to a new variable, `d`. Next, you changed the `sampleProperty` value of `d` to `20`. When you print out the `sampleProperty` value of `c`, `20` is printed in the Debug area, showing that any changes made to `c` or `d` are affecting the same `SampleReferenceType` instance.

Now, the question is, which should you use, classes or structures? Let's explore that in the next section.

Deciding between classes and structures

You've seen that you can use either a class or a structure to represent a complex object. So, which should you use?

It is recommended to use structures unless you need something that requires classes, such as subclasses. This actually helps to prevent some subtle errors that may occur due to classes being reference types.

Fantastic! Now that you have learned about classes and structures, let's take a look at **enumerations**, which allow you to group related values together, in the next section.

Understanding enumerations

Enumerations allow you to group related values together, for example:

- Compass directions (E, W, N, and S)
- Traffic light colors
- The colors of a rainbow

To understand why enumerations would be ideal for this purpose, let's consider the following example.

Imagine you're programming a traffic light. You can use an integer variable to represent different traffic light colors where `0` is red, `1` is yellow and `2` is green, like this:

```
var trafficLightColor = 2
```

Although this is a possible way to represent a traffic light, what happens when you assign 3 to `trafficLightColor`? This will cause problems as 3 does not represent a valid traffic light color. So, it would be better if you could limit the possible values of `trafficLightColor` to the colors it can display.

Here's what an enumeration declaration looks like:

```
enum EnumName {
    case value1
    case value2
    case value3
}
```

Every enumeration has a descriptive name, and the body contains the associated values for that enumeration.

> **Important information**
>
> To learn more about enumerations, visit `https://docs.swift.org/swift-book/LanguageGuide/Enumerations.html`.

Let's look at how to work with enumerations. You'll learn how to create and manipulate them. You'll start by creating one to represent a traffic light color in the next section.

Creating an enumeration

Let's create an enumeration to represent a traffic light. Follow these steps:

1. Add the following code to your playground and run it:

    ```
    enum TrafficLightColor {
        case red
        case yellow
        case green
    }
    var trafficLightColor = TrafficLightColor.red
    ```

This creates an enumeration named `TrafficLightColor`, which groups together the red, yellow, and green values. As you can see, the value for the `trafficLightColor` variable is limited to red, yellow, and green; setting any other value will generate an error.

2. Just like classes and structures, enumerations can contain methods. Let's add a method to `TrafficLightColor`. Modify your code as shown to make `TrafficLightColor` return a string representing the traffic light color and run it:

```swift
enum TrafficLightColor {
    case red
    case yellow
    case green
    func description() -> String {
        switch self {
        case .red:
            return "red"
        case .yellow:
            return "yellow"
        default:
            return "green"
        }
    }
}
var trafficLightColor = TrafficLightColor.red
print(trafficLightColor.description())
```

The `description()` method returns a string depending on `trafficLightColor`'s value. Since `trafficLightColor`'s value is `TrafficLightColor.red`, red will appear in the Debug area.

You've learned how to create and use enumerations to store grouped values, and how to add methods to them. This concludes this chapter. Good job!

Summary

In this chapter, you learned how to declare complex objects using a class, create instances of a class, create a subclass, and override a class method. You've also learned how to declare a structure, create instances of a structure, and understand the difference between reference and value types. Finally, you learned how to use enumerations to represent a specific set of values.

You now know how to use classes and structures to represent complex objects, and how to use enumerations to group related values together in your own programs.

In the next chapter, you will study how to specify common traits in classes and structures using protocols, extend the capability of built-in classes using extensions, and handle errors in your programs.

8
Protocols, Extensions, and Error Handling

In the previous chapter, you've learned how to represent complex objects using classes or structures and how to use enumerations to group related values together.

To end the section on Swift, you'll learn about **protocols**, **extensions**, and **error handling**. Protocols define a blueprint of methods, properties, and other requirements that can be adopted by a class, structure, or enumeration. Extensions enable you to provide new functionality for an existing class, structure, or enumeration. Error handling covers how to respond to and recover from errors in your program.

By the end of this chapter, you'll be able to write your own protocols to meet the requirements of your apps, use extensions to add new capabilities to existing types, and handle error conditions in your apps without crashing.

The following topics will be covered in this chapter:

- Understanding protocols
- Understanding extensions
- Exploring error handling

Technical requirements

The Xcode playground for this chapter is in the `Chapter08` folder of the code bundle for this book, which can be downloaded here:

`https://github.com/PacktPublishing/iOS-15-Programming-for-Beginners-Sixth-Edition`

Check out the following video to see the code in action:

`https://bit.ly/3H1XWkQ`

If you wish to start from scratch, create a new playground and name it `Protocols, ExtensionsAndErrorHandling`. You can type in and run all of the code in this chapter as you go along. Let's start with protocols, which is a way of specifying properties and methods that a class, structure or enumeration should have.

Understanding protocols

Protocols are like blueprints that determine what properties or methods an object should have. After you've declared a protocol, classes, structures, and enumerations can adopt this protocol, and provide their own implementation for the required properties and methods.

Here's what a protocol declaration looks like:

```
protocol ProtocolName {
    var readWriteProperty1 {get set}
    var readOnlyProperty2 {get}
    methodName1()
    methodName2()
}
```

Just like classes and structures, protocol names start with an uppercase letter. Properties need to be declared using the `var` keyword. You use `{get set}` if you want a property that can be read from or written to, and `{get}` if you want a read-only property. Note that you just specify property and method names. The implementation is done within the adopting class, structure, or enumeration.

> **Important Information**
>
> For more information on protocols, visit: `https://docs.swift.org/swift-book/LanguageGuide/Protocols.html`.

To help you understand protocols, imagine an app used by a fast-food restaurant. The management has decided to show calorie counts for the meals being served. The app currently has the following class, structure, and enumeration, and none of them have calorie counts implemented:

- A Burger class

- A Fries structure

- A Sauce enumeration

Add the following code to your playground to declare the Burger class, the Fries structure, and the Sauce enumeration:

```
class Burger {
}
struct Fries {
}
enum Sauce {
    case chili
    case tomato
}
```

These represent the existing class, structure, and enumeration in the app. Don't worry about the empty definitions, as they are not required for this lesson. As you can see, none of them have calorie counts at present. Let's look at how to work with protocols to specify the properties and methods needed to implement calorie counts. You'll start by declaring a protocol that specifies the required properties and methods in the next section.

Creating a protocol declaration

Let's create a protocol that specifies a required property, calories, and a method, description(). Type the following into your playground above the class, structure, and enumeration declarations:

```
protocol CalorieCount {
    var calories: Int { get }
    func description() -> String
}
```

This protocol is named `CalorieCount`. It specifies that any object that adopts it must have a property, `calories`, that holds the calorie count, and a method, `description()`, that returns a string. `{ get }` means that you only need to be able to read the value stored in `calories`, and you don't have to write to it. Note that the definition of the `description()` method is not specified as that will be done in the class, structure, or enumeration. All you need to do to adopt a protocol is type a colon after the class name followed by the protocol name, and implement the required properties and methods.

To make the `Burger` class conform to this protocol, modify your code as follows:

```
class Burger: CalorieCount {
    let calories = 800
    func description() -> String {
        return "This burger has \(calories) calories"
    }
}
```

As you can see, the `calories` property and the `description()` method have been added to the `Burger` class. Even though the protocol specifies a variable, you can use a constant here because the protocol only requires that you can get the value for `calories`, and not set it.

Let's make the `Fries` structure adopt this protocol as well. Modify your code for the `Fries` structure as follows:

```
struct Fries: CalorieCount {
    let calories = 500
    func description() -> String {
        return "These fries have \(calories) calories"
    }
}
```

The same process that was used for the `Burger` class is used for the `Fries` structure, and it now conforms to the `CalorieCount` protocol as well.

You could modify the `Sauce` enumeration in the same way, but let's do it using extensions instead. Extensions extend an existing class's capabilities. You'll add the `CalorieCount` protocol to the `Sauce` enumeration using an extension in the next section.

Understanding extensions

Extensions allow you to provide extra capabilities to an object without modifying the original object definition. You can use them on Apple-provided objects (where you don't have access to the object definition) or when you wish to segregate your code for readability and ease of maintenance. Here's what an extension looks like:

```
class ExistingType {
    property1
    method1()
}
extension ExistingType : ProtocolName {
    property2
    method2()
}
```

Here, an extension is used to provide an additional property and method to an existing class.

> **Important Information**
>
> For more information on extensions, visit `https://docs.swift.org/swift-book/LanguageGuide/Extensions.html`.

Let's look at how to use extensions. You'll start by making the `Sauce` enumeration conform to the `CalorieCount` protocol using an extension in the next section.

Adopting a protocol via an extension

At present, the `Sauce` enumeration does not conform to the `CalorieCount` protocol. You'll use an extension to add the properties and methods required to make it conform. Type in the following code after the declaration for the `Sauce` enumeration:

```
enum Sauce {
    case chili
    case tomato
}
extension Sauce: CalorieCount {
    var calories: Int {
        switch self {
        case .chili:
```

```
        return 20
    case .tomato:
        return 15
    }
  }
  func description() -> String {
      return "This sauce has \(calories) calories"
  }
}
```

As you can see, no changes were made to the original definition for the `Sauce` enumeration. This is also really useful if you want to extend the capabilities of existing Swift standard types, such as `String` and `Int`.

Enumerations can't have stored properties, so a `switch` statement is used to return the number of calories based on the enumeration's value, using the `self` keyword. The `description()` method is the same as the one in the `Burger` class and the `Fries` structure.

At this point, all three objects have a `calories` property and a `description()` method. Great!

Let's see how you can put them in an array and perform an operation to get the total calorie count for a meal.

Creating an array of different types of objects

Ordinarily, an array's elements must be of the same type. However, since the `Burger` class, the `Fries` structure, and the `Sauce` enumeration all conform to the `CalorieCount` protocol, you can make an array that contains elements conforming to this protocol. Follow these steps:

1. To add instances of the `Burger` class, the `Fries` structure and the `Sauce` enumeration to an array, type in the following code after all the protocol and object declarations:

```
let burger = Burger()
let fries = Fries()
let sauce = Sauce.tomato
let foodArray: [CalorieCount] = [burger, fries, sauce]
```

2. To get the total calorie count, add the following code after the line where you created the `foodArray` constant:

```
var totalCalories = 0
for food in foodArray {
    totalCalories += food.calories
}
print(totalCalories)
```

The `for` loop iterates through each element in the `foodArray` array. For each iteration, the value in the `calories` property for each food item will be added to `totalCalories`, and the total amount, `1315`, will be displayed in the Debug area.

You have learned how to create a protocol and make a class, structure or enumeration conform to it, either within the class definition or via extensions. Let's look at error handling next, which looks at how to respond to or recover from errors in your program.

Exploring error handling

When you write apps, bear in mind that error conditions may happen, and error handling is how your app would respond to and recover from such conditions.

First, you create a type that conforms to Swift's `Error` protocol, which lets this type be used for error handling. Enumerations are normally used, as you can specify associated values for different kinds of errors. When something unexpected happens, you can stop program execution by throwing an error. You use the `throw` statement for this, and provide an instance of the type conforming to the `Error` protocol with the appropriate value. This allows you to see what went wrong.

Of course, it would be better if you can respond to an error without stopping your program. For this, you can use a `do-catch` block, which looks like this:

```
do {
    try expression1
    statement1
} catch {
    statement2
}
```

Here, you attempt to execute code in the do block using the `try` keyword. If an error is thrown, the statements in the `catch` block are executed. You can have multiple `catch` blocks to handle different error types.

> **Important Information:**
>
> For more information on error handling, visit `https://docs.swift.` `org/swift-book/LanguageGuide/ErrorHandling.html`.

As an example, let's say you have an app that needs to access a web page. However, if the server where that web page is located is down, it is up to you to write the code to handle the error, such as trying an alternative web server or informing the user that the server is down.

Let's create an enumeration that conforms to the `Error` protocol, use a `throw` statement to stop program execution when an error occurs, and use a `do-catch` block to handle an error. Follow these steps:

1. Type the following code into your playground:

    ```
    enum WebsiteError: Error {
        case noInternetConnection
        case siteDown
        case wrongURL
    }
    ```

    This declares an enumeration, `WebsiteError`, that adopts the `Error` protocol. It covers three possible error conditions; there is no internet connection, the website is down, or the URL could not be resolved.

2. Type in the following code to declare a function that checks if a website is up after the `WebpageError` declaration:

    ```
    func checkWebsite(siteUp: Bool) throws -> String {
        if siteUp == false {
            throw WebsiteError.siteDown
        }
        return "Site is up"
    }
    ```

    If `siteUp` is `true`, `"Site is up"` is returned. If `siteUp` is `false`, the program will stop executing and throw an error.

3. Type in the following code after the function declaration to call your function, and run your program:

```
let siteStatus = true
try checkWebsite(siteUp: siteStatus)
```

Since siteStatus is true, Site is up will appear in the Results area.

4. Change the value of siteStatus to false and run your program. Your program crashes and the following error message is displayed in the Debug area:

```
Playground execution terminated: An error was thrown and
was not caught:
__lldb_expr_5.WebsiteError.siteDown
```

5. Of course, it is always better if you can handle errors without making your program crash. You can do this by using a do-catch block. Modify your code as shown and run it:

```
let siteStatus = false
do {
    print(try checkWebsite(siteUp: siteStatus))
} catch {
    print(error)
}
```

The do block tries to execute the checkWebsite(siteUp:) function and prints the status if successful. If there is an error, instead of crashing, the statements in the catch block are executed, and the error message siteDown appears in the Debug area.

> **Tip**
>
> You can make your program handle different error conditions by implementing multiple catch blocks. See this link for details: https://docs.swift.org/swift-book/LanguageGuide/ErrorHandling.html.

You have learned how to handle errors in your app without making it crash. Give yourself a pat on the back; you have completed the first part of this book!

Summary

In this chapter, you learned how to write protocols and how to make classes, structures, and enumerations conform to them. You also learned how to extend the capabilities of a class by using an extension. Finally, you learned how to handle errors using the `do-catch` block.

It may seem rather abstract and hard to understand now, but as you will see in *Part 3* of this book, you will use protocols to implement common functionalities in different parts of your program instead of writing the same program over and over. You will see how useful extensions are in organizing your code, which makes it easy to maintain. Last but not least, you'll see how good error handling makes it easy to pinpoint the mistakes you made while coding your app.

In the next chapter, you will start writing your first iOS application by creating the screens for it using storyboards, which allow you to rapidly prototype an application without having to type a lot of code.

Part 2: Design

Welcome to *Part 2* of this book. At this point, you're familiar with the Xcode user interface, and you have a solid foundation of using Swift. In this part, you'll start creating the user interface of a restaurant reservation app, named *Let's Eat*. You will use Interface Builder to build the screens that your app will use, add elements such as buttons, labels, and fields to them, and connect them together, using segues. As you will see, you can do this with a minimum amount of coding.

This part comprises the following chapters:

- *Chapter 9, Setting Up the User Interface*
- *Chapter 10, Building Your User Interface*
- *Chapter 11, Finishing Up Your User Interface*
- *Chapter 12, Modifying and Configuring Cells*

By the end of this part, you'll be able to navigate the various screens of your app in the iOS Simulator, and you will know how to prototype the user interface of your own apps. Let's get started!

9

Setting Up the User Interface

In *Part 1* of this book, you studied about the Swift language and how it works. Now that you have a good working knowledge of the language, you can learn how to develop an iOS application. In this part, you will build the user interface of a restaurant reservation app, *Let's Eat*. You will use Xcode's **Interface Builder** for this, and coding will be kept to a minimum.

You'll start this chapter by learning useful terms used in iOS app development, which are used extensively throughout this book. Next, you will tour the screens used in the *Let's Eat* app and learn how the user would use the app. Finally, you will begin recreating the app's UI with Interface Builder, starting with the **tab bar**, which allows the user to select between the **Explore** and **Map** screens. You'll add navigation bars to the top of both screens. You'll also learn how to configure the **Launch** screen that is displayed when the app is started and how to use custom icons for the **Launch** screen and the **tab bar buttons**.

By the end of this chapter, you'll have learned common terms used in iOS app development, what the flow of your app will look like, how to add resources to your app, and how to use Interface Builder to add, configure and position UI elements.

The following topics will be covered:

- Learning useful terms in iOS development
- Touring the *Let's Eat* app
- Creating a new Xcode project
- Setting up a tab bar controller scene
- Setting up the **Launch** screen

Technical requirements

You will create a new Xcode project, LetsEat, in this chapter.

The resource files and completed Xcode project for this chapter are in the Chapter09 folder of the code bundle for this book, which can be downloaded here:

https://github.com/PacktPublishing/iOS-15-Programming-for-Beginners-Sixth-Edition

Check out the following video to see the code in action:

https://bit.ly/3qcB2kO

Before you create the project, you'll learn some common terms used in iOS development.

Learning useful terms in iOS development

As you begin your journey into iOS app development, you will encounter special terms and definitions. Here are some of the most commonly used terms and definitions. Just read through them for now. Even though you may not understand everything yet, it will become clearer as you go along:

- **View**: A view is an instance of the UIView class or one of its subclasses. Anything you see on your screen (buttons, text fields, labels, and so on) is a view. You will use views to build your UI.

- **Stack View**: A stack view is an instance of the UIStackView class, which is a subclass of UIView. It is used to group views together in a horizontal or vertical stack. This makes them easier to position on the screen using **Auto Layout**, which is described later in this section.

- **View Controller**: A view controller is an instance of the `UIViewController` class. It determines what a view displays to the user, and what happens when a user interacts with a view. Every view controller has a `view` property, which contains a reference to a view.

- **Table View Controller**: A table view controller is an instance of the `UITableViewController` class, which is a subclass of the `UIViewController` class. Its `view` property has a reference to a `UITableView` instance (**table view**), which displays a single column of `UITableViewCell` instances (**table view cells**).

The *Settings* app displays your device settings in a table view:

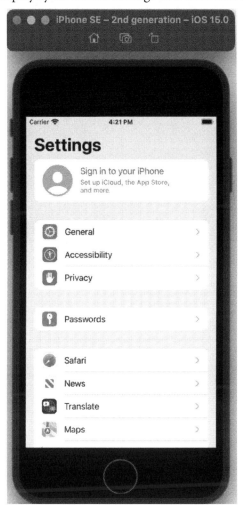

Figure 9.1: Settings app

As you can see, all of the different settings (**General**, **Accessibility**, **Privacy**, and so on) are displayed in table view cells inside the table view.

- **Collection View Controller**: A collection view controller is an instance of the `UICollectionViewController` class, which is a subclass of the `UIViewController` class. Its `view` property has a reference to a `UICollectionView` instance (**collection view**), which displays a grid of `UICollectionViewCell` instances (**collection view cells**).

The *Photos* app displays photos in a collection view:

Figure 9.2: Photos app

As you can see, thumbnail pictures are displayed in collection view cells inside the collection view.

- **Navigation Controller**: A navigation controller is an instance of the `UINavigationController` class, which is a subclass of the `UIViewController` class. It has a `viewControllers` property that holds an array of view controllers. The view of the last view controller in the array appears onscreen, along with a navigation bar at the top of the screen.

The table view controller in the *Settings* app is embedded in a navigation controller, and you can see the navigation bar above the table view:

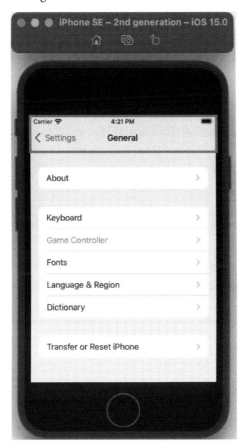

Figure 9.3: Navigation bar in Settings app

When you tap on a setting, the view controller for that setting is added to the array of view controllers assigned to the `viewControllers` property. The user sees the view for that view controller slide in from the right. Note the navigation bar at the top of the screen, which can hold a title and buttons. A < **Settings** button appears in the top left side of the navigation bar. Tapping this button returns you to the previous screen.

- **Tab Bar Controller**: A tab bar controller is an instance of the `UITabBarController` class, which is a subclass of the `UIViewController` class. It has a `viewControllers` property that holds an array of view controllers. The view of the first view controller in the array appears onscreen, along with a tab bar with buttons at the bottom. The button on the extreme left corresponds to the first view controller in the array and will be already selected. When you tap another button, the corresponding view controller is loaded, and its view appears on screen.

The *Photos* app uses a tab bar controller to display a row of buttons at the bottom of the screen:

Figure 9.4: Tab bar in Photos app

Tapping each button in the tab bar will display a different screen.

- **Model-View-Controller (MVC)**: This is a very common design pattern used in iOS app development. The user interacts with views onscreen. App data is stored in data model objects. Controllers manage the flow of information between views and data model objects. It will be discussed in detail in *Chapter 13, Getting Started with MVC and Collection Views.*

- **Storyboard**: A storyboard file contains a visual representation of what the user sees. Each screen of information is represented by a storyboard **scene**.

Open the `Exploring Xcode` project that you created in *Chapter 1, Getting Familiar with Xcode,* and click the `Main` storyboard file:

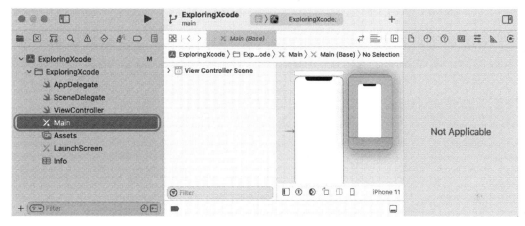

Figure 9.5: Exploring Xcode project showing Main storyboard file

You'll see one scene in it, and when you run your app in the iOS Simulator, the contents of this scene will be displayed on the screen. You can have more than one scene in a storyboard file.

- **Segue**: If you have more than one scene in an app, you use segues to move from one scene to another. The `ExploringXcode` project does not have any segues since there is just one scene in its storyboard, but you will see them in a later part of this chapter.

- **Auto Layout**: As a developer, you have to make sure that your app looks good on devices with different screen sizes. Auto Layout helps you lay out your user interface based on constraints you specify. For instance, you can set a constraint to make sure a button is centered on the screen regardless of screen size or make a text field expand when the device is rotated from portrait to landscape.

Now that you are familiar with the terms used in iOS app development, let's take a tour through the app you will build.

Touring the Let's Eat app

Let's take a quick tour of the app that you will build. The *Let's Eat* app is a restaurant app that allows users to explore a list of restaurants categorized by cuisine or view a map showing all restaurants in a particular area. You'll see all the screens used in the app and its overall flow in the next sections.

> **Tip**
>
> You can see a video version of this app tour at this link: `https://bit.ly/3G0Pv7U`.

Using the Explore screen

When the app is launched, you will see the **Explore** screen:

Figure 9.6: Explore screen

Let's study the different parts of this screen.

A `UITabBar` instance (tab bar) at the bottom of the screen displays **Explore** and **Map** buttons. The **Explore** button is selected, and you see a collection view displaying a list of cuisines in collection view cells. A `UICollectionReusableView` instance (section header) containing a **LOCATION** button is at the top of the screen.

Before you can pick a cuisine, you have to select a location by tapping the **LOCATION** button.

Using the Locations screen

When you tap the **LOCATION** button, you will see the **Locations** screen:

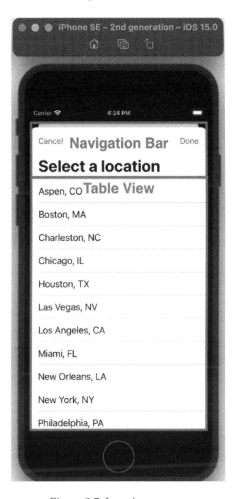

Figure 9.7: Locations screen

Let's study the different parts of this screen.

A navigation bar at the top of the screen contains **Cancel** and **Done** buttons. A table view displays a list of locations in table view cells.

You have to tap a row to select a location and tap the **Done** button to confirm. Once you tap **Done**, you are returned to the **Explore** screen and can then pick a cuisine. You can also tap **Cancel** to return to the **Explore** screen without choosing a location.

Using the Restaurant List screen

Once a location has been set (**ASPEN, CO** in this case), you can tap a cuisine. This displays the **Restaurant List** screen:

Figure 9.8: Restaurant List screen

Let's study the different parts of this screen.

A navigation bar at the top of the screen contains a **Back** button. A collection view displays a list of restaurants at that location offering the selected cuisine, in collection view cells.

You have to tap a restaurant to see its details. You can also tap the **Back** button to return to the **Explore** screen without choosing a restaurant.

Using the Restaurant Detail screen

Tapping on a restaurant on the **Restaurant List** screen displays details of that restaurant on the **Restaurant Detail** screen:

Figure 9.9: Restaurant Detail screen

Let's study the different parts of this screen.

A navigation bar at the top of the screen contains a button showing the location (**ASPEN, CO** in this case). A table view displays the restaurant's location, rating, customer reviews, photo reviews, and a location map in table view cells.

You can tap the **ASPEN, CO** button to return to the **Restaurant List** screen or tap the **Add Review** or **Add Photo** button to display the **Review Form** or **Photo Filter** screens.

Using the Review Form screen

Tapping on the **Add Review** button displays the **Review Form** screen:

Figure 9.10: Review Form screen

Let's study the different parts of this screen.

A navigation bar at the top of the screen contains **Cancel** and **Save** buttons. A table view displays a rating and text fields in table view cells.

You can set a rating and write a review for the restaurant on this screen. You can then tap the **Save** button to save your rating and review or the **Cancel** button to return to the **Restaurant Detail** screen without saving.

Using the Photo Filter screen

Tapping on the **Add Photo** button displays the **Photo Filter** screen:

Figure 9.11: Photo Filter screen

Let's study the different parts of this screen.

A navigation bar at the top of the screen contains **Cancel**, **Camera** and **Save** buttons. An image view displays a picture, and a collection view displays photo filters in collection view cells.

You can choose a picture and apply a filter to it on this screen. You can then tap the **Save** button to save your picture or the **Cancel** button to return to the **Restaurant Detail** screen without saving.

Using the Map screen

Tapping the **Map** button in the tab bar displays the **Map** screen:

Figure 9.12: Map screen

Let's study the different parts of this screen.

A tab bar at the bottom of the screen displays **Explore** and **Map** buttons. The **Map** button is selected, and you see a `MKMapView` instance (map view) displaying a map on the screen, with pins indicating restaurant locations.

Tapping a pin will display an annotation and tapping the button in the annotation will display the **Restaurant Detail** screen for that restaurant.

This completes the tour of the app. Now, it's time to start building the UI for your app!

Creating a new Xcode project

Now that you know what the screens of the app are going to look like, you can start building your app. Let's begin by creating a new project. This is the same process you used to create the `ExploringXcode` project in *Chapter 1, Getting Familiar with Xcode.* Follow these steps:

1. Launch Xcode and click **Create a new Xcode project**.
2. **iOS** should already be selected. Choose **App** and click **Next**.
3. The **Choose options for your new project:** screen is displayed:

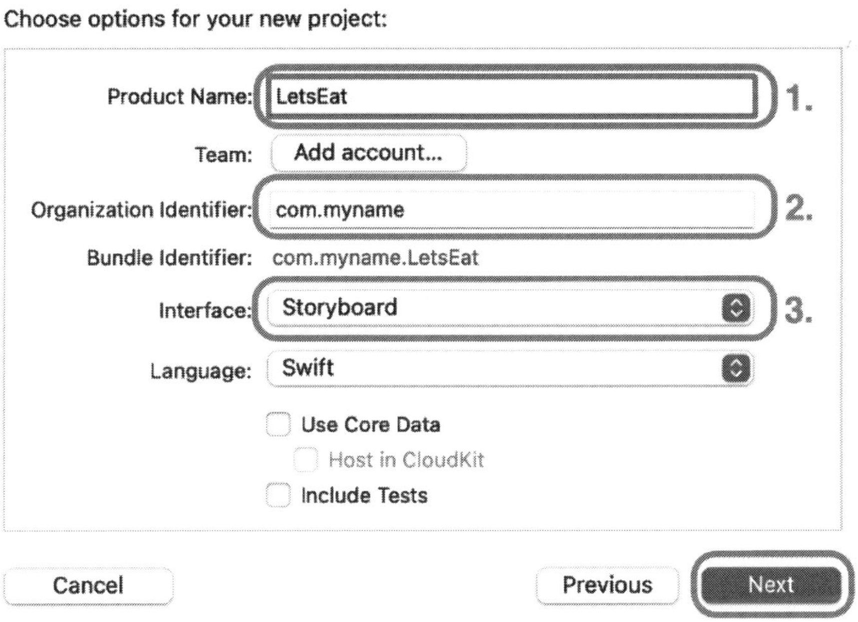

Figure 9.13: Choose options for your new project screen

Enter the information as shown:

Product Name: `LetsEat`

Organization Name: Your own name

Organization Identifier: `com.` followed by your own name

User Interface: `Storyboard`

Leave the rest of the settings at their default values. Click **Next**.

4. Choose a location to save your project and click **Create**.

5. You'll be using the iPhone SE (2nd generation) iOS simulator as a test device. In the **Scheme** menu, choose the **iPhone SE (2nd generation)** simulator.

Build and run your app. You will see a blank white screen. If you click the `Main` storyboard file in the Project navigator, you will see that it contains a single scene containing a blank view. This is why you only see a blank white screen when you run the app.

To configure the UI, you will modify the `Main` storyboard file using Interface Builder. Interface Builder allows you to add and configure scenes. Each scene represents a screen the user will see. You can add UI objects such as views and buttons to a scene, and configure them as required using the **Attributes inspector**.

> **Important Information**
>
> For more information on how to use Interface Builder, visit this link:
> `https://help.apple.com/xcode/mac/current/#/`
> `dev31645f17f.`

Now that you've created your project, you will add a tab bar controller scene to it. This scene displays a tab bar with two tabs at the bottom of the screen. Tapping a tab will display the screen associated with it. These screens correspond to the **Explore** and **Map** screens shown in the app tour. Let's see how to do this in the next section.

Setting up a tab bar controller scene

As you saw in the app tour, the *Let's Eat* app has a tab bar with two buttons at the bottom of the screen, which are used to display the **Explore** and **Map** screens. You will remove the existing view controller scene and the `ViewController` Swift file and add a tab bar controller scene with two buttons to your project. Follow these steps:

1. Click the `Main` storyboard file in the Project navigator:

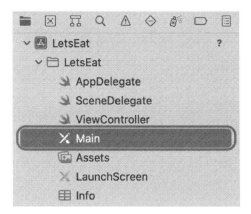

Figure 9.14: Project navigator with Main storyboard file selected

2. The contents of the `Main` storyboard file appear in the Editor area. Click the Document Outline button to collapse the document outline if it is present. This gives you more room to work with:

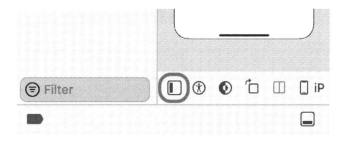

Figure 9.15: Editing area with the Document Outline button shown

3. Click the + button to open the **library**:

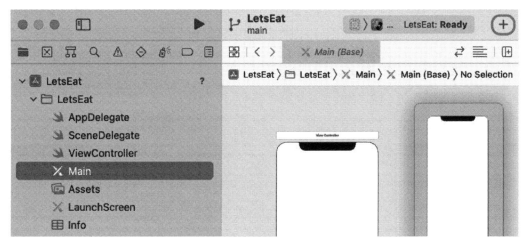

Figure 9.16: Toolbar with the Library button shown

The library allows you to pick UI objects to be added to a scene.

4. Type tabbar in the filter field. A **Tab Bar Controller** object will appear in the list of results:

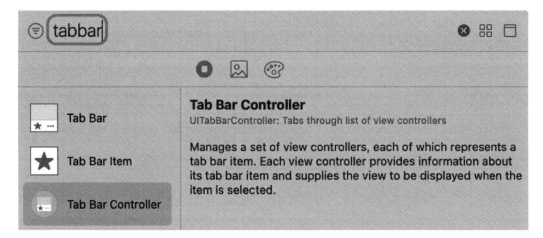

Figure 9.17: Library with Tab Bar Controller object selected

5. Drag the **Tab Bar Controller** object to the storyboard to add a new tab bar
    controller scene. It's okay if it covers the existing view controller scene. You can
    see it consists of a scene with two arrows representing segues leading to two
    more scenes:

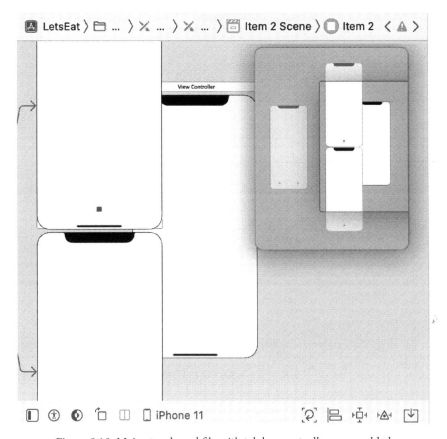

Figure 9.18: Main storyboard file with tab bar controller scene added

6. Click the - button to zoom out, and rearrange the scenes in the storyboard so that both the tab bar controller scene and the view controller scene are visible:

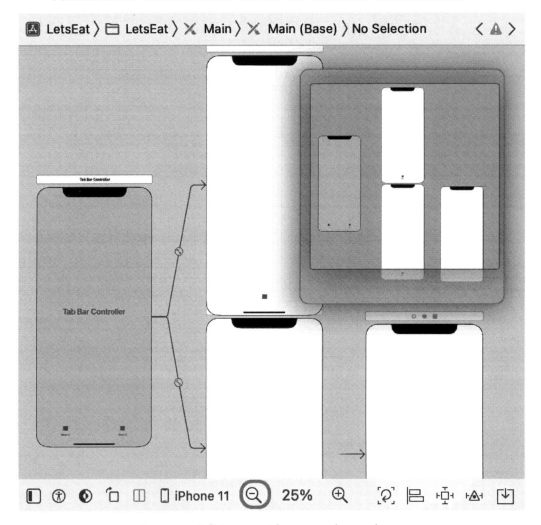

Figure 9.19: Editing area with zoom out button shown

7. Select the arrow pointing to the view controller scene as shown. This arrow determines the initial view controller scene of your app, making the view appear when the app is launched:

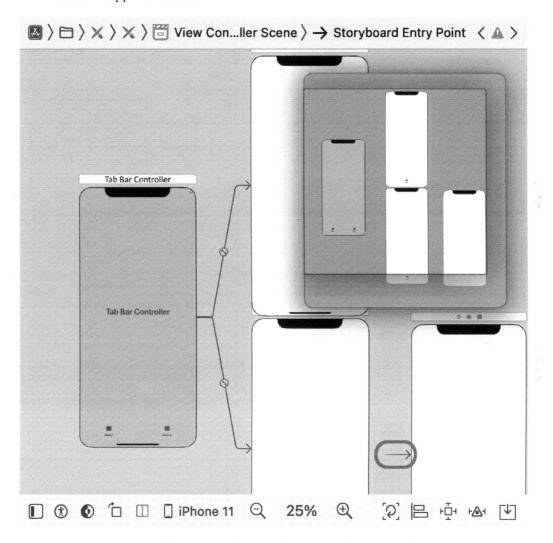

Figure 9.20: Editing area with arrow showing initial view controller scene

8. Drag the arrow from the view controller scene to the tab bar controller scene as shown. This makes the tab bar controller scene the initial scene, and the tab bar will appear when you launch the app:

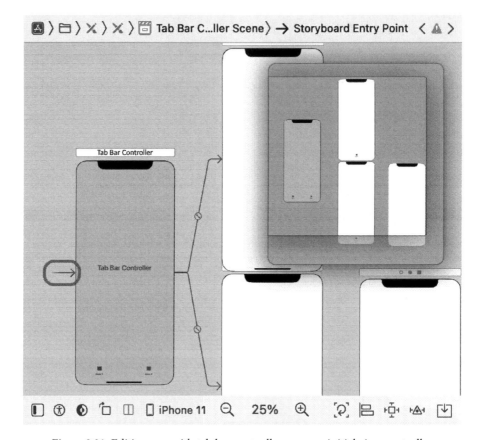

Figure 9.21: Editing area with tab bar controller scene as initial view controller

> **Tip**
>
> You can also make the tab bar controller scene the initial view controller scene by selecting it, clicking the Attributes inspector button, and ticking the **is Initial View Controller** checkbox. You'll learn more about the Attributes inspector in the next section.

9. Select the existing view controller scene in the storyboard and press *Delete* on the keyboard to remove it, as you won't be using it for this project.

10. Select the `ViewController` file in the Project navigator and press *Delete* on the keyboard to remove it, as you won't be using it for this project:

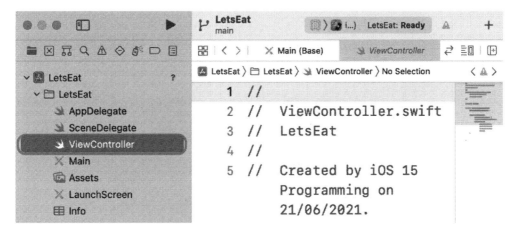

Figure 9.22: Project navigator showing the file to be deleted

11. Click **Move to Trash** in the dialog box that pops up:

Figure 9.23: Move to Trash dialog box

Build and run your app in the iOS simulator, and you'll see the tab bar with two buttons at the bottom of the screen:

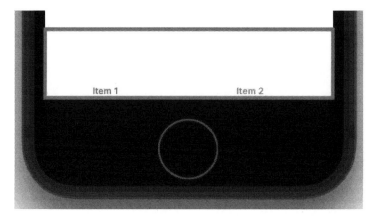

Figure 9.24: iOS simulator showing tab bar with two buttons

You have successfully added a tab bar to your project, but as you can see, the button titles are currently **Item 1** and **Item 2**. You will change them to **Explore** and **Map** in the next section.

Setting the titles of the tab bar's buttons

Your app now displays a tab bar at the bottom of the screen, but the button titles do not match those shown in the app tour. To make them match, you will configure the button titles to **Explore** and **Map** in the Attributes inspector. Follow these steps:

1. Click the Main storyboard file in the Project navigator. Click the Document Outline button to show the document outline. Click **Item 1 Scene** in the document outline:

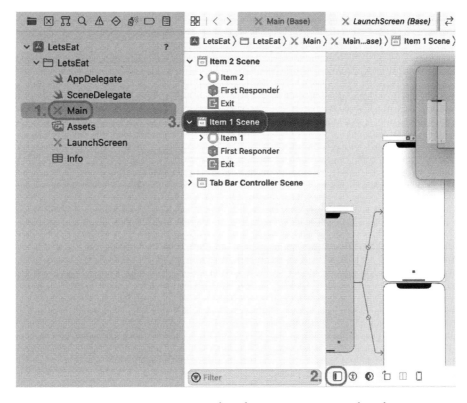

Figure 9.25: Document outline showing Item 1 scene selected

2.   Click the **Item 1** button under **Item 1 Scene**. Click the Attributes inspector button:

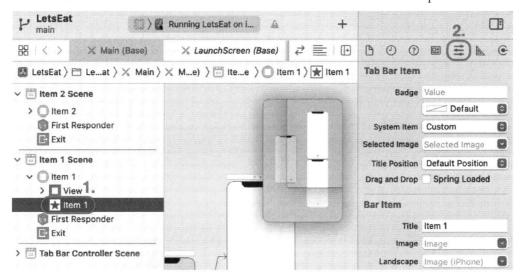

Figure 9.26: Attributes inspector selected

3.   Under **Bar Item**, set **Title** to `Explore`:

Figure 9.27: Attributes inspector with Title set to Explore

4.   Click the **Item 2** button in the **Item 2 Scene** and under **Bar Item**, set **Title** to `Map`:

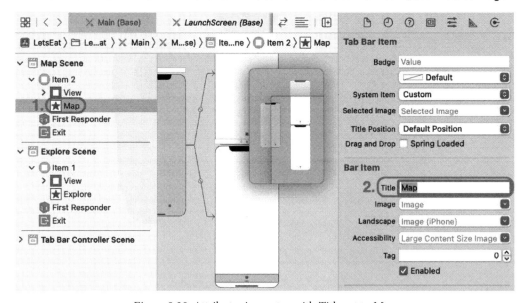

Figure 9.28: Attributes inspector with Title set to Map

Build and run your app in the Simulator. You'll see the titles for the buttons have changed to **Explore** and **Map**, respectively. Great!

Tapping the **Explore** and **Map** buttons will display the scenes for the **Explore** and **Map** screens. As shown in the app tour, if you tap the **LOCATION** button on the **Explore** screen, you will see a navigation bar at the top of the **Locations** screen containing the **Cancel** and **Done** buttons. You'll also see an empty navigation bar at the top of the **Map** screen. As you have seen in the app tour, some screens have titles and buttons in the navigation bar. In the next section, you will learn how to add navigation bars to your screens, so you can add buttons and titles to them later as required.

Embedding view controllers in navigation controllers

As you saw in the app tour, the **Explore** and **Map** screens both have a navigation bar at the top of the screen. To add the navigation bars for both screens, you will embed the view controllers of the **Explore** and **Map** scenes in a navigation controller. This will make navigation bars appear at the top of the screen when the **Explore** and **Map** screens are displayed. Follow these steps:

1. Click **Explore Scene** in the document outline:

Figure 9.29: Document outline with Explore Scene selected

2. Choose **Editor | Embed In | Navigation Controller**:

Figure 9.30: Editor menu with Embed In | Navigation Controller selected

3. A navigation controller scene appears between the **Tab Bar Controller Scene** and the **Explore Scene**:

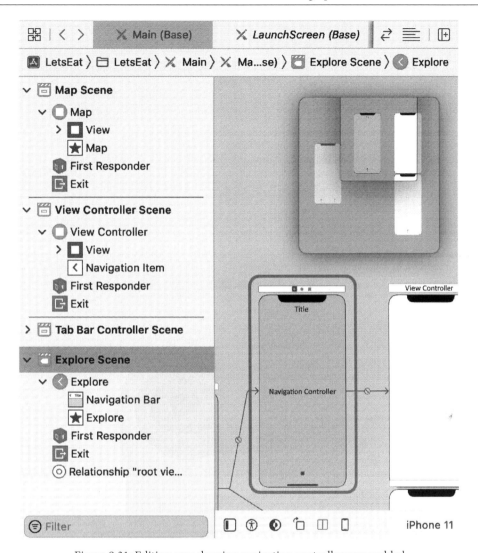

Figure 9.31: Editing area showing navigation controller scene added

Build and run your app. The **Explore** screen now has a navigation bar but since it is the same color as the background, it is not apparent on the screen.

Embedding a view controller in a navigation controller adds that view controller to the navigation controller's `viewControllers` array. The navigation controller then displays the view controller's view on the screen. The navigation controller also displays a navigation bar at the top of the screen.

The **Map** screen does not have a navigation bar yet. Let's add one now. Follow these steps:

1. Click **Map Scene** in the document outline:

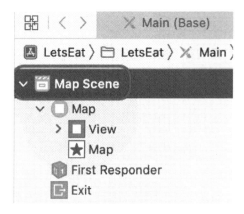

Figure 9.32: Document outline with Map Scene selected

2. Choose **Editor | Embed In | Navigation Controller**.

3. A navigation controller scene appears between the **Tab Bar Controller Scene** and the **Map Scene**:

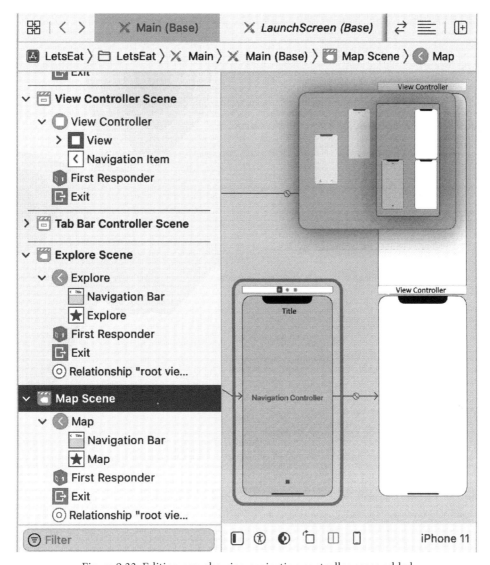

Figure 9.33: Editing area showing navigation controller scene added

Build and run your app. Both Explore and Map screens now have a navigation bar, even though you can't see them right now.

The tab bar buttons can switch between the **Explore** and **Map** screens, and each screen now has a navigation bar. The button titles are correct but the buttons themselves do not have icons. To get the button icons, you will add a file containing all of the graphics assets required for your project in the next section.

Adding the Assets.xcassets file

The `Assets.xcassets` file contains resources, such as app icons and custom images, for your project. It is currently empty as you just created this project. You will need to download the `Assets.xcassets` file in the `Chapter09` folder (which contains all of the resources for the *Let's Eat* app) from this link if you have not yet done so:

`https://github.com/PacktPublishing/iOS-15-Programming-for-Beginners-Sixth-Edition`

Once you have downloaded the file, you can add it to your project by following these steps:

1. You have to remove the existing `Assets.xcassets` file (shown as **Assets** in the Project navigator) from your project. Select it in the Project navigator and press the *Delete* key to remove it:

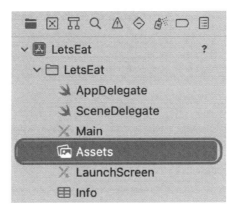

Figure 9.34: Project navigator showing file to be removed

2. Click **Move to Trash** in the dialog box that pops up.

3. Open the `Chapter09` folder inside the code bundle files you downloaded. You will see `Assets.xcassets` inside:

Figure 9.35: Assets.xcassets file from the downloaded code bundle

4. Drag the new `Assets.xcassets` file to the Project navigator area. The **Choose options for adding these files** dialog box appears. Tick the **Copy items if needed** checkbox. Tick the **Create groups** radio button. Leave the rest of the settings at their default values. Click **Finish**:

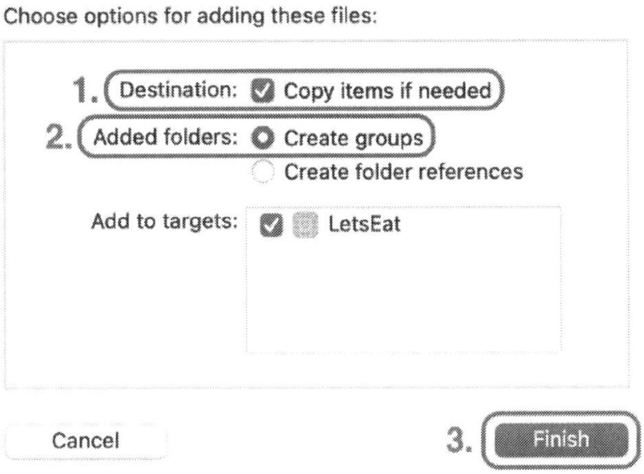

Choose options for adding these files:

1. Destination: ✅ Copy items if needed
2. Added folders: ⬤ Create groups
   ◯ Create folder references

Add to targets: ✅ 🔲 LetsEat

Cancel

3. Finish

Figure 9.36: Choose options for adding these files dialog box

5. The `Assets.xcassets` file has been added to your project. Note that it appears as `Assets` in the Project navigator. Click it to see its contents:

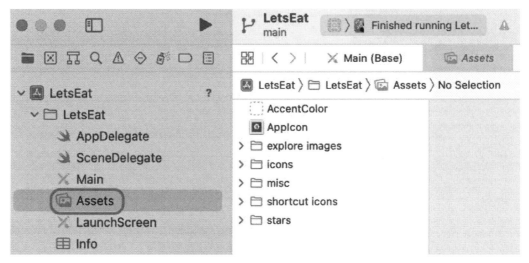

Figure 9.37: Project navigator with Assets.xcassets selected

Among the graphics assets included are icons for the tab bar buttons. You'll add the icons for the **Explore** and **Map** buttons in the next section.

Adding the icons for the Explore and Map buttons

The **Explore** and **Map** buttons currently do not have icons. These icons are in the `Assets.xcassets` folder. Add them to the buttons now by following these steps:

1. Click the `Main` storyboard file. Click the **Explore** button under **Explore Scene** in the document outline. Click the Attributes inspector button:

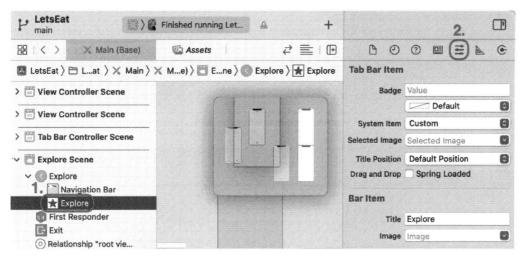

Figure 9.38: Attributes inspector for the Explore button selected

2.   Under **Bar Item**, set **Image** to `icon-explore-on`:

Figure 9.39: Attributes inspector with Image set to icon-explore-on

3. Click the **Map** button under **Map Scene**. Under **Bar Item**, set **Image** to `icon-map-on`:

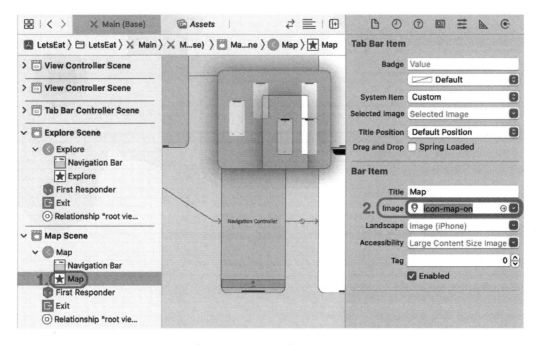

Figure 9.40: Attributes inspector with Image set to icon-map-on

Build and run your app. You can see the Explore and Map buttons now have icons:

Figure 9.41: iOS simulator showing Explore and Map buttons with icons

Congratulations! You've just configured the tab bar for your app!

When your app is launched, you may see a white screen briefly before you see the tab bar. This screen is called the **Launch** screen, and it's displayed briefly as your app is starting. You'll learn how to configure this screen to display a custom color and app logo in the next section.

Setting up the Launch screen

The **Launch** screen refers to the screen that is displayed briefly as your app is starting up. You can configure it by modifying the LaunchScreen storyboard file in your project. This file is automatically created when you create an Xcode project.

You will create a new custom color for this screen, add an icon from the Assets. xcassets folder, and set the icon's location using Auto Layout constraints.

> **Important Information**
>
> For more information on Auto Layout and how to use it, see this link: https://developer.apple.com/library/archive/ documentation/UserExperience/Conceptual/ AutolayoutPG/.

You'll start by creating a new custom color in the next section.

Configuring the Launch screen's background color

The Attributes inspector can be used to modify the colors of the UI elements on screen. You can specify the precise color you want by using custom red, green and blue values. You'll set a custom color for the Launch screen by following these steps:

1. Click the Launchscreen storyboard file in your Project navigator:

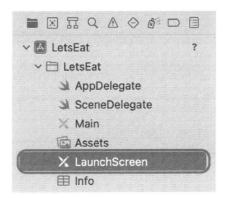

Figure 9.42: Project navigator with LaunchScreen storyboard selected

2. Select **View** in the document outline. Click the Attributes inspector button. Under **View**, click the **Background** pop-up menu:

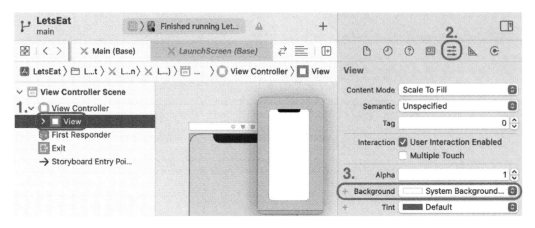

Figure 9.43: Attributes inspector with Background attribute selected

3. Choose **Custom...** from the pop-up menu:

Figure 9.44: Background pop-up menu with Custom... selected

4. In the color picker, choose the second tab (the one with the three sliders):

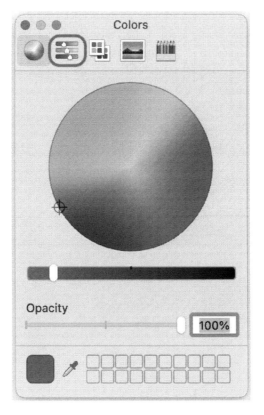

Figure 9.45: Color picker with the second tab selected

5. Select **RGB Sliders** from the pop-up menu and enter 4A4A4A in the
    Hex Color # box:

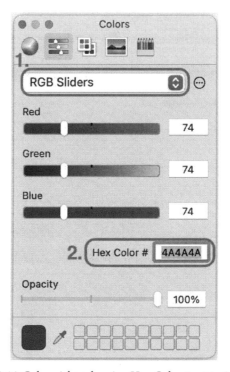

Figure 9.46: Color picker showing Hex Color # set to 4A4A4A

A color consists of red, green and blue. The range of values for each color from 0 to
255. This hex value sets the red, green and blue values to 74, resulting in a pleasant
dark gray color.

Build and run your app. You should briefly see a dark gray screen before the tab bar
appears. Cool!

In the next section, you'll add a logo to this screen, and use Auto Layout constraints
to position it in the exact center of the screen regardless of the device and orientation.
Adding a logo informs the user that the app is launching and is one way to make your app
look good.

Adding a logo and constraints to the Launch screen

Your **Launch** screen is rather plain, so let's add a logo to it. You will find the logo for the *Let's Eat* app inside the `Assets.xcassets` file you added to your project earlier. You'll also use Auto Layout constraints to position the logo in the center of the screen. Follow these steps:

1. The `LaunchScreen` storyboard file should still be selected in the Project navigator. Click the + button to display the library:

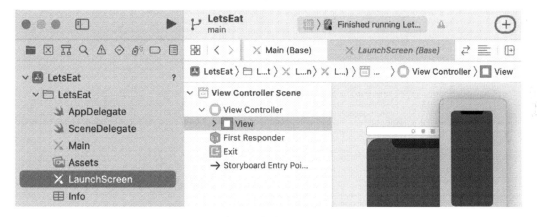

Figure 9.47: Toolbar with the Library button shown

2. Click the Media button to show all of the graphic files in your project:

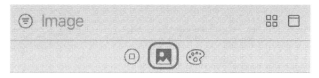

Figure 9.48: Library with the Media button selected

3. Type `detail` in the filter field. You'll see `detail-logo` in the results:

Figure 9.49: Library with detail-logo selected

4. Drag `detail-logo` into the view of your view controller scene and center it vertically and horizontally. You'll see blue guidelines to help you. Click the Auto Layout Align button when you're done:

Figure 9.50: The Launchscreen storyboard's view controller scene with logo added

> **Tip**
>
> If you don't see the Auto Layout Align button, click the Inspector button in the toolbar to hide the Inspector area.

5. Tick **Horizontally in Container** and **Vertically in Container**. Click **Add 2 Constraints**:

Figure 9.51: Auto Layout align pop-up dialog box

6. The constraints have been added to `detail-logo` and are visible in the document outline:

Figure 9.52: Document outline showing constraints for the logo

What the constraints do is specify the position of the logo in relation to the view controller's view. The view controller's view is the container in this case. **Horizontally in Container** calculates the logo's horizontal position relative to the left and the right sides of the container, and **Vertically in Container** calculates the logo's vertical position relative to the top and bottom of the container.

Build and run your app. You'll see the logo in the middle of the screen. Even if you try running the app in the iOS simulator with a different screen size, the logo will still be in the exact center of the screen.

Congratulations! You have successfully configured the **Launch** screen of your app!

You may have noticed that the screens represented in Interface Builder don't match the iPhone model you selected in the iOS simulator, and you may find the minimap display gets in the way of arranging screens in your app. Let's do some additional configuration for Interface Builder to fix that.

Configuring Interface Builder

Even though you have configured iPhone SE (2nd generation) as the iOS simulator for your app, you may find that the scenes shown in Interface Builder are for a different iPhone model. You may also wish to hide the minimap display. Let's configure Interface Builder to use the screens from the iPhone SE (2nd generation) and to hide the minimap display. Follow these steps:

1. The Launchscreen storyboard file should still be selected. To configure Interface Builder, click the device configuration button:

Figure 9.53: Editing area with device configuration button shown

2. A pop-up window displaying different device screens will appear:

Figure 9.54: Editing area with device pop-up window

Note that **iPhone 11** is selected.

3. Choose **iPhone SE (2nd generation)** from this pop-up window:

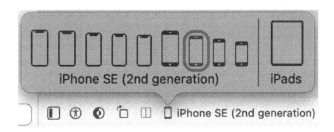

Figure 9.55: Device pop-up window with iPhone SE (2nd generation) selected

4. After iPhone SE (2nd generation) has been set in the device pop-up window, note the scene has changed to reflect the iPhone SE (2nd generation)'s screen. The logo is still located at the exact center of the **Launch** screen:

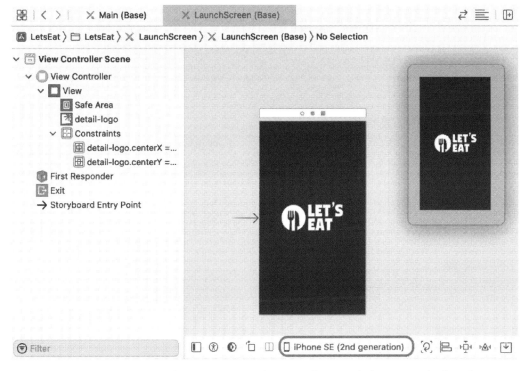

Figure 9.56: Device configuration button showing iPhone SE (2nd generation) selected

5. Click the Main storyboard file in the Project navigator. Configure the storyboard here to use iPhone SE (2nd generation) as well:

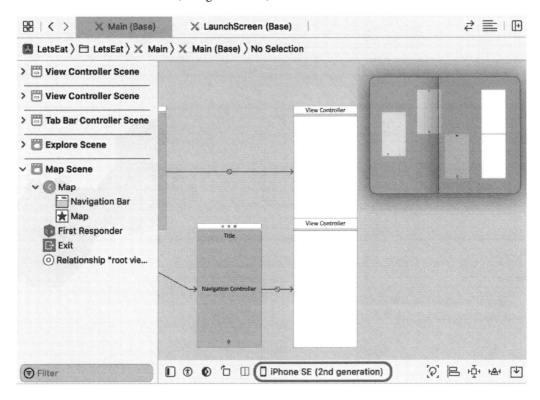

Figure 9.57: Device configuration button showing iPhone SE (2nd generation) selected for the Main storyboard file

6. If you wish to hide the minimap, choose **Editor | Minimap** from Xcode's menu bar to deselect it:

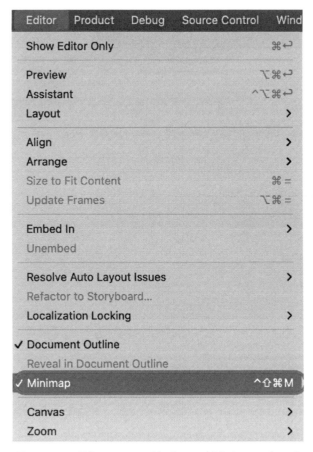

Figure 9.58: Editor menu with Canvas | Minimap selected

7. Verify that you have the following scenes in the `Main` storyboard file:

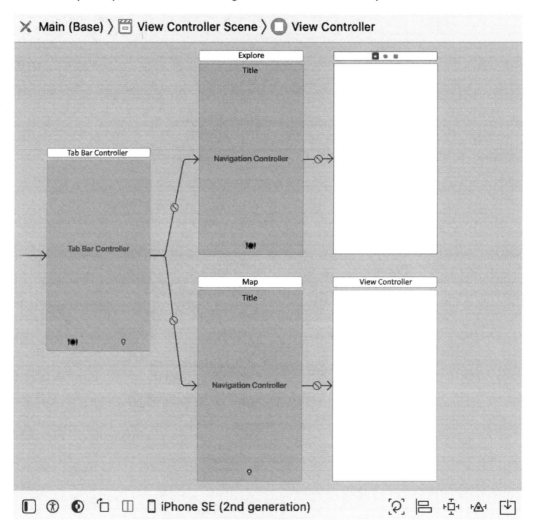

Figure 9.59: Editor area showing completed Main storyboard file

Build and run your app. It should work just as it did before.

You have created the **Explore** and **Map** screens for your app! Well done!

Summary

In this chapter, you learned some useful terms used in iOS app development. This will make it easier for you to understand the remainder of this book, as well as other books or online resources on the subject.

Next, you also learned about the different screens used in the *Let's Eat* app and how the user would use the app. As you recreate the app's user interface from scratch, you'll be able to compare what you're doing to what the actual app looks like.

Finally, you learned how to use Interface Builder and storyboards to add a tab bar controller scene to your app, configure the button titles, and configure the navigation bar for the **Explore** and **Map** screens. You also added an `Assets.xcassets` file that contains all of the graphic files required for your project, configured custom tab bar button icons, and configured the **Launch** screen for your app with a custom color and icon. This will familiarize you with adding UI elements, configuring them and setting their constraints for your own apps.

In the next chapter, you will continue setting up your app's user interface and become familiar with more UI elements. You will configure the **Explore** screen to display a collection view displaying collection view cells and a collection view section header containing a button that displays another view when tapped.

Invitation to join us on Discord

Book club is a great platform to learn from other iOS developers and share your iOS app prototype for feedback and invite others to build with you.

Join the iOS community to ask questions, share advice, collaborate with professionals and participate in Ask Me Anything sessions and more events with the author.

Scan the QR code or visit the link to join the community.

https://packt.link/iosdevelopment

10
Building Your User Interface

In the previous chapter, you created a new Xcode project, added a tab bar to your app that allowed the user to select between the **Explore** and **Map** screens, added an `Assets.xcassets` file that contains resources for your app, and modified the **Launch** screen of your app with a custom color and icon. When your app is launched, you should see the **Launch** screen briefly. After that, the **Explore** screen is displayed, but it is currently blank.

As you saw in the app tour in *Chapter 9, Setting Up the User Interface*, the **Explore** screen should display a collection view showing a list of cuisines in collection view cells and a collection view section header containing a **LOCATION** button. Tapping the **LOCATION** button should display a **Locations** screen containing a list of locations.

In this chapter, you will make the **Explore** screen display a **collection view** containing 20 empty **collection view cells**, as well as a **collection view section header** containing a button that will display a view representing the **Locations** screen when tapped. You'll also configure a **Cancel** button to dismiss this view and return you to the **Explore** screen.

You'll be adding a small amount of code to your app, but don't worry too much about this—you'll learn more about it in the next part of this book.

By the end of this chapter, you'll have learned how to add view controllers to a storyboard scene, link outlets in view controllers to scenes, set up collection view cells and collection view section headers, and present a view controller modally.

In this chapter, you'll cover the following topics:

- Adding a collection view to the **Explore** screen
- Connecting storyboard elements to outlets in a view controller
- Configuring data source methods for the collection view
- Adding a collection view section header to the collection view
- Configuring storyboard element sizes
- Presenting a view modally

Technical requirements

You will continue working on the `LetsEat` project that you created in the previous chapter.

The completed Xcode project for this chapter is in the `Chapter10` folder of the code bundle for this book, which can be downloaded here:

`https://github.com/PacktPublishing/iOS-15-Programming-for-Beginners-Sixth-Edition`

Check out the following video to see the code in action:

`https://bit.ly/3kjIKFQ`

Let's start by adding a collection view to the **Explore** scene, which will eventually display the list of cuisines and the **LOCATION** button.

Adding a collection view to the Explore screen

A collection view is an instance of the `UICollectionView` class. Like a spreadsheet program, it displays a grid of cells. Each cell in a collection view is a collection view cell, which is an instance of the `UICollectionViewCell` class. You'll start by adding a collection view to the view controller scene for the **Explore** screen in the `Main` storyboard file, then you'll add Auto Layout constraints to make it fill the screen.

> **Important Information**
>
> For more information on Auto Layout and how to use it, go to https://
> developer.apple.com/library/archive/documentation/
> UserExperience/Conceptual/AutolayoutPG/.

Open the LetsEat project you created in the previous chapter and run the app to make sure everything still works as it should, then follow these steps:

1. Click the Main storyboard file in the Project navigator, and click the Library button:

Figure 10.1: Toolbar with the Library button shown

2. The library will appear. Make sure the Objects button is selected, then type collec in the filter field. A **Collection View** object will appear as one of the results. Drag it to the middle of the view of the **View Controller Scene** for the **Explore** screen:

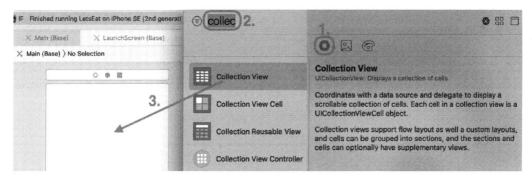

Figure 10.2: Library with Collection View object selected

The collection view (containing a single prototype cell) has been added, but it only takes up a small part of the screen. As shown in the app tour in the previous chapter, it should fill the screen.

3. You will use the **Auto Layout Add New Constraints** button to bind the edges of the collection view to the edges of its enclosing view. Make sure the collection view is selected. Click the Auto Layout Add New Constraints button:

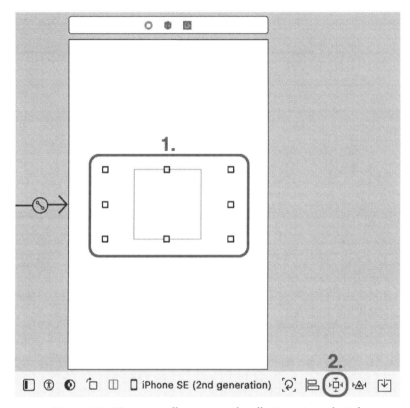

Figure 10.3: View controller scene with collection view selected

4. Type 0 in the top, left, right, and bottom edge constraint fields and click all the pale red struts. Make sure all the struts have turned bright red. Click the **Add 4 Constraints** button:

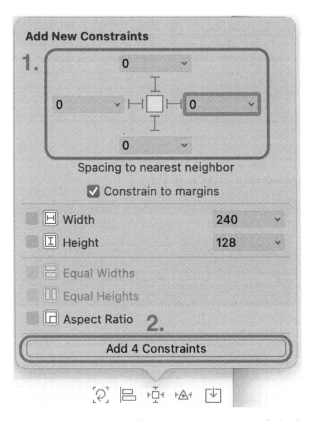

Figure 10.4: Auto Layout add new constraints pop-up dialog box

This sets the space between the edges of the collection view and the edges of the enclosing view to 0, binding the collection view's edges to those of the enclosing view. Now the collection view will fill the screen, regardless of device and orientation.

5. Verify that all four sides of the collection view are now bound to the edges of the screen as shown:

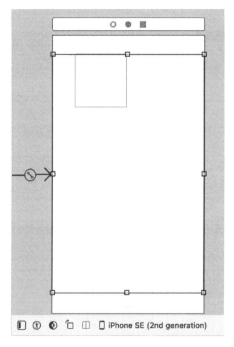

Figure 10.5: View controller scene with collection view filling the screen

You have added a collection view to the view of the view controller scene for the **Explore** screen, and used Auto Layout constraints to make it fill the screen, but the **Explore** screen will still be blank when you run the app.

In the next section, you will add a **Cocoa Touch Class** file to your project so that you can implement the code for the `ExploreViewController` class, and you'll connect outlets in this class to the UI elements in the **Explore** screen. This will enable an instance of the `ExploreViewController` class to control what is displayed by the **Explore** screen.

Connecting storyboard elements to outlets in a view controller

You've added a collection view to the **Explore** screen, but it won't be able to display anything yet. You'll need to implement a view controller to manage the view in the **Explore** screen. To do so, you'll add a Cocoa Touch Class file to your project, declare and define a `UIViewController` subclass in that file, and connect UI elements in the **Explore** screen to the code in your `UIViewController` subclass.

> **Important Information**
> The Model-View-Controller design pattern and collection view controllers will be explained in more detail in *Chapter 13, Getting Started with MVC and Collection Views*.

Let's start by adding a Cocoa Touch Class file to your project so you can declare and define a `UIViewController` subclass in the next section.

Adding a Cocoa Touch Class file to your project

Cocoa Touch is the application development environment for building apps for iOS, iPadOS, watchOS, and tvOS. A Cocoa Touch Class file makes it easy for you to implement any Cocoa Touch class or subclass. It contains boilerplate code based on the superclass that you specified when you create it. You'll add a Cocoa Touch Class file to your project in this section.

First, you will make a new `Explore` group in your project to keep things organized. Next, you will create and add a Cocoa Touch Class file, `ExploreViewController`, to this group. You'll declare and define a subclass of the `UIViewController` class named `ExploreViewController` in this file and make an instance of this class the view controller for the **Explore** screen. You'll add properties and methods to this class to manage the collection view that you added in the previous section. Follow these steps:

1. Right-click on the `LetsEat` group in the Project navigator and choose **New Group**.

2. The name of the group will be highlighted. Change it to `Explore` and press *Return* on the keyboard when you're done:

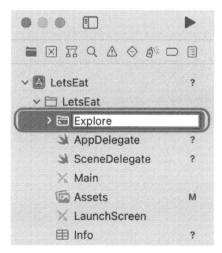

Figure 10.6: Project navigator with Explore group selected

If you make a mistake, press *Return* once more. This makes the field editable so that you can make changes to the name.

3. Right-click on the `Explore` group in the Project navigator and choose **New File...**

4. **iOS** should already be selected. Choose **Cocoa Touch Class** and click **Next**:

Figure 10.7: Choose a template for your new file screen

5. The **Choose options for your new file** screen will appear:

Figure 10.8: Choose options for your new file screen

6. Enter the following in the **Class** and **Subclass of** fields:

Class: ExploreViewController

Subclass of: UIViewController

Click **Next**.

7. Click **Create** to add the file to your project. You will see that the
ExploreViewController file has been added to the project inside the
Explore folder in the Project navigator. Review the code in the Editor area. Note
that ExploreViewController is a subclass of UIViewController, which
means it inherits properties and methods from the UIViewController class.
There is one method, viewDidLoad(), inside the class definition, but it won't be
used right now.

8. Remove the commented code after the viewDidLoad() class from the
ExploreViewController file so that it looks like this:

```
LetsEat ⟩ LetsEat ⟩ Explore ⟩ ExploreViewController ⟩ No Selection
1  //
2  //  ExploreViewController.swift
3  //  LetsEat
4  //
5  //  Created by iOS 15 Programming on 29/11/2021.
6  //
7
8  import UIKit
9
10 class ExploreViewController: UIViewController {
11
12     override func viewDidLoad() {
13         super.viewDidLoad()
14
15         // Do any additional setup after loading the
                view.
16     }
17
18 }
                                              Line: 18 Col: 2
```

Figure 10.9: Editing area showing ExploreViewController.swift's contents

You have just added the ExploreViewController file containing the
ExploreViewController class declaration and definition to your app.

The next step is to assign the ExploreViewController class as the identity of the
view controller for the **Explore** screen and assign an **outlet** for the collection view that
you added to the view controller scene earlier. You'll see how this is done in the
next section.

Connecting storyboard elements to the view controller

Let's review where you are now. In the `Main` storyboard file, you have a view controller scene for the **Explore** screen. Inside it, there's a view containing a collection view. In the `ExploreViewController` file, you have code that declares and defines the `ExploreViewController` class.

You need to assign the `ExploreViewController` class as the identity for the **Explore** screen's view controller and connect the collection view to an outlet in this class. You can think of outlets as a connection between your user interface and code. This will make an instance of the `ExploreViewController` class the view controller for the **Explore** screen when you run your app and enable you to manage what is displayed by the collection view. Follow these steps:

1. Click on the `Main` storyboard file in the Project navigator. Make sure the **View Controller Scene** for the **Explore** screen is selected. Click the **View Controller** icon in the document outline and click on the Identity inspector button:

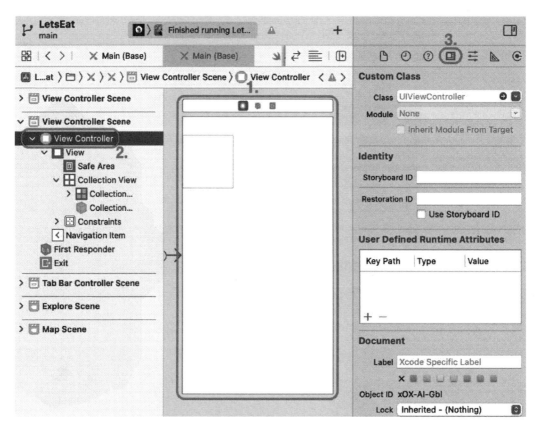

Figure 10.10: Identity inspector selected

2. Under **Custom Class**, set **Class** to `ExploreViewController`:

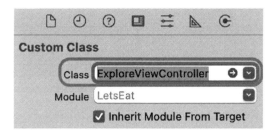

Figure 10.11: Identity inspector with Class set to ExploreViewController

This creates an instance of `ExploreViewController` as the view controller for this scene when you run the app. Note that the scene name has changed from **View Controller Scene** to **Explore View Controller Scene**.

Now let's create the outlet for the collection view.

3. Click the Navigator and Inspector buttons to hide the Navigator and Inspector areas so you have more room to work:

Figure 10.12: Toolbar showing Navigator and Inspector buttons

4. Click the Adjust Editor Options button:

Figure 10.13: Adjust Editor Options button

5. Choose **Assistant** from the pop-up menu:

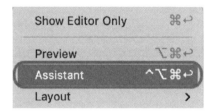

Figure 10.14: Adjust Editor Options menu with Assistant selected

This will display any Swift files associated with this scene in an assistant editor.

6. As you can see, the `Main` storyboard file's content appears on the left and the `ExploreViewController` class definition appears on the right-hand side of the Editor area. Look at the bar just above the code. Verify that `ExploreViewController.swift` is selected:

Figure 10.15: Bar showing ExploreViewController.swift selected

7. If you don't see `ExploreViewController.swift` selected, click the bar and select `ExploreViewController.swift` from the pop-up menu.

8. To connect the collection view in the **Explore View Controller Scene** to an outlet in the `ExploreViewController` class, *Ctrl + Drag* from the collection view to the `ExploreViewController` file, just below the class name declaration:

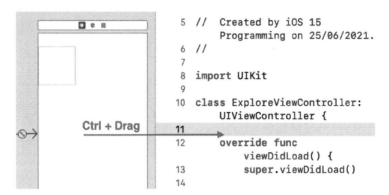

Figure 10.16: Editing area

9. A small pop-up dialog box will appear. Type the name of the outlet, `collectionView`, into the **Name** text field, set **Storage** to **Strong**, and click **Connect**:

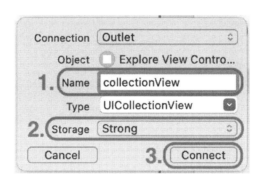

Figure 10.17: Pop-up dialog box for outlet creation

10. Verify that the code that creates the `collectionView` outlet has been automatically added to the `ExploreViewController` file. Note the `IBOutlet` keyword, which indicates that `collectionView` is an outlet. After you have done so, click the **x** to close the assistant editor window:

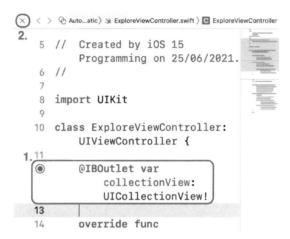

Figure 10.18: Editing area showing collectionView outlet

The `ExploreViewController` class now has an outlet, `collectionView`, for the collection view in the **Explore** screen. This means an `ExploreViewController` instance can manage what the collection view displays.

It is common to make mistakes when using *Ctrl + Drag* to drag from an element in a storyboard scene to a Cocoa Touch Class file. If you make a mistake while doing so, this may cause a crash to occur when the app is launched. To check if there are any errors in the connection between the collection view and `ExploreViewController` class, follow these steps:

1. Click the Navigator and Inspector buttons to display the Navigator and Inspector areas.

2. With **Explore View Controller** in the **Explore View Controller Scene** selected, click the **Connections inspector** button:

Figure 10.19: Connections inspector selected

The Connections inspector displays the links between your UI objects and your code. You should be able to see the `collectionView` outlet connected to the collection view in the **Outlets** section.

3. If you see a tiny error icon, click on the **x** to break the connection:

Figure 10.20: Connections inspector showing collectionView outlet

4. Under **Outlets**, drag from the **collectionView** outlet back to the collection view to re-establish the connection:

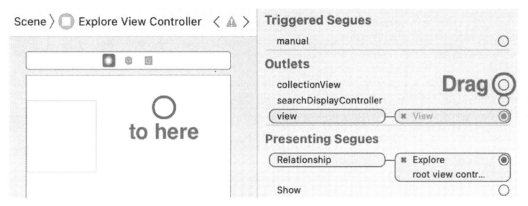

Figure 10.21: Editing area showing collection view to be connected

At this point, you've assigned the `ExploreViewController` class as the identity for the **Explore** screen's view controller and created an outlet in the `ExploreViewController` class for the collection view.

In order to display collection view cells on screen, you will need to implement data source methods for the collection view by adding some code to the `ExploreViewController` class. You will do this in the next section.

Configuring data source methods for the collection view

When your app is running, an instance of the `ExploreViewController` class acts as the view controller for the **Explore** screen. It is responsible for loading and displaying all the views in that screen, including the collection view you added earlier. The collection view needs to know how many collection view cells to display and what to display in each cell. Normally, the view controller is responsible for providing this information. Apple has already created a protocol, `UICollectionViewDataSource`, for this purpose. All you need to do is connect the collection view's `dataSource` outlet to the `ExploreViewController` class and implement the required methods of this protocol.

The collection view also needs to know what to do if the user taps on a collection view cell. Again, the view controller for the collection view is responsible, and Apple has created the `UICollectionViewDelegate` protocol for this purpose. You will connect the collection view's `delegate` outlet to the `ExploreViewController` class, but you won't be implementing any methods from this protocol yet.

> **Tip**
> Protocols are covered in *Chapter 8, Protocols, Extensions, and Error Handling.*

You will need to type in a small amount of code in this chapter. Don't worry about what it means; you'll learn more about collection view controllers and their associated protocols in *Chapter 13, Getting Started with MVC and Collection Views.*

In the next section, you'll use the Connections inspector to assign the collection view's `dataSource` and `delegate` outlets to the `ExploreViewController` class.

Setting the delegate and data source properties of the collection view

An instance of the `ExploreViewController` class will provide the data that the collection view will display, as well as the methods that will be executed when the user interacts with the collection view. You need to connect the collection view's `dataSource` and `delegate` properties to outlets in the `ExploreViewController` class for this to work. Follow these steps:

1. Click the Navigator and Inspector buttons to display the Navigator and Inspector areas again if you haven't done so already.

2. The `Main` storyboard file should still be selected. Click the **Collection View** for the **Explore View Controller Scene** in the document outline to select it. Click the Connections inspector button. Look at the **Outlets** section. Note that there are two empty circles next to the `dataSource` and `delegate` outlets. Drag from each empty circle to the **ExploreViewController** icon in the document outline:

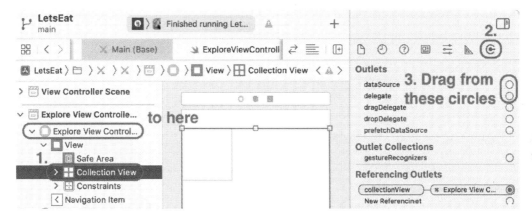

Figure 10.22: Connections Inspector selected

3. Verify the `dataSource` and `delegate` properties of the collection view have been connected to outlets in the `ExploreViewController` class:

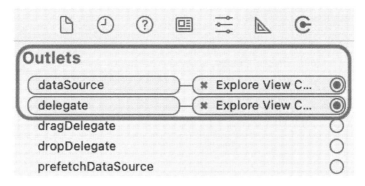

Figure 10.23: Connections Inspector with dataSource and delegate outlets set

In the next section, you will add some code to make the `ExploreViewController` class conform to the `UICollectionViewDataSource` protocol, and configure the collection view to display 20 collection view cells when you run your app.

Adopting the UICollectionViewDataSource and UICollectionViewDelegate protocols

So far, you've made the `ExploreViewController` class the data source and delegate for the collection view. The next step is to make it adopt the `UICollectionViewDataSource` and `UICollectionViewDelegate` protocols and implement any required methods. You'll also change the color of the collection view cells to make them visible on screen. Follow these steps:

1. Click **Collection View Cell** in the document outline. This represents the collection view cells that the collection view will display. Make sure the Attributes inspector is selected:

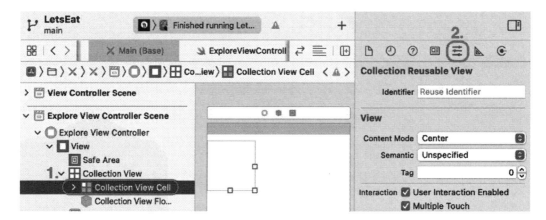

Figure 10.24: Attributes inspector selected

2. Under **Collection Reusable View**, set **Identifier** to `exploreCell` and press Return. The name **Collection View Cell** will change to **exploreCell**. Under **View**, set **Background** to `Light Gray Color` so that you can see them when you run the app:

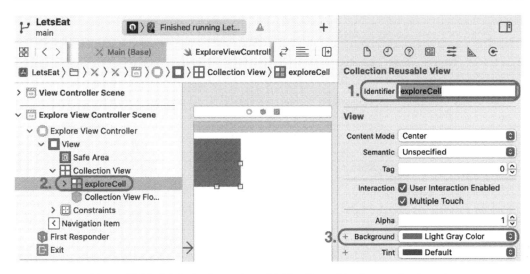

Figure 10.25: Attributes inspector with identity and background color set

3. Click on the `ExploreViewController` file in the Project navigator.
    Type in the following code after the class declaration to make the
    `ExploreViewController` class adopt the `UICollectionViewDataSource`
    and `UICollectionViewDelegate` protocols:

```
class ExploreViewController: UIViewController,
UICollectionViewDataSource, UICollectionViewDelegate {
```

After a few seconds, an error will appear. Click on it to display an error message.

4. The error message says that **Type 'ExploreViewController' does not
    conform to protocol 'UICollectionViewDataSource'. Do you want to
    add protocol stubs?**. This means you need to implement the required
    methods for the `UICollectionViewDataSource` protocol to make
    `ExploreViewController` conform to it. Click **Fix** to automatically add stubs
    for the required methods into the `ExploreViewController` class.

5. Verify the stubs for the two required methods for the
   `UICollectionViewDataSource` protocol have been automatically inserted
   into the `ExploreViewController` file as shown:

```
11
12  func collectionView(_ collectionView:
        UICollectionView,
        numberOfItemsInSection section: Int) ->
        Int {
13      code
14  }
15
16  func collectionView(_ collectionView:
        UICollectionView, cellForItemAt
        indexPath: IndexPath) ->
        UICollectionViewCell {
17      code
18  }
19
```

Figure 10.26: Editing area showing UICollectionViewDataSource method stubs

The first method tells the collection view how many cells to display, while the
second method tells the collection view what to display in each collection view cell.

6. Replace the `code` text in the first method with `20` (the `return` keyword is optional
   if it's just a single line of code). This tells the collection view to display 20 cells:

```
11
12  func collectionView(_ collectionView:
        UICollectionView,
        numberOfItemsInSection section: Int) ->
        Int {
13      20
14  }
```

Figure 10.27: Editing area showing code to display 20 cells

7. Replace the `code` text in the second method with the following code:

```
let cell = collectionView.
dequeueReusableCell(withReuseIdentifier: "exploreCell",
for: indexPath)
return cell
```

Don't worry about what this means for now as you'll learn more about collection views in *Chapter 13, Getting Started with MVC and Collection Views*.

Build and run your app. You should see the simulator display a grid of 20 light gray collection view cells as shown:

Figure 10.28: iOS Simulator showing 20 collection view cells

As you saw in the app tour in *Chapter 9, Setting Up the User Interface*, there should be a **LOCATION** button at the top right of this screen. You will enable the section header for the collection view to house this button in the next section.

Adding a section header to the collection view

A collection view can be configured with a section header and a section footer. Both of them are instances of the `UICollectionReusableView` class. You'll enable the section header for the collection view in the **Explore** screen, so you'll have a place to put the **LOCATION** button. Follow these steps:

1. Click the `Main` storyboard file in the Project navigator and click the **Collection View** in the document outline. Click the Attributes inspector button. Under **Collection View,** tick the checkbox for **Section Header:**

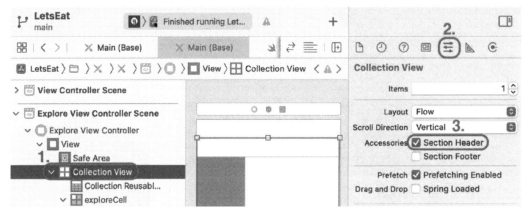

Figure 10.29: Attributes inspector with Section Header checkbox ticked

This enables the section header for the collection view.

2. Note that **Collection Reusable View** appears in the document outline. This represents the collection view section header. Click on **Collection Reusable View** in the document outline. In the Attributes inspector under **Collection Reusable View,** set **Identifier** to `header` and press *Return* when you're done:

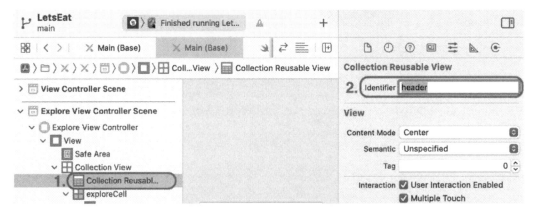

Figure 10.30: Attributes inspector with Identifier set to header

3. Click on the `ExploreViewController` file in the Project navigator. Just before the data source methods, type in the following code:

```
func collectionView(_ collectionView: UICollectionView,
viewForSupplementaryElementOfKind kind: String, at
indexPath: IndexPath) -> UICollectionReusableView {
    let headerView =
    collectionView.dequeueReusableSupplementaryView(
    ofKind: kind, withReuseIdentifier: "header",
    for: indexPath)
    return headerView
}
```

This method returns the instance of `UICollectionReusableView` with the identifier `header` that you just configured, which will be displayed onscreen.

Build and run your app. You should see the collection view section header as a white space between the collection view cells and the navigation bar:

Figure 10.31: iOS Simulator showing collection view section header

Before you add the **LOCATION** button, you'll need to increase the collection view section header's height and the collection view cell size to make them match the **Explore** screen shown in the app tour (refer to *Chapter 9, Setting Up the User Interface*). You will set the cell size and the header height using the **Size inspector** in the next section.

Configuring storyboard element sizes

The Size inspector is used to change the size of storyboard elements. You will use it to change the size of the collection view cell and collection view section header to make them match the **Explore** screen that was shown in the app tour in *Chapter 9, Setting Up the User Interface*. Follow these steps:

1. Click the `Main` storyboard file in the Project navigator and click the **Collection View** in the document outline. Click the Size inspector button:

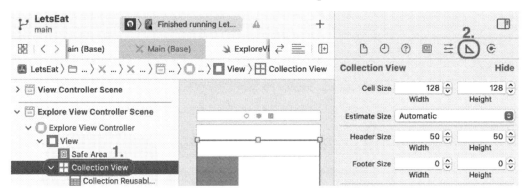

Figure 10.32: Size inspector selected

2. The collection view size settings will be displayed in the Size inspector as shown:

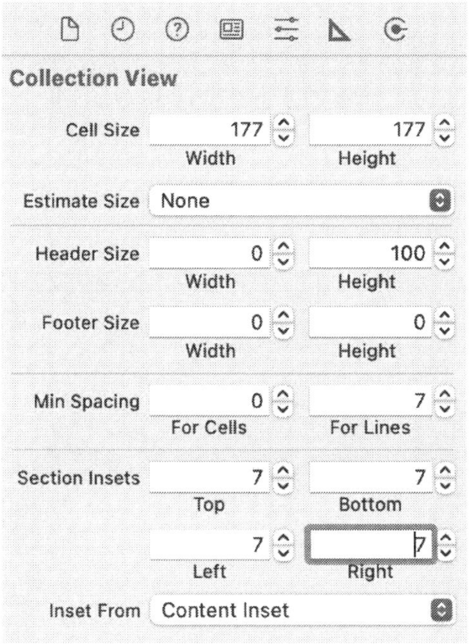

Figure 10.33: Size inspector showing size settings for the collection view

3. Configure the collection view size settings, as follows:

Cell Size: Set **Width** to `177` and **Height** is `177`.

Estimate Size: **None**.

Header Size: Set **Width** to `0` and **Height** to `100`.

Min Spacing: Set **For Cells** to `0` and **For Lines** to 7.

Section Insets: Set **Top**, **Bottom**, **Left**, and **Right** to 7.

Remember to press *Return* after changing each value.

The units that are used in the Size inspector are points. Each point may refer to one or more pixels on the device screen. For the iPhone SE (2nd generation), the screen is 375 points wide and 667 points high, although the actual screen resolution is 750 x 1,334 pixels.

Cell Size determines the size of the collection view cell. **Header Size** determines the size of the collection view section header. **Min Spacing** determines the space between cells. **Section Insets** determines the space between the section containing the cells to the sides of the enclosing view. These settings are specific to the iPhone SE (2nd generation). In *Chapter 22, Getting Started with Mac Catalyst*, you will calculate the optimum cell size based on the dimensions of the device screen.

Build and run your app, and you should see the **Explore** screen display 20 collection view cells and a collection view section header:

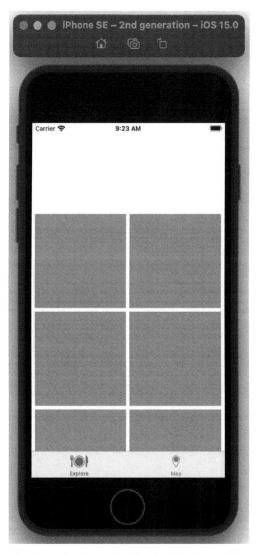

Figure 10.34: iOS simulator showing resized collection view cells and section header

Note that although there is no data in the cells and no button in the header, it looks similar to the **Explore** screen that was shown in the app tour in *Chapter 9, Setting Up the User Interface*. You will configure the cells to display data in the next part of this book. For now, let's add a button to the collection view section header, which will be used later to display the **Locations** screen.

Presenting a view modally

In this section, you will add a button to the collection view section header. When tapped, this button will display a view showing the **Locations** screen. This view will be from a new view controller scene embedded in a navigation controller, which you will add to the project. The view will be presented modally, which means you won't be able to do anything else until it is dismissed. To dismiss it, you'll add a **Cancel** button to the view's navigation bar. You'll also add a **Done** button, but you'll only implement its functionality in *Chapter 17, Getting Started with JSON Files*.

Let's start by adding a button from the library to the collection view section header.

Adding a button to the collection view header

As shown in the app tour in *Chapter 9, Setting Up the User Interface*, there is a **LOCATION** button at the top right-hand side of the screen. You'll add a button to represent the **LOCATION** button in the collection view section header. Follow these steps:

1. Click the Main storyboard file in the Project navigator. Make sure the **Explore View Controller Scene** is selected. Click the Library button to display the library:

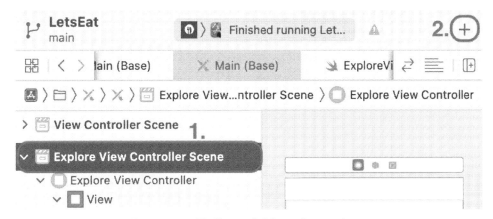

Figure 10.35: Toolbar with Library button shown

2. Type button in the filter field. A **Button** object will appear in the results. Drag the button to the collection view section header:

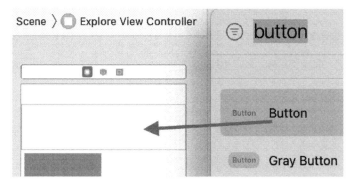

Figure 10.36: Library with Button object selected

3. Position the button to the right-hand side of the collection view section header:

Figure 10.37: Collection view section header with button added

Its exact placement isn't important right now as you will customize the button's position in *Chapter 12, Modifying and Configuring Cells.*

You now have a button in your collection view section header. Next, you will add a view controller scene to represent the **Locations** screen that will appear when the button is tapped.

Adding a new view controller scene

As shown in the app tour in *Chapter 9, Setting Up the User Interface*, when you tap the
LOCATION button, a list of locations will appear in the **Locations** screen. You'll add
a new view controller scene to your project to represent this screen. Follow these steps:

1. Click the Library button to display the library and type `view con` in the filter
    field. A **View Controller** object will be among the search results. Drag the **View
    Controller** object onto the storyboard:

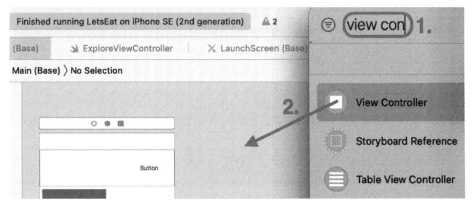

Figure 10.38: Library with View Controller object selected

2. Position it to the right of the **Explore View Controller Scene**:

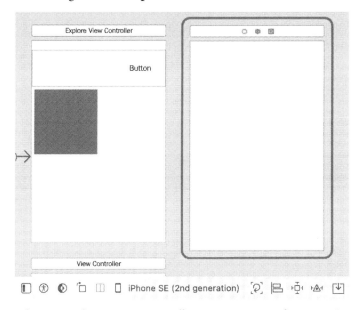

Figure 10.39: Editing area showing view controller scene next to Explore View Controller Scene

3. The newly added view controller scene should already be selected. In the document outline, click on the **View Controller** icon for this scene:

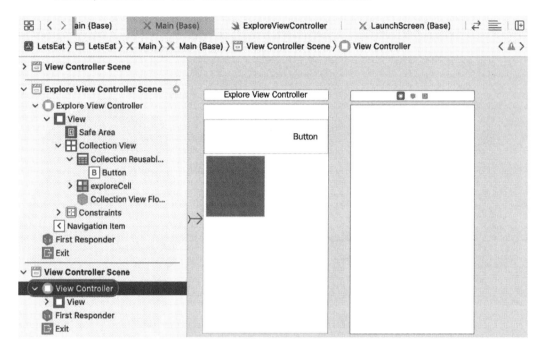

Figure 10.40: Document outline with View Controller selected

4. You will need space for the **Cancel** and **Done** buttons, so you will embed this view controller scene in a navigation controller to provide a navigation bar where the buttons can be placed. Choose **Embed In | Navigation Controller** from the **Editor** menu.

5. A navigation controller scene will appear to the left of the view controller scene:

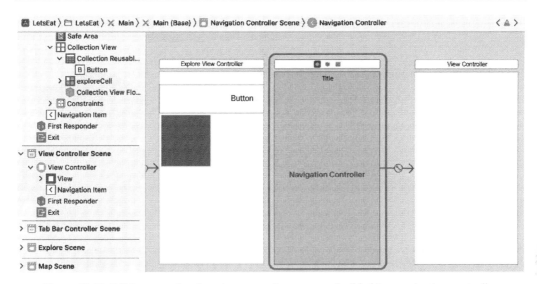

Figure 10.41: Editing area showing view controller scene embedded in a navigation controller

6. *Ctrl + Drag* from the button to the navigation controller scene:

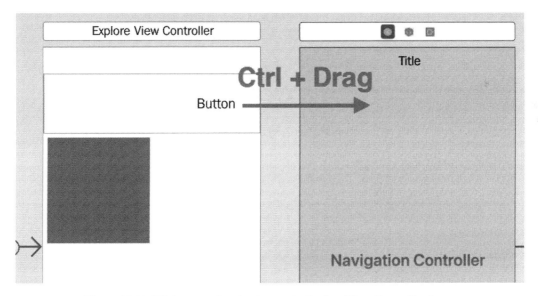

Figure 10.42: Editing area showing button in Explore View Controller Scene

7. The Segue pop-up menu will appear. Choose **Present Modally**:

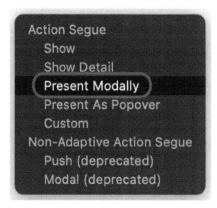

Figure 10.43: Segue pop-up menu with Present Modally selected

This makes the view controller's view slide up from the bottom of the screen when the button is tapped. You won't be able to interact with any other view until this view is dismissed.

8. Verify that a segue has linked the **Explore View Controller Scene** and the navigation controller scene together:

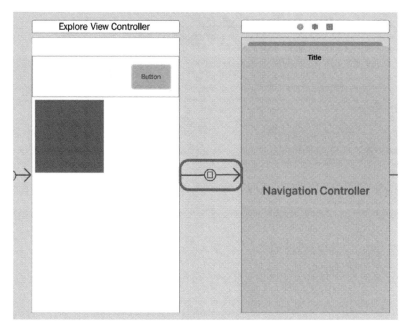

Figure 10.44: Editing area showing segue between Explore View Controller Scene and navigation controller scene

Build and run your app. If you click the button, the new view controller's view should slide up from the bottom of the screen:

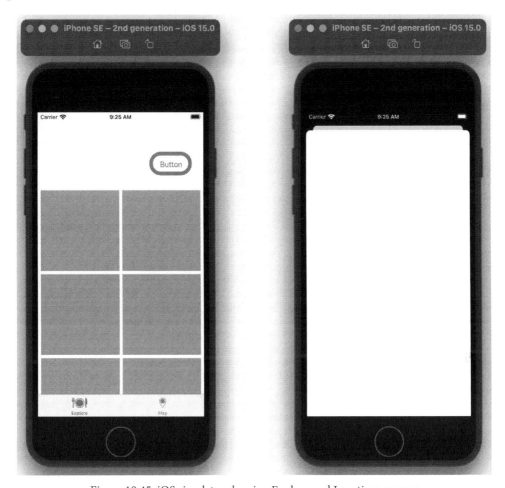

Figure 10.45: iOS simulator showing Explore and Locations screens

At the moment, you can't dismiss this view. In the next section, you will add a **Cancel** button to the navigation bar and program it to dismiss the view. You'll also add a **Done** button, but you won't program it yet.

Adding Cancel and Done buttons to the navigation bar

One of the benefits of embedding a view controller in a navigation controller is the navigation bar at the top of the screen. You can place buttons on its left- and right-hand sides. Follow these steps to add the **Cancel** and **Done** buttons to the navigation bar:

1. Click the **Navigation Item** for the **View Controller Scene** in the document outline. Click the Library button:

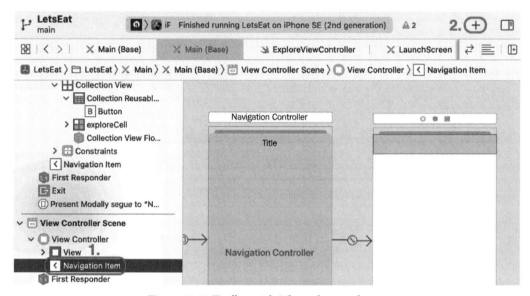

Figure 10.46: Toolbar with Library button shown

2. Type bar b into the filter field and drag two **Bar Button Item** objects to each side of the navigation bar:

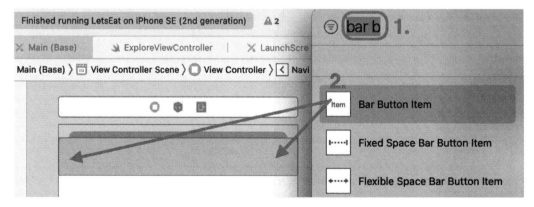

Figure 10.47: Library with Bar Button Item objects selected

3. Click the **Item** button on the right:

Figure 10.48: View controller scene with right button selected

4. Click the Attributes inspector button. Under **Bar Button Item**, choose **Done** from the **System Item** menu:

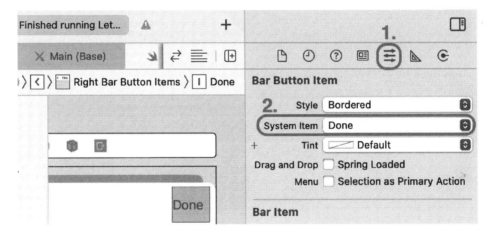

Figure 10.49: Attributes inspector with System Item set to Done

5. Click the **Item** button on the left and choose **Cancel** from the **System Item** menu:

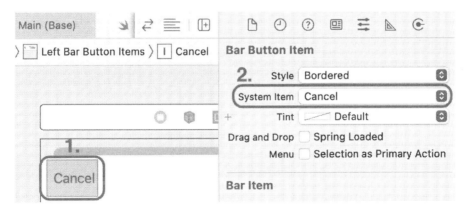

Figure 10.50: Attributes inspector with System Item set to Cancel

Remember that the navigation controller has a property, `viewControllers`, that holds an array of view controllers. When you click the button in the **Explore** screen, the new view controller is added to the `viewControllers` array and its view appears from the bottom of the screen, covering the **Explore** screen.

6. To dismiss the view, you will link the **Cancel** button to the scene exit and implement a method in the `ExploreViewController` class which will be executed when the **Explore** screen reappears. In the Project navigator, click the `ExploreViewController` file and add the following method at the bottom of the file, just before the last curly brace:

```
@IBAction func unwindLocationCancel(segue:
UIStoryboardSegue) {

}
```

7. Click on the `Main` storyboard file in the Project navigator. *Ctrl + Drag* from the **Cancel** button to the scene exit icon (the third icon) and choose **unwindLocationCancelWithSegue:** from the pop-up menu:

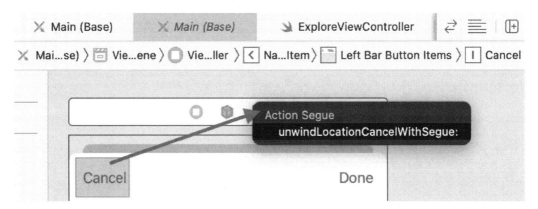

Figure 10.51: View controller scene showing Cancel button action being set

When your app is running, clicking the **Cancel** button will remove the view controller from the navigation controller's `viewControllers` array, making the view that is presented modally go away and executes the `unwindLocationCancel(segue:)` method. Note that this method doesn't do anything.

Build and run your app and click the button in the section header of the **Explore** screen. The new view will appear onscreen. When you click the **Cancel** button, the new view disappears:

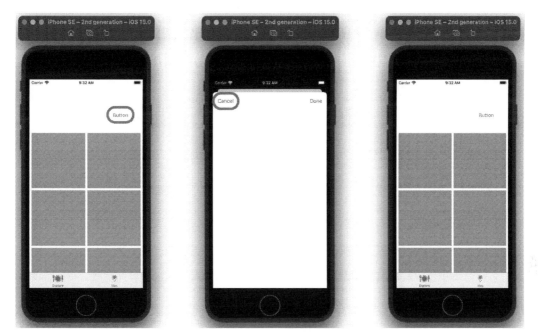

Figure 10.52: iOS Simulator showing Explore and Locations screens

Congratulations! You've completed the basic structure for the **Explore** screen.

Summary

In this chapter, you added a collection view to the **Explore** screen in the Main storyboard file and added a new file, ExploreViewController, which contains the implementation of the ExploreViewController class. You made the ExploreViewController class the view controller for the scene containing the collection view. Then, you modified the ExploreViewController class to have an outlet for the collection view in the storyboard, and made it the data source and delegate for the collection view. You added a collection view section header to the collection view and set the size for the collection view cells and collection view section header. Finally, you added a button to display a second view and configured a **Cancel** button to dismiss it.

At this point, you should be fairly proficient in using Interface Builder to add views and view controllers to a storyboard scene, link view controller outlets to UI elements in storyboards, set up collection view cells and section headers, and present views modally. This will be very useful when you're designing the user interface for your own apps.

In the next chapter, you'll configure the new view controller to display a table view, implement the remaining screens of your app, and implement a map view for the **Map** screen.

11
Finishing Up Your User Interface

In the previous chapter, you configured the **Explore** screen to display 20 empty collection view cells in a collection view, added a button to the collection view section header to present a view representing the **Locations** screen modally, and added a **Cancel** button to dismiss it.

In this chapter, you will implement the remaining screens that were shown in the app tour shown in *Chapter 9, Setting Up the User Interface*. First, you'll add a blank table view to the **Locations** screen. Next, you'll add the **Restaurant List** screen, which will be displayed when a cell in the **Explore** screen is tapped. You'll configure this screen to display a collection view containing a single collection view cell. After that, you'll add the **Restaurant Detail** screen, which will be displayed when the cell in the **Restaurant List** screen is tapped. You'll configure this screen to display a table view with static table view cells. You'll also add a button to one of the cells that displays a view representing the **Review Form** screen when tapped. Finally, you'll make the **Map** screen display a map.

By the end of this chapter, you'll have learned how to add and configure a table view to a storyboard scene, how to add segues between scenes, and how to add a map view to a scene. The basic user interface of your app will be complete, and you will be able to walk through all the screens in the simulator. None of the screens will be displaying data, but you will finish their implementation in *Part 3* of this book.

The following topics will be covered:

- Adding a table view to the **Locations** screen
- Implementing the **Restaurant List** screen
- Implementing the **Restaurant Detail** screen
- Adding a map view to the **Map** screen

Technical requirements

You will continue working on the LetsEat project that you created in the previous chapter.

The completed Xcode project for this chapter is in the Chapter11 folder of the code bundle for this book, which can be downloaded here:

https://github.com/PacktPublishing/iOS-15-Programming-for-Beginners-Sixth-Edition

Check out the following video to see the code in action:

https://bit.ly/3EYWb6i

To start, you'll add a table view to the **Locations** screen, which will eventually be used to display a list of restaurant locations.

Adding a table view to the Locations screen

When you tap the button in the collection view section header of the **Explore** screen, another view representing the **Locations** screen will be presented modally, but it is currently blank. Let's add a table view to this view. Follow these steps:

1. Build and run the LetsEat app to make sure everything still works as it should. Click the Main storyboard file in the Project navigator. In the document outline, select the **View Controller** icon in the **View Controller Scene** presented modally by the button in the **Explore View Controller Scene**. Click the Library button:

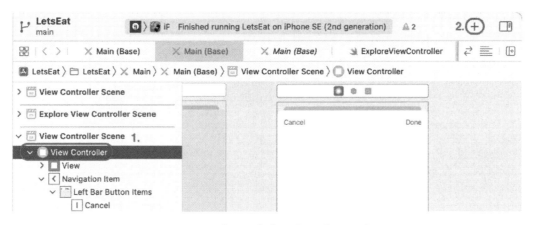

Figure 11.1: Toolbar with the Library button shown

2. The library will appear. Type `table` into the filter field. A **Table View** object will appear in the results.

3. Drag the **Table View** object to the view in the view controller scene:

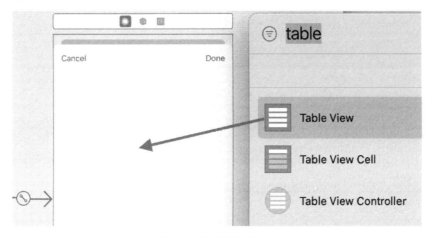

Figure 11.2: Library with Table View object selected

4. You'll add constraints to make the table view fill the whole screen. With the table view selected, click the Add New Constraints button:

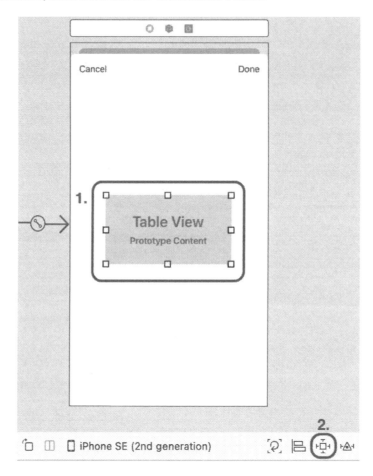

Figure 11.3: View Controller scene with Table View selected

5. Type 0 into all the **Spacing to nearest neighbor** fields and make sure that all the pale red struts are selected (they will turn bright red). Click the **Add 4 Constraints** button:

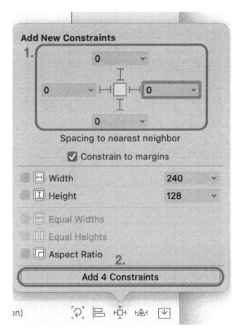

Figure 11.4: Auto Layout add new constraints pop-up dialog box

6. Verify that the table view's edges are now flush with the edges of the view in the view controller scene:

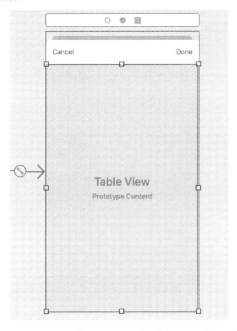

Figure 11.5: View controller scene with table view filling the screen

Build and run your app and tap the button in the section header. You'll see an empty table view in the **Locations** screen:

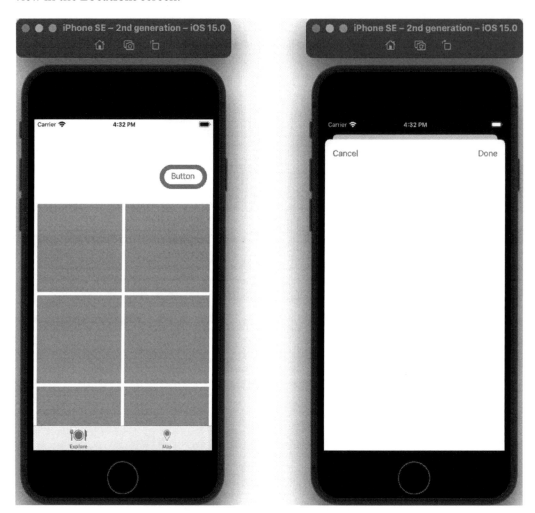

Figure 11.6: iOS Simulator showing Explore and Locations screens

You'll implement the view controller for the **Locations** screen in *Chapter 15, Getting Started with Table Views*. Eventually, this table view will display a list of restaurant locations, as shown in the app tour. As you can see, this process is similar to adding a collection view to the **Explore** screen, which you did in the previous chapter.

In the next section, you'll add a view controller scene to your storyboard to represent the **Restaurant List** screen.

Implementing the Restaurant List screen

As can be seen in the app tour in *Chapter 9, Setting Up the User Interface*, once you've set a location and tapped a cuisine in the **Explore** screen, the **Restaurant List** screen will appear, showing a list of restaurants.

To implement the **Restaurant List** screen, you'll add a new view controller scene to your storyboard and add a collection view to the view in this scene. You'll also add a new Cocoa Touch Class file, declare and define the `RestaurantListViewController` class, make it the view controller for the view controller scene's view, and connect the outlets of the collection view to this class. The steps are very similar to the one you followed in the previous chapter for the `ExploreViewController` class.

Let's start by adding the new view controller scene. Follow these steps:

1. In the `Main` storyboard file, move the navigation controller scene and view controller scene that you added in the previous chapter upward to make room for the new view controller scene that you will add:

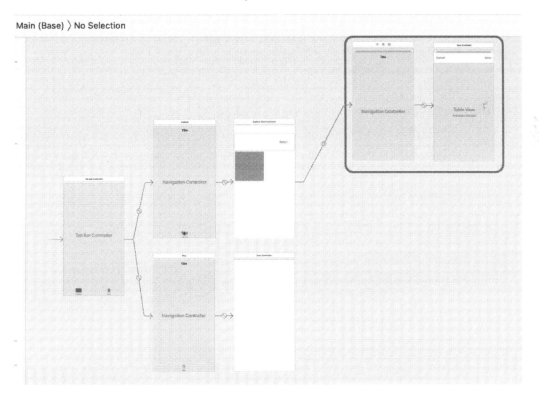

Figure 11.7: Editing area showing Main storyboard file contents

2. Click the Library button and type `view con` into the filter field. A **View Controller** object will be in the results. Drag the **View Controller** object into the storyboard to represent the **Restaurant List** screen:

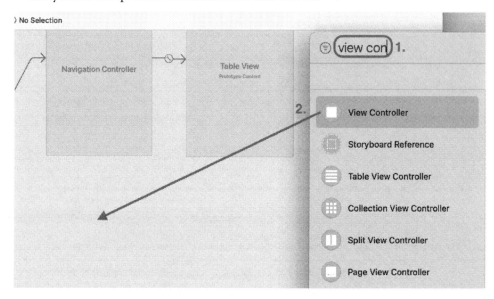

Figure 11.8: Library with View Controller object selected

3. Click the Library button and type `collec` into the filter field. A **Collection View** object will be in the results. Drag the **Collection View** object to the view in the view controller scene:

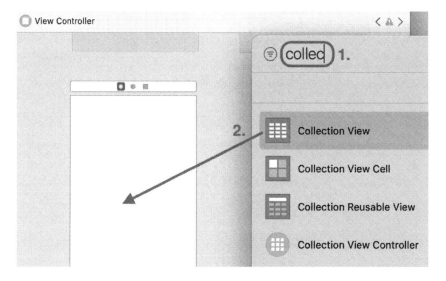

Figure 11.9: Library with Collection View object selected

4. You'll add constraints to make the collection view fill the whole screen. With the collection view selected, click the Add New Constraints button:

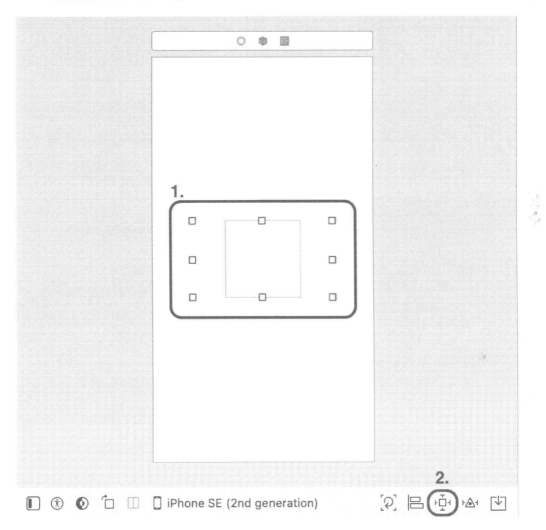

Figure 11.10: View controller scene with collection view selected

5. Type 0 into all the **Spacing to nearest neighbor** fields and make sure that all the pale red struts are selected (they will turn bright red). Click the **Add 4 Constraints** button. Verify that the edges of the collection view are now flush with the edges of the view in the view controller scene:

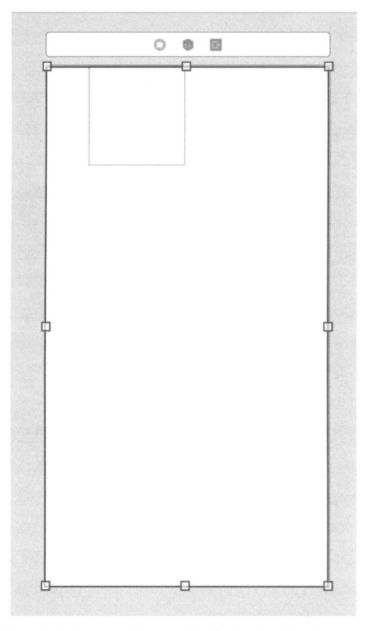

Figure 11.11: View controller scene with collection view filling the screen

The view controller scene for the **Restaurant List** screen has been added, but it does not have a view controller yet. You'll need one to make it display a collection view cell. In the next section, you'll add a new Cocoa Touch Class file to your app so that you can declare and define a new view controller class for this screen.

Declaring the RestaurantListViewController class

As you did in the previous chapter, you'll add a new Cocoa Touch Class file to your project, but this time, you'll implement the `RestaurantListViewController` class. You'll use an instance of this class as the view controller for the **Restaurant List** screen. Follow these steps:

1. Click the Navigator and Inspector buttons to turn on the Navigator and Inspector areas.

2. Right-click on the `LetsEat` group and choose **New Group** from the pop-up menu.

3. Name this new group `Restaurants`. If you make a mistake, click the name and press *Return* on your keyboard to make it editable again.

4. Right-click the `Restaurants` group and select **New File....**

5. **iOS** should already be selected. Select **Cocoa Touch Class** and click **Next**.

6. The **Choose options for your new file** screen will appear. Type the following into the **Class** and **Subclass of** fields:

   Class: `RestaurantListViewController`

   Subclass of: `UIViewController`

   Click **Next** when you're done.

7. On the next screen, click **Create**.

8. The `RestaurantListViewController` file has been added to the project, and you will see the boilerplate code for the `RestaurantListViewController` class in it. The `RestaurantListViewController` class is a subclass of the `UIViewController` class and contains a single method, `viewDidLoad()`. Like you did in the previous chapter, remove the commented code after the `viewDidLoad()` class in the `RestaurantListViewController` class until only the code shown in the following screenshot remains:

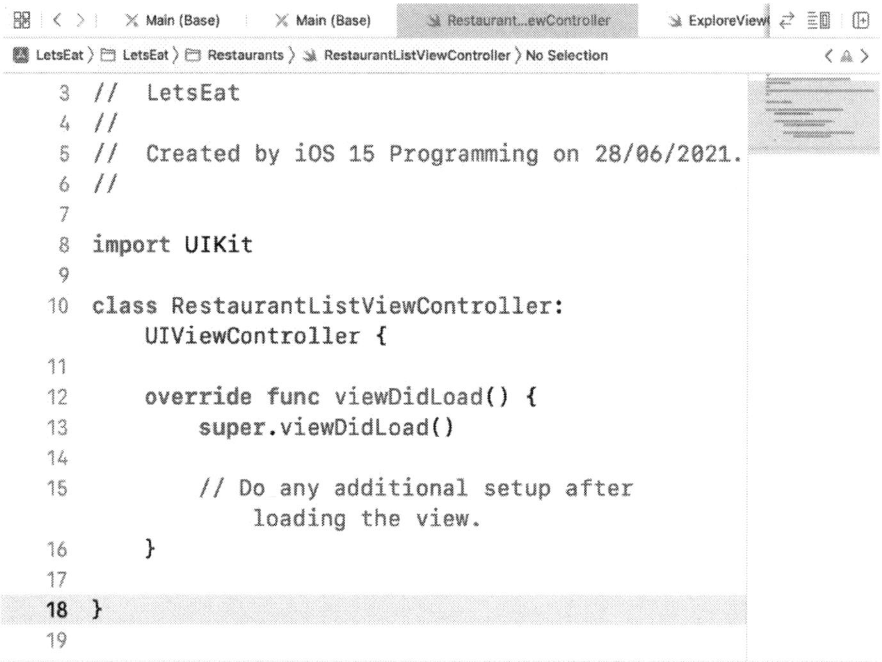

```
3  //   LetsEat
4  //
5  //   Created by iOS 15 Programming on 28/06/2021.
6  //
7
8  import UIKit
9
10  class RestaurantListViewController:
        UIViewController {
11
12      override func viewDidLoad() {
13          super.viewDidLoad()
14
15          // Do any additional setup after
                loading the view.
16      }
17
18  }
19
```

Figure 11.12: Editing area showing RestaurantListViewController file's contents

As you did before for the **Explore** screen, you'll make the `RestaurantListViewController` class the view controller for the view in the view controller scene and adopt the collection view data source and delegate protocols. You'll also add an outlet for the collection view manually in the class definition and use the Connections inspector to connect the outlet to the collection view in the storyboard. You'll do this in the next section.

Adopting the delegate and data source protocols

You will modify the RestaurantListViewController class to make it conform
to the UICollectionViewDataSource and UICollectionViewDelegate
protocols and add any required protocol methods. You'll also add an outlet for the
collection view and make an instance of the RestaurantListViewController class
the view controller for the view. Follow these steps:

1. Modify the RestaurantListViewController class declaration as
   shown to make it adopt the UICollectionViewDataSource and
   UICollectionViewDelegate protocols:

   ```
   class RestaurantListViewController: UIViewController,
   UICollectionViewDataSource, UICollectionViewDelegate {
   ```

2. When the error icon appears, click it.

3. You'll see this error because the methods required to conform to the protocols you
   added are not present in the class definition. Click the **Fix** button to add stubs for
   the required methods to your class definition.

4. Verify that the method stubs have been added to the file. Rearrange everything so
   that the stubs are after the viewDidLoad() method:

   ```
   13          super.viewDidLoad()
   14
   15          // Do any additional setup after
   16              loading the view.
           }
   17
   18          func collectionView(_ collectionView:
                   UICollectionView,
                   numberOfItemsInSection section: Int) ->
                   Int {
   19              code
   20          }
   21
   22          func collectionView(_ collectionView:
                   UICollectionView, cellForItemAt
                   indexPath: IndexPath) ->
                   UICollectionViewCell {
   23              code
   24          }
   ```

   Figure 11.13: Editing area showing UICollectionViewDataSource method stubs

5. Modify the method stubs as shown to make the collection view display a single collection view cell on the screen when the app is run:

```
func collectionView(_ collectionView: UICollectionView,
numberOfItemsInSection section: Int) -> Int {

    1

}
func collectionView(_ collectionView: UICollectionView,
cellForItemAt indexPath: IndexPath) ->
UICollectionViewCell

{

    collectionView.dequeueReusableCell(
    withReuseIdentifier: "restaurantCell",
    for: indexPath)

}
```

6. Verify that your code looks like this:

```
17
18          func collectionView(_ collectionView:
                UICollectionView,
                numberOfItemsInSection section: Int) ->
                Int {
19              (1)
20          }
21
22          func collectionView(_ collectionView:
                UICollectionView, cellForItemAt
                indexPath: IndexPath) ->
                UICollectionViewCell {
23              collectionView
                    .dequeueReusableCell
                    (withReuseIdentifier:
                    "restaurantCell", for: indexPath)
24          }
25
```

Figure 11.14: Editing area showing code to display a single cell

7. Add an outlet, `collectionView`, just after the class declaration:

```
@IBOutlet var collectionView: UICollectionView!
```

You will link this to the collection view in the storyboard later.

8.   Verify that your code looks like this:

```
10  class RestaurantListViewController :
        UIViewController,
        UICollectionViewDataSource,
        UICollectionViewDelegate {
11
        @IBOutlet var collectionView:
            UICollectionView!
13
14      override func viewDidLoad() {
15          super.viewDidLoad()
16
```

Figure 11.15: Editing area showing collectionView outlet

You won't be using the assistant editor to link the outlet to the collection view, like you did in the previous chapter. This is a matter of personal preference—you are free to choose whichever method suits you best.

9.   Click the Main storyboard file and click the **View Controller** icon of the newly added **View Controller Scene** in the document outline. Click the Identity inspector button:

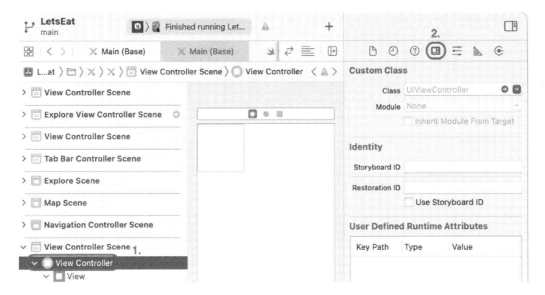

Figure 11.16: Identity inspector selected

10. To make an instance of the `RestaurantListViewController` class the view controller for this scene, select `RestaurantListViewController` in the **Class** field:

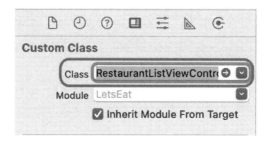

Figure 11.17: Identity inspector with Class set to RestaurantListViewController

Note that the name of the view controller scene has changed to **Restaurant List View Controller Scene**.

11. Click the Connections inspector button. To assign the collection view in the **Restaurant List View Controller Scene** to the outlet in the `RestaurantListViewController` class definition, drag from the circle next to the `collectionView` outlet to the collection view in the **Restaurant List View Controller Scene**:

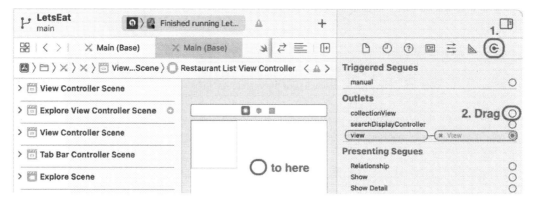

Figure 11.18: Editing area showing collection view to be connected

12. Verify that the collection view in the **Restaurant List View Controller Scene** and the `collectionView` outlet in the `RestaurantListViewController` class definition are now connected:

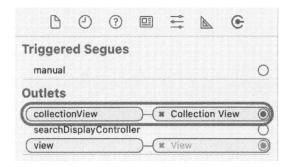

Figure 11.19: Connections inspector showing collectionView outlet

13. Click the **Collection View** in the document outline and click the Connections inspector. To make an instance of the `RestaurantListViewController` class the data source and delegate object for the collection view, drag from the circles next to the `dataSource` and `delegate` outlets to the **Restaurant List View Controller** icon in the document outline:

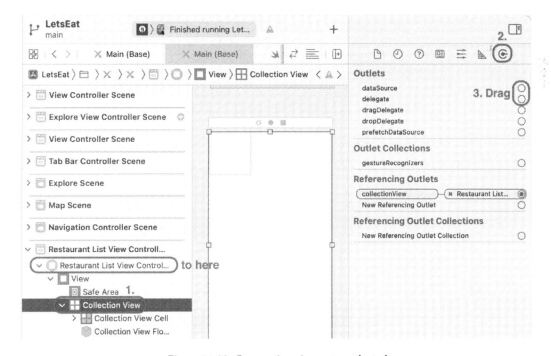

Figure 11.20: Connections inspector selected

14. Verify that the `dataSource` and `delegate` outlets are now connected:

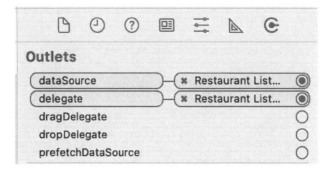

Figure 11.21: Connections inspector with dataSource and delegate outlets set

15. Click the **Collection View Cell** in the document outline. Click the Attributes inspector button to set the identifier and color of the collection view cell (you'll learn more about identifiers in *Chapter 13, Getting Started with MVC and Collection Views*):

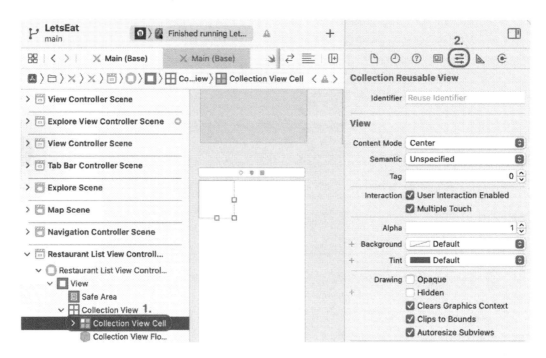

Figure 11.22: Attributes inspector selected

16. Set the **Identifier** of the collection view cell to `restaurantCell` and set the **Background** color to `Light Gray Color`:

Figure 11.23: Attributes inspector with identifier and background color set

The **Restaurant List View Controller Scene** setup is now complete. Now, you need to display this screen when a cell in the **Explore** screen is tapped. To do this, you will add a segue between the **Explore** screen and the **Restaurant List** screen in the next section.

Presenting the Restaurant List screen

In the previous chapter, you added a segue to make the **Locations** screen appear when a button in the **Explore** screen is tapped. To display the **Restaurant List** screen when a cell in the **Explore** screen is tapped, you'll use a segue as well. Follow these steps:

1.   Click **Explore View Controller Scene** in the document outline. *Ctrl + Drag* from `exploreCell` in the document outline to the **Restaurant List View Controller Scene** to add a segue between them:

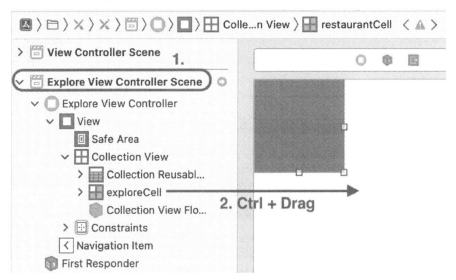

Figure 11.24: Document outline showing exploreCell

2.   The **Segue** menu will appear. Choose **Show** from the menu:

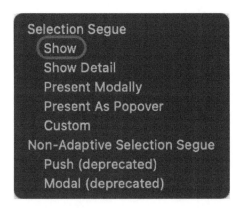

Figure 11.25: Segue pop-up menu with Show selected

This makes the **Restaurant List** screen slide in from the right when a cell in the **Explore** screen is tapped. A <**Back** button will appear in the navigation bar.

Build and run your app. In the **Explore** screen, tap a cell. You should see the **Restaurant List** screen appear with a collection view containing a single cell inside it. Tapping the <**Back** button in the navigation bar will dismiss the **Restaurant List** screen:

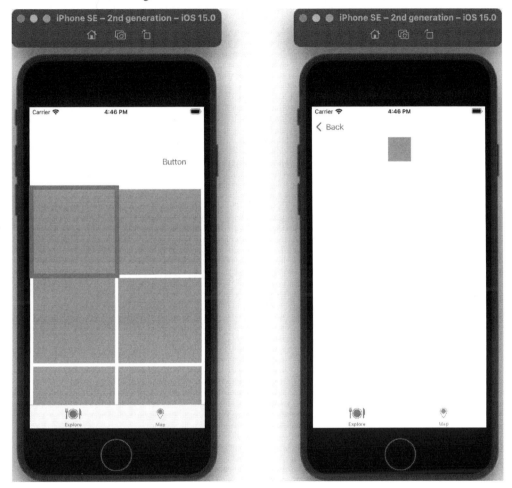

Figure 11.26: iOS Simulator showing Explore and Restaurant List screens

The implementation of the **Restaurant List** screen is now complete, and you can navigate from the **Explore** screen to the **Restaurant List** screen and back. Eventually, the collection view in this screen will display a list of restaurants at a particular location, as shown in the app tour. Great! The next thing you will do is add a view controller scene to represent the **Restaurant Detail** screen. This screen will be displayed when a cell in the **Restaurant List** screen is tapped. You'll do this in the next section.

Implementing the Restaurant Detail screen

As shown in the app tour in *Chapter 9, Setting Up the User Interface*, when you tap a restaurant in the **Restaurant List** screen, a **Restaurant Detail** screen containing the details of that restaurant will appear. Tapping the **Add Review** button will display the **Review Form** screen where you can add reviews and tapping the **Add Photo** button will display the **Photo Filter** screen where you can add photos and apply filters to them.

In this section, you'll add a new table view controller scene to your storyboard to represent the **Restaurant Detail** screen and add a second view controller scene to represent the **Review Form** screen. You'll place a button in one of the table view cells to present the **Review Form** screen.

Let's start by adding the new view controller scene. Follow these steps:

1. Click the Library button, type `table` in the filter field, and drag a **Table View Controller** object to the storyboard next to the **Restaurant List View Controller Scene**:

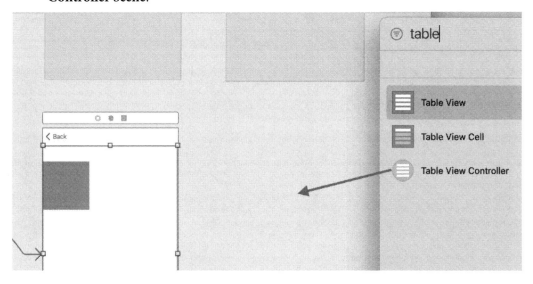

Figure 11.27: Library with Table View Controller object selected

This will represent the **Restaurant Detail** screen.

2.   Verify that the **Table View Controller Scene** has been added:

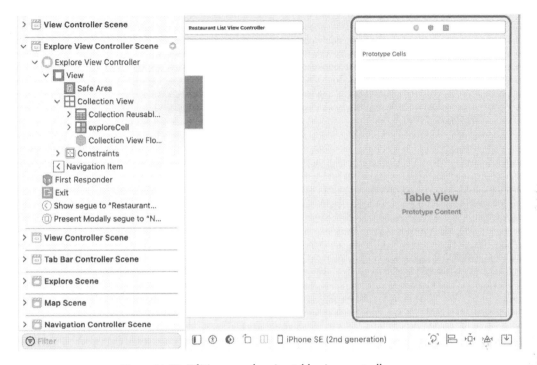

Figure 11.28: Editing area showing table view controller scene
next to Restaurant List View Controller Scene

Note that it already has a table view inside it, so you don't need to add a table view to the scene, like you did in the previous section.

3. To display the **Restaurant Detail** screen when a cell in the **Restaurant List** screen is tapped, *Ctrl + Drag* from `restaurantCell` (in the document outline under the **Restaurant List View Controller Scene**) to the table view to add a segue between them:

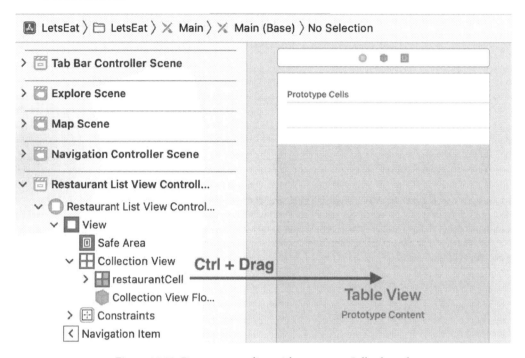

Figure 11.29: Document outline with restaurantCell selected

4. Select **Show** from the **Segue** menu. This makes the **Restaurant Detail** screen slide in from the right when a cell in the **Restaurant List** screen is tapped. A <**Back** button will appear in the navigation bar.

5. Verify that a segue has appeared between the two scenes:

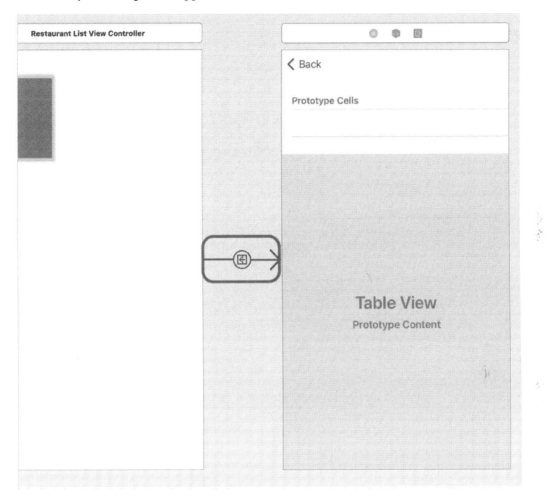

Figure 11.30: Editing area showing segue between Restaurant List View Controller Scene
and the table view controller scene

6. The **Restaurant Detail** screen always displays a fixed number of cells. In the document outline, click **Table View** under **Table View Controller Scene** and click the Attributes inspector button:

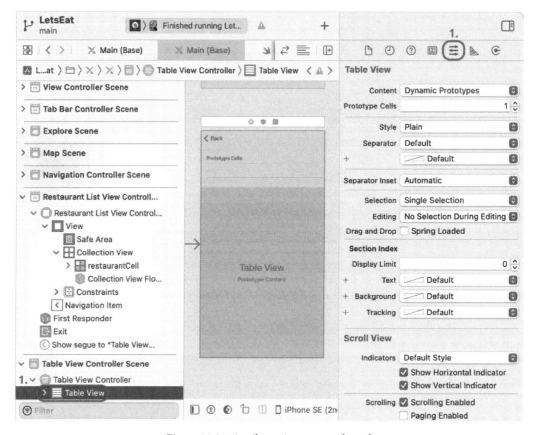

Figure 11.31: Attributes inspector selected

7. Set **Content** to **Static Cells** to make the **Restaurant Detail** screen display a fixed number of cells:

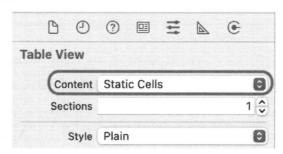

Figure 11.32: Attributes inspector with Content set to Static Cells

You're doing this because the **Restaurant Detail** screen always uses the same number of cells to display restaurant details.

Build and run your app. Click on a cell in the **Explore** screen to display the **Restaurant List** screen. Then, click on a cell in the **Restaurant List** screen to display the **Restaurant Detail** screen:

Figure 11.33: iOS simulator showing Restaurant Detail screen

Click the **Back** button to go back.

In the next section, you will implement a button inside one of the table view cells to display a screen that represents the **Review Form** screen.

Implementing the Review Form screen

In this section, you will implement a new view controller scene to represent the **Review Form** screen and configure a button in the **Restaurant Detail** screen to display it. Follow these steps:

1. You need a button in the **Restaurant Detail** screen to display the **Review Form** screen when tapped. Click the Library button and type button into the filter field. A **Button** object appears as one of the results. Drag it to the top static cell in the table view controller scene representing the **Restaurant Detail** screen:

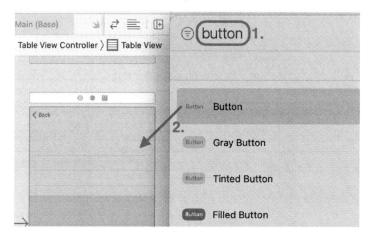

Figure 11.34: Library with Button object selected

2. Position it on the right-hand side of the cell:

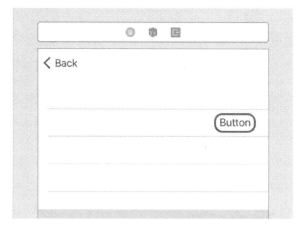

Figure 11.35: Editing area showing table view controller scene with button

3. Click the Library button and type `view con` in the filter field. A **View Controller** object will appear as one of the results. Drag it next to the table view controller scene to represent the **Review Form** screen:

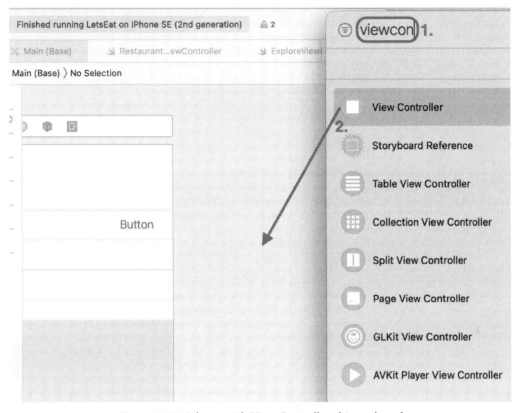

Figure 11.36: Library with View Controller object selected

4. Verify that the new view controller scene has been added:

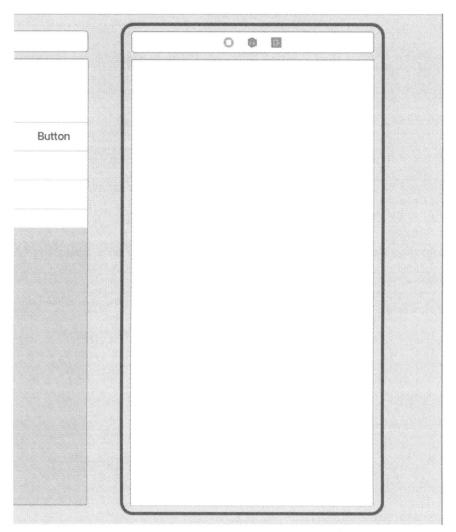

Figure 11.37: Editing area showing view controller scene next to table view controller scene

5. Click the Library button and type `label` in the filter field. A **Label** object appears as one of the results. Drag it to the center of the new view controller scene to represent a review:

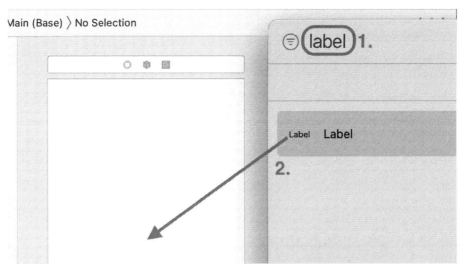

Figure 11.38: Library with Label object selected

6. Change the label text to Reviews. Click the Align button to add horizontal and vertical constraints to it:

Figure 11.39: Editing area showing view controller scene with label

7. Tick the **Horizontally in Container** and **Vertically in Container** checkboxes. Click the **Add 2 Constraints** button. Verify the constraints have been added:

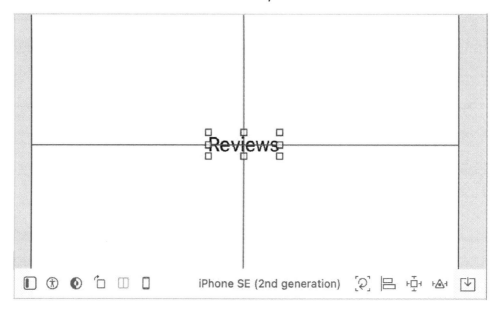

Figure 11.40: Editing area showing label constraints set

These constraints ensure that the **Reviews** label will always be in the middle of the screen when the app is run, regardless of orientation or screen size.

8. *Ctrl + Drag* from the button in the table view cell to the newly added view controller scene and select **Show** from the pop-up menu. This makes the **Review Form** screen appear when the button is tapped:

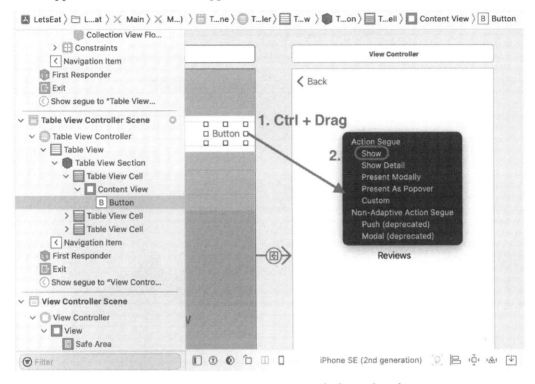

Figure 11.41: Segue pop-up menu with Show selected

Build and run your app. Click on a cell in the **Explore** screen, then click on a cell in the
Restaurant List screen. Click the button in the **Restaurant Detail** screen to display the
Review Form screen:

Figure 11.42: iOS simulator showing Review Form screen

Fantastic! All the screens that are accessible from the **Explore** tab, except for the **Photo Filter** screen, have now been implemented, with hardly any coding required! If you wish, you can repeat the steps in this section to add the **Photo Filter** screen.

The last thing to do is make the **Map** screen display a map. You'll do this in the next section.

Implementing the Map screen

When you launch the app, the **Explore** screen is displayed. Tapping the **Map** button in the tab bar makes the **Map** screen appear, but it is blank. To make the **Map** screen display a map, you'll add a map view to the view in the view controller scene for the **Map** screen. Follow these steps:

1. Select the view controller scene for the **Map** screen:

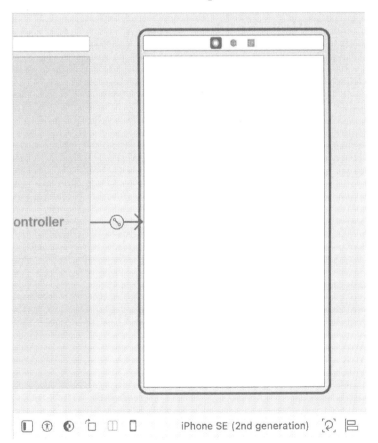

Figure 11.43: Editing area showing view controller scene

2. To make this scene display a map, click the Library button and type map in the filter field. A **Map Kit View** object appears as one of the results. Drag it to the view in the view controller scene:

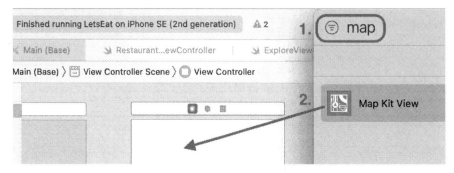

Figure 11.44: Library with Map Kit View object selected

3. The map should fill the whole screen. With the map view selected, click the Add New Constraints button:

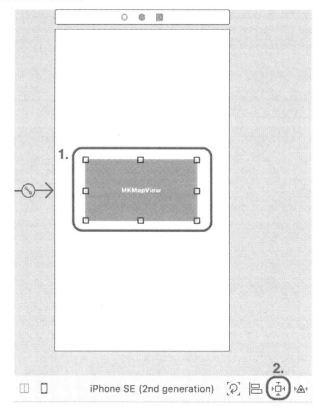

Figure 11.45: View controller scene with map view selected

4. Type 0 into all the **Spacing to nearest neighbor** fields and make sure that the pale red struts are selected (they will turn bright red). Click the **Add 4 Constraints** button. Verify that the map view fills the entire screen:

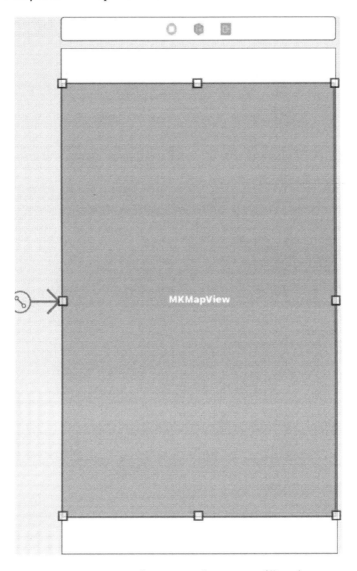

Figure 11.46: View controller scene with map view filling the screen

Build and run your app. Click the **Map** button. You should see a map similar to the one shown:

Figure 11.47: iOS Simulator showing Map screen

If you look at the Main storyboard file at this point, you should see something like this:

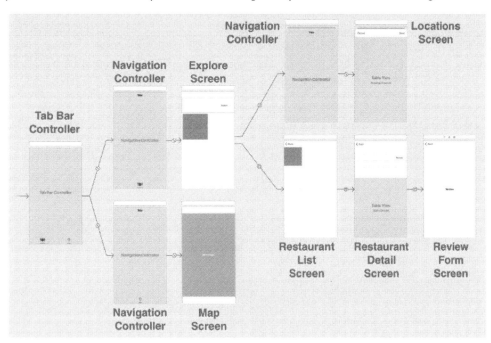

Figure 11.48: Editing area showing all the scenes in Main storyboard file

Verify that you have all the scenes shown in the preceding screenshot, and you can also run your app in the simulator to check that all the screens are working properly.

Wonderful! You've now completed the basic user interface for your app!

Summary

In this chapter, you completed the basic structure of your app. First, you added a blank table view to the **Locations** screen. You also added a new view controller scene to your storyboard to represent the **Restaurant List** screen, added and configured a collection view for this screen, and implemented a segue that displays it when a cell in the **Explore** screen is tapped. You added a new table view controller scene to represent the **Restaurant Detail** screen, configured a table view with static cells for this screen, and implemented a segue that will display this screen when a cell in the **Restaurant List** screen is tapped. You also added a button to one of the rows in the **Restaurant Detail** screen, added a table view controller scene to represent the **Review Form** screen, and configured the button you added to display it. Finally, you added a map view to the view controller scene for the **Map** screen, and it now displays a map when the **Map** button is tapped.

You have successfully implemented all the screens required for your app, and you'll be able to test your app's flow when you run it in the simulator. You should also be more proficient with Interface Builder. You now know how to add and configure a table view to a storyboard scene, how to add segues between scenes and how to add a map view to a scene. This will be useful as you implement your own apps that contain table views, use segues to navigate between different screens, and display maps. Great!

In the next chapter, you'll modify the cells inside the **Explore** screen, the **Restaurant List** screen, and the **Locations** screen so that they match the designs that were shown in the app tour.

12
Modifying and Configuring Cells

In the previous chapter, you implemented all the screens required for your app, but the cells in the **Explore**, **Restaurant List** and **Locations** screens still need work. For example, the **Explore** screen's collection view section header and collection view cells do not match the design shown in the app tour in *Chapter 9, Setting Up the User Interface*.

In this chapter, you'll modify and configure the **Explore**, **Restaurant List**, and **Locations** screens to match the design shown in the app tour. For the **Explore** screen, you'll add labels and views to the collection view section header and configure the button's appearance. You'll also modify the exploreCell collection view cell by adding an image view and a label to it. For the **Restaurant List** screen, you'll modify the restaurantCell collection view cell by adding labels, buttons and an image view to it. You'll also configure the image view to show a default image. For the **Locations** screen, you'll configure a prototype cell for the table view and set an identifier, locationCell, for the table view cells.

By the end of this chapter, you will be proficient in adding and positioning user interface elements and will know how to use constraints to determine their position relative to one another.

The following topics will be covered:

- Modifying the **Explore** screen's collection view section header
- Modifying the `exploreCell` collection view cell
- Modifying the `restaurantCell` collection view cell
- Configuring the `locationCell` collection view cell

Technical requirements

You will continue working on the `LetsEat` project that you modified in the previous chapter.

The completed Xcode project for this chapter is in the `Chapter12` folder of the code bundle for this book, which can be downloaded here:

`https://github.com/PacktPublishing/iOS-15-Programming-for-Beginners-Sixth-Edition`

Check out the following video to see the code in action:

`https://bit.ly/3kjQVSD`

Let's start by adding UI elements to the collection view section header in the **Explore** screen, to make it match the one shown in the app tour.

Modifying the Explore screen section header

Let's see what the collection view section header for the **Explore** screen looks like in the app tour:

Figure 12.1: The collection view section header for the completed Let's Eat app

There are four elements in this collection view section header: two labels (title and subtitle), a button, and a view (the gray line underneath the title and button).

You have already added a button to the collection view section header of the **Explore** screen's collection view in *Chapter 10, Building Your User Interface*. You will now add labels and views and then modify all elements to match the collection view section header shown in the app tour. Follow these steps:

1. First, turn on **bounds rectangles** in the Editor area. This will highlight the bounds of the user interface elements in blue and make them easier to see. Choose **Canvas | Bounds Rectangles** from the **Editor** menu to turn them on:

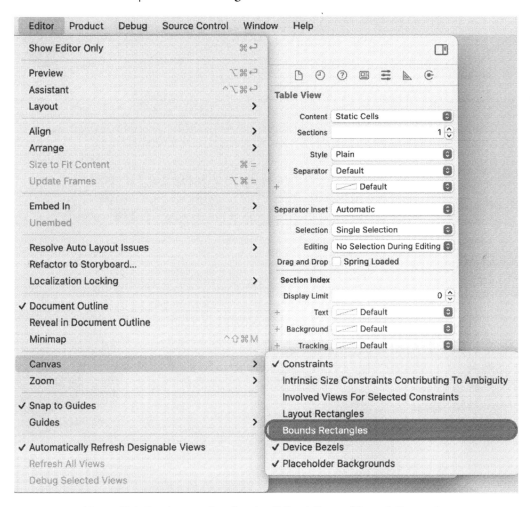

Figure 12.2: Xcode menu bar showing Editor | Canvas | Bounds Rectangles

2. Verify that the collection view section header's size has been set properly. In the
    `Main` storyboard file, find **Explore View Controller Scene**. Select **Collection
    Reusable View** in the document outline (remember, this is the collection view
    section header). Click the Size inspector button. Update the values in the **Size**
    section if required:

Width: 0

Height: 100

Figure 12.3: Size inspector settings for the collection view section header

Remember that the units used are points. Setting the width of the collection view
section header to 0 will automatically make it the same width as the screen.

3. You'll add a view to the collection view section header to act as a container to all the
    other user interface elements you will add. Click the Library button. Type `uiview`
    in the filter field. A **View** object will appear in the results. Drag it to the collection
    view section header:

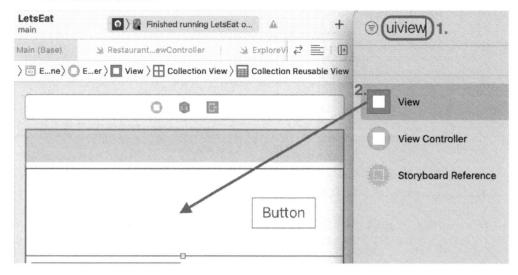

Figure 12.4: Library with View object selected

4. In the document outline, drag the **View** up to make it the first item in the **Collection Reusable View**'s list of subviews. The first item in the list of subviews will be drawn onscreen first, and this ensures it doesn't overlap the button:

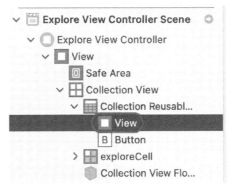

Figure 12.5: Document outline showing View position

5. You'll make the view the same size as the collection view section header. With the **View** selected in the document outline, click the Size inspector button. In the **View** section, update the following values:

    X: 0

    Y: 0

    Width: 375

    Height: 100

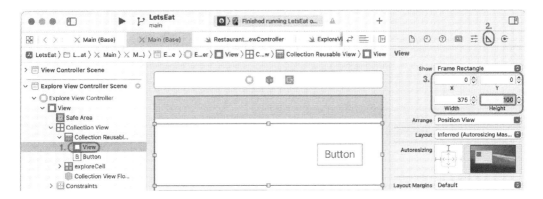

Figure 12.6: Size inspector settings for the view

The **X** and **Y** values determine the horizontal and vertical offset of the view relative to the top-left corner of the collection view section header, and the **Width** and **Height** values determine the width and height of the view. This makes the position of the top-left corner of this view the same as the top-left corner of the collection view section header, sets the width of the view to the same width as the screen (375 points), and sets the height of the view to 100 points. This will make it easier to add constraints later, as you will be positioning the views you will add relative to this container view.

6. You'll need labels to display **PLEASE SELECT A LOCATION** and **EXPLORE** in the collection view section header. Click the Library button. Type label in the filter field. A **Label** object will appear in the results. Drag two **Label** objects into the view you dragged in earlier:

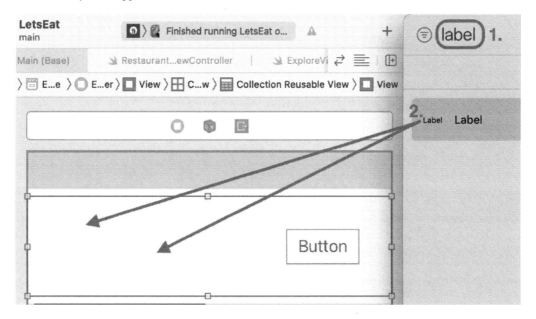

Figure 12.7: Library with Label object selected

7. Both labels have to be subviews of the container view as you will apply constraints to them relative to their position in the container view. In the document outline, verify both **Label** objects are subviews of the **View**, and the **View** is a subview of the **Collection Reusable View**:

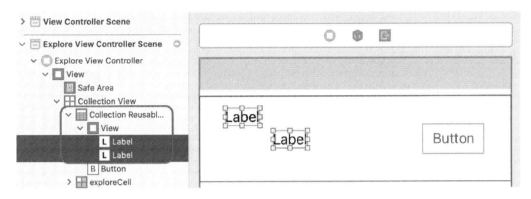

Figure 12.8: View containing two labels

8. The button has to be a subview of the container view as well, as it will also have constraints applied to it relative to the container view. Select the **Button** in the document outline and drag it to the **View** to make it a subview of the **View**. When you are done, it should look like this:

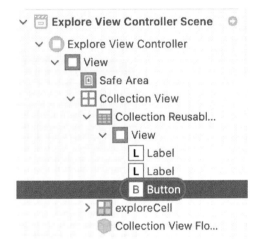

Figure 12.9: Document outline showing Collection Reusable View's subviews

9. One of the labels in the collection view section header should be set to a custom gray color. You will create a folder in your asset catalog and add new custom colors to it. Click the `Assets.xcassets` file. Right-click in the clear white space of the document outline as shown:

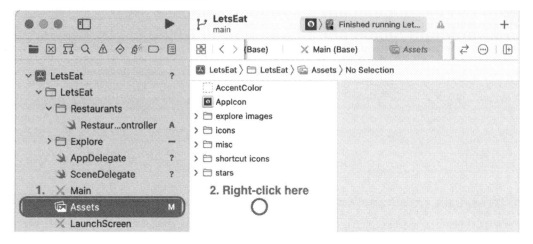

Figure 12.10: Assets.xcassets folder showing document outline

10. Choose **New Folder** from the pop-up menu to create a new folder:

Figure 12.11: Pop-up menu with New Folder selected

11. Change the name of the folder to `colors`:

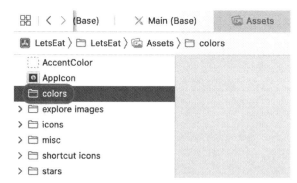

Figure 12.12: Assets.xcassets folder showing colors folder

You'll put all your custom colors in this folder.

12. Now you will add a new custom color to your project. Right-click the `colors` folder and choose **New Color Set**:

Figure 12.13: Pop-up menu with New Color Set selected

13. Click the newly created color set. Make sure **Any Appearance** is selected. In the Attributes inspector, name the color `LetsEat Light Gray`, set the **Input Method** to `8-bit Hexadecimal` and type `#AFAFB2` into the **Hex** field, pressing *Return* when you're done:

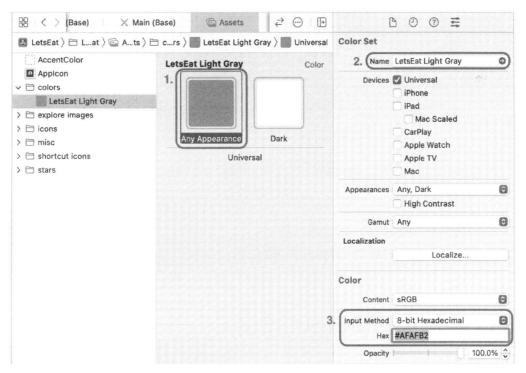

Figure 12.14: Attributes inspector settings for LetsEat Light Gray

Note that next to the **Any Appearance** color box, there is a **Dark Appearance** color box. The color in the **Dark Appearance** color box is used if the user switches on **Dark Mode**. Leave it at the default value.

> **Important Information**
>
> To learn more about Dark Mode, visit this link: `https://support.apple.com/en-us/HT210332`.

14. You'll create a second color, which you will use when you're modifying the **Restaurant Detail** screen later. Repeat *steps 12* and *13*, but this time, name the color `LetsEat Dark Gray` and set the **Hex** value in the **Color** section to #AAAAAA:

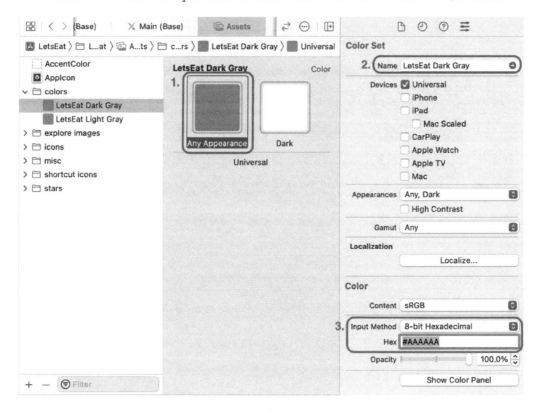

Figure 12.15: Attributes inspector settings for LetsEat Dark Gray

15. For `LetsEat Dark Gray`, you'll change the **Dark Appearance** color to a darker gray. Click the **Dark Appearance** color box and click the **Show Color Panel** button:

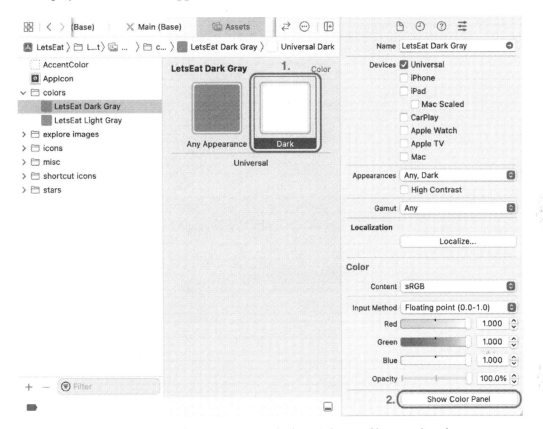

Figure 12.16: Attributes inspector with Show Color Panel button selected

16. To set the color, choose the sliders pane, choose **Grayscale Slider** from the pop-up menu and click the second gray shade from the left as shown:

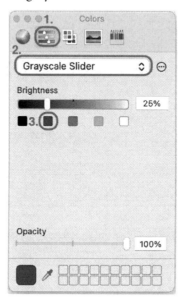

Figure 12.17: Color Panel settings for LetsEat Dark Gray Dark Appearance

17. Verify that the contents of the colors folder are as follows:

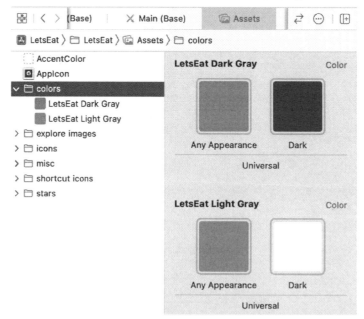

Figure 12.18: Assets.xcassets showing contents of colors folder

18. To configure a label as a subtitle, click the `Main` storyboard file and select one of the labels. Click the Attributes inspector button and update the following values:

Text: `Plain` and then add `PLEASE SELECT A LOCATION` in the empty text field below it

Color: `LetsEat Light Gray`

Font: `System Semibold 13.0`

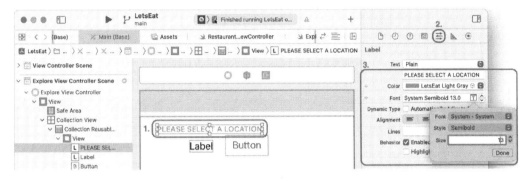

Figure 12.19: Attributes inspector settings for subtitle label

19. With the label still selected, click the Size inspector button. Update the following values in the **View** section:

X: 8

Y: 24

Width: 359

Height: 21

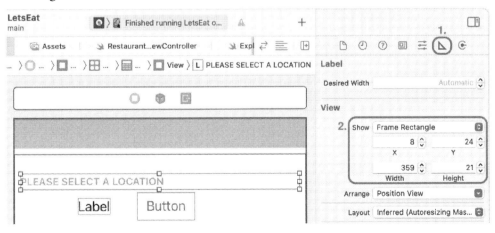

Figure 12.20: Size inspector settings for subtitle label

This label is a subview of the container view you added earlier to the collection view section header. This means the position of the label will be relative to this view. The top-left corner of the label will be offset by 8 points horizontally and 24 points vertically, appearing below and to the right of the top-left corner of the collection view section header. The width of the label will be 359 points and the height will be 21 points.

20. To make the other label a title, select it and click the Attributes inspector button. Update the following values:

Text: `Plain` and then add `EXPLORE` in the empty text field below it

Font: `System Heavy 40.0`

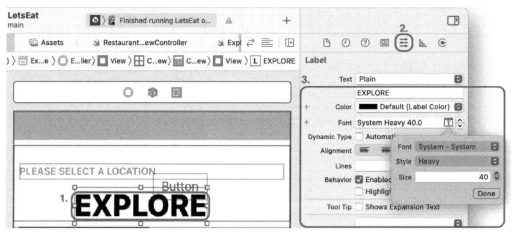

Figure 12.21: Attributes inspector settings for title label

21. With the label still selected, click the Size inspector button. Update the following values in the view section:

X: 8

Y: 45

Width: 255

Height: 37

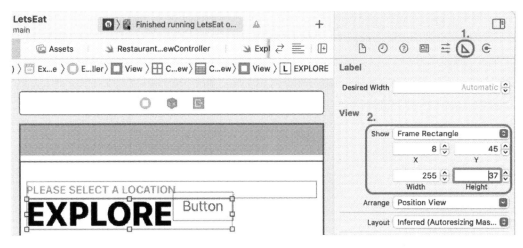

Figure 12.22: Size inspector settings for title label

These settings offset this label by 8 points to the right and 45 points below the top-left corner of the container view, positioning it just below the first label. Note that it does not extend all of the way to the right, leaving some space for the button which will be added later.

22. To configure a custom image for the button, select it and in the Attributes inspector, update the following values in the **Button** section:

Type: Custom and remove the text from the field under the **Title** pop-up menu

Image: btn-location

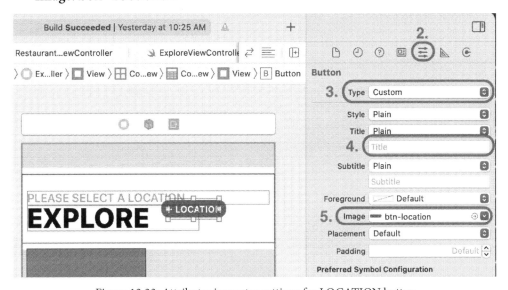

Figure 12.23: Attributes inspector settings for LOCATION button

This image is included in the `Assets.xcassets` file you added to your app in *Chapter 9, Setting Up the User Interface.*

23. With the button still selected, click the Size inspector button. Update the following values in the **View** section to position the button to the right of the **EXPLORE** label:

X: 271

Y: 50

Width: 96

Height: 25

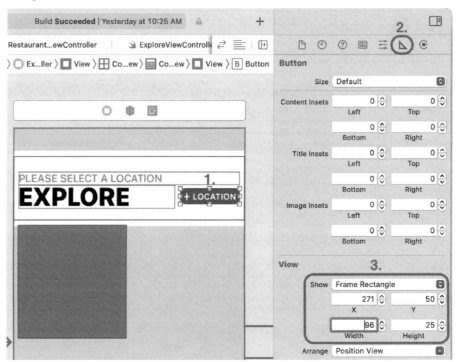

Figure 12.24: Size inspector settings for LOCATION button

24. The last thing you will add is the thin gray line at the bottom of the collection view section header. Click the Library button. Type `uiview` in the filter field. A **View** object will appear in the results. Drag the **View** object into the container view:

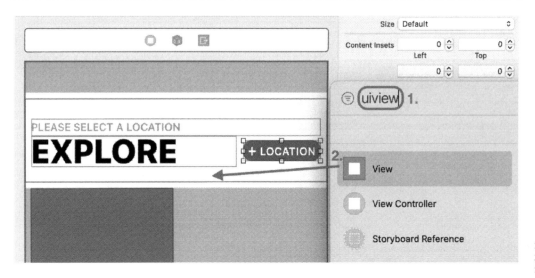

Figure 12.25: Library with View object selected

25. To position the newly added view in the right place, click the Size inspector button and update the following values in the **View** section:

X: 8

Y: 89

Width: 359

Height: 1

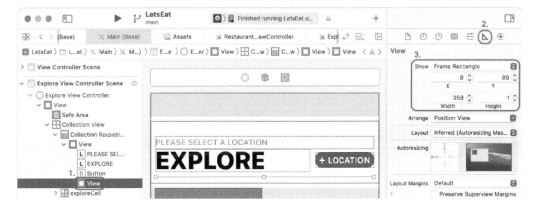

Figure 12.26: Size inspector settings for gray line view

This places the view below all of the other elements, but it is invisible.

26. To set a color for the view, click the Attributes inspector button and set **Background** to `LetsEat Light Gray`:

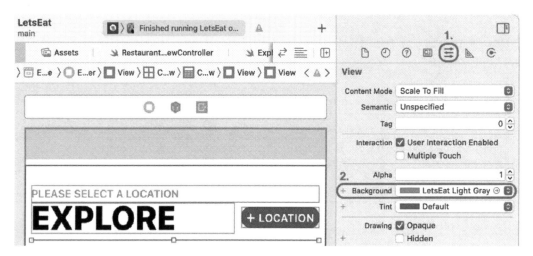

Figure 12.27: Attributes inspector settings for gray line view

All the required user interface elements have been added. Build and run your app. Your collection view section header should now look like this:

Figure 12.28: iOS Simulator showing completed collection view section header

As you can see, the collection view section header now matches the design shown in the app tour. It works great using the iPhone SE (2nd generation) simulator, but to make sure it works in other screen sizes, you will add Auto Layout constraints. You'll do this in the next section.

Adding Auto Layout to the Explore screen's section header

If you build and run your app now in the iPhone SE (2nd generation) simulator, the collection view section header will look great, but if you switch to a simulator with a larger screen, you'll see some graphic elements are not positioned correctly. As you have seen in previous chapters, Auto Layout ensures that the UI adapts to the device's screen size and orientation. For example, the *Let's Eat* app logo on the Launch screen stays in the exact center of the screen regardless of device, and the table view in the **Locations** screen takes up all of the available screen space even when the device is rotated.

So far, you've only used Auto Layout constraints with single user interface elements. In this section, you will add them to multiple user interface elements inside the collection view section header. You will begin by adding constraints to the container view, then proceed to add constraints to all of the other items inside it. Follow these steps:

1. Select the **View** that contains the other views in the document outline:

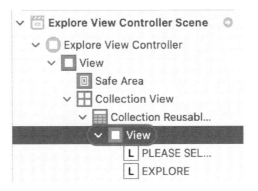

Figure 12.29: Document outline showing container view

2. Click the Add New Constraints button and enter the following values to set the constraints for this view:

Top: 0

Left: 0

Right: 0

Height: 90

When done, click the **Add 4 Constraints** button. This binds the top, left, and right edges of the container view to the edges of the collection view section header. The height of the view is set to 90 points, which determines the position of the bottom edge.

3. Select the **PLEASE SELECT A LOCATION** label in the document outline:

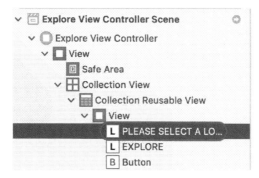

Figure 12.30: Document outline showing subtitle label

4. Click the Add New Constraints button and enter the following values to set the constraints for this label:

Top: 24

Left: 8

Right: 8

Height: 21

When done, click the **Add 4 Constraints** button. The space between the top, left, and right edges of the label and the corresponding edges of the container view are set to 24 points, 8 points, and 8 points respectively. Note the width of the label is not set, allowing it to change if you run it on a simulator with a smaller or larger screen. As before, setting the height constraint determines the position of the bottom edge of the label.

5. Select the **LOCATION** button in the document outline:

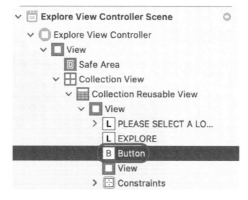

Figure 12.31: Document outline showing LOCATION Button

6. Click the Add New Constraints button and enter the following values to set the constraints for this button:

   Top: 5

   Right: 8

   Width: 96

   Height: 25

   When done, click the **Add 4 Constraints** button. Since the **LOCATION** button is under the **PLEASE SELECT A LOCATION** label, the top constraint determines the space between the top edge of the **LOCATION** button and the bottom edge of the label, not the top edge of the container view. The space between the right edge of the **LOCATION** button and the right edge of the container view is set to 8 points, and the width and height constraints determine the position of the **LOCATION** button's left and bottom edges.

7. Select the gray line **View** in the document outline:

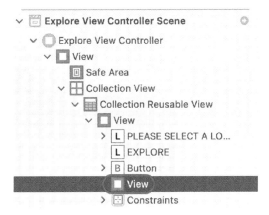

Figure 12.32: Document outline showing gray line view

8. Click the Add New Constraints button and enter the following values to set the constraints for this view:

   Left: 8

   Right: 8

   Bottom: 0

   Height: 1

When done, click the **Add 4 Constraints** button. The space between the left and right edges of the view and the left and right edges of the container view are set to 8 points, and the bottom edge of the view is bound to the bottom edge of the container view. The height constraint determines the position of the top edge of the view.

9. Select the **EXPLORE** label in the document outline:

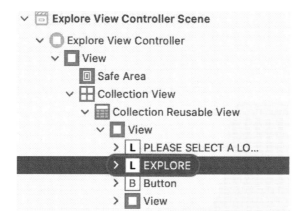

Figure 12.33: Document outline showing title label

10. Click the Add New Constraints button and enter the following values to set the constraints for this label:

Top: 0

Left: 8

Right: 8

Height: 3 7

When done, click the **Add 4 Constraints** button. The top edge of the label is bound to the bottom edge of the **PLEASE SELECT A LOCATION** label. The space between the left edge of the label and the left edge of the container view is 8 points. The space between the right edge of the label and the left edge of the **LOCATION** button is 8 points. The height constraint determines the position of the bottom edge of the label.

You have completed adding Auto Layout constraints to all of the views in the **Explore** screen's collection view section header. Try running your app using different simulators to see the user interface adapt to different screen sizes. Cool!

You may be wondering why you needed to set the position of the user interface elements using the Size inspector before adding constraints. Actually, you don't have to, but by doing that, it makes it much easier to add constraints, as the constraint values that you see when you click the Add New Constraints button are derived from the current space between the user interface elements.

Working with Auto Layout can be challenging for novice developers. Take your time doing it. If it doesn't work properly, clear all of the constraints and start over. To do this, click the Resolve Auto Layout Issues button at the bottom of the screen and choose **Clear Constraints**:

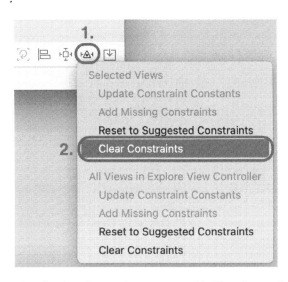

Figure 12.34: Resolve Auto Layout issues menu with Clear Constraints selected

You have added all the required user interface elements and constraints to the collection view section header in the **Explore** screen. Now that you've completed modifying the collection view section header, let's modify the `exploreCell` collection view cell in the next section. You'll add some user interface elements to make it match the cell shown in the app tour.

Modifying the exploreCell collection view cell

Let's take a look at what the `exploreCell` collection view cell looks like in the app tour:

Figure 12.35: The exploreCell collection view cell for the completed Let's Eat app

In the previous chapter, you set the background color for the `exploreCell` collection view cell and configured the collection view to display a grid of 20 cells. You'll now remove the background color and add user interface elements to the `exploreCell` collection view cell to match the design shown in the app tour. Follow these steps:

1. Before you begin, check the initial settings for the `exploreCell` collection view cell. Select `exploreCell` in the document outline of the **Explore View Controller Scene**. Click the Attributes inspector button. Confirm **Identifier** is set to `exploreCell`. Set **Background** to `Default`:

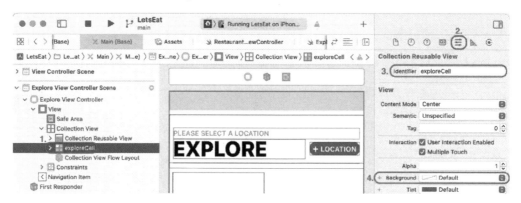

Figure 12.36: Attributes inspector settings for exploreCell collection view cell

2.   You'll add a container view to the `exploreCell` collection view cell. Click the Library button. Type `uiview` into the filter field. A **View** object will appear in the results. Drag it into the prototype cell:

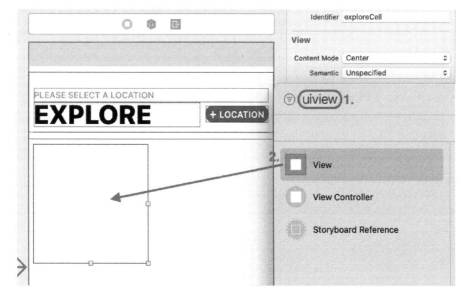

Figure 12.37: Library with View object selected

3.   To ensure the constraints for the newly added view can be set properly, verify the **View** you just added is a subview of the `exploreCell` **Content View**, and is selected:

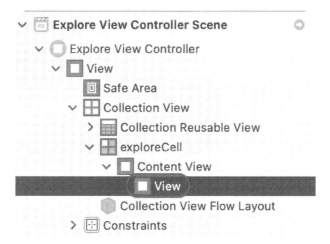

Figure 12.38: Document outline with View selected

4. Click the Add New Constraints button and enter the following values to set the constraints for the newly added view:

    Top: 0

    Left: 0

    Right: 0

    Bottom: 40

    When done, click the **Add 4 Constraints** button. This binds the view's top, left, and right edges to corresponding edges of the exploreCell collection view cell. The position of the bottom edge is determined by the bottom constraint, which sets the distance between the bottom edge of the view and the bottom edge of the exploreCell collection view cell. You'll add a label in this space later.

5. You'll add an image view to display a photo of a cuisine. Click the Library button. Type image into the filter field. An **Image View** object will appear in the results. Drag it on top of the view you added earlier:

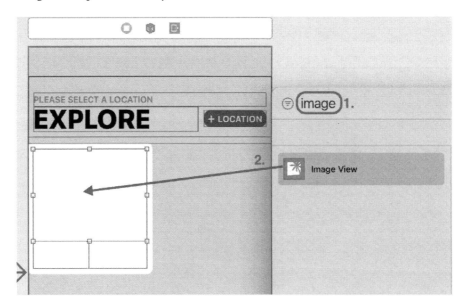

Figure 12.39: Library with Image View object selected

6. To ensure the constraints for the image view can be set properly, verify the **Image View** is a subview of the **View** you added earlier, and is selected:

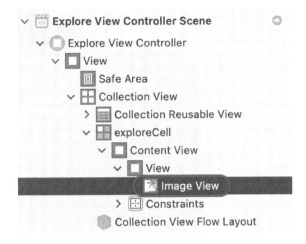

Figure 12.40: Document outline with Image View selected

7. Click the Add New Constraints button and enter the following values to set the constraints for the image view:

Top: 0

Left: 0

Right: 0

Bottom: 0

When done, click the **Add 4 Constraints** button. This binds the edges of the image view to the edges of the view you added earlier.

8. You'll add a label to display the cuisine type. Click the Library button. Type `label` into the filter field. A **Label** object will appear in the results. Drag it to the space between the image view you just added and the bottom of the cell:

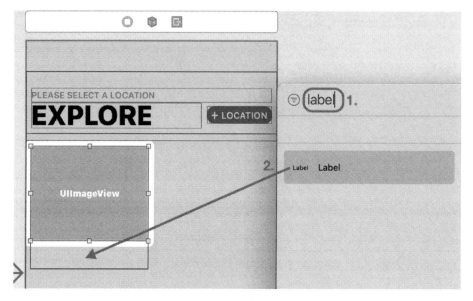

Figure 12.41: Library with Label object selected

9. To ensure the constraints for the label can be set properly, verify the **Label** is selected and is a subview of the `exploreCell` collection view cell's **Content View**, and not a subview of the **View** you added earlier:

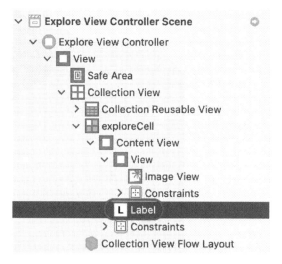

Figure 12.42: Document outline with Label selected

10. Click the Add New Constraints button and enter the following values to set the constraints for the label:

Top: 9

Left: 8

Right: 8

Height: 21

When done, click the **Add 4 Constraints** button. The space between the top edge of the label and the bottom edge of the view you added earlier is set to 9 points. The space between the left and right edges of the label and the corresponding edges of the exploreCell content view are both set to 8 points. The height constraint determines the position of the bottom edge of the label by setting the space between the top and bottom edges of the label.

All the necessary constraints have been added. Build and run your app:

Figure 12.43: iOS Simulator showing completed exploreCell collection view cell

As you can see, the **Explore** screen now more closely matches the design shown in the app tour. Each cell now has an image view and a label just under it, and all of the necessary constraints have been added. Fantastic!

Note that unlike the previous section, you did not set the position of the user interface elements using the Size inspector before adding constraints. You can do this as you are only adding a few elements to the cell, and the relative positions of each element to one another are unambiguous.

You have added all the required user interface elements and constraints to the exploreCell collection view cell. Now that you've completed modifying the exploreCell collection view cell, let's modify the restaurantCell collection view cell next by adding some user interface elements to it in the next section.

Modifying the restaurantCell collection view cell

Let's take a look at what the restaurantCell collection view cell looks like in the app tour:

Figure 12.44: The restaurantCell collection view cell for the completed Let's Eat app

As you can see, the restaurantCell collection view cell has many elements. You will now modify it to match the design shown in the app tour. A summary of the changes required is as follows:

- Change the size of the restaurantCell collection view cell to make it larger and change the background color to the default.

- Add a view, then add a label and a stack view containing three buttons to show the available reservation times.

- Add a view, then add an image view to show a photo of the restaurant.

- Add a label at the top-left corner to show the restaurant's name.

- Add a label just under the name label to show the cuisine the restaurant offers.

You'll be using the Size inspector to position all of the elements, and this will make it easier to add the necessary Auto Layout constraints later. Take your time doing this to reduce the chances of making a mistake. Follow these steps:

1. You'll start by setting the size of the `restaurantCell` collection view cell. In the `Main` storyboard file, click the **Collection View** for the **Restaurant List View Controller Scene** in the document outline. Click the Size inspector button. Under **Cell Size**, set **Width** to 335 and **Height** to 312. Set **Estimate Size** to None:

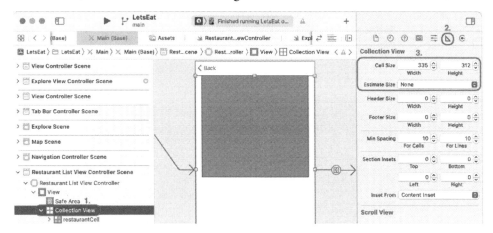

Figure 12.45: Size inspector settings for restaurantCell collection view cell

2. To check the identifier and background color for the `restaurantCell` collection view cell, click `restaurantCell` in the document outline. Click the Attributes inspector button. Confirm the **Identifier** is set to `restaurantCell`. Set **Background** to Default:

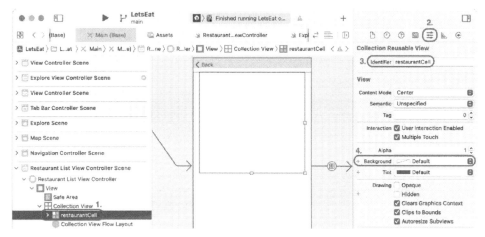

Figure 12.46: Attributes inspector settings for restaurantCell collection view cell

3. You'll add a container view for the **Available Times** label and reservation buttons. Click the Library button. Type `uiview` in the filter field. A **View** object will appear in the results. Drag it into the prototype cell:

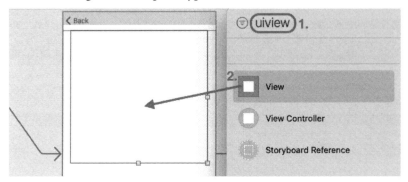

Figure 12.47: Library with View object selected

4. With the newly added view selected, click the Size inspector button. Update the following values for the **View** section to position it within the cell:

X: 55

Y: 245

Width: 224

Height: 56

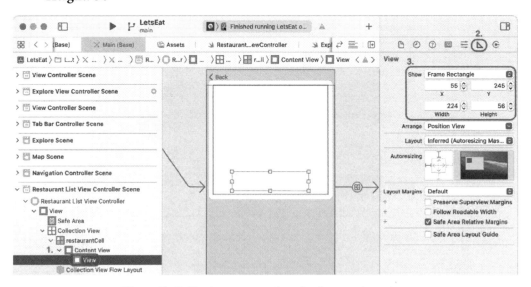

Figure 12.48: Size inspector settings for the container view

5. You'll add a label containing the text **Available Times** to the view. Click the Library button. Type `label` in the filter field. A **Label** object will appear in the results. Drag it into the view you just added:

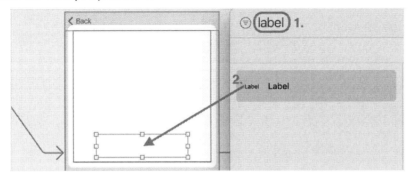

Figure 12.49: Library with Label object selected

6. With the label selected, click the Size inspector button. Update the following values in the **View** section to set the label's position within the view:

X: 0

Y: 2

Width: 224

Height: 21

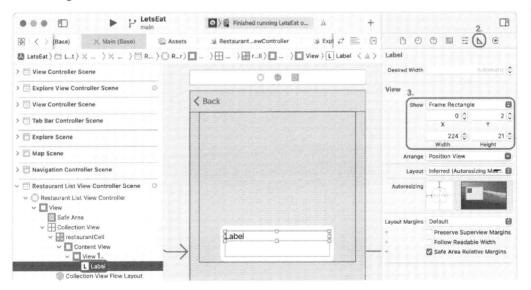

Figure 12.50: Size inspector settings for Available Times label

7. To set and configure the **Available Times** text for the label, click the Attributes inspector button. Update the following values:

Text: Plain and then add Available Times in the empty text field below it

Alignment: Center

Font: System Bold 17.0

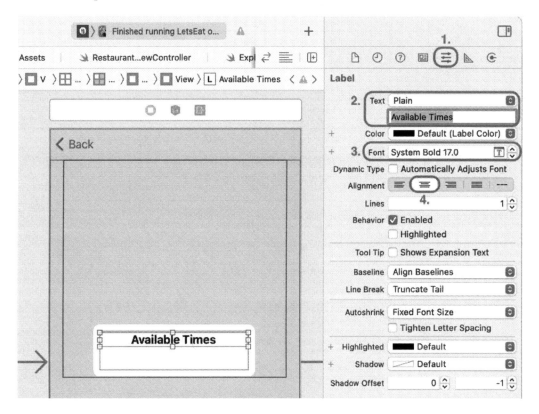

Figure 12.51: Attributes inspector settings for Available Times label

8. You'll add buttons with reservation times to the view. Click the Library button. Type button in the filter field. A **Button** object will appear in the results. Drag it into the same view where the **Available Times** label was:

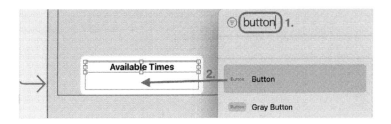

Figure 12.52: Library with Button object selected

9. To set the button's text and background, select it and click the Attributes inspector button. Update the following values:

Type: System

Style: Default

Title: Plain and then add 7:30pm in the empty text field below it

Font: System Bold 15.0

Text Color: White Color

Background: time-bg

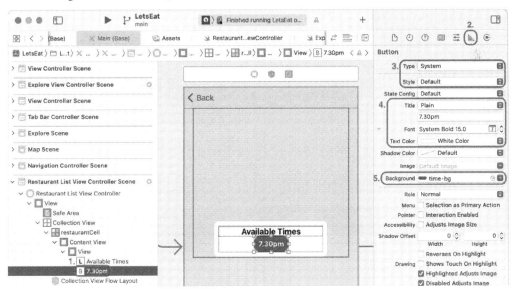

Figure 12.53: Attributes inspector settings for reservation buttons

10. To verify the button's width and height, click the Size inspector button. Update the following values in the **View** section if necessary:

Width: 68

Height: 27

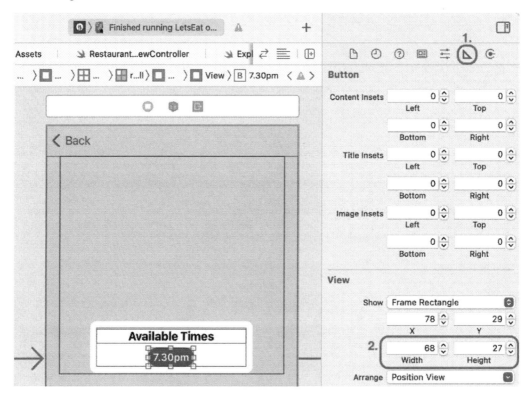

Figure 12.54: Size inspector settings for reservation buttons

11. As seen in the app tour, there are three reservation buttons. Select the button and hit *Command + C* to copy. Hit *Command + V* twice to paste. You should now have three buttons. Arrange them as follows:

Figure 12.55: View showing button arrangement

12. Embedding user interface elements in stack views makes them easier to manage. You'll embed all the buttons in a stack view. Click one button, then press *Shift* and click the other two. All three buttons should now be selected:

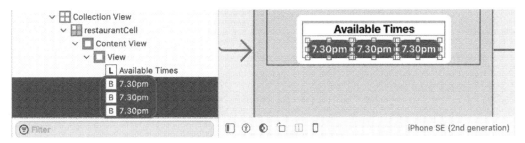

Figure 12.56: View showing all buttons selected

13. Choose **Embed In | Stack View** from the **Editor** menu. This will put all three buttons into a stack view that has a grid of cells with 1 row and 3 columns.

14. Verify all the buttons are now subviews of the stack view by checking the **Stack View**'s subviews in the document outline:

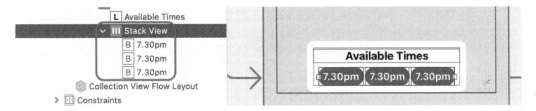

Figure 12.57: View showing all buttons embedded in a stack view

---

Important Information

You can learn more about Stack Views at this link: `https://developer.apple.com/documentation/uikit/uistackview`.

---

15. Select **Stack View** in the document outline. Click the Attributes inspector button. Update the following values to evenly space the buttons:

Axis: Horizontal

Alignment: Fill

Distribution: Equal Spacing

Spacing: 10

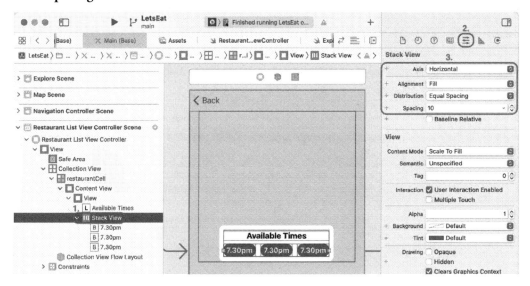

Figure 12.58: Attributes inspector settings for the stack view

16. To position the stack view within the enclosing view, click the Size inspector button. Update the following values in the **View** section:

X: 0

Y: 29

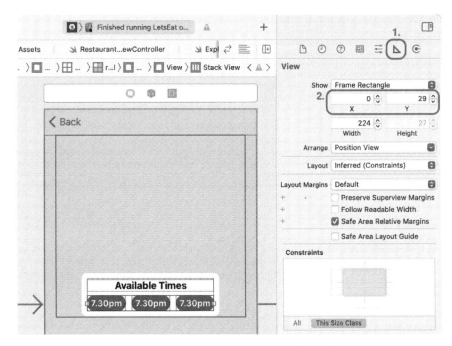

Figure 12.59: Size inspector settings for the stack view

17. You'll add a container view to the `restaurantCell` collection view cell. This view will enclose an image view showing a photo of the restaurant. Click the Library button. Type `uiview` in the filter field. A **View** object will appear in the results. Drag it into the prototype cell:

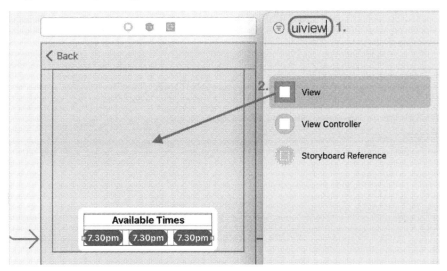

Figure 12.60: Library with View object selected

18. With the view selected, click the Size inspector button. Update the following values in the **View** section to position the view within the cell:

    X: 11

    Y: 42

    Width: 316

    Height: 200

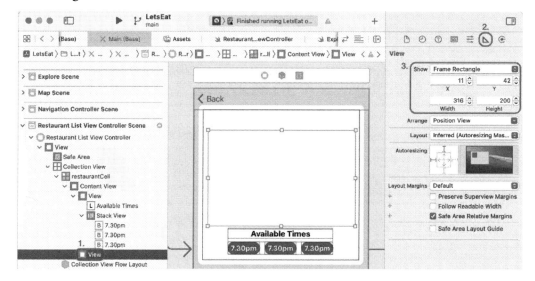

Figure 12.61: Size inspector settings for the container view

19. You'll add an image view to the container view you added earlier. Click the Library button. Type image into the filter field. An **Image View** object will appear in the results. Drag it into the view you just added:

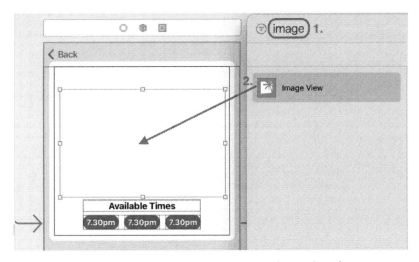

Figure 12.62: Library with Image View object selected

20. To set a temporary placeholder image for the image view, select it and click the Attributes inspector button. Set **Image** to american.

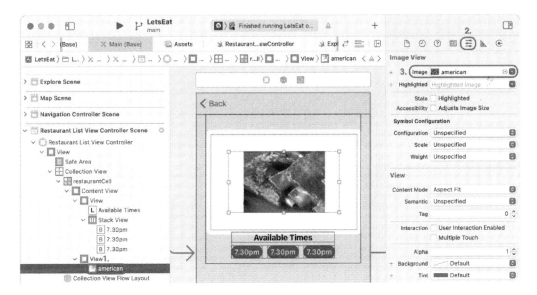

Figure 12.63: Attributes inspector settings for the image view

You will load images using code in *Chapter 14, Getting Data into Collection Views.*

21. To position the image view within its container view, select it and click the Size inspector button. Update the following values in the **View** section:

X: 0

Y: 0

Width: 316

Height: 200

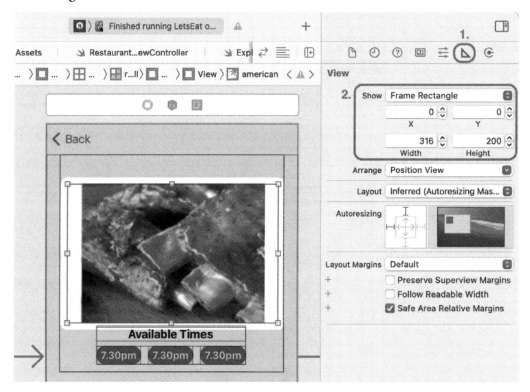

Figure 12.64: Size inspector settings for the image view

22. You'll add labels that will be used to display the restaurant's name and the type of cuisine it offers. Click the Library button. Type `label` into the filter field. A **Label** object will appear in the results. Drag two **Label** objects into the prototype cell:

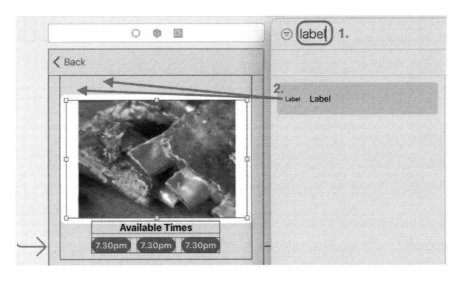

Figure 12.65: Library with Label object selected

23. One of the labels will be used for the restaurant name. Select a label and click the Attributes inspector button. Set **Font** to `System Bold 17.0` to configure the font style for this label.

Figure 12.66: Attributes inspector settings for the name label

24. To position this label within the `restaurantCell` collection view cell, select the label and click the Size inspector button. Update the following values in the **View** section:

    X: 10

    Y: 3

    Width: 315

    Height: 19

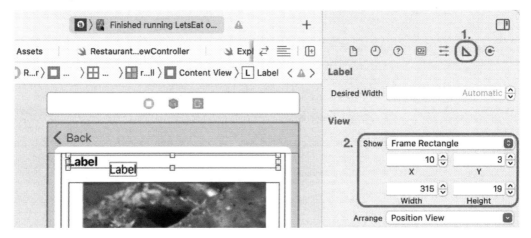

Figure 12.67: Size inspector settings for the name label

25. The other label will be used to display the cuisine offered by the restaurant. Select the other label and click the Attributes inspector button. Update the following values to configure the font and color for it:

    Color: LetsEat Dark Gray

    Font: System 14.0

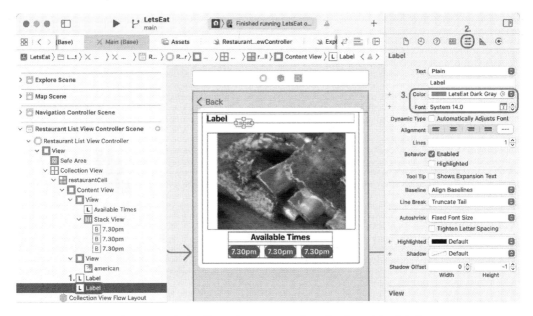

Figure 12.68: Attributes inspector settings for the cuisine label

26. This label should be under the label showing the restaurant name. With the label selected, click the Size inspector button. Update the following values in the **View** section to position this label within the `restaurantCell` collection view cell:

X: 10

Y: 22

Width: 315

Height: 16

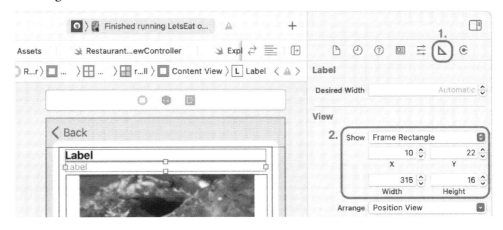

Figure 12.69: Size inspector settings for the cuisine label

You have added all of the elements for `restaurantCell` and set their positions using the Size inspector. Now, you need to add Auto Layout constraints to them to ensure the user interface adapts to device screen size and orientation. You'll do this in the next section.

Adding Auto Layout constraints to the restaurantCell collection view cell

As you did before for the `exploreCell` collection view cell, you will now add Auto Layout constraints to all of the elements in `restaurantCell`. As you have used the Size inspector to position the elements, their positions relative to one another and the values of the constraints should already be correctly set, making it easy for you to add the constraints. Since there are many elements in `restaurantCell`, take your time during this section. Follow these steps:

1.   To set the constraints for the label containing the restaurant's name, select the top **Label** in the document outline:

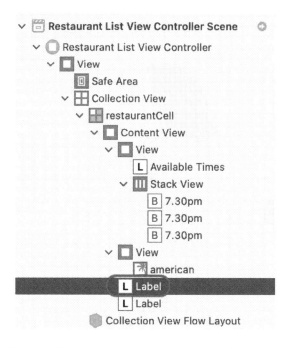

Figure 12.70: Document outline with name Label selected

Tip:

The **Label** position in the document outline does not determine the label position in the restaurantCell collection view cell. Verify the correct label has been selected. It should be black and not light gray.

2. Click the Add New Constraints button and enter the following values:

Top: 3 (the space between the top edge and the top edge of the enclosing view)

Left: 10 (the space between the left edge and the left edge of the enclosing view)

Right: 10 (the space between the right edge and the right edge of the enclosing view)

Height: 19 (the space between the top and bottom edges)

Click the **Add 4 Constraints** button when done.

3. To set the constraints for the label containing the restaurant's cuisine, select the **Label** under the previous **Label** in the document outline:

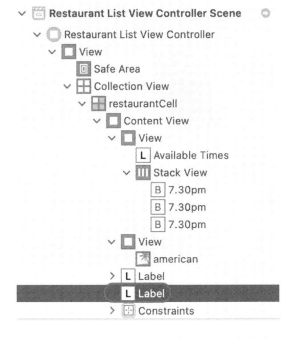

Figure 12.71: Document outline with cuisine Label selected

> **Tip:**
> The **Label** position in the document outline does not determine the label position in the `restaurantCell` collection view cell. Verify the correct label has been selected. It should be light gray and not black.

4. Click the Add New Constraints button and enter the following values:

   Top: 0 (binds the top edge to the bottom edge of the previous label)

   Left: 10 (the space between the left edge and the left edge of the enclosing view)

   Right: 10 (the space between the right edge and the right edge of the enclosing view)

   Height: 16 (the space between the top and bottom edges)

   Click the **Add 4 Constraints** button when done.

5. To set the constraints for the view containing the image view with the restaurant's photo, select the **View** that contains the image view in the document outline:

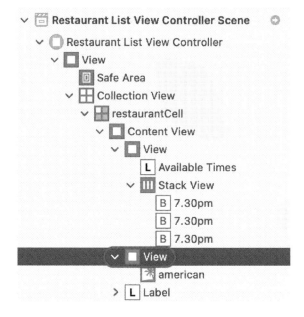

Figure 12.72: Document outline with container View selected

6. Click the Add New Constraints button and enter the following values:

   Top: 4 (the space between the top edge and the bottom edge of the label)

   Width: 316 (the space between the left and right edges)

   Height: 200 (the space between the top and bottom edges)

   Click the **Add 3 Constraints** button when done. Note that the horizontal position of this view has not been set yet.

7. Click the Align button, tick **Horizontally in Container** and enter the following value: 0. Click the **Add 1 Constraint** button when done. This sets the horizontal position of the view to the center of the enclosing view. Since the width of this view is set, the position of the left and right edges can be determined automatically.

8. To set the constraints for the image view containing the restaurant photo, select **american** in the document outline:

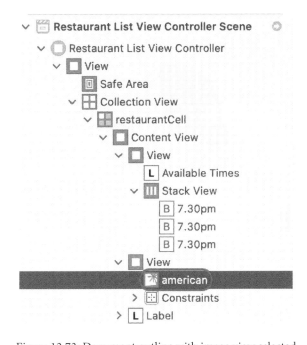

Figure 12.73: Document outline with image view selected

9. Click the Add New Constraints button and enter the following values:

Top: 0

Left: 0

Right: 0

Bottom: 0

Click the **Add 4 Constraints** button when done. This binds the edges of the image view to the enclosing view.

10. To set the constraints for the view containing the label and buttons, select the **View** containing the **Available Times** label and the **Stack View** in the document outline:

Figure 12.74: Document outline with container view selected

11. Click the Add New Constraints button and enter the following values:

Top: 3 (the space between the top edge and the bottom edge of the view containing the image view)

Width: 224 (the space between the left and right edges)

Height: 56 (the space between the top and bottom edges)

Click the **Add 3 Constraints** button when done. Note that the horizontal position of the view has not been set yet.

12. Click the Align button. tick **Horizontally in Container** and enter the following value: 0. Click the **Add 1 Constraint** button when done. This sets the horizontal position of the view to the center of the **Content View**. Since the width of this view is set, the position of the left and right edges can be determined automatically.

13. To set the constraints for the stack view containing the buttons, select the **Stack View** in the document outline:

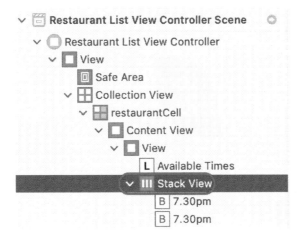

Figure 12.75: Document outline with Stack View selected

14. Click the Add New Constraints button and enter the following values:

Top: 6 (the space between the top edge and the bottom edge of the **Available Times** label)

Left: 0 (the space between the left edge and the left edge of the enclosing view)

Right: 0 (the space between the right edge and the right edge of the enclosing view)

Height: 27 (the space between the top and bottom edges)

Click the **Add 4 Constraints** button when done.

15. To set the constraints for the **Available Times** label, select the **Available Times** label in the document outline:

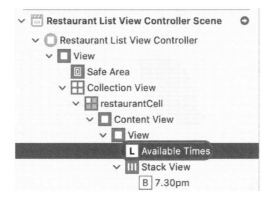

Figure 12.76: Document outline with Available Times label selected

16. Click the Add New Constraints button and enter the following values:

Top: 2 (the space between the top edge and the top edge of the enclosing view)

Left: 0 (binds the left edge to the left edge of the enclosing view)

Right: 0 (binds the right edge to the right edge of the enclosing view)

Height: 21 (the space between the top and bottom edges)

Click the **Add 4 Constraints** button when done.

All of the Auto Layout constraints for the `restaurantCell` collection view cell have been set up. Build and run your app and go to the **Restaurant List** screen. You should see the following:

Figure 12.77: iOS Simulator showing completed restaurantCell collection view cell

As you can see, the **Restaurant List** screen now more closely matches the design shown in the app tour. The `restaurantCell` collection view cell now looks just like the app tour design, and all of the necessary constraints have been added. Awesome!

You have added all the required user interface elements and constraints to `restaurantCell`. Now that you've completed modifying `restaurantCell`, let's modify the table view cells in the **Locations** screen in the next section.

Configuring the locationCell table view cell

The last thing to do in this chapter is to configure the table view cells inside the **Locations** screen. As you have seen in the app tour, each table view cell just contains text, so all you need to do now is to enable the prototype cell for the table view and set the identifier for the table view cell to `locationCell`. Follow these steps:

1. Find the view controller scene triggered by the button in the **Explore View Controller Scene**. Select the **Table View** in the document outline. Click the Attributes inspector button. Set **Prototype Cells** to 1:

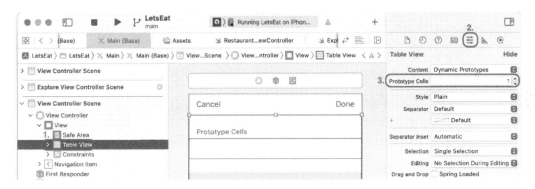

Figure 12.78: Attributes inspector settings for the table view

A prototype table view cell will appear in the table view.

2. To set the style and identifier for the cell, click **Table View Cell** in the document outline. Click the Attributes inspector button and enter the following values:

Style: `Basic`

Identifier: `locationCell`

Figure 12.79: Attributes inspector settings for locationCell table view cell

Note that the name of the prototype table view cell will change to `locationCell`. When you change the style from `Custom` to `Basic`, the word `Title` should appear in the cell. This is just a placeholder. You will change this value in code later.

3. To set the cell's font size, click **Title** inside `locationCell`'s **ContentView** in the document outline. In the Attributes inspector, change the **Font size** to `20`:

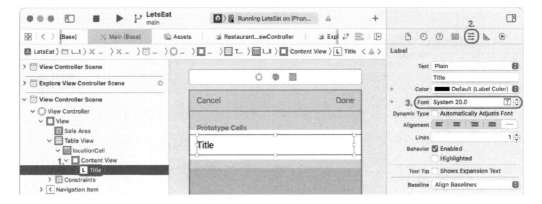

Figure 12.80: Attributes inspector settings for text in locationCell table view cell

If you build and run your app now and go to the **Locations** screen, it will still appear blank, as you have not yet added any code to display data in the cells. You will do so in *Chapter 15, Getting Started with Table Views*.

Summary

In this chapter, you modified the cells inside the **Explore, Restaurant List**, and **Locations** screens to match the design shown in the app tour. For the **Explore** screen, you added labels and a view to the collection view section header, configured the button with a custom image, and modified the `exploreCell` collection view cell by adding an image view and a label to it, as well as the required constraints. For the **Restaurant List** screen, you modified the `restaurantCell` collection view cell by adding labels, buttons and an image view to it, configured it to show a default image, and added the necessary constraints. For the **Locations** screen, you configured a prototype cell for the table view and set the identifier for the table view cells to `locationCell`.

You now know how to use Interface Builder to add and configure multiple user interface elements, set their sizes and positions using the Size inspector, and apply the necessary constraints using the Add New Constraints and Align buttons to ensure compatibility with different screen sizes and orientations. This will be useful when you design your own user interfaces. You should also be able to easily prototype the appearance and flow of your own apps.

At this point, you're now finished with the storyboard and design setup. You can go through every screen that your app is supposed to have and see what they look like, even though none of the screens have actual data in them. If this app was a house being built, it's as though you've built all of the walls and floors, and the house is now ready to have the interior done. Great job!

This concludes *Part 2* of this book. In the next part, you'll begin to type in all of the code required for your app to work. In the next chapter, you'll start by learning more about the **Model-View-Controller** design pattern. You'll also learn how collection views work, which are crucial for understanding how the **Explore** and **Restaurant List** screens work.

Part 3: Code

Welcome to *Part 3* of this book. With your user interface complete, you will then add code to implement your app's functionality. To display your data in a grid, you will use collection views, and to display your data in a list, you will use table views. You will also look at how to add basic and custom annotations to a map. After that, you will learn about JSON files, and how to use them to get actual restaurant data into your collection views, table views, and map. Next, you will add code that allows users to add restaurant reviews and photos, and to rate a restaurant. Finally, you'll make restaurant reviews and photos persistent, using Core Data.

This part comprises the following chapters:

- *Chapter 13, Getting Started with MVC and Collection Views*
- *Chapter 14, Getting Data into Collection Views*
- *Chapter 15, Getting Started with Table Views*
- *Chapter 16, Getting Started with MapKit*
- *Chapter 17, Getting Started with JSON Files*
- *Chapter 18, Displaying Data in a Static Table View*
- *Chapter 19, Getting Started with Custom UIControls*
- *Chapter 20, Getting Started with Cameras and Photo Libraries*
- *Chapter 21, Understanding Core Data*

By the end of this part, you'll have completed the *Let's Eat* app. You'll have the experience of building a complete app from scratch, which will be useful as you build your own apps. Let's get started!

13
Getting Started with MVC and Collection Views

In the previous chapter, you modified the cells inside the **Explore** screen, the **Restaurant List** screen, and the **Locations** screen to match the app tour in *Chapter 9, Setting Up the User Interface*. You have completed the initial UI for the *Let's Eat* app, and this concludes *Part 2* of this book.

This chapter begins *Part 3* of this book, where you will focus on the code that makes your app work. In this chapter, you will learn about the **Model-View-Controller (MVC)** design pattern and how the different parts of an app interact with one another. Then, you'll implement a collection view programmatically (which means implementing it using code instead of storyboards) using a playground, to understand how collection views work. Finally, you'll revisit the collection views you implemented in the **Explore** and **Restaurant List** screens, so you can see what the differences are between implementing them in storyboard and implementing them programmatically.

By the end of this chapter, you'll understand the MVC design pattern, learn how a create a collection view controller programmatically and learn how to use collection view delegates and data source protocols.

The following topics will be covered:

- Understanding the Model-View-Controller design pattern
- Exploring controllers and classes

Technical requirements

The resource files and completed Xcode project for this chapter are in the `Chapter13` folder of the code bundle for this book, which can be downloaded here:

`https://github.com/PacktPublishing/iOS-15-Programming-for-Beginners-Sixth-Edition`

Take a look at the following video to see the code in action:

`https://bit.ly/3wsOeCZ`

Create a new playground and call it `CollectionViewBasics`. You can use this playground to type in and run all the code in this chapter as you go along. Before you do, let's take a look at the Model-View-Controller design pattern, an approach commonly used to write iOS apps.

Understanding the Model-View-Controller design pattern

The **Model-View-Controller** (**MVC**) design pattern is a common approach used to build iOS apps. MVC divides an app into three different parts:

- **Model**: This handles data storage and representation, and data processing tasks.
- **View**: This includes all the things that are on the screen that the user can interact with.
- **Controller**: This manages the flow of information between model and view.

One notable feature of MVC is that view and model do not interact with one another; instead, all communication is managed by the controller.

For example, imagine you're at a restaurant. You look at a menu and choose something you want. Then, a waiter comes, takes your order, and sends it to the cook. The cook prepares your order, and, when it is done, the waiter takes the order and brings it out to you. In this scenario, the menu is the view, the waiter is the controller, and the cook is the model. Also, note that all interactions between you and the kitchen are only through the waiter; there is no interaction between you and the cook.

> **Important Information**
>
> To find out more about MVC, go to `https://en.wikipedia.org/wiki/Model-view-controller`.

To see how MVC works, let's learn more about controllers and classes. You will see what it takes to implement a view controller that is required to manage a collection view, which is used in the **Explore** screen and the **Restaurant List** screen.

Exploring controllers and classes

So far, you have implemented view controller scenes in `the Main storyboard file` using Interface Builder. You added `ExploreViewController`, a view controller that manages the collection view inside the **Explore** screen, and `RestaurantListViewController`, a view controller that manages the collection view inside the **Restaurant List** screen, to your project. However, you still haven't learned how the code you added to each view controller works, so let's look at that now.

> **Tip**
>
> You may wish to re-read *Chapter 10, Building Your User Interface*, where you created the `ExploreViewController` class, and *Chapter 11, Finishing Up Your User Interface*, where you created the `RestaurantListViewController` class.

When a typical iOS app is launched, the view controller for the first screen to be displayed is loaded. The view controller has a `view` property, and automatically loads the view instance assigned to its `view` property. That view may have subviews, which are also loaded. If one of the subviews is a collection view, it will have `dataSource` and `delegate` properties. The `dataSource` property is assigned to an object that provides data to the collection view. The `delegate` property is assigned to an object that handles user interaction with the collection view. Typically, the view controller for the collection view will also be assigned to the collection view's `dataSource` and `delegate` properties. The method calls that a collection view will send to its view controller are declared in the `UICollectionViewDataSource` and `UICollectionViewDelegate` protocols. Remember that protocols only provide method declarations; the implementation of those method calls are in the view controller. The view controller will then provide the requested data for the collection view or handle the user interaction.

Let's take a closer look at collection views and collection view protocols in the next section.

Understanding collection views

A collection view displays an ordered collection of collection view cells using customizable layouts.

> **Important Information**
>
> To learn more about collection views, you can refer to `https://developer.apple.com/documentation/uikit/uicollectionview`.

The layout for the collection view is dictated by `UICollectionViewFlowLayout`. It determines the flow direction and size of the elements in a collection view.

> **Important Information**
>
> To learn more about `UICollectionViewFlowLayout`, you can refer to `https://developer.apple.com/documentation/uikit/uicollectionviewflowlayout`.

The data displayed by a collection view is normally provided by a view controller. A view controller providing data for a collection view must conform to the `UICollectionViewDataSource` protocol. This protocol declares a list of methods that tells the collection view how many cells to display and what to display in each cell. It also covers the creation and configuration of supplementary views (such as the collection view section header).

> **Important Information**
>
> To learn more about the `UICollectionViewDataSource` protocol, you can refer to `https://developer.apple.com/documentation/uikit/uicollectionviewdatasource`.

To provide user interaction, a view controller for a collection view must also conform to the `UICollectionViewDelegate` protocol, which declares a list of methods which are triggered when a user interacts with the collection view.

> **Important Information**
>
> To learn more about the `UICollectionViewDelegate` protocol, you can refer to `https://developer.apple.com/documentation/uikit/uicollectionviewdelegate`.

To understand how collection views work, you'll implement a view controller that controls a collection view in your `CollectionViewBasics` playground. You will then compare this with the implementation for the view controllers in the **Explore** and **Restaurant List** screens in the next section. As there is no storyboard in the playground, you can't add UI elements the way you have done in previous chapters. Instead, you will add them programmatically.

> **Important Information**
>
> Adding model objects to a collection view will be covered in the next chapter, *Chapter 14, Getting Data into Collection Views*.

You'll start by creating the `CollectionViewExampleController` class, an implementation of a view controller that manages a collection view. After that, you'll create an instance of `CollectionViewExampleController` and make it display a collection view containing a single collection view cell in the playground's live view. Follow these steps:

1. Open your `CollectionViewBasics` playground that you have created at the beginning of this chapter. At the very top of the playground, remove the `var` statement and add an `import PlaygroundSupport` statement. Your playground should now contain the following:

```
import UIKit
import PlaygroundSupport
```

The first `import` statement imports the API for creating iOS apps. The second statement enables the playground to display a live view, which you will use to display the collection view.

2. Add the following code after the `import` statements to declare the `CollectionViewExampleController` class:

```
class CollectionViewExampleController: UIViewController {

}
```

This class is a subclass of `UIViewController`, a class that Apple provides to manage views on the screen.

3. Add the following code inside the curly braces to add an optional property, `collectionView`, to the `CollectionViewExampleController` class:

```
var collectionView: UICollectionView?
```

An instance of a collection view will be assigned to this property later.

4. Verify that your code looks like the following:

```
class CollectionViewExampleController: UIViewController {
    var collectionView: UICollectionView?
}
```

In the next section, you'll learn how to set the number of cells for a collection view to display, and how to set the contents of each cell.

Conforming to the UICollectionViewDataSource protocol

A collection view displays a grid of collection view cells on the screen. However, before it can do this, it needs to know how many cells to display, and what to put in each cell. To provide this information to the collection view, you will make the `CollectionViewExampleController` class conform to the `UICollectionViewDataSource` protocol.

This protocol has two required methods:

- `collectionView(_:numberOfItemsInSection:)` is called by the collection view to determine how many collection view cells should be displayed.

- `collectionView(_:cellForItemAt:)` is called by the collection view to determine what to display in each collection view cell.

Let's add some code to make `CollectionViewExampleController` conform to the `UICollectionViewDataSource` protocol. Follow these steps:

1. To make `CollectionViewExampleController` adopt the `UICollectionViewDataSource` protocol, type a comma after the superclass declaration and then type `UICollectionViewDataSource`. When you are done, your code should look like the following:

```
class CollectionViewExampleController: UIViewController,
UICollectionViewDataSource {
    var collectionView:UICollectionView?
}
```

2. An error will appear because you have not yet implemented the two required methods. Click on the error icon:

Figure 13.1: Editing area showing error icon

3. The error message states that the required methods for the
    `UICollectionViewDataSource` protocol are missing. Click on the **Fix** button
    to add the required methods:

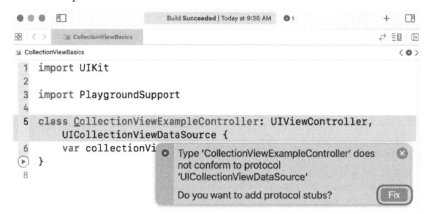

Figure 13.2: Error explanation and Fix button

4. Verify that your code looks like the following:

```
class CollectionViewExampleController: UIViewController,
UICollectionViewDataSource {
    func collectionView(_ collectionView:
    UICollectionView, numberOfItemsInSection
    section: Int) -> Int {
        code
    }
    func collectionView(_ collectionView:
    UICollectionView, cellForItemAt indexPath:
    IndexPath) -> UICollectionViewCell{
        code
    }
    var collectionView:UICollectionView?
}
```

5. In a class definition, convention dictates that properties are declared at the top
    of the class, before any method declarations. Rearrange the code so that the
    `collectionView` property declaration is at the top, as follows:

```
class CollectionViewExampleController: UIViewController,
UICollectionViewDataSource {
```

```
var collectionView:UICollectionView?
func collectionView(_ collectionView:
UICollectionView, numberOfItemsInSection
section: Int) -> Int {
    code
}
```

6. In collectionView(_:numberOfItemsInSection:), click on the word code and type 1. The completed method should look as follows:

```
func collectionView(_ collectionView:
UICollectionView, numberOfItemsInSection
section: Int) -> Int {
    1
}
```

This will tell the collectionView instance to display a single collection view cell. Typically, the number of cells to be displayed will be provided by a model object. You will learn more about them in *Chapter 14, Getting Data into Collection Views*.

7. In collectionView(_:cellForItemAt:), click on the word code and modify the method as follows:

```
func collectionView(_ collectionView:
UICollectionView, cellForItemAt indexPath:
IndexPath) -> UICollectionViewCell{
    let cell = collectionView.dequeueReusableCell
    (withReuseIdentifier: "BoxCell", for: indexPath)
    cell.backgroundColor = .red
    return cell
}
```

Here is how this method works. Imagine you have 1,000 items to display in a collection view. You don't need 1,000 collection view cells; you only need just enough to fill the screen. Collection view cells that scroll off the top of the screen can be reused to display items that appear at the bottom of the screen. To make sure you are using the right type of cell, you use a reuse identifier to identify a cell type. The reuse identifier needs to be registered with the collection view, which you will do later. The next line of code sets the cell's background color to red, and the line after that returns the cell, which is then displayed on the screen. The process is repeated for the number of cells given in the first method, which, in this case, is 1.

8. Verify that your `CollectionViewExampleController` class looks like the following:

```
class CollectionViewExampleController:
UIViewController, UICollectionViewDataSource {
    var collectionView: UICollectionView?
    func collectionView(_ collectionView:
    UICollectionView, numberOfItemsInSection
    section: Int) -> Int {
        1
    }
    func collectionView(_ collectionView:
    UICollectionView, cellForItemAt indexPath:
    IndexPath) -> UICollectionViewCell{
        let cell = collectionView.dequeueReusableCell
        (withReuseIdentifier: "BoxCell", for: indexPath)
        cell.backgroundColor = .red
        return cell
    }
}
```

You have completed the implementation of the `CollectionViewExampleController` class. In the next section, you'll learn how to create an instance of this class.

Creating a CollectionViewExampleController instance

Now that you have declared and defined the `CollectionViewExampleController` class, you will write a method to create an instance of it. Follow these steps:

1. Type in the following code after the `collectionView` variable declaration to declare a new method:

```
func createCollectionView() {

}
```

This declares a new method, `createCollectionView()` which you'll use to create an instance of a collection view and assign it to the `collectionView` property.

2. Type in the following code after the opening curly brace to define the body of this method:

```
self.collectionView = UICollectionView(
frame: CGRect(x: 0, y: 0, width:
self.view.frame.width, height:
self.view.frame.height),
collectionViewLayout: UICollectionViewFlowLayout())
```

This creates a new collection view instance and assigns it to `collectionView`. The dimensions of this collection view are exactly the same as its enclosing view, with the default flow layout. The flow layout dictates the order the collection view cells are displayed, which is left to right.

3. Go to the next line, and then type in the following code to set the collection view's `dataSource` property to an instance of `CollectionViewExampleController`:

```
self.collectionView?.dataSource = self
```

The `dataSource` property of a collection view will specify which object contains the implementation of the required `UIViewControllerDataSource` methods.

4. Go to the next line, and then type in the following code to set the collection view's background color to white:

```
self.collectionView?.backgroundColor = .white
```

5. Go to the next line, and then type in the following code to set the identifier for the collection view cells in the collection view to `BoxCell`:

```
self.collectionView?.register(UICollectionViewCell.self,
forCellWithReuseIdentifier:"BoxCell")
```

This identifier will be used in the `collectionView(_:cellForItemAt:)` method to identify the type of collection view cells to be reused.

6. Go to the next line, and then type in the following code to add the collection view as a subview to the view of the `CollectionViewExampleController` instance:

```
self.view.addSubview(self.collectionView!)
```

When an instance of a view controller is loaded into memory, its view is also loaded, along with any subviews. In this case, the `CollectionViewExampleController` instance will automatically load its view, and since the collection view is a subview of its view, the collection view will also be loaded.

7. Verify that the completed method looks like the following:

```
func createCollectionView() {
    self.collectionView = UICollectionView(frame:
    CGRect(x: 0, y: 0, width: self.view.frame.width,
    height: self.view.frame.height),
    collectionViewLayout:
    UICollectionViewFlowLayout())
    self.collectionView?.dataSource = self
    self.collectionView?.backgroundColor = .white
    self.collectionView?.register(
    UICollectionViewCell.self,
    forCellWithReuseIdentifier: "BoxCell")
    self.view.addSubview(self.collectionView!)
}
```

Now you need a suitable place to call this method. View controllers have a `view` property. The view assigned to the `view` property will be automatically loaded when the view controller is loaded. After a view has been loaded successfully, the view controller's `viewDidLoad()` method will be called. You will override the `viewDidLoad()` method in your `CollectionViewControllerExample` class to call `createCollectionView()`. Follow these steps:

1. Type in the following code just before the `createCollectionView()` method:

```swift
override func viewDidLoad(){
    super.viewDidLoad()
    self.view.bounds = CGRect(x: 0, y: 0, width: 375,
    height: 667)
    createCollectionView()
}
```

This sets the size of the live view, creates a collection view instance, assigns it to `collectionView` and adds it as a subview to the view of the `CollectionViewExampleController` instance. The collection view then calls the data source methods to determine how many collection view cells to display, and what to display in each cell.

`collectionView(_:numberOfItemsInSection:)` returns 1, so a single collection view cell will be displayed.

`collectionView(_:cellForItemAt:)` creates the cell, sets the background color of the cell to red, and returns it for display.

2. Verify that your completed playground looks like this:

```swift
import UIKit
import PlaygroundSupport
class CollectionViewExampleController:
UIViewController, UICollectionViewDataSource{
    var collectionView: UICollectionView?
    override func viewDidLoad(){
        super.viewDidLoad()
        self.view.bounds = CGRect(x: 0, y: 0,
        width: 375, height: 667)
        createCollectionView()
    }
    func createCollectionView(){
```

```
    self.collectionView = UICollectionView(frame:
CGRect(x: 0, y: 0, width: self.view.frame.width,
height: self.view.frame.height),
collectionViewLayout:
UICollectionViewFlowLayout())
    self.collectionView?.dataSource = self
    self.collectionView?.backgroundColor = .white
    self.collectionView?.register(
UICollectionViewCell.self,
forCellWithReuseIdentifier: "BoxCell")
    self.view.addSubview(self.collectionView!)
}
func collectionView(_ collectionView:
UICollectionView, numberOfItemsInSection
section: Int) -> Int {
    1
}
func collectionView(_ collectionView:
UICollectionView, cellForItemAt indexPath:
IndexPath) -> UICollectionViewCell {
    let cell = collectionView.dequeueReusableCell(
    withReuseIdentifier: "BoxCell", for: indexPath)
    cell.backgroundColor = .red
    return cell
}
}
```

3. Now it's time to see it in action. Type the following after all the other code in the playground:

```
PlaygroundPage.current.liveView =
CollectionViewExampleController()
```

This command creates the instance of `CollectionViewExampleController` and displays its view in the playground's live view. The `createCollectionView()` method will create a collection view and add it as a subview to the `CollectionViewExampleController` instance's view, and it will appear on the screen.

4. Run the playground. If you don't see a representation of the collection view on your screen, you will need to turn on the playground's live view. Click the Adjust Editor Options button:

Figure 13.3: Adjust Editor Options button

5. Make sure that **Live View** is selected:

Figure 13.4: Adjust Editor Options menu with Live View selected

6. You will see the collection view displaying one red collection view cell in the live view:

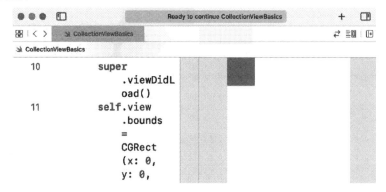

Figure 13.5: Playground live view showing collection view with one collection view cell

You've just created a view controller for a collection view, created an instance of it and displayed a collection view in the playground's live view. Good job!

In the next section, you'll revisit how collection view controllers are used in the **Explore** and **Restaurant List** screens, which you implemented in *Chapter 10, Building Your User Interface*, and *Chapter 11, Finishing Up Your User Interface*. Using what you have learned in this section as a reference, you should be able to understand how they work.

Revisiting the Explore and Restaurant List screens

Remember the ExploreViewController class that you added in *Chapter 10, Building Your User Interface*, and the RestaurantListViewController class that you added in *Chapter 11, Finishing Up Your User Interface*? Both of these are examples of view controllers that manage a collection view. Note that the code in both of them is very similar to that in your playground. The differences are as follows:

- You set the cell background color programmatically in collectionView(_:cellForItemAt:), instead of setting it in the Attributes inspector.

- You created and assigned the collection view to the collectionView property in CollectionViewExampleController programmatically.

- You set the dimensions of the collection view programmatically in UICollectionView(frame: collectionViewLayout:), instead of using the Size inspector.

- You connected the data source outlet to the view controller programmatically, instead of using the Connections inspector.

- You set the background color of the collection view programmatically, instead of using the Attributes inspector.

- You set the reuse identifier for the collection view cell programmatically, instead of using the Attributes inspector.

- You added the collection view as a subview of the view for `CollectionViewExampleController` programmatically, instead of dragging in a **Collection View** object from the Library.

Open the `LetsEat` project. Review *Chapter 10, Building Your User Interface* and *Chapter 11, Finishing Up Your User Interface,* once more, in order to compare and contrast the implementation of the collection view using the storyboard, and by doing the implementation programmatically as you have done in this chapter.

Summary

In this chapter, you learned about the MVC design pattern and collection view controllers in detail. You then revisited the collection views used in the **Explore** and **Restaurant List** screens and learned how they work.

You should now understand the MVC design pattern, how to create a collection view controller, and how to use the collection view data source protocol. This will enable you to implement collection view controllers for your own apps.

Up to this point, you have set up the views and view controllers for the **Explore** and **Restaurant List** screens, but the **Explore** screen just displays a grid of cells, and the **Restaurant List** screen displays a single cell with a placeholder image. In the next chapter, you're going to implement the model objects for the **Explore** screen so it can display a list of cuisines. To do this, you will read data from a file stored on your iOS device, create structures to store that data, and finally, provide it to the `ExploreViewController` instance so that it may be displayed by the collection view in the **Explore** screen.

14
Getting Data into Collection Views

In the previous chapter, you learned about the Model-View-Controller (MVC) design pattern and about collection views. You've also revisited the **Explore** and **Restaurant List** screens, and you have seen how the collection views in both screens work. At this point, though, both screens just display cells that do not contain any data. As shown in the app tour in *Chapter 9, Setting Up the User Interface*, the **Explore** screen should display a list of cuisines, and the **Restaurant List** screen should display a list of restaurants.

In this chapter, you're going to implement the model objects for the **Explore** screen to make it display a list of cuisines. You'll start by learning about model objects that you will use. Next, you'll learn about property lists, and see how they are used to store cuisine data, and you'll create a Swift structure that can store cuisine instances. After that, you'll create a data manager class that reads data from the property list and populates an array of structures. This array of structures will then be used as the data source for the collection view in the **Explore** screen.

By the end of this chapter, you'll have learned how property lists are used to store data, how to create model objects, how to create a data manager class that can load data from a property list into an array of model objects, how to configure view controllers to provide model objects to collection view, and how to configure collection views to display data on screen.

The following topics will be covered:

- Understanding model objects
- Understanding .plist files
- Creating a structure to represent a cuisine
- Implementing a data manager class to read data from a .plist file
- Displaying data in a collection view

Technical requirements

You will continue working on the LetsEat project that you modified in *Chapter 12, Modifying and Configuring Cells.*

The resource files and completed Xcode project for this chapter are in the Chapter14 folder of the code bundle for this book, which can be downloaded here:

https://github.com/PacktPublishing/iOS-15-Programming-for-Beginners-Sixth-Edition

Check out the following video to see the code in action:

https://bit.ly/3mWQ8sJ

Let's start by looking at the different model objects that are required to hold the initial data, load the data into the app, and store the data within the app.

Understanding model objects

As you learned in *Chapter 13, Getting Started with MVC and Collection Views*, a common design pattern for iOS apps is Model-View-Controller, or MVC. To recap, MVC divides an app into three different parts:

- **Model**: This handles data storage, representation, and data processing tasks.
- **View**: This is anything on the screen that the user can interact with.
- **Controller**: This manages the flow of information between model and view.

Let's revisit the design of the **Explore** screen that you saw during the app tour, which looks like this:

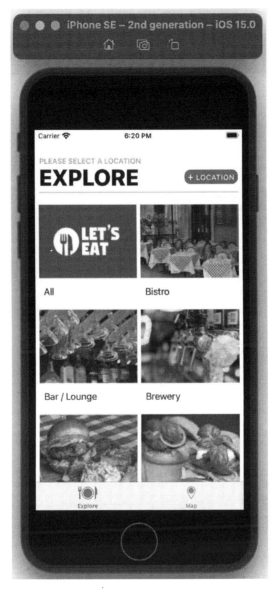

Figure 14.1: iOS Simulator showing the Explore screen from the app tour

Build and run your app, and the **Explore** screen will look like this:

Figure 14.2: iOS Simulator showing the Explore screen from your app

As you can see, all of the cells are currently empty. Based on the MVC design pattern, you have completed the implementation of the views (collection view section header and collection view) and the controller (the `ExploreViewController` class). Now, you will add model objects that will provide the data to be displayed.

First, you'll add a property list, `ExploreData.plist`, to your project, which contains the name and the image filename for each cuisine. The cuisine images themselves are already present in your `Assets.xcassets` folder. Next, you'll create a model object, `ExploreItem`, which will be a structure with two properties. One property will be used to store cuisine names, and the other will be used to store image filenames. After that, you will create a data manager class, `ExploreDataManager`, which will load the data from `ExploreData.plist`, put it into an array of `ExploreItem` instances and provide the array to the `ExploreViewController` instance. Finally, you will modify the `ExploreViewController` class so it can provide data for the collection view to display.

To learn more about property list files, let's add `ExploreData.plist` to your project now and see how it stores cuisine data.

Understanding .plist files

Apple developed property lists to store data structures or object states for later reconstitution and transmission. They are commonly used to store preferences for applications. Property list files use the `.plist` filename extension, and hence are often referred to as `.plist` files. You will be using a `.plist` file containing cuisine data, `ExploreData.plist`, in your project.

You will need to download the code bundle for this book to get the `ExploreData.plist` file. After that, you can use Xcode to view its contents. Follow these steps:

1. If you have not yet done so, download the resource files and completed Xcode project for this from this link: `https://github.com/PacktPublishing/iOS-15-Programming-for-Beginners-Sixth-Edition`.

2. Open the `Chapter14` folder and look inside the `resources` folder to find `ExploreData.plist`. This file stores cuisine names and image filenames.

3. Open the `LetsEat` project, right-click on the `Explore` folder in the Project navigator, and choose **New Group**.

4. Rename the new group that you just added `Model`.

5. Drag `ExploreData.plist` into this group.

6. Make sure **Copy items if needed** is ticked and click **Finish**.

When you click on `ExploreData.plist` in the Project navigator, you'll see an array that contains dictionaries, as shown:

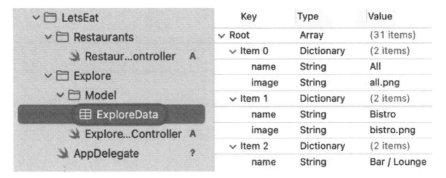

Figure 14.3: Editor area showing contents of ExploreData.plist

Each dictionary has two elements. The first element has a key, name, and a value describing a type of cuisine. The second element has a key, `image`, and a value containing the filename of a cuisine image. All of the cuisine images are stored in the `Assets.xcassets` file in your project.

To use the data contained in `ExploreData.plist`, you'll need to create a structure to hold it in the app so it can be accessed later by the `ExploreViewController` instance. You will create it in the next section.

Creating a structure to represent a cuisine

To create a model object that can represent a cuisine in your app, you will add a new file to your project, `ExploreItem`, and declare an `ExploreItem` structure that has properties for a cuisine's name and image. Follow these steps:

1. Right-click on the `Model` folder and select **New File**.

2. **iOS** should already be selected. Choose **Swift File**, then click **Next**.

3. Name the file `ExploreItem` and then click **Create**. It will appear in the Project navigator and its contents will appear in the Editor area. The only line in this file is an `import` statement.

> **Important Information**
>
> The `import` statement allows you to import other code libraries into your project, giving you the ability to use classes, properties, and methods from them. `Foundation` is one of Apple's core frameworks, and you can learn more about it here: `https://developer.apple.com/documentation/foundation`.

4. Add the following code to the file to declare a structure named `ExploreItem`:

```
struct ExploreItem {


}
```

5. Add the following code before the last curly brace to add two optional `String` properties to the `ExploreItem` structure:

```
Struct ExploreItem {
    let name: String?
    let image: String?
}
```

The `name` property will store the cuisine name, and the `image` property will store the filename of an image from the `Assets.xcassets` file.

> **Important Information**
> Structures are covered in *Chapter 7, Classes, Structures, and Enumerations.*

Structures automatically get a default initializer. You can create an instance of `ExploreItem` by using the following statement:

```
let myExploreItem = ExploreItem(name:"name",
image:"image")
```

However, the name and image filename in `ExploreData.plist` are stored as dictionary elements, as shown in the following example:

```
["name": "All", "image": "all.png"]
```

> **Important Information**
> Dictionaries are covered in *Chapter 5, Collection Types.*

You'll create a custom initializer that takes a dictionary as a parameter and assigns the values obtained from the dictionary elements to the properties in an `ExploreItem` instance. You'll use an extension to add this custom initializer to the `ExploreItem` structure.

> **Important Information**
> Extensions are covered in *Chapter 8, Protocols, Extensions, and Error Handling.*

Follow these steps:

1. Type the following after the `ExploreItem` structure declaration to add an extension:

    ```
    extension ExploreItem {

    }
    ```

    You'll use this extension to add the initializer method to the `ExploreItem` structure.

2. Add the following between the curly braces of the extension to declare a custom initializer method:

    ```
    init(dict: [String: String]) {

    }
    ```

    Ignore the error that appears, as you will fix it shortly. This initializer takes a dictionary as an argument. Note that both key and value are strings.

3. Add the following between the curly braces of the initializer:

    ```
    self.name = dict["name"]
    self.image = dict["image"]
    ```

    This assigns the value of the dictionary item with the key `"name"` to the `name` property, and the value of the dictionary item with the key `"image"` to the `image` property.

    The completed extension should look as follows:

    ```
    extension ExploreItem {
        init(dict: [String: String]) {
            self.name = dict["name"]
            self.image = dict["image"]
        }
    }
    ```

At this point, you have a structure, `ExploreItem`, with two `String` properties, `name` and `image`. When you create an instance of this structure, you will pass in a dictionary containing elements with keys and values of type `String`. The value for the `name` key will be assigned to the `name` property, and the value of the `image` key will be assigned to the `image` property.

In the next section, you'll implement a data manager class. This will read the array of dictionaries from the `ExploreData.plist` file and assign the values of the dictionary elements to `ExploreItem` instances.

Implementing a data manager class to read data from a .plist file

You have added a `.plist` file, `ExploreData.plist`, to your project containing the cuisine data, and you have created a structure, `ExploreItem`, that can store details of each cuisine. Now, you need to create a new class, `ExploreDataManager`, that can read the data in the `.plist` file and store it in an array of `ExploreItem` instances. You'll refer to this class as a data manager class. Follow these steps:

1. Right-click on the **Model** folder and select **New File**.

2. **iOS** should already be selected. Choose **Swift File**, then click **Next**.

3. Name the file `ExploreDataManager` and then click **Create** to display its contents in the Editor area.

4. Type the following code in the file to declare the `ExploreDataManager` class:

```
class ExploreDataManager {


}
```

5. Type in the following code between the curly braces. This implements a method, `loadData()`, which will read the contents of the `ExploreData.plist` file and return an array of dictionaries:

```
private func loadData() -> [[String: String]] {
    let decoder = PropertyListDecoder()
    if let path = Bundle.main.path(forResource:
    "ExploreData", ofType: "plist"),
    let exploreData = FileManager.default.contents(
    atPath: path),
    let exploreItems = try? decoder.decode([[String:
    String]].self, from: exploreData) {
        return exploreItems
    }
```

```
    return [[:]]
}
```

Let's break this method down:

```
private
```

The `private` keyword means that the method may only be used within this class.

```
func loadData() -> [[String: String]]
```

The `loadData()` method declaration has no arguments and returns an array of dictionaries, and each dictionary contains elements with keys and values of type `String`.

```
let decoder = PropertyListDecoder()
```

This statement creates an instance of a property list decoder that will be used to decode the data in the `ExploreData.plist` file.

```
if let path = Bundle.main.path(forResource:
"ExploreData", ofType: "plist"),
```

When you build your app, the result is a folder with all of the app resources inside it, called the application bundle. `ExploreData.plist` is inside this bundle. This statement attempts to get the path to the `ExploreData.plist` file and assign it to a constant, `path`.

```
let exploreData = FileManager.default.contents(
atPath: path),
```

This statement attempts to get the `ExploreData.plist` file stored at `path` and assign it to a constant, `exploreData`.

```
let exploreItems = try? decoder.decode([[String:
String]].self, from: exploreData) {
```

If you click `ExploreData.plist` in your project, note that the root level object is an array, and each item in the array is a dictionary, as shown:

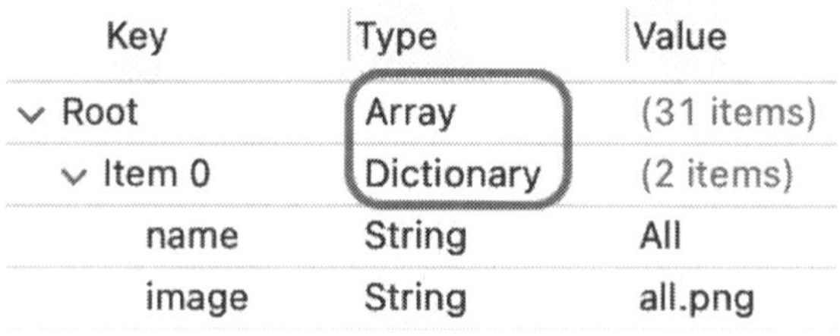

Key	Type	Value
∨ Root	Array	(31 items)
∨ Item 0	Dictionary	(2 items)
name	String	All
image	String	all.png

Figure 14.4: Editor area showing arrays and dictionaries in ExploreData.plist

This statement attempts to create an array from the contents of the `ExploreData.plist` file and assign it to a constant, `exploreItems`:

```
    return exploreItems
}
```

If the optional binding is successful, this statement returns `exploreItems` as an array of dictionaries, and each dictionary is of the `[String: String]` type:

```
    return [[:]]
}
```

If the optional binding is unsuccessful, an empty array of dictionaries is returned.

At this point, you have a data manager class, `ExploreDataManager`, containing a method that loads data from the `ExploreData.plist` file and assigns it to an array, `exploreItems`. In the next section, you will look at how to use the dictionaries inside this array to initialize `ExploreItem` instances, which will eventually be passed to the `ExploreViewController` instance managing the **Explore** screen.

Using the data manager to initialize ExploreItem instances

At present, you have a data manager class, `ExploreDataManager`. This class contains a method, `loadData()`, which reads data from `ExploreData.plist` and returns an array of dictionaries. You'll add a method that creates and initializes `ExploreItem` instances with the dictionaries in that array. Follow these steps:

1. In the `ExploreDataManager` class definition, add the following code before the `loadData()` method to implement a `fetch()` method:

```
func fetch() {
    for data in loadData() {
        print(data)
    }
}
```

This method will call `loadData()`, which returns an array of dictionaries. The `for` loop is then used to print the contents of each dictionary in the array to the Debug area to ensure that the `ExploreData.plist` file has been read successfully.

2. Click the `ExploreViewController` file in the Project navigator. Add
    the following code to the `viewDidLoad()` method. This creates an
    `ExploreDataManager` instance and calls its `fetch()` method when the
    `ExploreViewController` instance loads its view:

```
override func viewDidLoad() {
    super.viewDidLoad()
    let manager = ExploreDataManager()
    manager.fetch()
}
```

Build and run your app. The contents of the `ExploreData.plist` file are read
and printed in the Debug area, as shown:

Figure 14.5: Debug area displaying contents of ExploreData.plist

Now, you'll assign the `name` and `image` strings from each dictionary in the array to
an `ExploreItem` instance.

3. Click on the `ExploreDataManager` file. Add a property declaration to store an
    array of `ExploreItem` instances just before the `fetch()` method:

```
private var exploreItems: [ExploreItem] = []
```

This adds a property, `exploreItems`, to the `ExploreDataManager` class and
assigns an empty array to it.

4. Inside the `fetch()` method, replace the `print()` statement with the following
    statement that initializes `ExploreItem` instances and appends them to the
    `exploreItems` array:

```
exploreItems.append(ExploreItem(dict: data))
```

The custom initializer in the `ExploreItem` class assigns the `name` and `image`
strings in each dictionary read from `ExploreData.plist` to the `name` and
`image` properties of an `ExploreData` instance.

5. Verify that the `ExploreDataManager` file's contents looks like this:

```
import Foundation
class ExploreDataManager {
    private var exploreItems: [ExploreItem] = []
    func fetch() {
        for data in loadData() {
            exploreItems.append(ExploreItem(dict:
            data))
        }
    }

    private func loadData() -> [[String: String]] {
        let decoder = PropertyListDecoder()
        if let path = Bundle.main.path(forResource:
        "ExploreData", ofType: "plist"),
        let exploreData =
        FileManager.default.contents(atPath: path),
        let exploreItems = try?
        decoder.decode([[String: String]].self,
        from: exploreData) {
            return exploreItems
        }
        return [[:]]
    }
}
```

At this point, you have an `ExploreDataManager` class that reads data from
`ExploreData.plist` and stores it in `exploreItems`, an array of `ExploreItem`
instances. This array will be the data source for the collection view managed by the
`ExploreViewController` instance. The cuisine information it contains will eventually
be displayed in the **Explore** screen.

Displaying data in a collection view

You've implemented a data manager class, `ExploreDataManager`, that reads cuisine data from the `ExploreData.plist` file and stores it in an array of `ExploreItem` instances. Now, you will modify the `ExploreViewController` class to use that array as the data source for the collection view in the **Explore** screen.

At present, the collection view in the **Explore** screen displays 20 collection view cells, with each cell containing an empty image view and a label. You need a way to set the values for the image view and the label in the cells, so you will create a new class, `ExploreCell`, for this purpose. You can then configure the view controller for the collection view, `ExploreViewController`, to get cuisine details from the `ExploreDataManager` instance and provide it to the collection view for display. To create `ExploreCell`, follow these steps:

1. Right-click on the `Explore` folder in the Project navigator and choose **New Group**.

2. Rename the new group `View`.

3. Right-click on the `View` folder and select **New File**.

4. **iOS** should already be selected. Choose **Cocoa Touch Class**, then click **Next**.

5. Configure the class as shown here:

    Class: `ExploreCell`

    Subclass: `UICollectionViewCell`

    Also create XIB: `Unchecked`

    Language: `Swift`

    Click **Next**.

6. Click **Create**.

7. A new file, `ExploreCell`, will be added to your project. Inside it you will see the following:

```
import UIKit
class ExploreCell: UICollectionViewCell {

}
```

> **Important Information**
>
> UIKit provides the infrastructure required for iOS apps. You can read more about it here: https://developer.apple.com/documentation/uikit.

8. You'll now assign the ExploreCell class as the identity of the exploreCell collection view cell. Click the Main storyboard file in the Project navigator and click exploreCell inside the **Explore View Controller Scene** in the document outline. Click the Identity inspector button:

Figure 14.6: Identity inspector selected

9. Under the **Custom Class** section, set **Class** to ExploreCell. This sets an ExploreCell instance as the manager for exploreCell. Press *Return* when done:

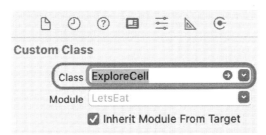

Figure 14.7: Identity inspector showing Class settings for exploreCell

You've just declared and defined the ExploreCell class, and assigned it as the manager for the exploreCell collection view cell. Now, you'll create outlets in this class that will be connected to the image view and the label in the exploreCell collection view cell, so you can control what they display.

Connecting the outlets in exploreCell

To manage what is being displayed by the collection view cells in the **Explore** screen, you'll connect the image view and label in the `exploreCell` collection view cell to outlets in the `ExploreCell` class. You'll use the assistant editor for this. Follow these steps:

1. Click the Navigator and Inspector buttons to hide the Navigator and Inspector areas. This will give you more room to work:

Figure 14.8: Toolbar showing Navigator and Inspector buttons

2. Click the Adjust Editor Options button to display a menu:

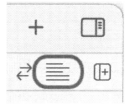

Figure 14.9: Adjust Editor Options button

3. Choose **Assistant** from the menu to display the assistant editor:

Figure 14.10: Adjust Editor Options menu with Assistant selected

4. To create the outlets for the `ExploreCell` class, the assistant editor path should be set to `Automatic | ExploreCell.swift`. If you don't see `ExploreCell.swift` in the path, select the `exploreCell` collection view cell's **Label** in the document outline and select `ExploreCell.swift` from the assistant editor's path drop-down menu:

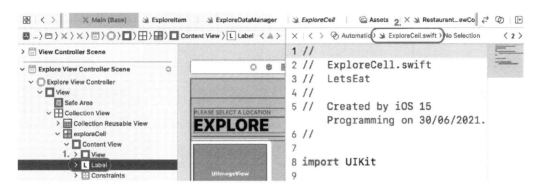

Figure 14.11: Assistant editor bar showing ExploreCell.swift

5. *Ctrl + Drag* from the **Label** element in the collection view cell to the space between the curly braces as shown. This creates an outlet for it:

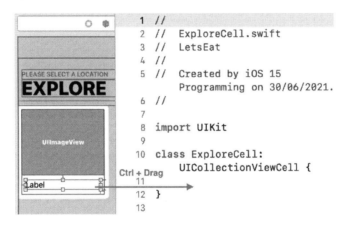

Figure 14.12: Editor area showing ExploreCell.swift

6. In the pop-up dialog, enter `exploreNameLabel` in the **Name** field to set the outlet's name:

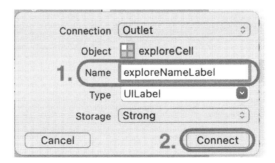

Figure 14.13: Pop-up dialog box for exploreNameLabel outlet creation

7. *Ctrl + Drag* from the **UIImageView** element in the collection view cell to the space just after the `exploreNameLabel` property. This creates an outlet for it:

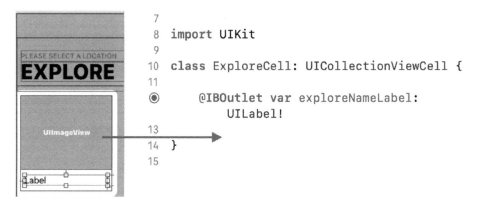

```
 7
 8  import UIKit
 9
10  class ExploreCell: UICollectionViewCell {
11
       @IBOutlet var exploreNameLabel:
          UILabel!
13
14  }
15
```

Figure 14.14: Editor area showing ExploreCell.swift

8. In the pop-up dialog, enter `exploreImageView` in the **Name** field to set the outlet's name:

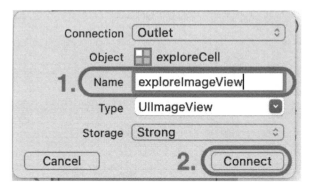

Figure 14.15: Pop-up dialog box for exploreImageView outlet creation

9. The `exploreNameLabel` and `exploreImageView` outlets have been added to the `ExploreCell` class and connected to the `exploreCell` collection view cell's image view and label elements, as shown:

```
 7
 8  import UIKit
 9
10  class ExploreCell: UICollectionViewCell {
11
◉       @IBOutlet var exploreNameLabel:
            UILabel!
13      |
◉       @IBOutlet var exploreImageView:
            UIImageView!
15
```

Figure 14.16: Editor area showing exploreNameLabel and exploreImageView outlets

10. Click the **x** button to close the assistant editor:

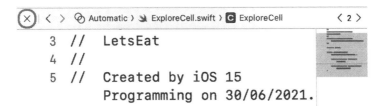

Figure 14.17: Assistant editor close button

The exploreCell collection view cell in the Main storyboard file has now been set up with a class, ExploreCell. The outlets for the collection view cell's image view and label have also been created and assigned. Now, you can set the exploreNameLabel and exploreImageView outlets in the ExploreCell instance to display a cuisine image and name in each cell when the app is run.

> **Tip**
>
> You can check whether the outlets are connected properly in the
> Connections inspector.

In the next section, you will add code to ExploreDataManager to provide the number of cells to be displayed by collectionView, and provide an ExploreItem instance whose properties will be used to determine what image and label the cell will display.

Implementing additional data manager methods

As you learned in *Chapter 13, Getting Started with MVC and Collection Views*, a collection view needs to know how many cells to display and what to put in each cell. You will add two methods to the `ExploreDataManager` class that will provide the number of `ExploreItem` instances in the `exploreItems` array and return an `ExploreItem` instance at a specified array index. Click the `ExploreDataManager` file in the Project navigator and add these two methods after the `loadData()` method:

```
func numberOfExploreItems() -> Int {
    exploreItems.count
}
func exploreItem(at index: Int) -> ExploreItem {
    exploreItems[index]
}
```

The first method, `numberOfExploreItems()`, will determine the number of cells to be displayed by the collection view.

The second method, `exploreItem(at:)`, will return an `ExploreItem` instance that corresponds to a cell's position in the collection view.

In the next section, you'll update the collection view data source methods in the `ExploreViewController` class to provide the number of cells to be displayed in the collection view, and to provide the cuisine name and image for each cell.

Updating the data source methods in ExploreViewController

The data source methods in the `ExploreViewController` class are currently set to display 20 cells, each cell containing an empty image view and label. You'll update them to get the number of cells to display, and the data to put in each cell, from the `ExploreDataManager` instance. Follow these steps:

1. Click the `ExploreViewController` file and find the `viewDidLoad()` method. It should look like this:

```
override func viewDidLoad() {
    super.viewDidLoad()
    let manager = ExploreDataManager()
    manager.fetch()
}
```

This means the `ExploreDataManager` instance is only accessible within the `viewDidLoad()` method. You need to make it available to the entire class.

2. Move the `let manager = ExploreDataManager()` line to just after the `collectionView` property declaration to make the `ExploreDataManager` instance available to all methods within the `ExploreViewController` class, as shown:

```
@IBOutlet var collectionView: UICollectionView!
let manager = ExploreDataManager()
```

3. Update `collectionView(_:numberOfItemsInSection:)` as shown. This will make the collection view display a cell for each element in the `items` array:

```
func collectionView(_ collectionView: UICollectionView,
numberOfItemsInSection section: Int) -> Int {
    manager.numberOfExploreItems()
}
```

4. Update `collectionView(_:cellForItemAt:)` as shown to set the image view and label for each cell using data from the corresponding element in the `items` array:

```
func collectionView(_ collectionView: UICollectionView,
cellForItemAt indexPath: IndexPath) ->
UICollectionViewCell {
    let cell = collectionView.dequeueReusableCell(
    withReuseIdentifier: "exploreCell", for:
    indexPath) as! ExploreCell
    let exploreItem = manager.exploreItem(at:
    indexPath.row)
    cell.exploreNameLabel.text = exploreItem.name
    cell.exploreImageView.image = UIImage(named:
    exploreItem.image!)
    return cell
}
```

Let's break this down:

```
let cell = collectionView.dequeueReusableCell(
withReuseIdentifier:"exploreCell", for: indexPath)
as! ExploreCell
```

Specifies the cell that is dequeued is an instance of `ExploreCell`.

```
let exploreItem = manager.exploreItem(at:
indexPath.row)
```

Gets the `ExploreItem` instance that corresponds to the current cell in the collection view. In other words, the first cell in the collection view corresponds to the first `ExploreItem` instance in the `exploreItems` array, the second cell corresponds to the second `ExploreItem` instance, and so on.

```
cell.exploreNameLabel.text = exploreItem.name
```

Sets the `text` property of the cell's `nameLabel` to the name of the `ExploreItem` instance.

```
cell.exploreImageView.image = UIImage(named:
exploreItem.image!)
```

Gets the `image` string from the `ExploreItem` instance, gets the corresponding image from the `Assets.xcassets` file, and assigns it to the `image` of the cell's `imgExplore` property.

Build and run the app. You'll see the collection view in the **Explore** screen display images and text of different cuisines. Tapping a collection view cell will display the **Restaurant List** screen:

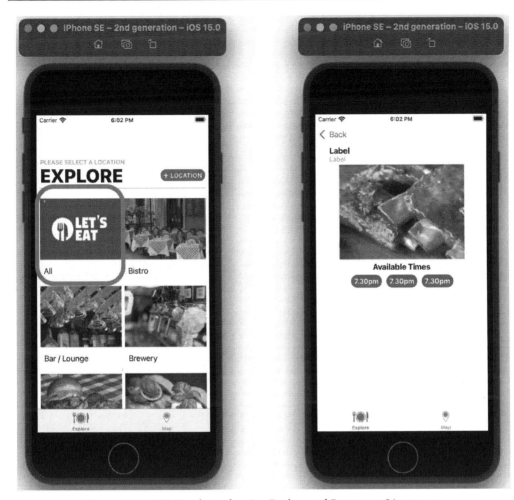

Figure 14.18: iOS Simulator showing Explore and Restaurant List screens

At this point, the **Explore** screen displays images and text of different cuisines based on the data obtained from the ExploreData.plist file. In *Chapter 17, Getting Started with JSON Files*, you will modify the RestaurantListViewController class to make the **Restaurant List** screen display a list of restaurants offering the selected cuisine. But before you can do that, you'll need to set a location in the **Locations** screen, which will provide a list of all available restaurants at that location. This will be covered in the next chapter.

Summary

In this chapter, you added a property list file, `ExploreData.plist`, to your project. You implemented the `ExploreItem` structure, the model objects for the **Explore** screen. You created a data manager class, `ExploreDataManager`, to read data from `ExploreData.plist`, put the data into an array of `ExploreItem` instances, and provide it to `ExploreViewController`. You created a class for the `exploreCell` collection view cell. Finally, you configured the data source methods in the `ExploreViewController` class to use data from the array of `ExploreItem` instances to populate the collection view, and the **Explore** screen now displays a list of cuisines. Great job!

You now know how to provide data to an app using `.plist` files, create model objects, create data manager classes that load `.plist` files into model objects, configure collection views to display data that has been loaded, and configure view controllers for collection views. This will be useful should you wish to create your own apps that use collection views.

In the next chapter, you will look at table views, which are similar in some ways to collection views, and configure the **Locations** screen to display a list of locations in a table view when you tap the **LOCATION** button in the **Explore** screen.

15
Getting Started with Table Views

In the previous chapter, you configured the `ExploreViewController` class, the view controller for the **Explore** screen, to display cuisine information provided by `ExploreData.plist` in a collection view.

In this chapter, you'll start by learning about table views and table view controllers. You'll implement a table view programmatically (which means implementing it using code instead of storyboards) using a playground, to understand how table views work. Next, you'll create a table view controller for the **Locations** screen, create a `.plist` file from scratch to hold a list of locations, create a data manager class to read data from the `.plist` file, and configure the table view controller to get data from the data manager and provide it to the table view. The **Locations** screen will then display a list of restaurant locations.

By the end of this chapter, you'll have learned how to create `.plist` files, and how to implement table view controllers. This will enable you to implement `.plist` files and table views that use `.plist` files for a data source in your own apps.

The following topics will be covered in this chapter:

- Understanding table views
- Creating the `LocationViewController` class
- Adding location data for the table view
- Creating the `LocationDataManager` class

Technical requirements

You will start by working in a playground, then you will continue working on the `LetsEat` project that you modified in the previous chapter.

The playground and completed Xcode project for this chapter are in the `Chapter15` folder of the code bundle for this book, which can be downloaded here:

`https://github.com/PacktPublishing/iOS-15-Programming-for-Beginners-Sixth-Edition`

Check out the following video to see the code in action:

`https://bit.ly/3obiApY`

Let's begin by learning more about how a table view works by implementing a view controller that manages a table view in a playground. Create a new playground and name it `TableViewBasics`. You can type in and run all the code shown in the upcoming sections as you go along.

Understanding table views

The *Let's Eat* app uses a table view in the **Locations** screen to display a list of restaurant locations. A table view presents table view cells using rows arranged in a single column.

> **Important Information**
>
> To learn more about table views, visit `https://developer.apple.com/documentation/uikit/uitableview`.

The data displayed by a table view is normally provided by a view controller. A view controller providing data for a table view must conform to the `UITableViewDataSource` protocol. This protocol declares a list of methods that tells the table view how many cells to display and what to display in each cell.

> **Important Information**
>
> To learn more about the `UITableViewDataSource` protocol, visit
> `https://developer.apple.com/documentation/uikit/`
> `uitableviewdatasource`.

To provide user interaction, a view controller for a table view must also conform to the `UITableViewDelegate` protocol, which declares a list of methods which are triggered when a user interacts with the table view.

> **Important Information**
>
> To learn more about the `UITableViewDelegate` protocol, visit
> `https://developer.apple.com/documentation/uikit/`
> `uitableviewdelegate`.

To learn how table views work, you'll implement a view controller subclass that controls a table view in your `TableViewBasics` playground. Since there is no storyboard in the playground, you can't add the UI elements using the library, as you did in the previous chapters. Instead, you will do everything programmatically. Follow these steps:

1. Open your `TableViewBasics` playground that you have created at the beginning of this chapter. At the very top of the playground, remove the `var` statement and add an `import PlaygroundSupport` statement.

   Your playground should now contain the following:

   ```
   import UIKit
   import PlaygroundSupport
   ```

   The first `import` statement imports the API for creating iOS apps. The second allows the playground to display a live view, which you will use to display the table view.

2. Add the following code after the `import` statements to declare the `TableViewExampleController` class:

   ```
   class TableViewExampleController: UIViewController {

   }
   ```

   This class is a subclass of `UIViewController`, a class that Apple provides to manage views on the screen.

3. Add the following code inside the curly braces to declare a table view property and an array property to the `TableViewExampleController` class:

```
class TableViewExampleController: UIViewController {
    var tableView: UITableView?
    var names: [String] = ["Divij","Aamir","Shubham"]
}
```

The `tableView` property is an optional property that will be assigned a `UITableView` instance. The `names` array is the model object that will be used to provide data to the table view.

A table view displays a single column of rows on the screen, and each row contains a table view cell instance. Similar to collection views, table views need to know how many rows to display and what to put in each row. To provide this information to the table view, you will make the `TableViewExampleController` class conform to the `UITableViewDataSourceProtocol`.

This protocol has two required methods:

*   `tableview(_:numberOfRowsInSection:)` is called by the table view to determine how many table view cells to display.

*   `tableView(_:cellForRowAt:)` is called by the table view to determine what to display in each table view cell.

Let's add some code to make the `TableViewExampleController` class conform to the `UITableViewDataSource` protocol. Follow these steps:

1. To make the `TableViewExampleController` class adopt the `UITableViewDataSource` protocol, type a comma after the superclass name and then type `UITableViewDataSource`. Your code should look like this:

```
class TableViewExampleController: UIViewController,
UITableViewDataSource {
```

2. An error will appear because you haven't implemented the two required methods. Click the error icon:

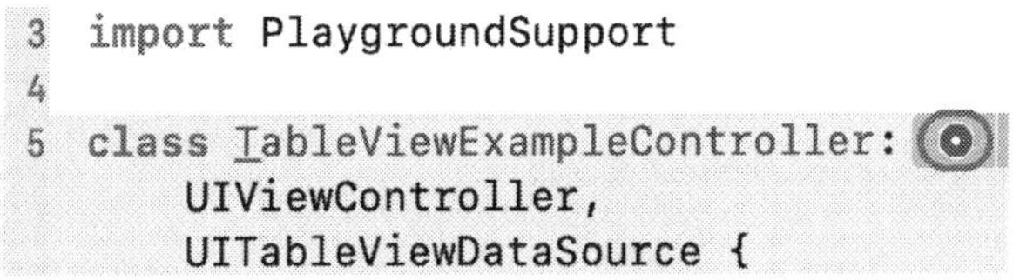

```
3  import PlaygroundSupport
4
5  class TableViewExampleController: ⊚
       UIViewController,
       UITableViewDataSource {
```

Figure 15.1: Editor area showing error icon

3. The error message that appears states that the required methods for the UITableViewDataSource protocol are missing. Click the **Fix** button to add the required method stubs to the class:

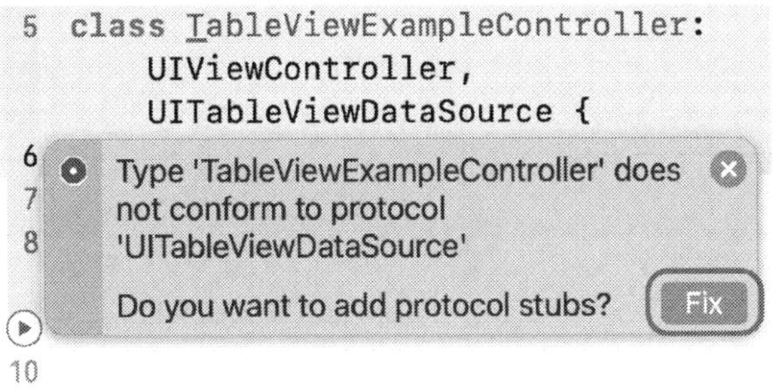

```
5  class TableViewExampleController:
       UIViewController,
       UITableViewDataSource {

6  ⊚  Type 'TableViewExampleController' does  ⊗
7      not conform to protocol
8      'UITableViewDataSource'

       Do you want to add protocol stubs?   [ Fix ]
⊙
10
```

Figure 15.2: Error explanation and Fix button

4. Verify that your code looks like this:

```
class TableViewExampleController: UIViewController,
UITableViewDataSource {
    func tableView(_ tableView: UITableView,
    numberOfRowsInSection section: Int) -> Int {
        code
    }
    func tableView(_ tableView: UITableView,
    cellForRowAt indexPath: IndexPath) ->
    UITableViewCell {
        code
    }
    var tableView: UITableView?
    var names: [String] = ["Divij","Aamir","Shubham"]
}
```

5. In a class definition, convention dictates that properties are declared at the top before any method declarations. Rearrange the code so that the property declarations are at the top, as follows:

```
class TableViewExampleController: UIViewController,
UITableViewDataSource {
    var tableView: UITableView?
    var names: [String] = ["Divij","Aamir","Shubham"]
    func tableView(_ tableView: UITableView,
    numberOfRowsInSection section: Int) -> Int {
```

6. To make the table view display a row for each element inside the names array, click the word code inside the tableView(_:numberOfRowsInSection:) method definition and type in names.count. The completed method should look like this:

```
func tableView(_ tableView: UITableView,
numberOfRowsInSection section: Int) -> Int {
    names.count
}
```

names.count returns the number of elements inside the names array. Since there are three names in it, this will make the table view display three rows.

7. To make the table view display names in each cell, click the word code inside the tableView(_:cellForRowAt:) method definition and type the following:

```
func tableView(_ tableView: UITableView, cellForRowAt
indexPath: IndexPath) -> UITableViewCell {
    let cell = tableView.dequeueReusableCell(
    withIdentifier: "Cell", for: indexPath)
    let name = names[indexPath.row]
    cell.textLabel?.text = name
    return cell
}
```

Let's break this down:

```
let cell = tableView.dequeueReusableCell(
withIdentifier: "Cell", for: indexPath)
```

This creates a new table view cell or reuses an existing table view cell, and assigns it to `cell`. Imagine you have 1,000 items to display in a table view. You don't need 1,000 rows containing 1,000 table view cells—you only need just enough to fill the screen. Table view cells that scroll off the top of the screen can be reused to display items that appear at the bottom of the screen. To make sure you are using the right type of cell, you set the reuse identifier to `Cell`. This reuse identifier will be registered with the table view later.

```
let name = names[indexPath.row]
```

The `indexPath` value locates the row in the table view. The first row has an `indexPath` containing section 0 and row 0. `indexPath.row` returns 0 for the first row, so `name` is assigned the first element in the `names` array.

```
cell.textLabel?.text = name
```

This assigns `name` to the `text` property of the table view cell's `textLabel`.

```
return cell
```

This returns the table view cell, which is then displayed on the screen.

This method is executed for each row in the table view.

8. Verify that your `TableViewExampleController` class looks like this:

```
class TableViewExampleController: UIViewController,
UITableViewDataSource {
    var tableView: UITableView?
    var names: [String] = ["Divij","Aamir","Shubham"]
    func tableView(_ tableView: UITableView,
    numberOfRowsInSection section: Int) -> Int {
        names.count
    }
    func tableView(_ tableView: UITableView,
    cellForRowAt indexPath: IndexPath) ->
    UITableViewCell {
        let cell = tableView.dequeueReusableCell(
        withIdentifier: "Cell", for:indexPath)
        let name = names[indexPath.row]
        cell.textLabel?.text = name
        return cell
    }
}
```

You have completed the implementation of the `TableViewExampleController` class. Now you will write a method, `createTableView()`, to create an instance of it. Type in the following code after the property declarations to declare and define the `createTableView()` method:

```
func createTableView() {
    self.tableView = UITableView(frame: CGRect(x: 0, y: 0,
    width: self.view.frame.width,
    height: self.view.frame.height))
    self.tableView?.dataSource = self
    self.tableView?.backgroundColor = .white
    self.tableView?.register(UITableViewCell.self,
    forCellReuseIdentifier: "Cell")
    self.view.addSubview(self.tableView!)
}
```

Let's break this down:

```
self.tableView = UITableView(frame: CGRect(x: 0, y: 0, width:
self.view.frame.width, height: self.view.frame.height))
```

This creates a new instance of `UITableView` that is exactly the same size as its enclosing view, and assigns it to `tableView`.

```
self.tableView?.dataSource = self
```

This tells the table view that its data source is an instance of `TableViewExampleController`.

```
self.tableView?.backgroundColor = .white
```

This sets the table view's background color to white.

```
self.tableView?.register(UITableViewCell.self,
forCellReuseIdentifier: "Cell")
```

This sets the reuse identifier for the table view cells to `"Cell"`. This reuse identifier will be used in the `tableView(_:cellForRowAt:)` method to identify the cells that can be reused.

```
self.view.addSubview(self.tableView!)
```

This adds the table view as a subview to the view of the `TableViewExampleController` instance.

Now you have to call this method. The `UIViewController` class has a method, `viewDidLoad()`, that is called when its view is loaded. This method is inherited by the `TableViewExampleController` class, and you'll override it to call `createTableView()`. Follow these steps:

1. Type in the following code, before the `createTableView()` method:

```
override func viewDidLoad() {
    super.viewDidLoad()
    self.view.bounds = CGRect(x: 0, y: 0,
    width: 375, height: 667)
    createTableView()
}
```

This sets the size of the live view, creates a table view and adds it as a subview to the view of the `TableViewExampleController` instance. The data source methods are then used to determine how many table view cells to display, as well as what to put in each table view cell. `tableView(_:numberOfRowsInSection:)` returns 3, so three rows are displayed. `tableView(_:cellForRowAt:)` sets the text of each cell to the corresponding name in the `names` array.

2. Verify that your completed code looks like this:

```
import UIKit
import PlaygroundSupport
class TableViewExampleController: UIViewController,
UITableViewDataSource {
    var tableView: UITableView?
    var names: [String] = ["Divij","Aamir","Shubham"]
    override func viewDidLoad() {
        super.viewDidLoad()
        self.view.bounds = CGRect(x: 0, y: 0,
        width: 375, height: 667)
```

```
            createTableView()
    }
    func createTableView() {
        self.tableView = UITableView(frame: CGRect(x: 0,
        y: 0, width: self.view.frame.width, height:
        self.view.frame.height))
        self.tableView?.dataSource = self
        self.tableView?.backgroundColor = .white
        self.tableView?.register(UITableViewCell.self,
        forCellReuseIdentifier: "Cell")
        self.view.addSubview(self.tableView!)
    }
    func tableView(_ tableView: UITableView,
    numberOfRowsInSection section: Int) -> Int {
        names.count
    }
    func tableView(_ tableView: UITableView,
    cellForRowAt indexPath: IndexPath) ->
    UITableViewCell {
        let cell = tableView.dequeueReusableCell(
        withIdentifier: "Cell", for:indexPath)
        let name = names[indexPath.row]
        cell.textLabel?.text = name
        return cell
    }
}
```

3. Type the following after all the other code in the playground:

```
PlaygroundPage.current.liveView =
TableViewExampleController()
```

This command creates an instance of `TableViewExampleController` and displays its view in the playground's live view.

4. Run the playground. If you don't see the table view, click the Adjust Editor Options button:

Figure 15.3: Adjust Editor Options button

5. Make sure **Live View** is selected from the pop-up menu:

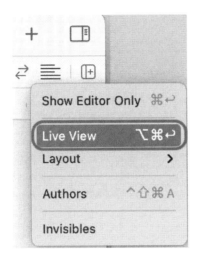

Figure 15.4: Adjust Editor Options menu with Live View selected

6. You will see the table view displaying a table with three rows containing names, as shown:

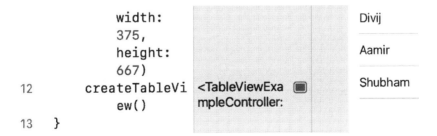

Figure 15.5: Playground Live View showing table view with names

Great! Now that you know how table views work, let's complete the implementation for the **Locations** screen. You'll start by creating a view controller for this screen in the next section, so that it can manage what the table view will display.

Creating the LocationViewController class

As shown in the app tour in *Chapter 9, Setting Up the User Interface*, the **Locations** screen displays a list of locations in a table view. At the end of *Chapter 12, Modifying and Configuring Cells*, you configured the **Locations** screen to display a table view and set the identifier of the table view cells to `locationCell`. Referring to the **Model-View-Controller (MVC)** design pattern, you have completed the required views, but you haven't completed the controller or the model yet.

At the moment, when you click the **LOCATION** button in the **Explore** screen, an empty table view is displayed:

Figure 15.6: iOS Simulator showing Locations screen from your app

You will create the `LocationViewController` class as the view controller for the **Locations** screen, add an outlet for the table view to it, and configure it as the table view's data source and delegate. Follow these steps:

1. Open your `LetsEat` project from the previous chapter. Create a new folder, `Location`, inside your project by right-clicking the `LetsEat` folder and choosing **New Group**. Create two more folders, `View` and `Model`, inside the `Location` folder. When you're done, you will see the following folder structure:

Figure 15.7: Project navigator showing Location folder and subfolders

2. Right-click on the `Location` folder and select **New File**.

3. **iOS** should already be selected. Choose **Cocoa Touch Class** and click **Next**.

4. Configure the class with the following details:

    Class: `LocationViewController`

    Subclass: `UIViewController`

    Also create XIB: `Unchecked`

    Language: `Swift`

    Click **Next**.

5. Click **Create**. The `LocationViewController` file appears in the Project navigator.

The `LocationViewController` file has been created, with the `LocationViewController` class declaration inside it. Now you'll set the identity of the view controller scene that's presented when you tap the **LOCATION** button to this class. Follow these steps:

1. Open the `Main` storyboard file in the Project navigator.

2. Choose the view controller scene that's presented when you click on the **LOCATION** button (it's the one with **Cancel** and **Done** buttons). Click the Identity inspector button and, under **Custom Class**, set **Class** to `LocationViewController`. Note the name of the scene will change to **Location View Controller Scene**:

Figure 15.8: Identity inspector settings for Location View Controller Scene

Cool! In the next section, let's connect the table view to an outlet in the `LocationViewController` class. By doing this, the `LocationViewController` instance for the **Locations** screen will be able to manage the table view.

Connecting the table view to the LocationViewController class

Currently, the `LocationViewController` instance for the **Locations** screen has no way of communicating with the table view in it. You'll create a new outlet in the `LocationViewController` class and assign the table view to it. Follow these steps:

1. Click the Navigator and Inspector buttons to hide the Navigator and Inspector areas, if necessary.

2. Click the Adjust Editor Options button and choose **Assistant** from the menu.

3. In the `Main` storyboard file, click the table view in the document outline. The assistant editor should be set to **Automatic > LocationViewController.swift** as shown:

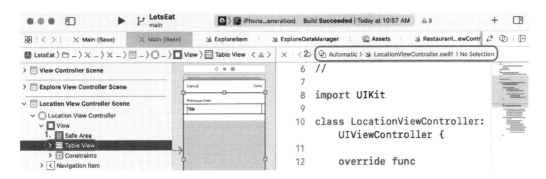

Figure 15.9: Assistant editor bar showing LocationViewController.swift

4. *Ctrl + Drag* from **Table View** to the space just above `viewDidLoad()`:

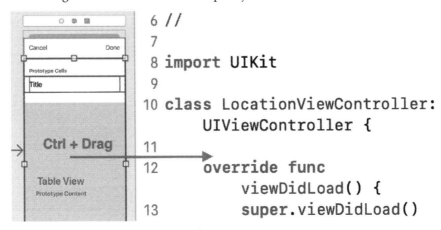

Figure 15.10: Editor area showing LocationViewController file contents

5. In the pop-up menu, enter `tableView` in the **Name** field and click **Connect**:

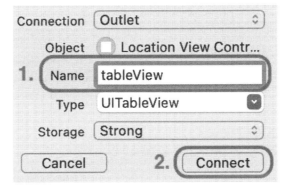

Figure 15.11: Pop-up dialog box for tableView outlet creation

6. Verify the `tableView` outlet has been added to the `LocationViewController` class and connected to the table view in the storyboard:

```
10 class LocationViewController:
       UIViewController {
11
◉       @IBOutlet var tableView:
           UITableView!
13
14       override func
```

Figure 15.12: Editor area showing LocationViewController file contents

7. Click the **x** button to close the assistant editor:

Figure 15.13: Assistant editor close button

You've connected the table view to an outlet in the `LocationViewController` class. In order for a table view to display data and respond to user interaction, the `LocationViewController` class has to conform to the `UITableViewDataSource` and `UITableViewDelegate` protocols and implement the required methods. You will do that in the next section.

Adding the data source and delegate methods

A view controller for a table view has to adopt the `UITableViewDataSource` and `UITableViewDelegate` protocols, as well as implement the required methods to allow data display and user interaction. In this section, you'll connect `LocationViewController` to the table view's `dataSource` and `delegate` outlets and implement the required data source methods. You will implement delegate methods in *Chapter 17, Getting Started with JSON Files*. Follow these steps:

1. Click the Navigator and Inspector buttons to show the Navigator and Inspector areas, if necessary.

2. In the `Main` storyboard file, make sure you have the table view selected in the document outline. Click the Connections inspector button. Click and drag from the `dataSource` and `delegate` outlets to the `LocationViewController` icon in the document outline:

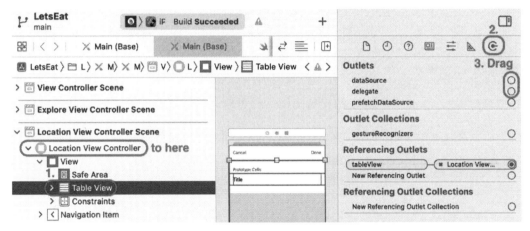

Figure 15.14: Connections Inspector showing outlets for the LocationViewController class

This connects the table view to outlets to the `LocationViewController` class.

3. Verify the `dataSource` and `delegate` properties of the table view have been connected to outlets in the `LocationViewController` class:

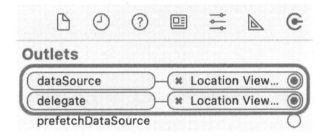

Figure 15.15: Connections Inspector with datasource and delegate outlets set

Next, you will make `LocationViewController` conform to the `UITableViewDataSource` protocol and implement the required methods for this protocol. Follow these steps:

1. Click the `LocationViewController` file in the Project navigator and remove all the commented code in the `LocationViewController` class definition so that only the following is left:

```
class LocationViewController: UIViewController {
    @IBOutlet weak var tableView: UITableView!
```

```
override func viewDidLoad(){
    super.viewDidLoad()
}
}
```

2. To make `LocationViewController` adopt the `UITableViewDataSource` protocol, type a comma after the superclass name, `UIViewController`, and type in `UITableViewDataSource`. When you are done, your code should look like this:

```
class LocationViewController: UIViewController,
UITableViewDataSource {
```

3. An error will appear because you haven't implemented the two required methods yet. Click the error icon to see the error message:

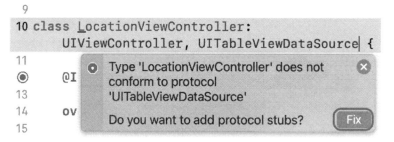

```
9
10 class LocationViewController:
    UIViewController, UITableViewDataSource {
11
    @IBOutlet weak var tableView: UITableView!
```

Figure 15.16: Editor area showing error icon

4. Click the **Fix** button to add the required method stubs to the class:

```
9
10 class LocationViewController:
    UIViewController, UITableViewDataSource {
11
    @I    Type 'LocationViewController' does not
13          conform to protocol
14    ov    'UITableViewDataSource'
15          Do you want to add protocol stubs?    Fix
```

Figure 15.17: Error explanation and Fix button

5. Rearrange the code so that the property declarations and the `viewDidLoad()` method are at the top. This follows general iOS development coding conventions and it makes your code easier to maintain. When you're done, verify that your code looks as follows:

```
class LocationViewController: UIViewController,
UITableViewDataSource {
    @IBOutlet var tableView: UITableView!
```

```
override func viewDidLoad() {
    super.viewDidLoad()
}
func tableView(_ tableView: UITableView,
    numberOfRowsInSection section: Int) -> Int {
    code
}
func tableView(_ tableView: UITableView,
    cellForRowAt indexPath: IndexPath) ->
UITableViewCell {
    code
}
}
```

6. Inside the first required method, click the word code and type 10. This will make the table view display 10 rows. The complete method should look like this:

```
func tableView(_ tableView: UITableView,
numberOfRowsInSection section: Int) -> Int {
    10
}
```

7. Inside the second required method, click the word code and type the following to make the table view display the string "A Cell" in each row:

```
func tableView(_ tableView: UITableView, cellForRowAt
indexPath: IndexPath) -> UITableViewCell {
    let cell = tableView.dequeueReusableCell(
    withIdentifier: "locationCell", for: indexPath)
    cell.textLabel?.text = "A Cell"
    return cell
}
```

Let's break this down:

```
let cell = tableView.dequeueReusableCell(
withIdentifier: "locationCell", for: indexPath)
```

This creates a new table view cell or reuses an existing table view cell with the `locationCell` identifier and assigns it to `cell`. You set this identifier in the **Location View Controller Scene** in the `Main` storyboard file in *Chapter 12, Modifying and Configuring Cells*.

```
cell.textLabel?.text = "A Cell"
```

This assigns a string, `"A Cell"` to the `text` property of the table view cell's `textLabel`.

```
return cell
```

This returns the cell, which is then displayed on the screen. This process is repeated for the number of cells that are given in the first method, which, in this case, is 10.

Build and run your project. Click the **LOCATION** button in the **Explore** screen. You should see the table view display 10 rows with each row containing `A Cell` as shown:

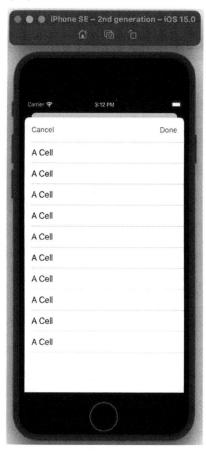

Figure 15.18: iOS Simulator showing table view cells

You have completed the implementation of the `LocationsViewController` class, and your table view is now displaying table view cells. Great! Now that your table view's view controller has been set up, let's create some model objects in the next section so that you can provide data for it.

Adding location data for the table view

At this point, you have created and configured the `LocationViewController` class. An instance of this class will act as the data source for the table view in the **Locations** screen. The views and the controller for this screen have been set up, so now you'll create model objects to make the table view display a list of actual locations. Just like you did in the previous chapter, you'll use a `.plist` file that contains location data, but instead of using an existing `.plist` file, you'll create one from scratch and add location data to it. Follow these steps:

1. Right-click the `Model` folder in the `Location` folder and choose **New File**.

2. **iOS** should already be selected. Type `proper` into the filter field; **Property List** will appear in the window. Choose **Property List** and click **Next**.

3. Name the file `Locations`, and click **Create**.

The `Locations.plist` file has been added to the project. In the previous chapter, you've seen how `ExploreData.plist` stores data as an array of dictionaries. You will configure `Locations.plist` so that it stores data for the **Locations** screen in the same format, and then add all the restaurant locations to it. Follow these steps:

1. Click on **Dictionary** in `Locations.plist` and change it to **Array**. Note that the disclosure triangle on the left should be pointing down. Click the + button:

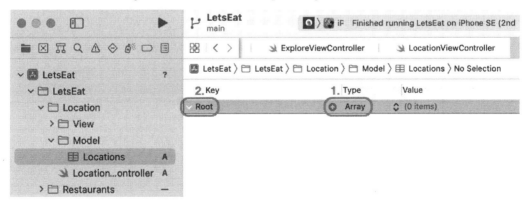

Figure 15.19: Editor area showing Locations.plist contents

2. A new item, **Item 0**, will be added to the array. Change the type to **Dictionary**. Click the disclosure triangle to make it point down. Click the + button:

Figure 15.20: Locations.plist with Item 0 added

3. A new item, **New Item**, will be added to the **Item 0** dictionary. Click the + button:

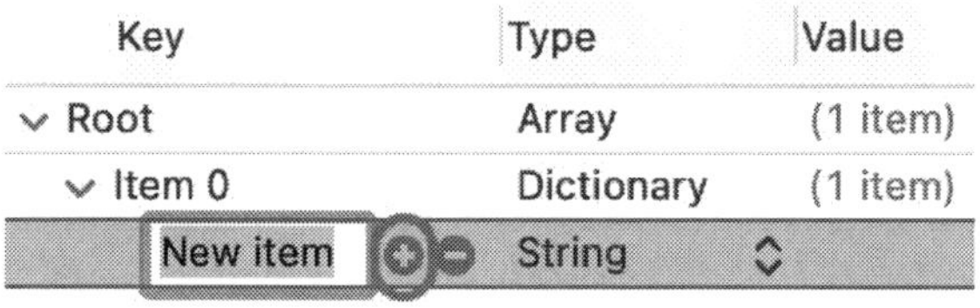

Key	Type	Value
∨ Root	Array	(1 item)
∨ Item 0	Dictionary	(1 item)
New item	String	

Figure 15.21: Locations.plist with New item added

4. A second item will be added to the **Item 0** dictionary. For the first item, change the key to `city` and the value to `Aspen`. For the second item, change the key to `state` and the value to `CO`:

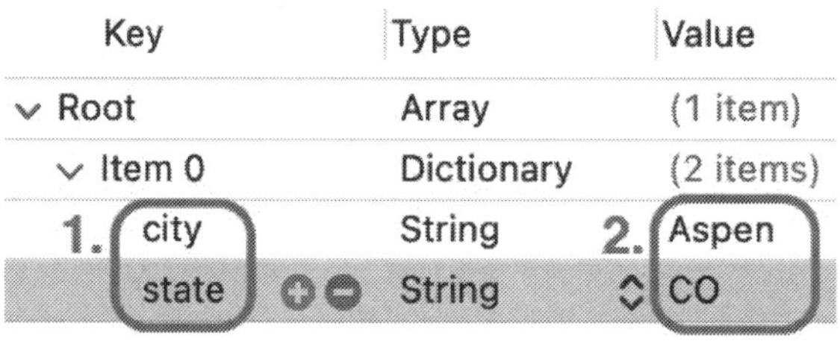

Key	Type	Value
∨ Root	Array	(1 item)
∨ Item 0	Dictionary	(2 items)
1. city	String	**2.** Aspen
state	String	CO

Figure 15.22: Locations.plist with city and state added to Item 0

5. Click the disclosure triangle next to the **Item 0** dictionary to collapse it:

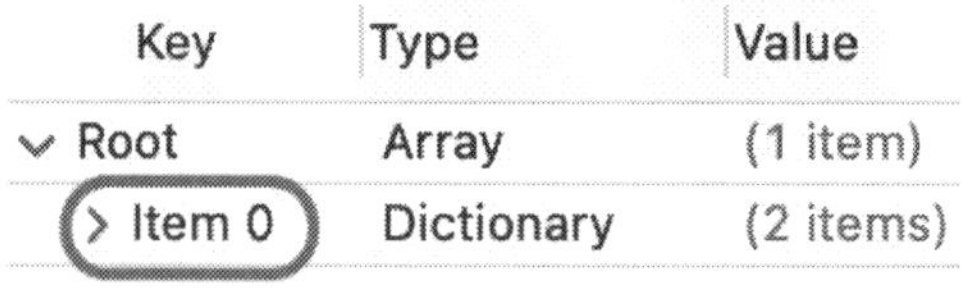

Key	Type	Value
∨ Root	Array	(1 item)
> Item 0	Dictionary	(2 items)

Figure 15.23: Locations.plist with Item 0 collapsed

6. Select **Item 0** and press *Command + C* on the keyboard to copy it and *Command + V* to paste. You will see a new item, **Item 1**:

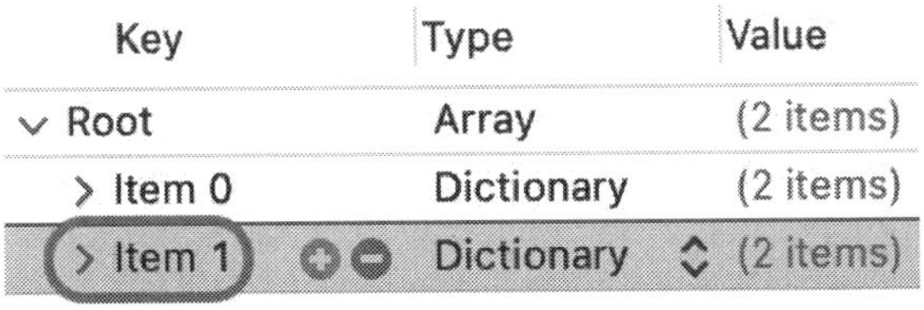

Key	Type	Value
∨ Root	Array	(2 items)
› Item 0	Dictionary	(2 items)
› Item 1	Dictionary	(2 items)

Figure 15.24: Locations.plist with Item 0 copied and pasted

7. Click the disclosure triangle next to the **Item 1** dictionary to expand it. Change the city to Boston and the state to MA:

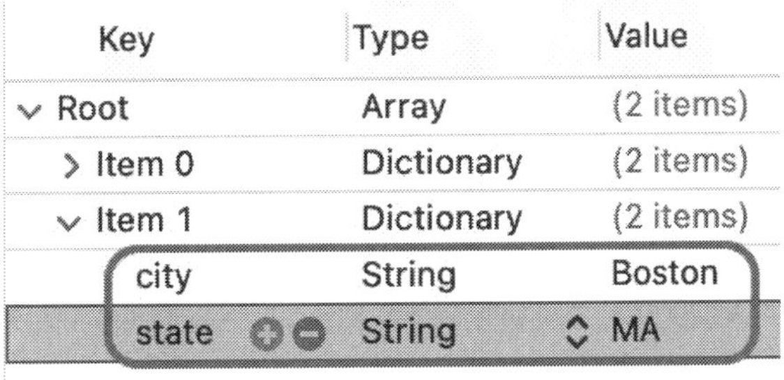

Key	Type	Value
∨ Root	Array	(2 items)
› Item 0	Dictionary	(2 items)
∨ Item 1	Dictionary	(2 items)
city	String	Boston
state	String	MA

Figure 15.25: Locations.plist with Item 1 configured

8. Continue with the same process by adding the following cities and states:

Item	City	State
Item 2	Charleston	NC
Item 3	Chicago	IL
Item 4	Houston	TX
Item 5	Las Vegas	NV
Item 6	Los Angeles	CA
Item 7	Miami	FL
Item 8	New Orleans	LA
Item 9	New York	NY
Item 10	Philadelphia	PA
Item 11	Portland	OR
Item 12	San Antonio	TX
Item 13	San Francisco	CA

The completed `.plist` file should look like this:

Key	Type	Value
⌄ Root	Array	(14 items)
⌄ Item 0	Dictionary	(2 items)
city	String	Aspen
state	String	CO
⌄ Item 1	Dictionary	(2 items)
city	String	Boston
state	String	MA
⌄ Item 2	Dictionary	(2 items)
city	String	Charleston
state	String	NC

Figure 15.26: Locations.plist completed

The `Locations.plist` file is complete. In the next section, you will create a data manager class, similar to the one you made in the previous chapter, that will read the `Locations.plist` file and provide it to the `LocationViewController` instance for the **Locations** screen.

Creating the LocationDataManager class

As what you've done in the previous chapter, you'll create a data manager class to load the location data from `Locations.plist` and provide it to the `LocationsViewController` instance for the **Locations** screen. The data will then be used to populate the table view in the **Locations** screen. Follow these steps:

1. Right-click the `Model` folder in the `Location` folder and select **New File**.

2. **iOS** should already be selected. Choose **Swift File** and click **Next**.

3. Name this file `LocationDataManager` and click `Create`.

4. Click on the `LocationDataManager` file in the Project navigator and after the `import` statement, type in the following to declare the `LocationDataManager` class:

```
class LocationDataManager {


}
```

5. Inside the curly braces, add an array property, `locations`, to hold the list of locations:

```
private var locations: [String] = []
```

The `private` keyword means that the `locations` property may only be accessed by methods in this class.

6. Add the following methods after the property declaration:

```
private func loadData() -> [[String: String]] {
    let decoder = PropertyListDecoder()
    if let path = Bundle.main.path(forResource:
    "Locations", ofType: "plist"),
    let locationsData = FileManager.default.contents(
    atPath: path),
    let locations = try? decoder.decode([[String:
    String]].self, from: locationsData) {
        return locations
    }
    return [[:]]
}
func fetch() {
    for location in loadData() {
        if let city = location["city"], let
        state = location["state"] {
            locations.append("\(city), \(state)")
        }
    }
}
func numberOfLocationItems() -> Int {
    locations.count
}
func locationItem(at index: Int) -> String {
    locations[index]
}
```

These methods are similar to those in `ExploreDataManager`. Let's break it down:

```
loadData()
```

Loads the contents of `Locations.plist` and returns an array of dictionaries. Each dictionary stores the city and state of a location.

```
fetch()
```

Takes the array provided by `loadData()`, concatenates the `city` and `state` for each element, and appends the resulting string to the `locations` array.

```
numberOfLocationItems()
```

Returns the number of elements in the `locations` array.

```
locationItem(at:)
```

Returns a string stored in the `locations` array at a given array index.

Now that the `LocationDataManager` class is complete, let's configure the `LocationViewController` class so that it can get data from the `LocationDataManager` instance and provide it to the table view. You will do this in the next section.

Displaying data in a table view

Currently, the **Locations** screen displays 10 cells containing the string `"A Cell"`. You will update the `LocationViewController` class to use the `LocationDataManager` instance as a data source. Follow these steps:

1. Click the `LocationViewController` file in the Project navigator. In the `LocationViewController` class definition before the `viewDidLoad()` method, create an instance of `LocationDataManager` and assign it to a property, `manager`, by typing the following:

    ```
    let manager = LocationDataManager()
    ```

2. Inside the `viewDidLoad()` method, fetch the data for the table view by calling `manager.fetch()`:

    ```
    override func viewDidLoad() {
        super.viewDidLoad()
        manager.fetch()
    }
    ```

3. Modify `tableView(_:numberOfRowsInSection:)` so it can get the number of rows to display in the table view from `manager`:

```
func tableView(_ tableView: UITableView,
numberOfRowsInSection section: Int) -> Int {
    manager.numberOfLocationItems()
}
```

4. Modify `tableView(_:cellForRowAt:)` as shown to make the table view display a string containing the city and state in every table view cell:

```
func tableView(_ tableView: UITableView, cellForRowAt
indexPath: IndexPath) -> UITableViewCell {
    let cell = tableView.dequeueReusableCell(
    withIdentifier: "locationCell", for: indexPath)
    cell.textLabel?.text =
    manager.locationItem(at: indexPath.row)
    return cell
}
```

This sets the `text` property of the table view cell's `textLabel` to the corresponding element in the `locations` array. The `indexPath` returns the section and row number of a particular row in a table view. For example, the first row has an `indexPath` containing section 0 and row 0. `indexPath.row` returns 0 for the first row, so `manager` returns the string stored at index 0 in the `locations` array. This string is then assigned to the `text` property of the first table view cell's `textLabel`.

Build and run your app. You should see the locations from `ExploreData.plist` displayed in the table view:

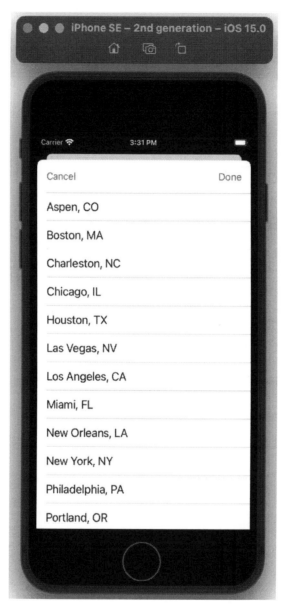

Figure 15.27: iOS Simulator showing completed Locations screen

You've completed the implementation of the **Locations** screen. Good job!

Summary

In this chapter, you learned about table views and table view controllers, and you implemented a view controller for a table view in a playground. Next, you implemented the `LocationViewController` class, a table view controller for the **Locations** screen, and created a `.plist` file from scratch called `Locations.plist` to hold a list of locations. You created a data manager class, `LocationDataManager`, to read data from the `.plist` file. Finally, you configured the `LocationViewController` class to get data from the `LocationDataManager` instance and provide it to the table view so that the **Locations** screen displays a list of restaurant locations.

This will enable you to create `.plist` files from scratch to store data, and to implement table views that use `.plist` files as a data source for your own apps. Awesome!

In the next chapter, you will add a map view to the **Map** screen and configure it to display restaurant locations. You'll also set up custom annotations for the **Map** screen and set up the **Restaurant Detail** screen, which will be displayed when a button in the annotation callout is tapped.

16
Getting Started with MapKit

In the previous chapter, you learned about table views and table view controllers, and completed the implementation of the **Locations** screen. It now displays a list of restaurant locations.

In this chapter, you'll display restaurant locations on the **Map** screen using custom pins. When you tap on a pin, you'll see a screen that shows details of a particular restaurant. Apple provides a `MKAnnotation` protocol, which allows you to associate the classes you create with a specific map location. You'll create a new class, `RestaurantItem`, that conforms to this protocol. Next, you'll create `MapDataManager`, a data manager class that loads restaurant data from a `.plist` file and puts it into an array of `RestaurantItem` instances. You'll create a new `DataManager` protocol to read `.plist` files and update both the `MapDataManager` and `ExploreDataManager` classes to avoid redundant code (refactoring). After that, you'll create a `MapViewController` class, a view controller for the **Map** screen, and configure it to display custom pins. You'll configure the pins to display callouts and configure buttons in the callouts to display the **Restaurant Detail** screen when tapped. You'll then create the `RestaurantDetailViewController` class, a view controller for the **Restaurant Detail** screen, and pass restaurant data to it from the `MapViewController` instance. Finally, you'll clean up and organize your code using extensions to make it easier to read and maintain.

By the end of this chapter, you'll have learned how to create custom map annotation views and add them to a map, how to use storyboard references to link storyboards together, and how to use extensions to organize your code, making it easier to read.

The following topics will be covered:

- Understanding and creating annotations

- Adding annotations to a map view

- Going from the map view to the **Restaurant Detail** screen

- Organizing your code

Technical requirements

You will continue working on the LetsEat project that you modified in the previous chapter.

The resource files and completed Xcode project for this chapter are in the Chapter16 folder of the code bundle for this book, which can be downloaded here:

https://github.com/PacktPublishing/iOS-15-Programming-for-Beginners-Sixth-Edition

Check out the following video to see the code in action:

https://bit.ly/3kEKEB7

Now let's learn about map annotations, which are used to mark restaurant locations on the **Map** screen.

Understanding and creating annotations

In *Chapter 11, Finishing Up Your User Interface*, you added a map view to the **Map** screen. A map view is an instance of the MKMapView class. You can see what it looks like in the Apple *Maps* app.

> **Important Information**
>
> To learn more about MKMapView, see https://developer.apple.com/documentation/mapkit/mkmapview.

When you build and run your app, you will see a map on the screen. The part of the map that is visible onscreen can be specified by setting the `region` property of the map.

> **Important Information**
>
> To learn more about regions and how to make them, see `https://` `developer.apple.com/documentation/mapkit/` `mkmapview/1452709-region`.

Pins on the **Map** screen are used to mark specific locations, and are instances of the `MKAnnotationView` class. To add a pin to a map view, you need an object that conforms to the `MKAnnotation` protocol. This protocol allows you to associate an object with a specific map location.

> **Important Information**
>
> To learn more about the `MKAnnotation` protocol, see `https://` `developer.apple.com/documentation/mapkit/` `mkannotation`.

Any object can conform to the `MKAnnotation` protocol by implementing a `coordinate` property, which contains a map location. Optional `MKAnnotation` protocol properties are `title`, a string containing the annotation's title, and `subtitle`, a string containing the annotation's subtitle.

When an object conforming to the `MKAnnotation` protocol is in the area of the map that is visible onscreen, the map view asks its delegate (usually a view controller) to provide a corresponding instance of the `MKAnnotationView` class. This instance appears as a pin on the map.

> **Important Information**
>
> To learn more about `MKAnnotationView`, see `https://developer.` `apple.com/documentation/mapkit/mkannotationview`.

If the user scrolls the map and the `MKAnnotationView` instance goes off screen, it will be put into a reuse queue and recycled later, similar to the way table view cells and collection view cells are recycled. An `MKAnnotationView` instance can be customized to display custom icons and can display callout bubbles when tapped. Callout bubbles can have buttons that perform actions, such as displaying a screen.

For your app, you will create a new class, `RestaurantItem`, that conforms to the `MKAnnotation` protocol. Let's see how to create this class in the next section.

Creating the RestaurantItem class

To represent restaurant locations on the **Map** screen, you will create a class, `RestaurantItem`, that conforms to the `MKAnnotation` protocol. This class will have a `coordinate` property to store the restaurant's location, a `title` property to store the restaurant name, and a `subtitle` property to store the cuisines it offers.

You need the restaurant location to set the `coordinate` property of the `RestaurantItem` instance. The restaurant data (including its location) will be provided as a `.plist` file. Before you create the `RestaurantItem` class, you need to import this `.plist` file into your app. Follow these steps:

1. Open the `LetsEat` project. In the Project navigator, right-click the `LetsEat` folder and create a new group called `Map`.

2. Right-click the `Map` folder and create a new group called `Model`.

3. If you have not yet done so, download the completed project and project resources from `https://github.com/PacktPublishing/iOS-15-Programming-for-Beginners-Sixth-Edition` and find the `Maplocations.plist` file inside the `resources` folder in the `Chapter16` folder.

4. Drag the `Maplocations.plist` file to the `Model` folder in your project, and click it to view its contents. You'll see that it is an array of dictionaries, with each dictionary containing a restaurant's details (including its location). You'll create properties in your `RestaurantItem` class for the data that you will use, which will eventually be displayed on the **Restaurant Detail** screen:

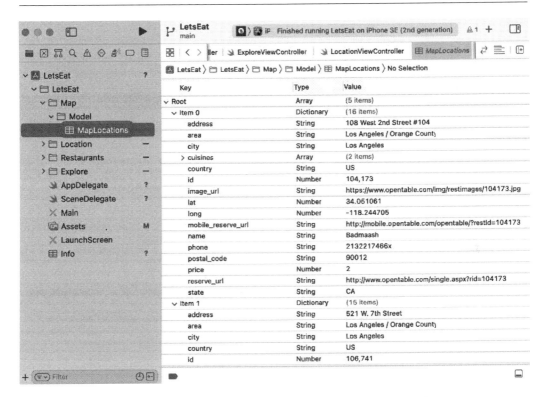

Figure 16.1: Editor area showing the contents of MapLocations.plist

Let's create the `RestaurantItem` class by following these steps:

1. Right-click the `Model` folder and select **New File**.

2. **iOS** should already be selected. Choose **Cocoa Touch Class** and then click **Next**.

3. Configure the file as follows:

   Class: `RestaurantItem`

   Subclass: `NSObject`

   Also create XIB: Greyed out

   Language: `Swift`

   Click **Next**.

4. Click **Create**. The `RestaurantItem` file appears in the Project navigator.

5. In the `RestaurantItem` file, type the following after the `import UIKit` statement to import the `MapKit` framework:

```
import MapKit
```

This gives you access to protocols such as `MKAnnotation` and `MKMapViewDelegate`.

6.   Modify the class declaration as follows to adopt the `MKAnnotation` protocol:

```
class RestaurantItem: NSObject, MKAnnotation {
```

You'll see an error, because you have not yet implemented the `coordinate` property, which is required to conform to `MKAnnotation`. You will do so shortly.

7.   Type the following between the curly braces:

```
let name: String?
let cuisines: [String]
let lat: Double?
let long: Double?
let address: String?
let postalCode: String?
let state: String?
let imageURL: String?
let restaurantID: Int?
```

These properties will hold the data you get from the `Maplocations.plist` file. Let's see what they are for:

`name` stores the name of the restaurant.

`cuisines` stores the cuisines offered by the restaurant.

`lat` and `long` stores the latitude and the longitude of the restaurant location.

`address` stores the restaurant's address.

`postalCode` stores the restaurant's postal code.

`state` stores the state in which the restaurant is located.

`imageURL` stores a a link to a photo of the restaurant.

`restaurantID` stores a unique number used as an identifier for the restaurant.

Note that you haven't created properties to store every detail of a restaurant contained in the `Maplocations.plist` file, and that's fine. You only need to create properties for the details that will appear on the **Restaurant Detail** screen.

8. You'll use a custom initializer to initialize `RestaurantItem` instances with data from the `.plist` file. Type the following after the last property declaration:

```
init(dict: [String: AnyObject]) {
    self.lat = dict["lat"] as? Double
    self.long = dict["long"] as? Double
    self.name = dict["name"] as? String
    self.cuisines = dict["cuisines"] as? [String] ?? []
    self.address = dict["address"] as? String
    self.postalCode = dict["postalCode"] as? String
    self.state = dict["state"] as? String
    self.imageURL = dict["image_url"] as? String
    self.restaurantID = dict["id"] as? Int
}
```

Even though this initializer looks complicated, it's actually quite straightforward. Each line looks for a specific dictionary item key and assigns its value to the corresponding property. For example, the first line looks for the dictionary item with a key containing `lat` and assigns the associated value to the `lat` property.

9. You'll use the `lat` and `long` properties to create the value for the `coordinate` property, which is required to conform to `MKAnnotation`. Type the following after the `init(dict:)` method to implement it:

```
var coordinate: CLLocationCoordinate2D {
    guard let lat = lat, let long = long else {
        return CLLocationCoordinate2D()
    }
    return CLLocationCoordinate2D(latitude: lat,
    longitude: long)
}
```

The `coordinate` property is of type `CLLocationCoordinate2D`, and it holds a geographical location. The value of the `coordinate` property is not assigned directly; the `guard` statement gets the latitude and longitude values from the `lat` and `long` properties, which are then used to create the value for the `coordinate` property. Such properties are called **computed properties**.

10. Implement the `title` property by adding the following code after the `coordinate` property:

```
var title: String? {
    name
}
```

`title` is a computed property that returns the contents of the `name` property.

11. Finally, implement the `subtitle` property by adding the following code after the `title` property:

```
var subtitle: String? {
    if cuisines.isEmpty {
        return ""
    } else if cuisines.count == 1 {
        return cuisines.first
    } else {
        return cuisines.joined(separator: ", ")
    }
}
```

`subtitle` is also a computed property. The first line checks to see whether the `cuisines` property is empty, and if so, returns an empty string. If the `cuisines` property contains a single item, that item will be returned. If the `cuisines` property has more than a single item, each item is added to a string, with a comma in between items. For example, if `cuisines` contained the `["American", "Bistro", "Burgers"]` array, the generated string would be `"American, Bistro, Burgers"`.

Your `RestaurantItem` class is now complete and free of errors and should look like this:

```
import UIKit
import MapKit
class RestaurantItem: NSObject, MKAnnotation {
    let name: String?
    let cuisines: [String]
    let lat: Double?
    let long: Double?
    let address: String?
    let postalCode: String?
```

```swift
    let state: String?
    let imageURL: String?
    let restaurantID: Int?
    init(dict: [String: AnyObject]) {
        self.lat = dict["lat"] as? Double
        self.long = dict["long"] as? Double
        self.name = dict["name"] as? String
        self.cuisines = dict["cuisines"] as? [String]
        ?? []
        self.address = dict["address"] as? String
        self.postalCode = dict["postalCode"] as? String
        self.state = dict["state"] as? String
        self.imageURL = dict["image_url"] as? String
        self.restaurantID = dict["id"] as? Int
    }
    var coordinate: CLLocationCoordinate2D {
        guard let lat = lat, let long = long else {
            return CLLocationCoordinate2D()
        }
        return CLLocationCoordinate2D(latitude: lat,
        longitude: long)
    }
    var title: String? {
        name
    }
    var subtitle: String? {
        if cuisines.isEmpty {
            return ""
        } else if cuisines.count == 1 {
            return cuisines.first
        } else {
            return cuisines.joined(separator: ", ")
        }
    }
}
```

At this point, you've added the `Maplocations.plist` file to your app, and you have created the `RestaurantItem` class. Next, let's create a data manager class that reads restaurant data from the `Maplocations.plist` file and puts it into an array of `RestaurantItem` instances for use by your app.

Creating the MapDataManager class

As you have done in previous chapters, you'll create a data manager class, `MapDataManager`, that will load restaurant data from the `Maplocations.plist` file and put the data into an array of `RestaurantItem` instances. Follow these steps:

1. Right-click the `Model` folder inside the `Map` folder and select **New File**.

2. **iOS** should already be selected. Choose **Swift File** and then click **Next**.

3. Name this file `MapDataManager`. Click **Create**. The `MapDataManager` file appears in the Project navigator.

4. In the `MapDataManager` file, add the following after the `import` statement to declare the `MapDataManager` class:

```
class MapDataManager {


}
```

5. Add the following properties between the curly braces to store the `RestaurantItem` instances that will be read from the `.plist` file:

```
private var items: [RestaurantItem] = []
var annotations: [RestaurantItem] {
    items
}
```

The `items` array will contain `RestaurantItem` instances. `private` makes the `items` array only accessible within the `MapDataManager` class, and `annotations` is a computed property that returns a copy of the `items` array when accessed. This allows the contents of the `items` array to be accessed, but not modified, by other objects.

6. Add the following methods after the property declarations to load the `.plist` file, read the data inside, and store it in an array of `RestaurantItem` instances:

```
private func loadData() -> [[String: AnyObject]] {
    guard let path = Bundle.main.path(forResource:
```

```
        "MapLocations", ofType: "plist"),
    let itemsData = FileManager.default.contents(
    atPath: path),
    let items = try! PropertyListSerialization
    .propertyList(from: itemsData, format: nil) as?
    [[String: AnyObject]] else {
        return [[:]]
    }
    return items
}
func fetch(completion: (_ annotations:
[RestaurantItem]) -> ()){
    if !items.isEmpty {
        items.removeAll()
    }
    for data in loadData() {
        items.append(RestaurantItem(dict: data))
    }
    completion(items)
}
```

The `loadData()` and `fetch(completion:)` methods perform the same tasks as the `loadData()` and `fetch()` methods in the `ExploreDataManager` class.

> **Tip**
> You may wish to re-read *Chapter 14, Getting Data into Collection Views*, to refresh your memory on the `ExploreDataManager` class.

However, the `loadData()` method used here is able to return an array containing dictionaries where the values are of the `AnyObject` type. This is necessary since the `MapLocations.plist` file, unlike the `ExploreData.plist` file, does not exclusively contain dictionaries of the `[String: String]` type. Also, the `fetch(completion:)` method used here has a completion closure as a parameter, which can accept any function or closure that takes an array of `RestaurantItems` as a parameter:

```
(_ annotations:[RestaurantItem]) -> ())
```

Sometimes, you don't know when an operation will be finished. For example, you need to do an action after you've downloaded a file from the internet, but you don't know how long it would take to download. You can specify a completion closure to be applied once the operation has been completed. In this case, the completion closure will process the `items` array once all the data from the `.plist` file has been read.

Now consider the `MapLocations.plist` file once more:

Key	Type	Value
∨ Root	Array	(5 items)
∨ Item 0	Dictionary	(16 items)
address	String	108 West 2nd Street #104
area	String	Los Angeles / Orange County
city	String	Los Angeles

Figure 16.2: Editor area showing array and dictionaries in MapLocations.plist

This file has the same structure as `ExploreData.plist`. The `Root` item is an array that contains dictionaries. Since both `ExploreData.plist` and `MapLocations.plist` have an array of dictionaries, it would be more efficient if you could create a single method to load `.plist` files and use it wherever it was needed. You will do this in the next section.

Creating the DataManager protocol

Instead of creating a method in each class to load a `.plist` file, you will create a new protocol, `DataManager`, to handle `.plist` file loading. This protocol will implement a method to load `.plist` files using an extension.

> **Tip**
> You may wish to re-read *Chapter 8, Protocols, Extensions, and Error Handling*, which covers protocols and extensions.

After you have created the `DataManager` protocol, any class that needs to load a `.plist` file can adopt it. You'll modify both `ExploreDataManager` and `MapDataManager` classes to adopt this protocol. Follow these steps:

1. Right-click the `LetsEat` folder and create a new group called `Misc`.

2. Right-click on the `Misc` folder and choose **New File**.

3. **iOS** should already be selected. Choose **Swift File** and then click **Next**.

4. Name this file `DataManager`. Click **Create**.

5. Click the `DataManager` file in the Project navigator and declare the `DataManager` protocol as follows:

```
import Foundation
protocol DataManager {
    func loadPlist(file name: String) ->
    [[String: AnyObject]]
}
```

This protocol requires any conforming object to have a method named `loadPlist(file:)` that takes a string as a parameter and returns an array of dictionaries. The string will hold the name of the `.plist` file to be loaded.

6. Add an extension containing the implementation of the `loadPlist(file:)` method after the protocol declaration:

```
import Foundation
protocol DataManager {
    func loadPlist(file name: String) ->
    [[String: AnyObject]]
}
extension DataManager {
    func loadPlist(file name: String) ->
    [[String:AnyObject]] {
        guard let path = Bundle.main.path(forResource:
        name, ofType: "plist"),
        let itemsData = FileManager.default
        .contents(atPath: path),
        let items = try! PropertyListSerialization
        .propertyList(from: itemsData, format: nil)
        as? [[String: AnyObject]] else {
            return [[:]]
        }
        return items
    }
}
```

Any class that adopts this protocol will get the `loadPlist(file:)` method. This method looks for a `.plist` file specified in the `name` parameter inside the application bundle. If the file is not found, an empty array of dictionaries is returned. Otherwise, the contents of the `.plist` file are loaded into an array of dictionaries of type `[String: AnyObject]` and returned.

Now that you have this protocol, you will modify the `MapDataManager` and `ExploreDataManager` classes to adopt it. When you take existing code and modify it to accomplish the same thing more efficiently, this process is called **refactoring**.

You will start with refactoring the `MapDataManager` class to conform to the `DataManager` protocol in the next section.

Refactoring the MapDataManager class

The `MapDataManager` class already has a `loadData()` method, which is hardcoded to read `Maplocations.plist`. Now that you have created the `DataManager` protocol, you will modify the `MapDataManager` class to use it instead. Follow these steps:

1. With the `MapDataManager` file selected in the Project navigator, find and delete the `loadData()` method. You'll see an error because the `fetch()` method calls the `loadData()` method, which you just removed. You'll fix this shortly.

2. Add the `DataManager` protocol to the class declaration as follows:

```
class MapDataManager: DataManager
```

This makes the `loadPlist(file:)` method available to the `MapDataManager` class.

3. Modify the `for data in loadData()` line in the `fetch()` method as follows to fix the error:

```
for data in loadPlist(file: "MapLocations")
```

Your updated `MapDataManager` class should look like this:

```
import Foundation
class MapDataManager: DataManager {
    private var items: [RestaurantItem] = []
    var annotations: [RestaurantItem] {
        items
    }
    func fetch(completion: (_ annotations:
    [RestaurantItem]) -> ()){
```

```
        if !items.isEmpty {
            items.removeAll()
        }
        for data in loadPlist(file: "MapLocations") {
            items.append(RestaurantItem(dict: data))
        }
        completion(items)
    }
}
```

The error should be gone. In the next section, you will refactor the
ExploreDataManager class as well to make it conform to the DataManager protocol.

Refactoring the ExploreDataManager class

Like the MapDataManager class, the ExploreDataManager class has a loadData()
method, which is hardcoded to read ExploreData.plist.

> **Tip**
> You may wish to re-read *Chapter 14, Getting Data into Collection Views*, to
> refresh your memory on the ExploreDataManager class.

You need to make the same changes to the ExploreDataManager class that you made
to the MapDataManager class. Follow these steps:

1. With the ExploreDataManager file selected in the Project navigator, find and
    delete the loadData() method. Ignore the error because it will be fixed shortly.

2. Add the DataManager protocol to the class declaration as follows:

    ```
    class ExploreDataManager: DataManager
    ```

    This makes the loadPlist(file:) method available to the
    ExploreDataManager class.

3. Modify the `fetch()` method as follows to fix the error:

```
func fetch() {
    for data in loadPlist(file: "ExploreData") {
        exploreItems.append(ExploreItem(dict: data
        as! [String: String]))
    }
}
```

Note that `data` is cast as `[String: String]` so that it can be used to initialize instances of the `ExploreItem` class.

You can now make any class that needs to load a `.plist` file containing an array of dictionaries adopt the `DataManager` protocol, as you did here with the `MapDataManager` and `ExploreDataManager` classes. It's not always clear when you should refactor, but the more experience you have, the easier it becomes. One indication that you need to refactor is when you are writing the same code in more than one class.

You have completed the implementation of the `MapDataManager` class, created the `DataManager` protocol, and refactored both the `MapDataManager` and `ExploreDataManager` classes to conform to this protocol. With the `MapDataManager` class, you can load data from the `MapLocations.plist` file and return an array of `RestaurantItem` instances. Now, let's see how to use this array to add annotations to a map view, which will be displayed as pins in the **Map** screen.

Adding annotations to a map view

In *Chapter 11, Finishing Up Your User Interface*, you added a map view to the **Map** screen. In previous sections, you added the `MapLocations.plist` file to your project and created the `RestaurantItem` and `MapDataManager` classes. Remember the MVC design pattern? At this point, you have created the views and models for the **Map** screen, so all you need now is the view controller.

The view controller will be responsible for the following tasks:

- Adding `RestaurantItem` instances, which conform to the `MKAnnotation` protocol, to the map view.

- For `RestaurantItem` instances within the region displayed in the map view, provide `MKAnnotationView` instances requested by the map view.

- Provide custom `MKAnnotationView` instances that display a callout bubble containing a button when tapped, and present the **Restaurant Detail** screen when the button is tapped.

You'll start by creating the `MapViewController` class as the view controller for the **Map** screen in the next section.

Creating the MapViewController class

You've created the view and model objects for the **Map** screen, and all that remains is to create the view controller for it. You'll create a new class, `MapViewController`, to be the view controller for the **Map** screen. Follow these steps:

1. Right-click the `Map` folder and select **New File**.

2. **iOS** should already be selected. Choose **Cocoa Touch Class** and then click **Next**.

3. Configure the file as follows:

   Class: `MapViewController`

   Subclass: `UIViewController`

   Also create XIB: Unchecked

   Language: `Swift`

   Click **Next**.

4. Click **Create**. The `MapViewController` file appears in the Project navigator.

5. In the `MapViewController` file, add the following line after `import UIKit` to import the `MapKit` framework:

```
import MapKit
```

6. Modify the class declaration as follows to make the `MapViewController` class adopt the `MKMapViewDelegate` protocol:

```
class MapViewController: UIViewController,
MKMapViewDelegate {
```

You have declared the `MapViewController` class. In the next section, you'll assign this class as the view controller for the **Map** screen, and create an outlet for the map view.

Connecting the outlets for the map view

The view controller scene for the **Map** screen displays a map, but there is currently no way to set the map region to be displayed and no way to display annotations. Let's assign the `MapViewController` class to be the view controller for the **Map** screen and add an outlet for the map view to it. Follow these steps:

1. Click the `Main` storyboard file. Click the **View Controller** icon in the **View Controller Scene** for the **Map** screen. In the Identity inspector, under **Custom Class**, set **Class** to `MapViewController`:

Figure 16.3: Identity inspector showing Class setting for MapViewController

2. Select the **Map View** in the document outline:

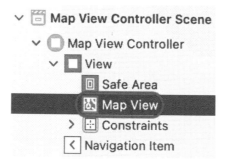

Figure 16.4: Document outline with Map View selected

3. Click the Adjust Editor Options button.

4. Choose Assistant in the pop-up menu.

5. The assistant editor appears, showing the contents of the `MapViewController` file. *Ctrl + Drag* from the map view to the space just under the class declaration:

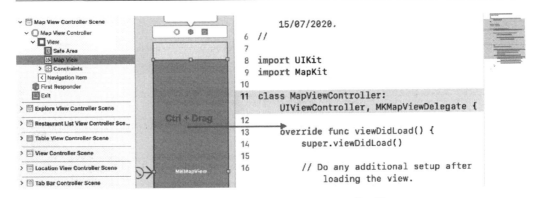

```
              15/07/2020.
  6  //
  7
  8  import UIKit
  9  import MapKit
 10
 11  class MapViewController:
         UIViewController, MKMapViewDelegate {
 12
 13     override func viewDidLoad() {
 14        super.viewDidLoad()
 15
 16        // Do any additional setup after
                loading the view.
```

Figure 16.5: Editor area showing MapViewController file contents

6. Type `mapView` in the **Name** field and click **Connect**:

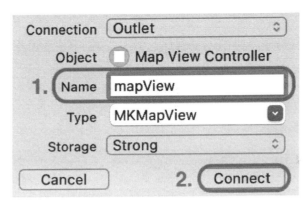

Figure 16.6: Pop-up dialog box for mapView outlet creation

7. The map view has been connected to the `mapView` outlet in the
    `MapViewController` class. Click the **x** button to close the assistant editor:

Figure 16.7: Assistant editor close button

The `MapViewController` class now has an outlet, `mapView`, that is linked to the map view in the **Map** screen. In the next section, you'll modify the `MapDataManager` class by adding a method to generate a new region based on the restaurant's location, so it can provide a map region for the map view to display.

Setting the map view region to be displayed

In a map view, the portion of the map that is visible on screen is called a region. To specify a region, you need the coordinates for the region's center point and the horizontal and vertical span representing the dimensions of the map to be displayed.

The `fetch(completion:)` method in the `MapDataManager` class returns an array of `RestaurantItem` instances. You will implement a method, `initialRegion(latDelta:longDelta:)`, to get the first `RestaurantItem` instance from this array, get the restaurant's coordinates, and use them to create a region. Follow these steps:

1. Click the `MapDataManager` file in the Project navigator. After the `import Foundation` statement, add `import MapKit`.

2. Just before the closing curly brace, implement the `initialRegion(latDelta:longDelta:)` method as follows:

```
func initialRegion(latDelta: CLLocationDegrees,
  longDelta: CLLocationDegrees) -> MKCoordinateRegion {
    guard let item = items.first else {
        return MKCoordinateRegion()
    }
    let span = MKCoordinateSpan(latitudeDelta:
    latDelta, longitudeDelta: longDelta)
    return MKCoordinateRegion(center: item.coordinate,
    span: span)
}
```

Let's break this down:

```
func initialRegion(latDelta: CLLocationDegrees,
  longDelta: CLLocationDegrees) -> MKCoordinateRegion
```

This method takes two parameters and returns an `MKCoordinateRegion`
instance. `latDelta` specifies the north-to-south distance (measured in degrees)
to display for the map region. One degree is approximately 69 miles. `longDelta`
specifies the amount of east-to-west distance (measured in degrees) to display for
the map region. The `MKCoordinateRegion` instance that is returned determines
the region that will appear onscreen.

```
guard let item = items.first else { return
MKCoordinateRegion() }
```

The `guard` statement gets the first item in the array of `RestaurantItem`
instances and assigns it to `item`. If the array is empty, an empty
`MKCoordinateRegion` instance is returned.

```
let span = MKCoordinateSpan(latitudeDelta: latDelta,
longitudeDelta: longDelta)
```

`latDelta` and `longDelta` are used to make an `MKCoordinateSpan` instance,
which is the horizontal and vertical span of the region to be created.

```
return MKCoordinateRegion(center: item.coordinate, span:
span)
```

An `MKCoordinateRegion` instance is created and returned using the coordinate
property of `item` and the `MKCoordinateSpan` instance.

Now that the map region has been determined, you can determine which
`RestaurantItem` instances are in this region based on their `coordinate` property.
Remember that the `RestaurantItem` class conforms to `MKAnnotation`. As the view
controller for the map view, the `MapViewController` class is responsible for providing
`MKAnnotationView` instances for any `RestaurantItem` instances in this region.

In the next section, you'll modify the `MapViewController` class to provide
`MKAnnotationViews` for the `RestaurantItem` instances in the region displayed by
the map view.

Displaying MKAnnotationView instances on the map view

At this point, you have the `MapViewController` class to manage the map view on the **Map** screen, and you can call the `initialRegion(latDelta:longDelta:)` method in the `MapDataManager` class to set the map region. You will now modify the `MapViewController` class to get an array of `RestaurantItem` instances from the `MapDataManager` class and add it to the map view. Follow these steps:

1. Click the `MapViewController` file in the Project navigator and remove the commented code.

2. Just after the `mapView` property declaration, add the following to create an instance of the `MapDataManager` class and assign it to `manager`:

   ```
   private let manager = MapDataManager()
   ```

3. Add the following method after `viewDidLoad()`. This method will add `RestaurantItem` instances (which conform to the `MKAnnotation` protocol) to the map view:

   ```
   func setupMap(_ annotations: [RestaurantItem]) {
       mapView.setRegion(manager.initialRegion(
       latDelta: 0.5, longDelta: 0.5), animated: true)
       mapView.addAnnotations(manager.annotations)
   }
   ```

   The `setupMap(_:)` method takes a parameter, `annotations`, which is an array of `RestaurantItem` instances. It sets the region of the map to be displayed in the map view using the `initialRegion(latDelta:longDelta:)` method of the `MapDataManager` class, then adds each `RestaurantItem` instance in the `annotations` array to the map view. The map view's delegate (the `MapViewController` class in this case) then automatically provides an `MKAnnotationView` instance for every `RestaurantItem` instance within the region.

4. Add the following method before the `setupMap(_:)` method. This calls the `fetch(completion:)` method of the `MapDataManager` instance and passes in the `setupMap(_:)` method as a completion closure:

   ```
   func initialize() {
       manager.fetch { (annotations) in
   ```

```
        setupMap(annotations)}
    }
```

The `fetch(completion:)` method loads the `MapLocations.plist` file and creates and assigns the array of `RestaurantItem` instances to the `items` array. The `annotations` property returns a copy of the `items` array. This array is then processed by the `setupMap(_:)` method that was passed in as the completion closure.

5. Call the `initialize()` method inside `viewDidLoad()` so it will be called when the map view is loaded:

```
override func viewDidLoad() {
    super.viewDidLoad()
    initialize()
}
```

Build and run the application. You should see pins (`MKAnnotationView` instances) on the **Map** screen:

Figure 16.8: iOS Simulator showing standard MKAnnotationView instances

An `MKAnnotationView` instance has been added for each `RestaurantItem` instance in the map region. Each `MKAnnotationView` instance is represented by a pin. You now have pins showing restaurant locations on your map, but you need to add code to display custom pins as shown in the app tour. You will do that in the next section.

Creating custom MKAnnotationView instances

Currently, the **Map** screen displays standard `MKAnnotationView` instances, which look like pins. You can replace the standard pin image with a custom image. There is a custom image in the `Assets.xcassets` file, and you'll configure the `MapViewController` class to use it. This will make the pins onscreen match the ones in the app tour. You'll also configure each pin to display a callout bubble when tapped. Follow these steps:

1. Click the `MapViewController` file in the Project navigator.

2. Add the following code inside the `initialize()` method after the opening curly brace. This makes the `MapViewController` class the delegate for the map view:

```
func initialize() {
    mapView.delegate = self
```

3. Add the following method after the `setupMap(_:)` method. This method returns a custom `MKAnnotationView` instance for every `MKAnnotation` instance in the region displayed by the map view:

```
func mapView(_ mapView: MKMapView, viewFor annotation:
MKAnnotation) -> MKAnnotationView? {
    let identifier = "custompin"
    guard !annotation.isKind(of: MKUserLocation.self)
    else {
        return nil
    }

    let annotationView: MKAnnotationView
    if let customAnnotationView =
    mapView.dequeueReusableAnnotationView(
    withIdentifier: identifier) {
        annotationView = customAnnotationView
        annotationView.annotation = annotation
    } else {
        let av = MKAnnotationView(annotation:
        annotation, reuseIdentifier: identifier)
```

```
         av.rightCalloutAccessoryView =
         UIButton(type: .detailDisclosure)
         annotationView = av
    }
    annotationView.canShowCallout = true
    if let image = UIImage(named:
         "custom-annotation") {
            annotationView.image = image
            annotationView.centerOffset = CGPoint(
         x: -image.size.width / 2,
         y: -image.size.height / 2)
    }
    return annotationView
}
```

Let's break this down:

```
func mapView(_ mapView: MKMapView, viewFor
annotation: MKAnnotation) -> MKAnnotationView?
```

This is one of the delegate methods specified in the `MKMapViewDelegate` protocol. It's triggered when an `MKAnnotation` instance is within the map region, and it returns an `MKAnnotationView` instance, which the user will see on the screen. You'll use this method to replace the default pins with custom pins.

```
let identifier = "custompin"
```

A constant, `identifier`, is assigned the `"custompin"` string. This will be the reuse identifier.

```
guard !annotation.isKind(of: MKUserLocation.self)
else {
    return nil
}
```

In addition to the annotations that you specify, an `MKMapView` instance will also add an annotation for the user location. This `guard` statement checks to see whether the annotation is the user location. If it is, `nil` is returned, as the user location is not a restaurant location.

```
let annotationView: MKAnnotationView
```

`annotationView` is a constant of the `MKAnnotationView` type. You create this so that you can configure and return it later.

```
if let customAnnotationView =
mapView.dequeueReusableAnnotationView (withIdentifier:
identifier) {
    annotationView = customAnnotationView
    annotationView.annotation = annotation
}
```

The `if` statement checks to see whether there are any existing annotations that were initially visible but are no longer on the screen. If there are, the `MKAnnotationView` instance for that annotation can be reused and is assigned to the `annotationView` variable. The `annotation` parameter is assigned to the `annotation` property of `annotationView`.

```
else {
    let av = MKAnnotationView(annotation: annotation,
    reuseIdentifier: identifier)
    av.rightCalloutAccessoryView =
    UIButton(type: .detailDisclosure)
    annotationView = av
}
```

The `else` clause is executed if there are no existing `MKAnnotationView` instances that can be reused. A new `MKAnnotationView` instance is created with the reuse identifier specified earlier (`custompin`). The `MKAnnotationView` instance is configured with a callout. When you tap a pin on the map, a callout bubble will appear showing the title (restaurant name), subtitle (cuisines), and a button. You'll program the button later to present the **Restaurant Detail** screen.

```
annotationView.canShowCallout = true
if let image = UIImage(named: "custom-annotation") {
    annotationView.image = image
    annotationView.centerOffset = CGPoint(
    x: -image.size.width / 2,
    y: -image.size.height / 2)
}
```

This configures the MKAnnotationView instance that you just created to display extra information in a callout bubble and sets the custom image to the custom-annotation image stored in Assets.xcassets. When adding a custom image, the annotation uses the center of the image as the pin point, so the centerOffset property is used to set the correct location of the pin point, at the tip of the pin.

```
return annotationView
```

The custom MKAnnotationView instance is returned.

Build and run your app. You can see the custom pins on your map:

Figure 16.9: iOS Simulator showing custom MKAnnotationView instances

You have configured the **Map** screen to display a region containing custom MKAnnotationView instances using the data obtained from the MapDataManager class. Tapping a pin displays a callout bubble showing the restaurant name and the cuisines it offers. Tapping the button in the callout bubble doesn't do anything yet. You'll configure the button to present the **Restaurant Detail** screen in the next section.

Going from the Map screen to the Restaurant Detail screen

The **Map** screen now displays your custom MKAnnotationView instances, and tapping one displays a callout bubble showing restaurant details. The button in the callout bubble doesn't work, though.

Inside the `resources` folder that you downloaded earlier, you'll find completed storyboards named `RestaurantDetail.Storyboard`, `PhotoFilter.Storyboard`, and `ReviewForm.Storyboard`, which you'll add to your project. These storyboards contain the scenes for the **Restaurant Detail** screen, the **Photo Filter** screen and the **Review Form** screen.

To present the **Restaurant Detail** screen from the callout button, you'll add a **storyboard reference** to your project, and link the `RestaurantDetail` storyboard file to it. You'll do this in the next section.

Creating and configuring a storyboard reference

There are a lot of scenes in the `Main` storyboard file. As your project grows, you'll find it more challenging to keep track of all the scenes in your app. One way to manage this is to create additional storyboard files, and use storyboard references to link them. You will add `RestaurantDetail`, `PhotoFilter` and `ReviewForm` storyboard files to your project, and you will link the `Main` storyboard file to the `RestaurantDetail` storyboard file using a storyboard reference. Follow these steps to add a storyboard reference to your project:

1. Open the `Main` storyboard file, and click the Library button.

2. Type `story` in the filter field. A **Storyboard Reference** object will appear in the results.

3. Drag the **Storyboard Reference** object into the `Main` storyboard file next to the **Map View Controller Scene**:

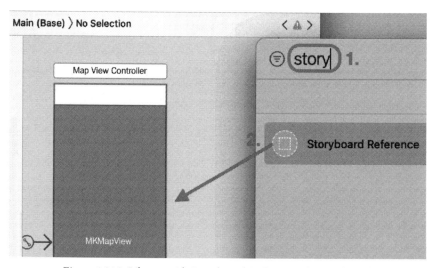

Figure 16.10: Library with Storyboard Reference object selected

4. Open the `resources` folder that you downloaded earlier, and locate the three storyboard files that you will add to your project in it (`RestaurantDetail.storyboard`, `PhotoFilter.storyboard`, and `ReviewForm.storyboard`):

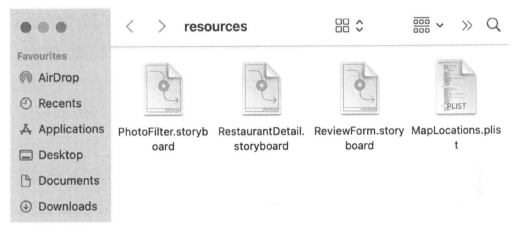

Figure 16.11: Contents of resources folder

5. In the Project navigator, create a new folder inside your `LetsEat` folder named `RestaurantDetail` and copy the `RestaurantDetail` storyboard file into it:

Figure 16.12: Project navigator showing RestaurantDetail folder and contents

6. Create a new folder inside your LetsEat folder named ReviewForm and copy the ReviewForm storyboard file into it, and create a new folder inside your LetsEat folder named PhotoFilter and copy the PhotoFilter storyboard file into it:

Figure 16.13: Project navigator showing PhotoFilter and ReviewForm folders and contents

7. Now you'll assign the RestaurantDetail storyboard file to the storyboard reference you added earlier to your project. Click the Main storyboard file, select the storyboard reference you added earlier, and click the Attributes inspector button. Under **Storyboard Reference**, set **Storyboard** to RestaurantDetail:

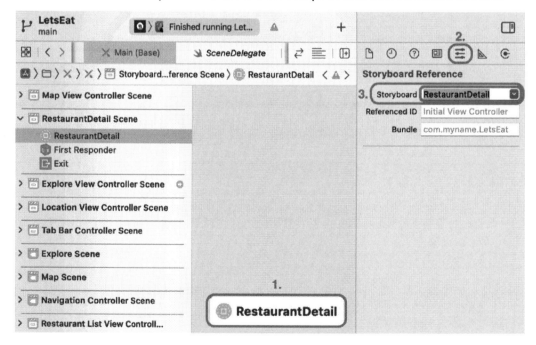

Figure 16.14: Attributes inspector settings for RestaurantDetail storyboard reference

8. *Ctrl + Drag* from the **Map View Controller** icon to the storyboard reference and choose **Show** from the pop-up menu to add a segue between the **Map View Controller Scene** and the storyboard reference:

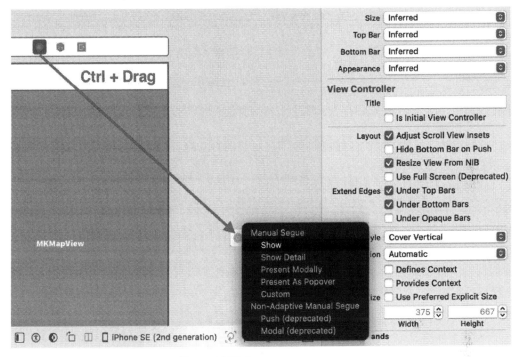

Figure 16.15: Segue pop-up menu

This is required to display the **Restaurant Detail** screen when you tap an MKAnnotationView instance's callout bubble button in the **Map** screen.

9. You will set an identifier for this segue. Later you'll add a method that performs the segue with this identifier when the callout bubble button is tapped. Select the segue connecting the **Map View Controller Scene** to the storyboard reference:

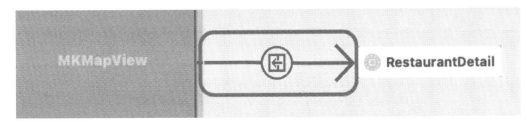

Figure 16.16: Segue between Map View Controller Scene and RestaurantDetail storyboard reference

10. In the Attributes inspector, under **Storyboard Segue**, set **Identifier** to `showDetail`:

Figure 16.17: Attributes inspector settings for showDetail segue

You have now linked the view controller scene for the **Map** screen with the view controller scene for the **Restaurant Detail** screen using a segue. In the next section, you'll implement a method to present the **Restaurant Detail** screen when the callout bubble button is tapped.

Performing the showDetail segue

You've linked the view controller scene for the **Map** screen to the view controller scene for the **Restaurant Detail** screen using a segue. You've also set the segue identifier to `showDetail`. Now you need a method to perform that segue, but before you implement it, you'll create an enumeration that contains all the segue identifiers for this project. This reduces potential errors by enabling autocompletion when you type the segue identifiers later in your code. Follow these steps:

1. Right-click on the `Misc` folder inside the `LetsEat` folder and choose **New File**.

2. **iOS** should already be selected. Choose **Swift File** and then click **Next**.

3. Name this file `Segue`. Click **Create**. The `Segue` file appears in the Project navigator.

4. Add the following after the `import` statement to declare and define the `Segue` enumeration:

```
enum Segue: String {
    case showDetail
    case showRating
    case showReview
    case showAllReviews
    case restaurantList
```

```
    case locationList
    case showPhotoReview
    case showPhotoFilter
}
```

Note that the `Segue` enum's type is `String`, so the raw values for each case are strings. For example, the raw value for case `showDetail` is `"showDetail"`.

Now you can add the method to perform the `showDetail` segue when the callout button is tapped. Click the `MapViewController` file in the Project navigator and add the following method after the `setupMap(_:)` method:

```
func mapView(_ mapView: MKMapView, annotationView view:
MKAnnotationView, calloutAccessoryControlTapped control:
UIControl) {
    self.performSegue(withIdentifier:
    Segue.showDetail.rawValue, sender: self)
}
```

`mapView(_:annotationView:calloutAccessoryControlTapped:)` is another method specified in the `MKMapViewDelegate` protocol. It is triggered when the user taps the callout bubble button.

`self.performSegue(withIdentifier: Segue.showDetail.rawValue, sender: self)` performs the segue with the `"showDetail"` identifier, which presents the **Restaurant Detail** screen.

Build and run your project. On the **Map** screen, tap a pin and tap the button inside the callout bubble:

Figure 16.18: iOS Simulator showing callout bubble button

The new **Restaurant Detail** screen appears, but it does not contain any details about the restaurant:

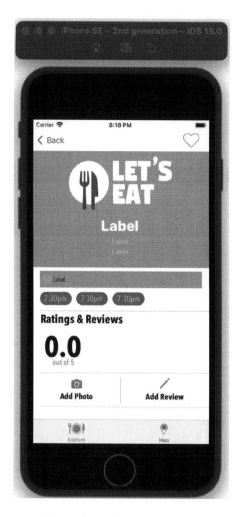

Figure 16.19: iOS Simulator showing Restaurant Detail screen

You will make the **Restaurant Detail** screen display the details of a restaurant in *Chapter 18, Displaying Data in a Static Table View*, but for now, let's just pass the data about the selected restaurant to the **Restaurant Detail** screen's view controller and print it to the Debug area. You will do this in the next section.

Passing data to the Restaurant Detail screen

The **Map** screen now displays custom MKAnnotationView instances that display callout bubbles when tapped. When the button in the callout bubble is tapped, the **Restaurant Detail** screen appears, but it does not contain any data about the restaurant. You'll need to pass restaurant data from the associated RestaurantItem instance to the view controller for the **Restaurant Detail** screen, which has not been created yet. Follow these steps to create it now:

1. Right-click the RestaurantDetail folder and select **New File**.

2. **iOS** should already be selected. Choose **Cocoa Touch Class** and then click **Next**.

3. Configure the file as follows:

    Class: RestaurantDetailViewController

    Subclass: UITableViewController

    Also create XIB: Unchecked

    Language: Swift

    Click **Next**.

4. Click **Create**. The RestaurantDetailViewController file appears in the Project navigator.

5. Remove all the commented code. Your file should look like this:

```
import UIKit
class RestaurantDetailViewController:
UITableViewController {
    override func viewDidLoad() {
        super.viewDidLoad()
    }
}
```

6. Declare a property named selectedRestaurant before the viewDidLoad() method:

```
var selectedRestaurant: RestaurantItem?
```

This property holds the RestaurantItem instance that will be passed to the RestaurantDetailViewController instance from the MapViewController instance:

7. Add the following code inside the `viewDidLoad()` method before the closing curly brace to print the `RestaurantItem` instance contents to the Debug area:

```
dump(selectedRestaurant as Any)
```

This confirms that the `MapViewController` instance has successfully passed the `RestaurantItem` instance to the `RestaurantDetailViewController` instance.

8. Verify your file looks like the following:

```
import UIKit
class RestaurantDetailViewController:
UITableViewController {
    var selectedRestaurant: RestaurantItem?
    override func viewDidLoad() {
        super.viewDidLoad()
        dump(selectedRestaurant as Any)
    }
}
```

9. Click the `RestaurantDetail` storyboard file inside the `RestaurantDetail` folder. Select the **Table View Controller Scene** in the storyboard. Click the Identity inspector button. Under **Custom Class**, set **Class** to `RestaurantDetailViewController`:

Figure 16.20: Identity inspector settings for Restaurant Detail View Controller scene

Note the scene name will change to **Restaurant Detail View Controller Scene**.

10. Click the `MapViewController` file in the Project navigator.

11. Add a property to hold a `RestaurantItem` instance after the `private let manager = MapDataManager()` statement:

```
var selectedRestaurant: RestaurantItem?
```

12. Add the following code into the `func mapView(_:annotationView:calloutAccessoryControlTapped:)` method, before the `self.performSegue(withIdentifier:sender:)` method call:

```
func mapView(_ mapView: MKMapView, annotationView
view: MKAnnotationView, calloutAccessoryControlTapped
control: UIControl) {
    guard let annotation =
    mapView.selectedAnnotations.first else {
        return
    }
    selectedRestaurant = annotation as? RestaurantItem
    self.performSegue(withIdentifier:
    Segue.showDetail.rawValue, sender: self)
}
```

This gets the `RestaurantItem` instance associated with `MKAnnotationView` instance that was tapped and assigns it to `selectedRestaurant`.

13. To pass the `RestaurantItem` instance from the `MapViewController` instance to the `RestaurantDetailViewController` instance, you'll override the `UIViewController` method named `prepare(for:sender:)`. Type in the following code after `viewDidLoad()`:

```
override func prepare(for segue: UIStoryboardSegue,
sender: Any?) {
    switch segue.identifier! {
        case Segue.showDetail.rawValue:
            showRestaurantDetail(segue: segue)
        default:
            print("Segue not added")
```

```
        }
    }
```

The `prepare(for:sender:)` method is executed by a view controller before transitioning to another view controller. In this case, this method is called before the **Map** screen transitions to the **Restaurant Detail** screen. If the segue's identifier is `showDetail`, which it is in this case, the `showRestaurantDetail(segue:)` method is called. This method will set the `selectedRestaurant` property for the `RestaurantDetailViewController` instance. You'll see an error because `showRestaurantDetail(segue:)` has not been created yet.

14. Add the following code after the `setupMap(_:)` method to implement `showRestaurantDetail(segue:)`:

```
func showRestaurantDetail(segue: UIStoryboardSegue) {
    if let viewController = segue.destination as?
    RestaurantDetailViewController, let restaurant =
    selectedRestaurant {
        viewController.selectedRestaurant = restaurant
    }
}
```

This checks to make sure the segue destination is a `RestaurantDetailViewController` instance. If it is, a temporary constant, `restaurant`, is assigned the `selectedRestaurant` property in the `MapViewController` instance. `restaurant` is then assigned to the `selectedRestaurant` property in the `RestaurantDetailViewController` instance.

In other words, the restaurant details that you get from the `RestaurantItem` instance is passed to the `RestaurantDetailViewController` instance.

Build and run your app. In the **Map** screen, tap a pin and then tap the callout button. The **Restaurant Detail** screen will appear. Click the Report navigator and click the first entry as shown. You should see the restaurant details in the Editor area:

Figure 16.21: Report navigator showing contents of first entry

You have added the storyboard for the **Restaurant Detail** screen to your project, connected it to the **Map** screen, and have successfully passed data from a selected restaurant in the **Map** screen to the **Restaurant Detail** screen. The `RestaurantDetailViewController` instance now has the data from the `RestaurantItem` instance that was selected on the **Map** screen. Great! You'll configure the **Restaurant Detail** screen to display that data in the next chapter.

You have done a lot of work in this chapter, so before you go on to the next chapter, let's organize the code that you have written to make it easier to understand. You will use extensions to do so in the next section.

Organizing your code

As your programs become more complex, you will use extensions (covered in *Chapter 8, Protocols, Extensions, and Error Handling*) to organize your code. Extensions can help you to make code more readable and avoid clutter.

You will organize four classes: `ExploreViewController`, `RestaurantListViewController`, `LocationViewController`, and `MapViewController`. You will segregate blocks of related code using extensions. Let's begin with the `ExploreViewController` class in the next section.

Refactoring the ExploreViewController class

You will divide the code in the `ExploreViewController` file into distinct sections using extensions. Follow these steps:

1. Click the `ExploreViewController` file in the Project navigator. After the final curly brace, add the following:

    ```
    // MARK: Private Extension
    private extension ExploreViewController {
        // code goes here
    }
    // MARK: UICollectionViewDataSource
    extension ExploreViewController:
    UICollectionViewDataSource {
        // code goes here
    }
    ```

    Here, you are creating two extensions. The first extension will be private, which means the contents of this extension are only accessible to the `ExploreViewController` class. The second extension will contain all of the `UICollectionViewDataSource` methods.

2. You'll get an error because `UICollectionViewDataSource` appears in two places. Delete `UICollectionViewDataSource` from the class declaration at the top of the file. Your class declaration should look like this:

    ```
    class ExploreViewController: UIViewController,
    UICollectionViewDelegate {
    ```

3. Move all the `UICollectionViewDataSource` methods into the second extension. It should look like this:

    ```
    // MARK: UICollectionViewDataSource
    extension ExploreViewController:
    UICollectionViewDataSource {
        func collectionView(_ collectionView:
        UICollectionView, viewForSupplementaryElementOfKind
        kind: String, at indexPath: IndexPath) ->
        UICollectionReusableView {
            let headerView = collectionView.
            dequeueReusableSupplementaryView( ofKind: kind,
    ```

```
    withReuseIdentifier: "header", for: indexPath)
    return headerView
}
func collectionView(_ collectionView:
UICollectionView, numberOfItemsInSection
section: Int) -> Int {
    manager.numberOfExploreItems()
}
func collectionView(_ collectionView:
UICollectionView, cellForItemAt indexPath:
IndexPath) -> UICollectionViewCell {
    let cell = collectionView.dequeueReusableCell(
    withReuseIdentifier: "exploreCell", for:
    indexPath) as! ExploreCell
    let exploreItem = manager.exploreItem(at:
    indexPath.row)
    cell.exploreNameLabel.text = exploreItem.name
    cell.exploreImageView.image = UIImage(
    named: exploreItem.image!)
    return cell
}
}
```

To keep `viewDidLoad()` as clean as possible, you will create an `initialize()` method inside the `private` extension, and put everything you need to initialize the view controller in there. After that, you will call `initialize()` in `viewDidLoad()`.

4. Add the `initialize()` method inside the `private` extension:

```
func initialize() {
    manager.fetch()
}
```

5. Move the `unwindLocationCancel(segue:)` method inside the `private` extension as well.

6. Verify that the private extension looks like this:

```
// MARK: Private Extension
private extension ExploreViewController {
    func initialize() {
        manager.fetch()
    }
    @IBAction func unwindLocationCancel(segue:
    UIStoryboardSegue) {
    }
}
```

7. Finally, modify `viewDidLoad()` as follows:

```
override func viewDidLoad() {
    super.viewDidLoad()
    initialize()
}
```

The benefits of segregating your code in this way may not seem obvious now, but as your classes become more complex, you will find it is easier to look for a specific method and to maintain your code. Before you do the same to the other files, let's see how the // MARK: syntax is used in the next section.

Using the // MARK: syntax

The // MARK: syntax is used to navigate easily between different parts of your code. Let's see what it does:

1. Look at the path that is visible just under the Toolbar and click on the last part as shown:

Figure 16.22: Editor area showing path

2. A menu is displayed, and you will see both **Private Extension** and
UICollectionViewDataSource in it, generated by the `// MARK:` syntax. This
enables you to easily jump to these sections:

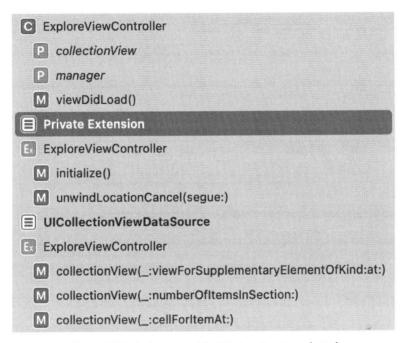

Figure 16.23: Path menu with Private extension selected

You have organized the `ExploreViewController` class, so let's do the
`RestaurantListViewController` class next by refactoring it and adding extensions.

Refactoring the RestaurantListViewController class

You will add two extensions to the `RestaurantListViewController` class, similar
to those you added to the `ExploreViewController` class. Follow these steps:

1. Click the `RestaurantListViewController` file in the Project navigator. After
the final curly brace, add the following:

```
// MARK: Private Extension
private extension RestaurantListViewController {
    // code goes here
}
// MARK: UICollectionViewDataSource
extension RestaurantListViewController:
```

```
UICollectionViewDataSource {
    // code goes here
}
```

You'll put private methods for the RestaurantListViewController class in the first extension, and all the UICollectionViewDataSource methods in the second extension.

2. Delete UICollectionViewDataSource from the class declaration at the top of the file. Your class declaration should look like this:

```
class RestaurantListViewController: UIViewController,
UICollectionViewDelegate {
```

3. Move all the UICollectionViewDataSource methods into the second extension. It should look like this when done:

```
// MARK: UICollectionViewDataSource extension
RestaurantListViewController:
UICollectionViewDataSource {
    func collectionView(_ collectionView:
    UICollectionView, numberOfItemsInSection
    section: Int) -> Int {
        1
    }
    func collectionView(_ collectionView:
    UICollectionView, cellForItemAt indexPath:
    IndexPath) -> UICollectionViewCell {
        collectionView.dequeueReusableCell(
        withReuseIdentifier: "restaurantCell",
        for: indexPath)
    }
}
```

You are done organizing the RestaurantListViewController class, so let's clean up the LocationViewController class in the next section.

Refactoring the LocationViewController class

As you did before, you will add two extensions to the `LocationViewController` file. Follow these steps:

1. Click the `LocationViewController` file in the Project navigator. After the final curly brace, add the following:

```
// MARK: Private Extension
private extension LocationViewController {
    // code goes here
}
// MARK: UITableViewDataSource
extension LocationViewController:
UITableViewDataSource {
    // code goes here
}
```

The first extension will contain private methods for the `LocationViewController` class. The second extension will contain all the `UITableViewDataSource` methods.

2. Delete `UITableViewDataSource` from the class declaration at the top of the file. Your class declaration should look like this:

```
class LocationViewController: UIViewController {
```

3. Move all the `UITableViewDataSource` methods into the second extension. It should look like this:

```
// MARK: UITableViewDataSource
extension LocationViewController: UITableViewDataSource
{
    func tableView(_ tableView: UITableView,
    numberOfRowsInSection section: Int) -> Int {
        manager.numberOfLocationItems()
    }
    func tableView(_ tableView: UITableView,
    cellForRowAt indexPath: IndexPath) ->
    UITableViewCell {
        let cell = tableView.dequeueReusableCell(
```

```
        withIdentifier: "locationCell", for: indexPath)
        cell.textLabel?.text =
        manager.locationItem(at: indexPath.row)
        return cell
    }
}
```

4. Just like you did in the `ExploreViewController` class, you will create an `initialize()` method inside the first extension, and put in it everything you need to initialize the `LocationViewController` class there. Add the following inside the first extension:

```
// MARK: Private Extension
private extension LocationViewController {
    func initialize() {
        manager.fetch()
    }
}
```

5. Modify `viewDidLoad()` as follows to call the `initialize()` method:

```
override func viewDidLoad() {
    super.viewDidLoad()
    initialize()
}
```

You are done organizing the `LocationViewController` class, so let's clean up the `MapViewController` class in the next section.

Refactoring the MapViewController class

As you did before for the other classes, you will add two extensions to the `MapViewController` class. Follow these steps:

1. Click the `MapViewController` file in the Project navigator. After the final curly brace, add the following:

```
// MARK: Private Extension
private extension MapViewController {
    // code goes here
}
```

```
// MARK: MKMapViewDelegate
extension MapViewController: MKMapViewDelegate {
    // code goes here
}
```

The first extension will contain private methods for the `MapViewController` class. The second one will contain all the `MKMapViewDelegate` methods.

2. Delete `MKMapViewDelegate` from the class declaration at the top of the file. Your class definition should look like this:

```
class MapViewController: UIViewController {
```

3. Move all the `MKMapViewDelegate` methods into the second extension. It should look like this:

```
// MARK: MKMapViewDelegate
extension MapViewController: MKMapViewDelegate {
    func mapView(_ mapView: MKMapView, annotationView
    view: MKAnnotationView,
    calloutAccessoryControlTapped control: UIControl){
        guard let annotation =
        mapView.selectedAnnotations.first else
        {
            return
        }
        selectedRestaurant = annotation as?
        RestaurantItem
        self.performSegue(withIdentifier:
        Segue.showDetail.rawValue, sender: self)
    }
    func mapView(_ mapView: MKMapView, viewFor
    annotation:MKAnnotation) -> MKAnnotationView? {
        let identifier = "custompin"
        guard !annotation.isKind(of:
        MKUserLocation.self) else {
            return nil
        }
        let annotationView: MKAnnotationView
        if let customAnnotationView = mapView.
```

```
dequeueReusableAnnotationView(withIdentifier:
identifier) {
    annotationView = customAnnotationView
    annotationView.annotation = annotation
} else {
    let av = MKAnnotationView(annotation:
    annotation, reuseIdentifier: identifier)
    av.rightCalloutAccessoryView =
    UIButton(type: .detailDisclosure)
    annotationView = av
}
annotationView.canShowCallout = true
if let image = UIImage(named: "custom-
annotation") {
    annotationView.image = image
    annotationView.centerOffset =
    CGPoint(x: -image.size.width / 2,
    y: -image.size height / 2 )
}
return annotationView
}
}
```

4. Move the `initialize()`, `setupMap(_:)`, and
   `showRestaurantDetail(segue:)` methods into the first extension. It should
   look like this:

```
// MARK: Private Extension
private extension MapViewController {
    func initialize() {
    mapView.delegate = self
    manager.fetch { (annotations) in
        setupMap(annotations)  }
    }
    func setupMap(_ annotations: [RestaurantItem]) {
        mapView.setRegion(manager.currentRegion(
        latDelta: 0.5, longDelta: 0.5), animated: true)
        mapView.addAnnotations(manager.annotations)
```

```
        }
    func showRestaurantDetail(segue:UIStoryboardSegue){
        if let viewController = segue.destination as?
        RestaurantDetailViewController, let restaurant
        = selectedRestaurant {
            viewController.selectedRestaurant
            = restaurant
        }
    }
}
```

You have organized all four view controllers (`ExploreViewController`, `RestaurantListViewController`, `LocationViewController`, and `MapViewController`) using extensions. Great job!

Summary

In this chapter, you created a new class, `RestaurantItem`, that conforms to the `MKAnnotation` protocol. Next, you created `MapDataManager`, a data manager class that loads restaurant data from a `.plist` file and puts it into an array of `RestaurantItem` instances. You created the `DataManager` protocol and refactored both `MapDataManager` and `ExploreDataManager` classes to use this protocol. After that, you created the `MapViewController` class, a view controller for the **Map** screen, and configured it to display custom annotations. You configured callout buttons in the custom annotations to present the **Restaurant Detail** screen. Next, you created the `RestaurantDetailViewController` class, a view controller for the **Restaurant Detail** screen, and passed data to it from the `MapViewController` instance. At this point, you know how to create objects that conform to the `MKAnnotation` protocol, how to add them to a map view, and how to create custom `MKAnnotationViews`, which enables you to add annotated maps to your own projects.

You also added storyboard files to your project, learned how to use storyboard references and organized your view controller classes (`ExploreViewController`, `RestaurantListViewController`, `LocationViewController`, and `MapViewController`) using extensions. This will help you organize storyboards and code for large projects, making it easier to read and maintain.

In the next chapter, you'll learn about **JSON** files, and how to load data from them so the **Restaurant List** and **Map** screens can display details about a particular restaurant.

17
Getting Started with JSON Files

In the previous chapter, you configured the **Map** screen to display a list of restaurants using data from a `.plist` file. You configured custom annotations for each restaurant location and configured the callout buttons in them to present the **Restaurant Detail** screen when tapped. You also organized your code using extensions to make it easier to read and maintain.

In this chapter, you will use data stored in **JavaScript Object Notation (JSON)** format to populate the **Map** and **Restaurant Detail** screens. You'll start by learning about the JSON format, create a data manager class that can load data from JSON files, and modify the **MapViewController** class to display a list of restaurants from a JSON file instead of a `.plist` file. Next, you'll configure the LocationViewController class to store the location selected by the user in the **Locations** screen and pass it to the ExploreViewController instance when the **Done** button is tapped. After that, you'll configure the ExploreViewController class to pass the selected location and cuisine to the RestaurantListViewController instance when a type of cuisine is selected. Finally, the RestaurantListViewController class will then be modified to get a list of restaurants from a JSON file corresponding to the selected location and cuisine and display them in the **Restaurant List** screen.

By the end of this chapter, you'll know how to load and parse data from JSON files for use in your own apps. You'll also learn about `UITableViewDelegate` methods and ways to pass data from one view controller to another.

The following topics will be covered:

- Getting data from JSON files

- Using data from JSON files in your app

- Configuring the `MapDataManager` instance to use data from the `RestaurantDataManager` instance

- Storing a user-selected location

- Passing location and cuisine information to the `RestaurantListViewController` instance

Technical requirements

You will continue working on the `LetsEat` project that you modified in the previous chapter.

The resource files and completed Xcode project for this chapter are in the `Chapter17` folder of the code bundle for this book, which can be downloaded here:

`https://github.com/PacktPublishing/iOS-15-Programming-for-Beginners-Sixth-Edition`

Check out the following video to see the code in action:

`https://bit.ly/3Hl8Ulz`

Let's start by learning how to read and parse JSON files to get data for use in your app.

Getting data from JSON files

In *Chapter 14, Getting Data into Collection Views*, you learned how to load a file, read data from it using a data manager class, and put it into objects in your app. In this chapter, you will also do the same thing, the difference is that you will be reading data from a JSON file instead of a `.plist` file. This will simulate reading data from an online web-based service, where JSON is a commonly used format. Let's start by learning more about JSON files and how they work.

Understanding the JSON format

JavaScript Object Notation (JSON) is a way to structure data in a file that can be easily read by both people and computers. Many iOS apps work with an online web-based service to access JSON files, which are then used to provide the app with data.

You will not be learning about how to connect to an online service in this chapter. Instead, you will use sample JSON files downloaded from `http://opentable.herokuapp.com`, which have been modified by Craig Clayton for this book. As you will see, working with JSON files is similar to working with `.plist` files.

To help you to understand the JSON format, you will add the sample JSON files to your project and look at the structure of one of them. Follow these steps:

1. In the Project navigator, create a new group inside the `Misc` folder and name it `JSON`.

2. If you have not yet downloaded the project files for this chapter, go ahead and download them from this link: `https://github.com/PacktPublishing/iOS-15-Programming-for-Beginners-Sixth-Edition`.

3. Unzip the folder and open the `resources` folder in the `Chapter17` folder. You should see several JSON files inside.

4. Drag all of the JSON files there into the `JSON` folder you just created.

5. Click **Finish** on the screen that appears.

6. Each JSON file contains restaurant details for a particular city. Click `Charleston.json` and you should see the following:

Figure 17.1: Editor area showing contents for Charleston.json

As you can see, the file starts with an opening square bracket, and each item inside consists of key-value pairs containing restaurant information, enclosed by curly braces and separated by commas. At the very end of the file, you can see a closing square bracket. The square brackets denote arrays, and the curly braces denote dictionaries. In other words, the JSON file contains an array of dictionaries, exactly the same as the .plist files you have been using earlier.

Now that you have seen what a JSON file looks like, let's create a data manager class to load data from JSON files into your app in the next section.

Creating the RestaurantDataManager class

You have learned how to create a data manager class to load data from a .plist file in *Chapter 14, Getting Data into Collection Views*. You will now create RestaurantDataManager, a data manager class that loads data from the JSON files that you added to your project earlier. As you will see, loading data from a JSON file will be similar to loading data from a .plist file.

> **Important Information**
>
> To learn more about parsing JSON files, watch the video available here: https://developer.apple.com/videos/play/wwdc2017/212/.

Before you create the RestaurantDataManager class, you'll need to modify the RestaurantItem class so it conforms to the Decodable protocol. Adopting this protocol allows you to use the JSONDecoder class to populate RestaurantItem instances using data from JSON files.

> **Important Information**
>
> To learn more about Decodable and the JSON Decoder class, see these links:
>
> https://developer.apple.com/documentation/foundation/archives_and_serialization/encoding_and_decoding_custom_types
>
> https://developer.apple.com/documentation/foundation/jsondecoder

To modify the `RestaurantItem` class so it conforms to the `Decodable` protocol, follow these steps:

1. In the Project navigator, click the `RestaurantItem` file inside the `Model` folder in the `Map` folder. Modify the class declaration for `RestaurantItem` as shown to adopt the `Decodable` protocol:

```
class RestaurantItem: NSObject, MKAnnotation,
Decodable {
```

2. Remove the `init()` method and add the following enumeration to make the `RestaurantItem` class conform to the `Decodable` protocol:

```
enum CodingKeys: String, CodingKey {
    case name
    case cuisines
    case lat
    case long
    case address
    case postalCode = "postal_code"
    case state
    case imageURL = "image_url"
    case restaurantID = "id"
}
```

The `CodingKeys` enumeration matches the `RestaurantItem` class properties to the keys in the JSON file. This allows the `JSONDecoder` instance to get values from the JSON file and assign them to properties in the `RestaurantItem` class. If the key name does not match the property name, you can map the key to the property, as shown in the preceding code block for `postalCode`, `imageURL`, and restaurantID.

After you modify the `RestaurantItem` class, you'll see an error in the `fetch(completion:)` method in the `MapDataManager` file. Don't worry about it as you will fix it in the next section.

Now let's create the `RestaurantDataManager` class, which will read the JSON file and put the data into an array of `RestaurantItem` instances. Follow these steps:

1. Right-click on the `Restaurants` folder and create a new group named `Model`. Then right-click on the `Model` folder and choose **New File**.

2. **iOS** should already be selected. Choose **Swift File** and then click **Next**.

3. Name this file `RestaurantDataManager`. Click **Create**. The `RestaurantDataManager` file appears in the Project navigator.

4. Add the following after the `import` statement to declare the `RestaurantDataManager` class:

```
class RestaurantDataManager {


}
```

5. Add the following property between the curly braces to hold an array of `RestaurantItem` instances:

```
private var restaurantItems: [RestaurantItem] = []
```

The `restaurantItems` array will store the `RestaurantItem` instances obtained from the JSON file. The `private` keyword means it is only accessible from within this class.

6. Add the following method after the `restaurantItems` property to read a JSON file and return an array of `RestaurantItem` instances:

```
func fetch(location: String, selectedCuisine:
String = "All", completionHandler: (_
restaurantItems: [RestaurantItem]) -> Void) {
    if let file = Bundle.main.url(forResource:
    location, withExtension: "json") {
        do {
            let data = try Data(contentsOf: file)
            let restaurants = try JSONDecoder().decode(
            [RestaurantItem].self, from: data)
            if selectedCuisine != "All" {
                restaurantItems = restaurants.filter {
                    ($0.cuisines.contains(selectedCuisine))
                }
```

```
        } else {
            restaurantItems = restaurants
        }
    } catch {
        print("There was an error \(error)")
    }
}
completionHandler(restaurantItems)
}
```

Let's break this down:

```
func fetch(location: String, selectedCuisine:
String = "All", completionHandler: (_ restaurantItems:
[RestaurantItem]) -> Void)
```

This method takes three parameters: `location`, a string containing the restaurant location, `selectedCuisine`, a string containing the cuisine selected by the user, and `completionHandler`, a closure used to process the result of this method when it has finished execution. If you do not provide a value for `selectedCuisine`, it will default to `"All"`.

```
if let file = Bundle.main.url(forResource: location,
withExtension: "json")
```

This gets the URL of the JSON file in the app bundle and assigns it to `file`.

`do` code block:

The first statement attempts to assign the contents of `file` to `data`. The next statement attempts to use a `JSONDecoder` instance to parse `data` and store it as an array of `RestaurantItem` instances, which is assigned to `restaurants`. In the next statement, if `selectedCuisine` is not `All`, the `filter` method is applied to the `restaurants` array using the `{ ($0.cuisines.contains(selectedCuisine)) }` closure. This results in an array of `RestaurantItem` instances where the `cuisines` property contains the user-selected cuisine, and this array is assigned to `restaurantItems`. Otherwise, the entire `restaurants` array is assigned to `restaurantItems`.

`catch` code block:

This prints an error message to the Debug area if the do code block fails.

```
completionHandler(restaurantItems)
```

This statement processes the restaurantItems array using the closure provided.

Note that when you call this method in Xcode, the autocomplete feature gives you two possible choices; one that includes the selectedCuisine: parameter (that takes a string containing the selected cuisine) and one that doesn't (selectedCuisine is set to All).

7. Add a method after the fetch(location:selectedCuisine:completionHandler:) method to return the number of items in the restaurantItems array:

```
func numberOfRestaurantItems() -> Int {
    restaurantItems.count
}
```

You'll call this method to determine the number of collection view cells to display in the **Restaurant List** screen.

8. Add a method just after the numberOfRestaurantItems() method to return a RestaurantItem instance from the restaurantItems array at the index provided:

```
func restaurantItem(at index: Int) ->
RestaurantItem {
    restaurantItems[index]
}
```

You'll call this method to configure the content of each collection view cell in the **Restaurant List** screen.

The RestaurantDataManager class has been created, which allows you to read data stored in JSON files and put it into an array of RestaurantItem instances. Before you can use it, you'll need to modify your project quite a bit. Let's see what's required to display restaurant information in the **Map** and **RestaurantList** screens in the next section.

Using data from JSON files in your app

Let's review how the app works. In the **Map** screen, the user will see all the restaurants near the user's location. Tapping a restaurant will display a callout bubble, and tapping the button in the callout button will display the details of said restaurant in the **Restaurant Detail** screen.

In the **Explore** screen, the user will tap the **LOCATION** button and select a location such as **Charleston, NC** on the **Locations** screen. After a location has been selected, the user taps **Done** and will be returned to the **Explore** screen. The user will then select a cuisine in the **Explore** screen, and a list of restaurants in that location that offer that cuisine will be displayed in the **Restaurant List** screen. Tapping a restaurant will display the details of said restaurant in the **Restaurant Detail** screen.

You will do the following:

- Configure the `MapViewController` class to get a list of restaurants from a JSON file instead of a `.plist` file. This will also fix the error in the `MapDataManager` class's `fetch(completion:)` method.

- Configure the `LocationViewController` class to store the location selected by the user.

- Pass the selected location to the `ExploreViewController` instance.

- Configure the `ExploreViewController` class to pass the selected location and cuisine to the `RestaurantListViewController` instance.

- Configure the `RestaurantListViewController` class to get a list of restaurants from a JSON file corresponding to the selected location.

- Configure the `RestaurantListViewController` class to display a list of restaurants based on the location and cuisine selected.

This may seem daunting, so you'll do things step by step. To start, you'll configure the `MapDataManager` class to read data from JSON files instead of `.plist` files.

Configuring the MapDataManager instance to use data from the RestaurantDataManager instance

Currently, there is an error in the `MapDataManager` file. This is because the `fetch(completion:)` method in your `MapDataManager` class calls the initializer method that you removed from the `RestaurantItem` class. You will now update the `MapDataManager` class to use the `RestaurantDataManager` instance as a data source, fixing the error in the process. Click the `MapDataManager` file (inside the `Model` folder in the `Map` folder) in the Project navigator and update the `fetch(completion:)` method as follows:

```
func fetch(completion: (_ annotations: [RestaurantItem]) -> ())
{
```

```
    let manager = RestaurantDataManager()
    manager.fetch(location: "Boston", completionHandler: {
        (restaurantItems) in self.items = restaurantItems
        completion(items)
    })
}
```

Let's break this down:

```
func fetch(completion: (_ annotations: [RestaurantItem]) -> ())
```

This method has a completion method parameter. The completion method will be used to process the result when the method has finished execution.

```
let manager = RestaurantDataManager()
```

This creates an instance of the `RestaurantDataManager` class and assigns it to `manager`.

```
manager.fetch(location: "Boston", completionHandler: {
    (restaurantItems) in self.items = restaurantItems
    completion(items)
})
```

This calls the `manager` instance's `fetch()` method to get a list of restaurants from `Boston.json`. This is hardcoded for now as the iOS Simulator does not have a functional GPS. To see restaurants at a different location, change the name of the JSON file used to another location. The array of `RestaurantItem` instances returned by this method is assigned to the `MapViewController` instance's `items` array, and the completion method that was passed in is used to process this array. As you saw in the previous chapter, this will generate the annotations that will be added to the map view in the **Map** screen.

> **Important Information**
>
> To learn more about how to determine your location, visit `https://developer.apple.com/documentation/mapkit/mkmapview/converting_a_user_s_location_to_a_descriptive_placemark`.

If you run your app now and select the **Map** screen, you should see pins for restaurants in Boston.

In the next section, you'll configure the `LocationViewController` class so it can store the location selected by the user.

Storing a user-selected location

At present, the `LocationDataManager` class loads data from `Locations.plist` and stores location information in an array of strings. You will create a new structure, `LocationItem`, and configure the `LocationDataManager` class to store locations in an array of `LocationItem` instances. After that, you'll modify the `LocationViewController` class so that it can store a `LocationItem` instance containing the user-selected location. You can then pass this instance to the `RestaurantListViewController` instance in your app. Follow these steps:

1. Right-click on the `Model` folder inside the `Location` folder and select **New File**.

2. **iOS** should already be selected. Choose **Swift File** and then click **Next**.

3. Name this file `LocationItem`. Click **Create**. The `LocationItem` file appears in the Project navigator.

4. Click the `LocationItem` file and add the following after the `import` statement to declare and define the `LocationItem` structure:

```swift
struct LocationItem {
    let city: String?
    let state: String?
}
extension LocationItem {
    init(dict: [String: String]) {
        self.city = dict["city"]
        self.state = dict["state"]
    }
    var cityAndState: String {
        guard let city = self.city, let state =
        self.state else {
            return ""
        }
        return "\(city), \(state)"
    }
}
```

The LocationItem structure has two String properties, city and state.

The init() method takes a dictionary, dict, as a parameter and assigns the values of the city and state keys to the city and state properties.

The cityAndState computed property returns a string made from combining the city and state values.

Now you'll update the LocationDataManager class so that it can store city and state information in an array of LocationItem instances instead of strings. Follow these steps:

1. Click the LocationDataManager in the Project navigator and modify the locations array to store LocationItem instances instead of strings:

    ```
    private var locations:[LocationItem] = []
    ```

2. The fetch() method will now show an error. Modify the fetch() method to work with LocationItem instances instead of strings:

    ```
    func fetch() {
        for location in loadData() {
            locations.append(LocationItem(dict: location))
        }
    }
    ```

    Each dictionary provided by the loadData() method is now used to initialize LocationItem instances instead of strings, which are then appended to the locations array. The loadData() method still uses the same Locations. plist file that you created in *Chapter 15, Getting Started with Table Views*.

3. The locationItem(at:) method now shows an error. Modify it so it returns a LocationItem instance instead of a string:

    ```
    func locationItem(at index: Int) ->
    LocationItem {
        locations[index]
    }
    ```

You are done with the `LocationDataManager` class at this point. Next, you'll update the `LocationViewController` class to use `LocationItem` instances instead of strings to populate the table view cells. Follow these steps:

1. Click the `LocationViewController` file in the Project navigator.

2. You will see an error in the `tableView(_:cellForRowAtIndexPath:)` method. This error is because you can't assign a `LocationItem` instance to the cell's `textLabel` property. Modify this method as follows:

```
func tableView(_ tableView: UITableView, cellForRowAt
indexPath: IndexPath) -> UITableViewCell {
    let cell = tableView.dequeueReusableCell(
    withIdentifier: "locationCell", for: indexPath)
    let location = manager.locationItem(at:
    indexPath.row)
    cell.textLabel?.text = location.cityAndState
    return cell
}
```

The `cityAndState` property of the `LocationItem` structure returns a string that combines a location's `city` and `state` strings, fixing the error.

3. You need a property to keep track of the user's selection. Add the following property declaration just after the `manager` declaration:

```
let manager = LocationDataManager()
var selectedCity: LocationItem?
```

To handle user interaction with the table view, you'll make the `LocationViewController` class conform to the `UITableViewDelegate` protocol.

> **Tip**
> The `UITableViewDelegate` protocol is covered in *Chapter 15, Getting Started with Table Views*.

The `UITableViewDelegate` protocol specifies the messages that a table view will send to its delegate when the user interacts with the rows in it. Follow these steps to adopt it:

1. Add the following extension after the `UITableViewDataSource` extension:

    ```
    // MARK: UITableViewDelegate
    extension LocationViewController:
    UITableViewDelegate {


    }
    ```

    The extension helps to keep your code organized, and the `// MARK:` syntax makes this extension easy to find in the Editor area.

2. The `UITableViewDelegate` method triggered when a user taps a row in the table view is `tableView(_:didSelectRowAt:)`. Add this method between the extension's curly braces. It should look like the following:

    ```
    // MARK: UITableViewDelegate
    extension LocationViewController: UITableViewDelegate
    {
        func tableView(_ tableView: UITableView,
        didSelectRowAt indexPath:IndexPath) {
            if let cell = tableView.cellForRow(at:
            indexPath) {
                cell.accessoryType = .checkmark
                selectedCity =
                manager.locationItem(at: indexPath.row)
            }
        }
    }
    ```

When the user taps a row in the **Locations** screen, a checkmark will appear in that row, and the `selectedCity` property is assigned the corresponding `LocationItem` instance in the `locations` array. For example, if you tap the third row, the `LocationItem` instance with the values `"Charleston"` and `"NC"` is assigned to `selectedCity`.

The `LocationViewController` class can now store a user-selected location, but when you choose a location in the **Locations** screen and tap **Done**, nothing happens. This is because you've not created or assigned an action to the **Done** button yet. Later you'll create an unwind action in the `ExploreViewController` class and assign it to the **Done** button, but before you do, you'll create a new view controller for the collection view section header in the **Explore** screen first. This will let you display the user-selected location in the **Explore** screen. You'll do this in the next section.

Adding a UICollectionReusableView subclass for the section header in the Explore screen

The **Explore** screen's collection view has a collection view section header, which contains a subtitle label, a title label, and the **LOCATION** button. There is currently no way to set the subtitle label text. You'll create a `UICollectionReusableView` subclass for the collection view section header, and set up an outlet for the subtitle label, so you can display the user-selected location in the collection view section header. Follow these steps:

1. Right-click the `View` folder inside the `Explore` folder and select **New File**.

2. **iOS** should already be selected. Choose **Cocoa Touch Class** and then click **Next**.

3. Configure the file as follows:

   Class: `ExploreHeaderView`

   Subclass: `UICollectionReusableView`

   Also create XIB: Unchecked

   Language: `Swift`

   Click **Next**.

4. Click **Create**. The `ExploreHeaderView` file appears in the Project navigator. Verify that it contains the following:

   ```
   class ExploreHeaderView: UICollectionReusableView {


   }
   ```

5. Click the `Main` storyboard file in the Project navigator. Select the **Collection Reusable View** in the **Explore View Controller Scene**. Click the Identity inspector button and under **Custom Class**, set **Class** to `ExploreHeaderView`:

Figure 17.2: Identity inspector with Class set to ExploreHeaderView

Note that **Collection Reusable View** will change to **Explore Header View** in the document outline.

The `ExploreHeaderView` class is now managing the collection view section header. In the next section, you will link the subtitle label in the collection view section header to an outlet in the `ExploreHeaderView` class, and add a property for the `ExploreHeaderView` class in the `ExploreViewController` class.

Connecting the section header's label to the ExploreViewController class

To display the user-selected city in the collection view section header, you'll connect the subtitle label to an outlet in the `ExploreHeaderView` class, then add a property for it in the `ExploreViewController` class. Follow these steps:

1. In the document outline, click the subtitle label for the **Explore Header View** (it is the label that has the text **PLEASE SELECT A LOCATION**):

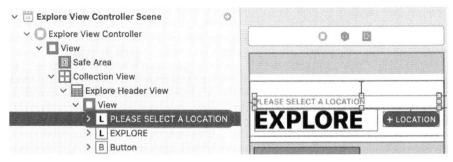

Figure 17.3: Document outline with PLEASE SELECT A LOCATION label selected

2. Click the Adjust Editor Options button and choose Assistant from the menu. An assistant editor appears on the right side of the screen. Make sure that it's showing the contents of the `ExploreHeaderView` file.

3. *Ctrl + Drag* from the **PLEASE SELECT A LOCATION** label to the space between the curly braces:

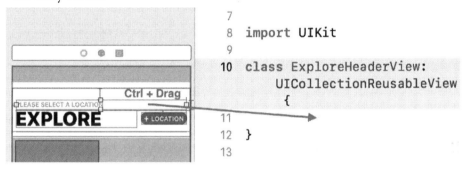

Figure 17.4: Editor area showing ExploreHeaderView file contents

4. In the box that appears, set the name to `locationLabel` and click **Connect**.

5. The `locationLabel` outlet has been created in the `ExploreHeaderView` class. Close the assistant editor by clicking the **x** button.

6. Click the `ExploreViewController` file in the Project navigator. Add the following property declaration after the `manager` declaration to store the location passed to the `ExploreViewController` instance by the `LocationViewController` instance:

```
let manager = ExploreDataManager()
var selectedCity: LocationItem?
```

7. After the `selectedCity` property declaration, declare a property that will be assigned an `ExploreHeaderView` instance, which will allow the `ExploreViewController` instance to set the value for `locationLabel`:

```
let manager = ExploreDataManager()
var selectedCity: LocationItem?
var headerView: ExploreHeaderView!
```

Next, let's configure the **Done** button to dismiss the **Locations** screen and set `locationLabel` to the user-selected city and state when tapped. The **Explore** screen will then appear with the selected city displayed in the collection view section header. You will do this in the next section.

Adding an unwind action method to the Done button

In *Chapter 10, Building Your User Interface*, you added an unwind action method for the **Cancel** button in the `ExploreViewController` class, which dismisses the **Locations** screen when it is tapped. Now, you'll add an unwind action method for the **Done** button, which dismisses the **Locations** screen and sets the `selectedCity` property in the `ExploreViewController` instance to the location selected by the user. Follow these steps:

1. Add the following just after the `unwindLocationCancel(segue:)` method to implement the unwind action for the **Done** button:

```
@IBAction func
unwindLocationDone(segue: UIStoryboardSegue) {
    if let viewController = segue.source as?
    LocationViewController {
        selectedCity = viewController.selectedCity
        if let location = selectedCity {
            headerView.locationLabel.text =
            location.cityAndState
        }
    }
}
```

You'll assign this method to the **Done** button later. The source view controller in this case is a `LocationViewController` instance and the destination view controller is an `ExploreViewController` instance. This method first checks to see if the source view controller is a `LocationViewController` instance. If it is, the value of the `LocationViewController` instance's `selectedCity` property is assigned to the `ExploreViewController` instance's `selectedCity` property, if it exists. If the `ExploreViewController` instance's `selectedCity` property has a value, it is assigned to `location`, and the text of the subtitle label is set to the `cityAndState` property of `location`.

2. Modify the `collectionView(_:viewForSupplementaryElementOf Kind:at:)` method as follows:

```
func collectionView(_ collectionView: UICollectionView,
viewForSupplementaryElementOfKind kind: String, at
indexPath: IndexPath) -> UICollectionReusableView {
    let header =
    collectionView.dequeueReusableSupplementaryView
    (ofKind: kind, withReuseIdentifier: "header", for:
    indexPath)
    headerView = header as? ExploreHeaderView
    return headerView
}
```

This method is one of the data source methods declared in the `UICollectionViewDataSource` protocol. It returns the view that will be used as the collection view section header. Here, the collection view section header in the **Explore** screen is set to an `ExploreHeaderView` instance.

Important Information

You can learn more about the `UICollectionViewDataSource` protocol at this link: `https://developer.apple.com/documentation/uikit/uicollectionviewdatasour ce/1618037-collectionview.`

---

3. Click the `Main` storyboard file. Select the **Location View Controller Scene**. To set the method to be triggered by the **Done** button, *Ctrl + Drag* from the **Done** button to the Exit icon in the Scene Dock:

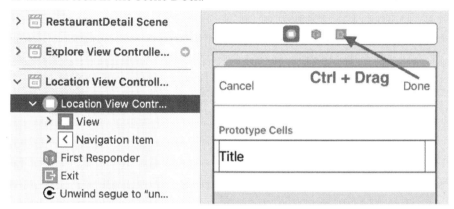

Figure 17.5: Location View Controller Scene showing Done button action being set

4. Choose `unwindLocationDoneWithSegue:` from the pop-up menu. This links the **Done** button to the `unwindLocationDone(segue:)` unwind action in the `ExploreViewController` class:

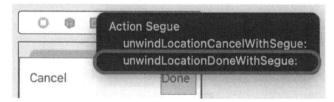

Figure 17.6: Pop-up menu with unwindLocationDoneWithSegue: selected

Build and run your app and tap the **LOCATION** button. Tap a city and a tick will appear in the row. Tap **Done**:

Figure 17.7: iOS Simulator showing Locations screen with location selected

The selected city name and state will replace the **PLEASE SELECT A LOCATION** text in the subtitle label inside the collection view section header:

Figure 17.8: iOS Simulator showing Explore screen with subtitle label set

Although this works, there are two issues that you need to fix when selecting a location. The first issue is that you can select multiple locations:

Figure 17.9: iOS simulator showing Locations screen with multiple locations selected

You want the user to only select one location, and if another is selected, the location selected earlier should be deselected.

The second issue is that the checkmark next to the user-selected location disappears if you click **Done** in the **Locations** screen and click the **LOCATION** button in the **Explore** screen again:

Figure 17.10: iOS simulator showing Locations screen with missing checkmark

The last selected location should have a checkmark when you go back to the **Locations** screen again.

Let's modify the `LocationDataManager` class to make sure only one location can be selected at a time in the next section.

Selecting only one location in the Locations screen

At present, you can select multiple locations in the **Locations** screen. You should only be able to select one location, and if another is selected, the previously selected location selected should be deselected. Follow these steps:

1. Click the `LocationItem` file. Make `LocationItem` conform to the `Equatable` protocol by modifying the `LocationItem` structure as follows:

    ```
    struct LocationItem: Equatable {
        let city: String?
        let state: String?
    }
    ```

    This allows you to check if two `LocationItem` instances are equal.

2. Click the `LocationViewController` file. After the `viewDidLoad()` method, add a method that sets a checkmark only on the row containing the selected city:

    ```
    private func setCheckmark(for cell: UITableViewCell,
    location: LocationItem) {
        if selectedCity == location {
            cell.accessoryType = .checkmark
        } else {
            cell.accessoryType = .none
        }
    }
    ```

    The `setCheckmark(for:location:)` method takes `cell`, a table view cell, and `location`, a `LocationItem` instance, as arguments. If `location` and `selectedCity` are equal, the checkmark for that row is set. Otherwise, the checkmark is not set.

3. In the `tableView(_:cellForRowAt:)` method, modify the code as follows to call `setCheckmark(for:location:)` after the line that sets the text for the cell's `textLabel` property:

```
func tableView(_ tableView: UITableView, cellForRowAt
indexPath: IndexPath) -> UITableViewCell {
    let cell = tableView.dequeueReusableCell(
    withIdentifier: "locationCell", for: indexPath)
    let location = manager.locationItem(at
    indexPath.row)
    cell.textLabel?.text = location.cityAndState
    setCheckmark(for: cell, location: location)
    return cell
}
```

This means `setCheckmark(for:at:)` will be called when each row in the table view is rendered, and the checkmark will only be set on the row containing the selected location.

4. In the `tableView(_:didSelectRowAt:)` method, modify the code in the `if` statement as follows to reload the table view (thus rendering all the rows in it) after a location has been selected:

```
if let cell = tableView.cellForRow(at: indexPath) {
    cell.accessoryType = .checkmark
    selectedCity = manager.locationItem(at:
    indexPath.row)
    tableView.reloadData()
}
```

Build and run your project. You should only be able to set one location now, and if you choose another location, the location you chose earlier will be deselected.

You'll fix the second issue in the next section so that once a location is selected, it will remain selected when you go back to the **Locations** screen. You'll also pass location and cuisine information to the `RestaurantListViewController` instance, so it can eventually display a list of restaurants at a particular location matching the cuisine selected by the user.

> **Tip**
> This is a long chapter, so you may wish to take a break here.

Passing location and cuisine information to the RestaurantListViewController instance

At present, you're able to set a location in the **Locations** screen and have that location appear in the collection view section header of the **Explore** screen. Now, you will add code so you can pass the location and cuisine values to the `RestaurantListViewController` instance, which will then display the restaurants at the selected location that offer the selected cuisine. You'll also make the checkmark next to your selected location reappear if you have selected a location in the **Locations** screen earlier. Follow these steps:

1. You'll add identifiers for each segue connected to the **Explore** screen so that you know which segue is occurring later. Open the `Main` storyboard file and click the **Explore View Controller Scene**. Select the segue between the **Explore View Controller Scene** and the **Location View Controller Scene**:

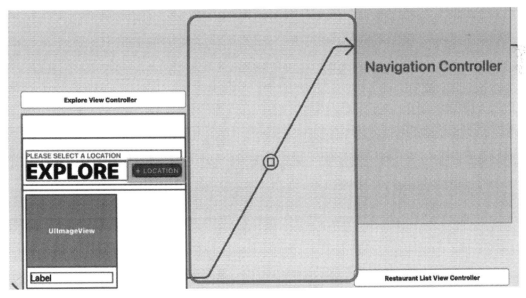

Figure 17.11: Editor area showing segue between Explore and Location screens selected

2. Click the Attributes inspector button. Under **Storyboard Segue**, set **Identifier** to `locationList`:

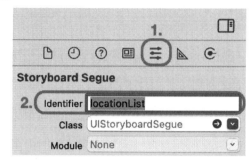

Figure 17.12: Attributes inspector with Identifier set to locationList

3. Select the segue between **Explore View Controller Scene** and the **Restaurant List View Controller Scene**. Click the Attributes inspector button. Under **Storyboard Segue**, set **Identifier** to `restaurantList`:

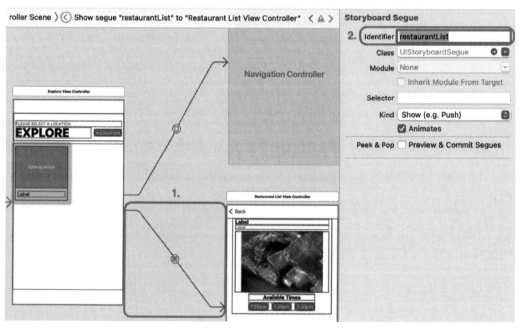

Figure 17.13: Attributes inspector identifier setting for the segue between
the Explore and Restaurant List screens

Once you know which segue is occurring, you can specify the methods to be executed for each segue. You'll create two methods, `showLocationList(segue:)` and `showRestaurantList(segue:)`, and you'll use the `prepare(for:sender:)` method to execute the desired method depending on which segue is occurring.

4. Click the `ExploreViewController` file in the Project navigator. Inside the `private` extension, declare and define the `showLocationList(segue:)` method before the `unwindLocationCancel()` method to pass the user-selected city back to the `LocationViewController` instance if it was set earlier:

```
func showLocationList(segue: UIStoryboardSegue) {
    guard let navController = segue.destination as?
    UINavigationController, let viewController =
    navController.topViewController as?
    LocationViewController else {
        return
    }
    viewController.selectedCity = selectedCity
}
```

The `showLocationList(segue:)` method will be called before the **Explore** screen transitions to the **Locations** screen. Let's see how it works.

Remember that in the `Main` storyboard file, you embedded the **Location View Controller Scene** in a navigation controller. A navigation controller has a `viewControllers` property that holds an array of view controllers, and the last view controller in the array has its view visible onscreen. You can access the last view controller in the array using the `topViewController` property of the navigation controller.

The `guard` statement checks whether the segue destination is a `UINavigationController` instance and whether `topViewController` is the `LocationViewController` instance. If it is, the `selectedCity` property of the `ExploreViewController` instance is checked to see if it contains a value. If it does, that value is assigned to the `selectedCity` property of the `LocationViewController` instance. Remember that the `setCheckmark(for:at:)` method of the `LocationViewController` instance will be called for each row in the table view, and this sets a checkmark on the row containing the selected city.

This will fix the second issue with the **Locations** screen. Now, let's add code to pass the location and cuisine to the `RestaurantListViewController` instance. Follow these steps:

1. Click the `RestaurantListViewController` file in the Project navigator. Add the following properties inside the `RestaurantListViewController` class just before the `@IBOutlet` declaration:

    ```
    var selectedRestaurant: RestaurantItem?
    var selectedCity: LocationItem?
    var selectedCuisine: String?
    @IBOutlet var collectionView: UICollectionView!
    ```

    `selectedRestaurant` will be set if you pick a restaurant in the **Restaurant List** screen, and will be passed to the **Restaurant Detail** screen later. You'll add code to do this in the next chapter.

    `selectedCity` stores the city you picked in the **Locations** screen.

    `selectedCuisine` stores the cuisine you picked in the **Explore** screen.

2. Add the following code after the `viewDidLoad()` method to print the selected city and cuisine to the Debug area when the view for the `RestaurantListViewController` instance appears onscreen:

    ```
    override func viewDidAppear(_ animated: Bool) {
        super.viewDidAppear(animated)
        print("selected city \(selectedCity as Any)")
        print("selected cuisine \(selectedCuisine as Any)")
    }
    ```

    `viewDidAppear()` is called every time a view controller's view appears onscreen, while `viewDidLoad()` is only called once when a view controller initially loads its view. `viewDidAppear()` is used here because the `RestaurantListViewController` instance will show a different list of restaurants each time its view appears onscreen, depending on the choices made by the user. At the moment, the code just prints the selected location and cuisine to the Debug area, so you can see that these values are being passed correctly.

> **Important Information**
> To learn more about the view controller lifecycle, see this link: https://
> developer.apple.com/documentation/uikit/
> uiviewcontroller.

3. Click the `ExploreViewController` file in the Project navigator.
    Declare and define the `showRestaurantList(segue:)` method
    after the `showLocationList(segue:)` method to set the
    `RestaurantListViewController` instance's `selectedCuisine` and
    `selectedCity` properties:

```swift
func showRestaurantList(segue: UIStoryboardSegue) {
    if let viewController = segue.destination as?
    RestaurantListViewController, let city =
    selectedCity, let index =
    collectionView.indexPathsForSelectedItems?.first?
    .row {
        viewController.selectedCuisine =
        manager.exploreItem(at: index).name
        viewController.selectedCity = city
    }
}
```

You will call this method before the **Explore** screen transitions to the **Restaurant
List** screen. The `if-let` statement checks to see whether the destination view
controller is the `RestaurantListViewController` instance, sets `city`
to the `selectedCity` value of the `ExploreViewController` instance
if it is, and gets the index of the collection view cell the user tapped. If the
statement is successful, the `RestaurantListViewController` instance's
`selectedCuisine` property is set to the name of the `ExploreItem`
instance located at that index in the `items` array. In the next line, the
`RestaurantListViewController` instance's `selectedCity` property will
be assigned the value stored in `city`.

For this method to work, the `selectedCity` property of the `ExploreViewController` instance has to be set first before transitioning to the **Restaurant Detail** screen. You will alert the user to set the city before choosing a cuisine. Follow these steps:

1. Click the `ExploreViewController` file in the Project navigator. Add the following method before `unwindLocationCancel()` to display an alert:

```
func showLocationRequiredAlert() {
    let alertController = UIAlertController(title:
    "Location Needed", message: "Please select a
    location.", preferredStyle: .alert)
    let okAction = UIAlertAction(title: "OK", style:
    .default, handler: nil)
    alertController.addAction(okAction)
    present(alertController, animated: true,
    completion: nil)
}
```

The `showLocationRequiredAlert()` method creates a `UIAlertController` instance with the title set to `"Location Needed"` and a message, `"Please select a location."`. A `UIAlertAction` instance with an OK button is then added to the `UIAlertController` instance. Finally, the alert is presented to the user, and tapping the OK button dismisses it.

2. Add the following code after `viewDidLoad()` to display this alert if a location has not been selected:

```
override func shouldPerformSegue(withIdentifier
identifier: String, sender: Any?) -> Bool {
    if identifier == Segue.restaurantList.rawValue,
    selectedCity == nil {
        showLocationRequiredAlert()
        return false
    }
    return true
}
```

The `shouldPerformSegue(withIdentifier:sender:)` method is used to check whether the **Explore** screen should transition to the **Restaurant List** screen. First, you check whether the segue identifier for the segue between these two screens matches `restaurantList` and if the `selectedCity` is set; if not, the `showLocationRequiredAlert()` method is called and `shouldPerformSegue(withIdentifier:sender:)` returns `false`. Otherwise, `shouldPerformSegue(withIdentifier:sender:)` returns `true`, and the **Restaurant List** screen appears.

Now that you've created the `showLocationList(segue:)` and the `showRestaurantList(segue:)` methods, you'll add code to implement the `prepare(for:sender:)` method after `viewDidLoad()` and before `shouldPerformSegue(withIdentifier:)`. This method calls `showLocationList(segue:)` or `showRestaurantList(segue:)` depending on the segue that will be executed:

```
override func prepare(for segue: UIStoryboardSegue, sender:
Any?) {
    switch segue.identifier! {
    case Segue.locationList.rawValue:
        showLocationList(segue: segue)
    case Segue.restaurantList.rawValue:
        showRestaurantList(segue: segue)
    default:
        print("Segue not added")
    }
}
```

When the **LOCATION** button is tapped, the segue identifier is `locationList`, so the `showLocationList(segue:)` method is executed before the transition to the **Locations** screen, which sets the checkmark for the selected city in the table view. When a cell in the **Explore** screen is tapped, the segue identifier is `restaurantList`, so the `showRestaurantListing(segue:)` method is executed before the transition to the **Restaurant List** screen. This sets the `selectedType` and `selectedCity` properties in the `RestaurantListViewController` instance, which will be printed to the Debug area.

Build and run your project. If you try to select a cuisine, you'll see this alert, stating you need to select a location:

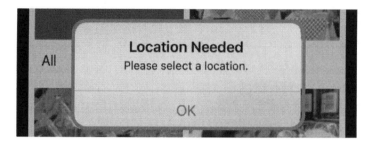

Figure 17.14: iOS Simulator showing alert

If you pick a location, tap **Done**, and tap the **LOCATION** button again the location you selected earlier should still be selected:

Figure 17.15: iOS simulator showing Locations screen with checkmark

If you pick a cuisine, you'll see the **Restaurant List** screen:

Figure 17.16: iOS Simulator showing Restaurant List screen

The location and cuisine you picked will appear in the Debug area:

Figure 17.17: Debug area showing location and cuisine you selected

Now that the `RestaurantListViewController` instance has a location, you can get the restaurant data for that location from the `RestaurantDataManager` instance. Click the `RestaurantListViewController` file in the Project navigator and update `viewDidAppear()` as follows. This prints the list of restaurants from the selected location that serves the selected cuisine:

```
override func viewDidAppear(_ animated: Bool) {
    super.viewDidAppear(animated)
    guard let city = selectedCity?.city, let cuisine =
    selectedCuisine else {
        return
    }
    let manager = RestaurantDataManager()
    manager.fetch(location: city, selectedCuisine: cuisine) {
        restaurantItems in if !restaurantItems.isEmpty {
            for restaurantItem in restaurantItems {
                if let restaurantName = restaurantItem.name {
                    print(restaurantName)
                }
            }
        } else {
            print("No data")
        }
    }
}
```

The `guard` statement checks to see if `city` and `cuisine` have been assigned values successfully, and returns if they have not. Next, an instance of `RestaurantDataManager` is created and assigned to `manager`. The `fetch(location:selectedCuisine:completion:)` method returns an array of `RestaurantItem` instances for the selected `city` and `cuisine`, and the `for` loop prints the restaurant names to the Debug area. If there are no restaurants matching the criteria, `No data` will be printed to the Debug area. Build and run your project, select a city, tap a cuisine, and note the results in the Debug area.

You can also see the results in the Report navigator. Click the Report navigator button and select the first entry as shown:

Figure 17.18: Report navigator showing list of restaurant names

You'll see either a list of restaurants or No data in the Editor area.

So, at this point, the RestaurantListViewController instance is successfully getting the data that it needs to display the list of restaurants. Now that you have this data, you need to configure the collection view to display it to the user. To do that, you will need to create a view controller for the collection view cells, and configure the RestaurantListViewController instance to populate them. You will do this in the next section.

Creating a view controller for the cells on the Restaurant List screen

At present the **Restaurant List** screen does not have a class to manage the collection view cells inside its collection view. You'll create a RestaurantCell class for this purpose. Follow these steps:

1. Right-click the Restaurants folder and choose **New Group**. Name it View.

2. Right-click the View folder and select **New File**.

3. **iOS** should already be selected. Choose **Cocoa Touch Class** and then click **Next**.

4. Configure the file as follows:

   Class: RestaurantCell

   Subclass: UICollectionViewCell

   Also create XIB: Unchecked

   Language: Swift

   Click **Next**.

5. Click **Create**. The `RestaurantCell` file appears in the Project navigator. It contains the implementation of the `RestaurantCell` class:

```
import UIKit

class RestaurantCell: UICollectionViewCell {


}
```

Now let's create the outlets for the collection view cell in the **Restaurant List** screen so their contents can be managed by the `RestaurantCell` class. You will do this in the next section.

Connecting the outlets for the RestaurantCell class

Now that you've created the `RestaurantCell` class, you'll need to create outlets in it and link them to the UI elements inside the collection view cells for the **Restaurant List** screen. This will allow `RestaurantCell` instances to manage what is displayed by the collection view cell. Follow these steps:

1. Click the `Main` storyboard file. Click `restaurantCell` in the **Restaurant List View Controller Scene**. In the Identity inspector, under **Custom Class**, set **Class** to `RestaurantCell`:

Figure 17.19: Identity inspector Class settings for restaurantCell

2. In **Restaurant List View Controller Scene**, click on the label with the text **Available Times** in the document outline. This is to ensure you can select the correct file (`RestaurantCell.swift`) to be displayed in the assistant editor when the Adjust Editor Options button is clicked:

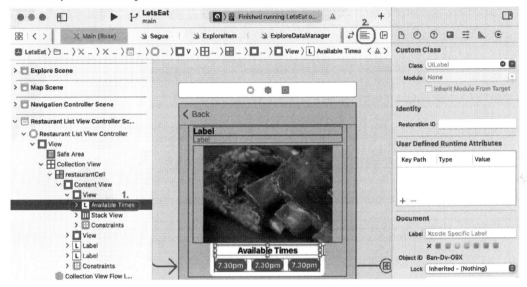

Figure 17.20: Document outline with Available Times label selected

3. Click the Adjust Editor Options button and choose **Assistant** from the menu.

4. The assistant editor appears. The path bar at the top should show **Automatic > RestaurantCell.swift**. If it does not, select it from the pop-up menu. *Ctrl + Drag* from the title **Label** to the space between the curly braces in the `RestaurantCell` file:

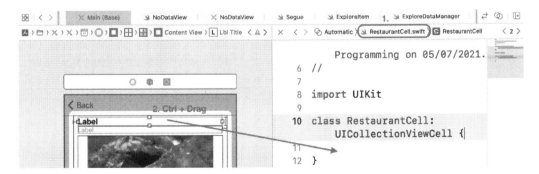

Figure 17.21: Assistant editor showing RestaurantCell.swift

5. In the box that appears, type `titleLabel` in the **Name** field and click **Connect**:

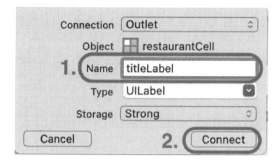

Figure 17.22: Dialog box showing label Name set to titleLabel

6. *Ctrl + Drag* from the subtitle **Label** to just after the `titleLabel` property you just created. In the box that appears, type `cuisineLabel` in the **Name** field and click **Connect**:

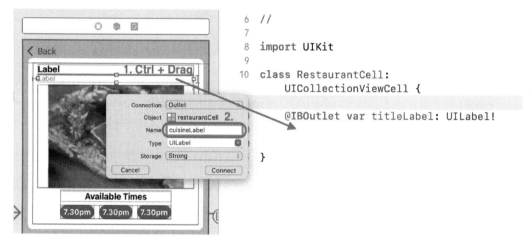

Figure 17.23: Dialog box showing label Name set to cuisineLabel

7. *Ctrl + Drag* from the `american` image view to just after the other properties you created. In the box that appears, type `restaurantImageView` in the **Name** field and click **Connect**:

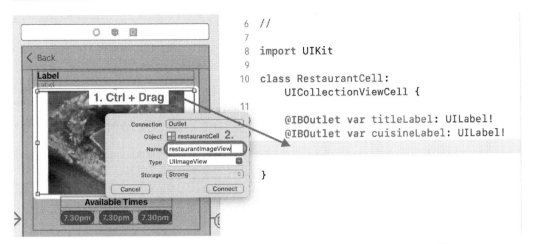

```
6  //
7
8  import UIKit
9
10 class RestaurantCell:
       UICollectionViewCell {
11
       @IBOutlet var titleLabel: UILabel!
       @IBOutlet var cuisineLabel: UILabel!


   }
```

Figure 17.24: Dialog box showing image view Name set to restaurantImageView

8.   Click the **x** button to close the assistant editor.

The outlets for the RestaurantCell class are now connected to the UI elements in the collection view cell. Later you'll configure the RestaurantListViewController instance to populate this collection view, but before you do, there is a possibility to consider. The user's choices for location and cuisine may not return any results, so you will implement a screen that informs the user when there is no data to be displayed. You'll do this in the next section.

Displaying a custom UIView to indicate no data is available

The location and cuisine choices the user makes on the **Explore** screen may not return any results. If this is the case, you will display a custom view stating that fact on the **Restaurant List** screen. To do this, you will create a UIView subclass and an accompanying **XIB** file. XIB stands for **Xcode Interface Builder** and XIB files were used to create the user interface before storyboards were implemented. Let's create both files now by following these steps:

1.   Right-click on the Misc folder and select **New Group**. Name it No Data.

2.   Right-click on the No Data folder and choose **New File**.

3.   **iOS** should already be selected. Choose **Cocoa Touch Class** and then click **Next**.

4. Configure the file as follows:

   Class: `NoDataView`

   Subclass: `UIView`

   Also create XIB: Grayed out

   Language: `Swift`

   Click **Next**.

5. Click **Create**. The `NoDataView` file appears in the Project navigator.

6. Right-click on the `No Data` folder and create a new file.

7. **iOS** should already be selected. Choose **View** and then click **Next**.

8. Name this file `NoDataView`. Click **Create**. The `NoDataView` XIB file appears in the Project navigator.

9. Click the `NoDataView` file in the Project navigator and declare and define the `NoDataView` class as follows:

```swift
class NoDataView: UIView {
    var view: UIView!
    @IBOutlet var titleLabel: UILabel!
    @IBOutlet var descLabel: UILabel!
    override init(frame: CGRect) {
        super.init(frame: frame)
        setupView()
    }
    required init?(coder: NSCoder) {
        super.init(coder: coder)
        setupView()
    }
    func loadViewFromNib() -> UIView {
        let nib = UINib(nibName: "NoDataView", bundle:
        Bundle.main)
        let view = nib.instantiate(withOwner: self,
        options: nil) [0] as! UIView
        return view
    }
    func setupView() {
        view = loadViewFromNib()
```

```
            view.frame = bounds
            view.autoresizingMask = [.flexibleWidth,
            .flexibleHeight]
            addSubview(view)
        }
        func set(title: String, desc: String) {
            titleLabel.text = title
            descLabel.text = desc
        }
    }
```

This class is a subclass of the `UIView` class, and it will manage the view in the `NoDataView` XIB file. Let's break this down:

```
var view: UIView!
@IBOutlet var titleLabel: UILabel!
@IBOutlet var descLabel: UILabel!
```

`view` will be assigned the view from the `NoDataView` XIB file during initialization.

`titleLabel` and `descLabel` will be assigned to two `UILabel` instances that will be placed in the `NoDataView` XIB file when you build the user interface in the next section.

```
override init(frame: CGRect) {
    super.init(frame:frame)
    setupView()
}
required init?(coder: NSCoder) {
    super.init(coder: coder)
    setupView()
}
```

The `NoDataView` class is a subclass of `UIView`. A `UIView` object has two `init` methods: the first handles view creation programmatically, and the second handles the loading of XIB files from the app bundle stored on the device. Here, both methods will call `setupView()`.

```
func loadViewFromNib() -> UIView {
    let nib = UINib(nibName: "NoDataView", bundle:
    Bundle.main)
```

```
let view = nib.instantiate(withOwner: self,
   options: nil) [0] as! UIView
return view
}
```

This method finds and loads the `NoDataView` XIB file from the app bundle and returns a `UIView` instance stored inside it.

```
func setupView() {
   view = loadViewFromNib()
   view.frame = bounds
   view.autoresizingMask = [.flexibleWidth, .flexibleHeight]
   addSubview(view)
}
```

This method calls `loadViewFromNib()`, configures the view so it is the same size as the device screen, makes the width and height of the view flexible to adapt to size and orientation changes, and adds it to the device view hierarchy so it is visible onscreen.

```
func set(title: String, desc: String) {
   titleLabel.text = title
   descLabel.text = desc
}
```

This method sets the text of the `titleLabel` and `descLabel` properties.

Now let's set up the `NoDataView` XIB file. You may want to refer to *Chapter 12, Modifying and Configuring Cells*, which covers using the Size inspector and the Auto Layout constraint menus in more detail. Follow these steps:

1. Click the `NoDataView` XIB file in the Project navigator.
2. Select **File's Owner** in the document outline. In the Identity inspector, under **Custom Class**, set **Class** to `NoDataView` and press *Return*.
3. Click the Library button to display the library. Type `label` in the filter field. A **Label** object appears in the results.
4. Drag two **Label** objects into the **View**, with one **Label** object above the other.

5. Select the top label to represent the title. In the Attributes inspector, update the following values:

    Text: Add `TITLE GOES HERE` to the text field under the **Text** setting

    Color: `Default (Label Color)`

    Alignment: `Center`

    Font: `System Bold 26.0`

6. With the same label selected, update the following values in the Size inspector:

    Width: `335`

    Height: `36`

7. Select the bottom label. This will represent the description. In the Attributes inspector, update the following values:

    Text: Add `Description goes here` to the text field under the **Text** setting

    Color: `Default (Label Color)`

    Alignment: `Center`

    Font: `System Thin 17.0`

8. In the Size inspector, update the following values:

    Width: `335`

    Height: `21`

9. Select both labels by clicking the first label and holding down the *Shift* key while selecting the second label.

10. With both labels still selected, click the **Editor** menu and choose **Embed In | Stack View**.

11. Select the **Stack View** in the document outline, and click the Attributes inspector button. Under **Stack View**, set the following values:

    Axis: `Vertical`

    Alignment: `Center`

    Spacing: `8`

12. With the **Stack View** selected, click the Add New Constraints button. Set the following values:

Left: 10

Right: 10

Click the **Add 2 constraints** button.

13. With the **Stack View** still selected, click the Align button. Set the following values:

Horizontally in Container (ticked)

Vertically in Container (ticked)

Click the **Add 2 Constraints** button.

14. Select **File's Owner** in the document outline.

15. Open the Connections inspector and connect titleLabel to the label that says TITLE GOES HERE.

16. Connect descLabel to the other label.

When you are done, you should see the following:

Figure 17.25: Editor area showing NoDataView XIB file contents

You have completed configuring NoDataView.xib. Now, let's put it all together so that the **Restaurant List** screen will display a list of restaurants based on the selected location and cuisine, or display the NoDataView if there aren't any restaurants offering the selected cuisine at a particular location. You will do this in the next section.

Displaying a list of restaurants on the Restaurant List screen

You now have everything you need to display a list of restaurants based on the selected location and cuisine on the **Restaurant List** screen. So, now it's time to put it all together. Follow these steps:

1. Click the `RestaurantListViewController` file in the Project navigator. Before the `selectedRestaurant` property, add the following to create an instance of `RestaurantDataManager` and assign it to a `manager` property:

```swift
private let manager = RestaurantDataManager()
var selectedRestaurant: RestaurantItem?
```

2. Add the following method inside the `private` extension to populate `manager`'s `items` array and to set the background view for the **Restaurant List** screen:

```swift
func createData() {
    guard let city = selectedCity?.city, let
    cuisine = selectedCuisine else {
        return
    }
    manager.fetch(location: city,
    selectedCuisine: cuisine) {restaurantItems in
        if !restaurantItems.isEmpty {
            collectionView.backgroundView = nil
        } else {
            let view = NoDataView(frame: CGRect(x: 0,
            y: 0, width: collectionView.frame.width,
            height: collectionView.frame.height))
            view.set(title: "Restaurants", desc:
            "No restaurants found.")
            collectionView.backgroundView = view
        }
        collectionView.reloadData()
    }
}
```

Let's break this down:

```
guard let city = selectedCity?.city, let cuisine =
selectedCuisine else {
    return
}
```

Checks to see whether the `selectedCity` and `selectedCuisine` properties are set; if they are, assign `selectedCity` to `city` and `selectedCuisine` to `cuisine`. Otherwise, exit the method.

```
manager.fetch(location: city, selectedCuisine: cuisine)
```

Calls the `fetch(location:selectedCuisine:completion:)` method of the `RestaurantDataManager` instance, which loads the appropriate `RestaurantItem` instances into its `restaurantItems` array.

```
{ restaurantItems in
    if !restaurantItems.isEmpty {
        collectionView.backgroundView = nil
    } else {
        let view = NoDataView(frame: CGRect(x: 0, y: 0,
        width: collectionView.frame.width, height:
        collectionView.frame.height))
        view.set(title: "Restaurants", desc:
        "No restaurants found.")
        collectionView.backgroundView = view
    }
```

If the `restaurantItems` array of the `RestaurantDataManager` instance is not empty, set `backgroundView` of the `collectionView` instance to `nil`. Otherwise, create an instance of `NoDataView`, set its title and description, and set it as the `backgroundView` property of the `collectionView` instance.

```
collectionView.reloadData()
```

Tells `collectionView` to refresh its view.

3. Update `collectionView(_:cellForItemAt:)` as follows to set the `RestaurantCell` instance's properties:

```
func collectionView(_ collectionView:
UICollectionView, cellForItemAt indexPath: IndexPath)
-> UICollectionViewCell {
```

```
    let cell = collectionView.dequeueReusableCell(
    withReuseIdentifier: "restaurantCell", for:
    indexPath) as! RestaurantCell
    let restaurantItem = manager.restaurantItem(at:
    indexPath.row)
    cell.titleLabel.text = restaurantItem.name
    if let cuisine = restaurantItem.subtitle {
        cell.cuisineLabel.text = cuisine
    }
    if let imageURL = restaurantItem.imageURL {
        if let url = URL(string: imageURL) {
            let data = try? Data(contentsOf: url)
            if let imageData = data {
                DispatchQueue.main.async {
                    cell.restaurantImageView.image =
                    UIImage(data: imageData)
                }
            }
        }
    }
    return cell
}
```

Let's break this down:

```
let restaurantItem = manager.restaurantItem(at:
indexPath.row)
```

Gets the `RestaurantItem` instance from the `restaurantItems` array of the `RestaurantDataManager` instance corresponding to the `RestaurantCell` instance's position.

```
cell.titleLabel.text = restaurantItem.name
```

This sets the text of the `RestaurantCell` instance's `titleLabel` to the value of the `RestaurantItem` instance's name.

```
if let cuisine = restaurantItem.subtitle {
    cell.cuisineLabel.text = cuisine
}
```

This sets the text of the `RestaurantCell` instance's `cuisineLabel` to the value of the `RestaurantItem` instance's `subtitle`.

```
if let imageURL = restaurantItem.imageURL {
    if let url = URL(string: imageURL) {
        let data = try? Data(contentsOf: url)
        if let imageData = data {
            DispatchQueue.main.async {
                cell.restaurantImageView.image =
                UIImage(data: imageData)
            }
        }
    }
}
```

This downloads the picture of the restaurant from the URL specified in the `RestaurantItem` instance's `imageURL` and assigns it to the `image` property of the `RestaurantCell` instance's `imgRestaurant` property.

```
    return cell
}
```

Returns the collection view cell.

> **Important Information**
>
> You will notice that scrolling is jerky, and if there is no internet connection, the **Restaurant List** screen will be blank. This is because downloading images from the internet takes time, and is interrupting the rendering of the collection view. These issues will be fixed in *Chapter 24, Swift Concurrency*.

4. Update `collectionView(_:numberOfItemsInSection:)` as follows to get the number of collection views to be displayed from `manager`:

```
func collectionView(_ collectionView: UICollectionView,
    numberOfItemsInSection section: Int) -> Int {
    manager.numberOfRestaurantItems()
}
```

5. Update `viewDidAppear()` as follows to call `createData()` when the collection view appears onscreen:

```
override func viewDidAppear(animated: Bool) {
    super.viewDidAppear(animated)
    createData()
}
```

Build and run your app. Set a location and click a cuisine. If there are restaurants that match the selected criteria, you'll see them displayed in the **Restaurant List** screen. Otherwise, the `NoDataView` instance will be displayed.

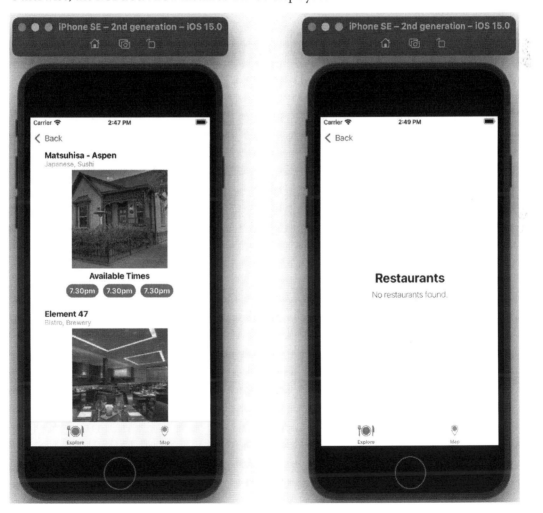

Figure 17.26: iOS simulator showing Restaurant List screen

Before you finish with the `RestaurantListViewController` class, there is just one more thing. It would be nice if the selected city were shown in the **Restaurant List** screen. Let's add code to display it at the top of the **Restaurant List** screen's navigation bar using large titles. Follow these steps:

1. In the `RestaurantListViewController` file, add the following method into the `private` extension after `createData()` to display the selected city in the navigation bar:

```
func setupTitle() {
    navigationController?.setNavigationBarHidden(
    false, animated: false)
    title = selectedCity?.cityAndState.uppercased()
    navigationController?.navigationBar.
    prefersLargeTitles = true
}
```

Every `UIViewController` instance has a `title` property, and if the navigation bar is visible, `title` will be visible as well. This method shows the navigation bar and sets the `RestaurantListViewController` instance's `title` to a string containing the city and state names in uppercase.

2. Call `setupTitle()` after `createData()` in the `viewDidAppear()` method:

```
override func viewDidAppear(_ animated: Bool) {
    super.viewDidAppear(animated)
    createData()
    setupTitle()
}
```

This calls the `setupTitle()` method when the **Restaurant List** screen appears.

Build and run your app. Select a location and cuisine. You should see the city and state in uppercase letters at the top of the **Restaurant List** screen:

Figure 17.27: iOS Simulator showing Restaurant List screen with title

You have completed the implementation of the **Restaurant List** screen, and you have finally reached the end of this chapter. Good job!

Summary

You have accomplished a lot in this chapter. You started by learning about the JSON format, and you created the `RestaurantDataManager` class, a data manager class that can load data from JSON files. You configured the `MapViewController` class to get data from a `RestaurantDataManager` instance to display a list of restaurants on the **Map** screen. Next, you configured the `LocationViewController` class to store the location selected by the user and pass it to an `ExploreViewController` instance when the **Done** button is tapped. After that, you configured the `ExploreViewController` class to pass the selected location and cuisine to the `RestaurantListViewController` instance when a type of cuisine is selected. Finally, you configured the `RestaurantListViewController` class to get a list of restaurants from the `RestaurantDataManager` instance, and display them in the **Restaurant List** screen, filtered by the selected cuisine. You also created a `NoDataView` class and view, which is displayed if there are no restaurants at a particular location offering the selected cuisine.

You are now able to load and read data from JSON files and pass that data between different view controllers in your app for display in collection views and map views. You also learned how to use `UITableViewController` delegate methods to handle user interaction with table views. This will be useful when you're creating your own apps.

In the next chapter, you'll implement the **Restaurant Detail** screen, which displays details of a specific restaurant using a table view containing static cells.

18
Displaying Data in a Static Table View

You've come a long way, and your app has data in all its screens except for the **Restaurant Detail** screen.

In this chapter, you'll configure the `RestaurantDetailViewController` class to manage the views in the **Restaurant Detail** screen. Next, you'll add methods to `viewDidLoad()` to populate the table view when the **Restaurant Detail** screen is displayed. Finally, you will pass the appropriate `RestaurantItem` instance from the `RestaurantListViewController` and `MapViewController` instances to the `RestaurantDetailViewController` instance, which will display the data from that `RestaurantItem` instance on the **Restaurant Detail** screen.

By the end of this chapter, you'll have learned how to make table views with static cells display data, and how to create a custom map image. By doing so, you'll be able to implement these features in your own apps.

The following topics will be covered in this chapter:

- Setting up outlets for the `RestaurantDetailViewController` class
- Displaying data in the static table view
- Passing data to the `RestaurantDetailViewController` instance

Technical requirements

You will continue working on the `LetsEat` project that you modified in the previous chapter.

The completed Xcode project for this chapter is in the `Chapter18` folder of the code bundle for this book, which can be downloaded here:

`https://github.com/PacktPublishing/iOS-15-Programming-for-Beginners-Sixth-Edition`

Check out the following video to see the code in action:

`https://bit.ly/3l2h6xq`

Let's start by creating outlets in the `RestaurantDetailViewController` class to enable it to manage the views in the **Restaurant Detail** screen.

Setting up outlets for the RestaurantDetailViewController class

Your app has data in all its screens except for the **Restaurant Detail** screen. This screen is accessed either by tapping a restaurant in the **Restaurant List** screen or by tapping the restaurant annotation view's callout bubble button in the **Map** screen. If you build and run your app, tapping a restaurant in the **Restaurant List** screen shows the placeholder **Restaurant Detail** screen:

Figure 18.1: iOS Simulator showing placeholder Restaurant Detail screen

Tapping the button in the restaurant annotation view's callout bubble in the **Map** screen shows the actual **Restaurant Detail** screen, but it does not contain any restaurant data:

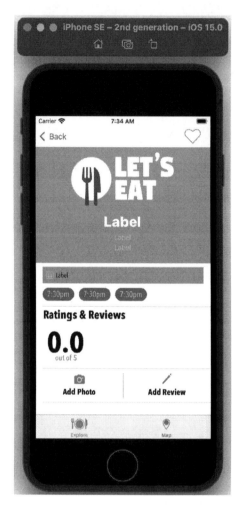

Figure 18.2: iOS Simulator showing Restaurant Detail screen

To fix this, let's set up the outlets for the `RestaurantDetailViewController` class. Click the `RestaurantDetailViewController` file in the Project navigator. Add the following outlets after the class declaration and before the `selectedRestaurant` property declaration:

```
// Nav Bar
@IBOutlet var heartButton: UIBarButtonItem!
// Cell One
```

```
@IBOutlet var nameLabel: UILabel!
@IBOutlet var cuisineLabel: UILabel!
@IBOutlet var headerAddressLabel: UILabel!
// Cell Two
@IBOutlet var tableDetailsLabel: UILabel!
// Cell Three
@IBOutlet var overallRatingLabel: UILabel!
// Cell Eight
@IBOutlet var addressLabel: UILabel!
// Cell Nine
@IBOutlet var locationMapImageView: UIImageView!
```

The outlets that you just set up are as follows:

- heartButton is the outlet for the heart-shaped button in the navigation bar. You won't be using it in this book, but it's something that you can work on later on your own.

- nameLabel is the outlet for the label that displays the name of the restaurant in the first cell.

- cuisineLabel is the outlet for the label that displays the cuisines offered by the restaurant in the first cell.

- headerAddressLabel is the outlet for the label that displays the address of the restaurant in the first cell.

- tableDetailsLabel is the outlet for the label that displays the table details of the restaurant in the second cell.

- overallRatingLabel is the outlet for the label that displays the overall rating for the restaurant in the third cell. You will calculate and set this value in *Chapter 21, Understanding Core Data*.

- addressLabel is the outlet for the label that displays the address of the restaurant in the eighth cell.

- locationMapImageView is the outlet for the image view that displays a location map for the restaurant in the ninth cell. You will write methods to generate this map later in this chapter.

Now that you've created the outlets, you'll connect them to the UI elements in the **Restaurant Detail View Controller Scene** in the `RestaurantDetail` storyboard file. Follow these steps:

1. Expand the `RestaurantDetail` folder in the Project navigator. Click the `RestaurantDetail` storyboard file. Then, click the **View Controller** icon in the **Restaurant Detail View Controller Scene**. Next, click the Identity inspector button. Under **Custom Class**, confirm that **Class** has been set to the `RestaurantDetailViewController` class:

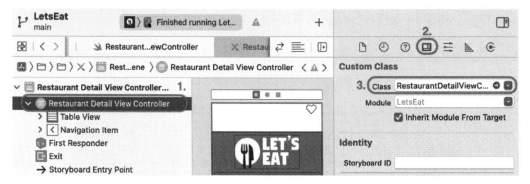

Figure 18.3: Identity inspector settings for Restaurant Detail View Controller

Note that the name of the view controller will change to **Restaurant Detail View Controller** once the class is set. Unlike the table view in the **Location View Controller Scene**, the table view in the **Restaurant Detail View Controller Scene** has static cells, meaning the number of cells is not dynamically generated based on data from a model object. As can be seen in the document outline, there are nine cells, and each cell has already been configured with the appropriate view objects. Clicking on each table view cell in the document outline will display that cell in the Editor area.

2. Click the Connections inspector button. You'll see all the outlets you added earlier in the `RestaurantDetailViewController` class:

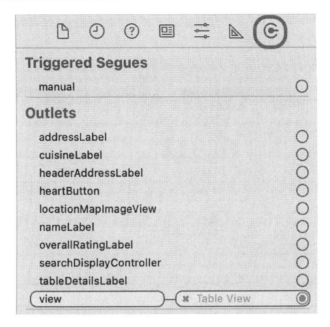

Figure 18.4: Connections inspector showing outlets for RestaurantDetailViewController class

3.   Click and drag from the `heartButton` outlet to the heart in the navigation bar:

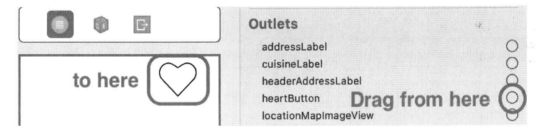

Figure 18.5: Connections inspector showing heartButton outlet

4. The `heartButton` outlet is now connected. Note that the description of the view will change to **Heart Button** in the document outline:

Figure 18.6: Document outline showing Heart Button view

5. Click on the last **Table View Cell** in the document outline to see the bottom of the table view and click **Restaurant Detail View Controller** (You may need to click a few times). You should see a **UIImageView**. Click and drag from the `locationMapImageView` outlet to the **Image View** in the last cell to connect them. Note that the name will change from **Image View** to **Location Map Image View** in the document outline:

Figure 18.7: Connections inspector showing locationMapImageView outlet

6. Click on the eighth **Table View Cell** in the document outline and click **Restaurant Detail View Controller**. Click and drag from the `addressLabel` outlet to the **Label** in the eighth cell to connect them. Note that the name will change from **Label** to **Address Label** in the document outline:

Figure 18.8: Connections inspector showing addressLabel outlet

7. Click on the first **Table View Cell** in the document outline and click **Restaurant Detail View Controller**. Click and drag from the `cuisineLabel` outlet to the second **Label** in the first cell to connect them. Note that the name will change from **Label** to **Cuisine Label** in the document outline:

Figure 18.9: Connections inspector showing cuisineLabel outlet

8. Click and drag from the `headerAddressLabel` outlet to the third **Label** in the first cell to connect them. Note that the name will change from **Label** to **Header Address Label** in the document outline:

Figure 18.10: Connections inspector showing headerAddressLabel outlet

9. Click and drag from the `nameLabel` outlet to the first **Label** in the first cell to connect them. Note that the name will change from **Label** to **Name Label** in the document outline:

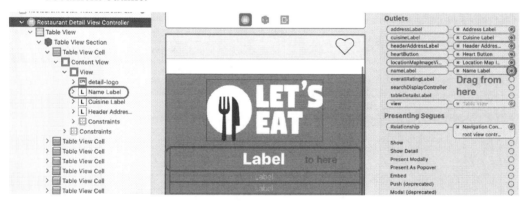

Figure 18.11: Connections inspector showing nameLabel outlet

10. Click on the third **Table View Cell** in the document outline and click **Restaurant Detail View Controller**. Click and drag from the `overallRatingLabel` outlet to the **Label** with the big black **0.0** inside it to connect them. Note that the name will change from **Label** to **Overall Rating Label** in the document outline:

Figure 18.12: Connections inspector showing overallRatingLabel outlet

11. Click on the second **Table View Cell** in the document outline and click **Restaurant Detail View Controller**. Click and drag from the `tableDetailsLabel` outlet to the **Label** just above the three red buttons in the second cell to connect them. Note that the name will change from **Label** to **Table Details Label** in the document outline:

Figure 18.13: Connections inspector showing tableDetailsLabel outlet

All the outlets for the `RestaurantDetailViewController` class have now been set up. In the next section, you'll modify the `RestaurantDetailViewController` class to receive restaurant data from the `RestaurantListViewController` and `MapViewController` instances and display it in the **Restaurant Detail** screen.

Displaying data in the static table view

You have successfully connected all the outlets in the `RestaurantDetailViewController` class to the user interface elements in the **Restaurant Detail** screen. Since this is a static table view, you won't be adopting the `UITableViewDataSource` protocol to populate the outlets. Instead, you will write custom methods to do so. Follow these steps:

1. Click the `RestaurantDetailViewController` file in the Project navigator.

2. Add code to import the `MapKit` framework after the existing `import` statement:

```
import MapKit
```

This is required since you will be using the `MapKit` framework's properties and methods to generate an image of a map for the image view in the last cell.

3. Add a private extension containing code to set the labels in the **Restaurant Detail** screen after the last curly brace:

```
private extension RestaurantDetailViewController {
    func setupLabels() {
        guard let restaurant =
        selectedRestaurant else {
            return
        }
        title = restaurant.name
        nameLabel.text = restaurant.name
        cuisineLabel.text = restaurant.subtitle
        headerAddressLabel.text = restaurant.address
        tableDetailsLabel.text = "Table for 7, tonight
        at 10:00 PM"
        addressLabel.text = restaurant.address
    }
}
```

The `setupLabels()` method is quite straightforward; it gets values from a `RestaurantItem` instance and puts them into the outlets in the `RestaurantDetailViewController` instance except for `tableDetailsLabel`, which is just assigned a string.

4. In the last cell, you will display an image of a map. To do this, you'll generate an image from a map region and set the `locationMapImageLabel` outlet to display that image. This image will also display the same custom annotation image you used in the **Map** screen. Add the following method after `setupLabels()` and before the last curly brace:

```
func createMap() {
    guard let annotation = selectedRestaurant, let long
    = annotation.long, let lat = annotation.lat else {
        return
    }

    let location = CLLocationCoordinate2D(latitude:
    lat, longitude: long)
```

```
    takeSnapshot(with: location)
}
```

This method creates a `CLLocationCoordinate2D` instance using the `selectedRestaurant` property's `lat` and `long` properties and assigns it to `location`. Then, it calls the `takeSnapshot(with:)` method, passing `location` as a parameter.

5. You'll see an error since `takeSnapShot(with:)` hasn't been implemented yet, so add the following code after the `createMap()` function to implement it:

```
func takeSnapshot(with location:
CLLocationCoordinate2D) {
    let mapSnapshotOptions = MKMapSnapshotter.Options()
    var loc = location
    let polyline = MKPolyline(coordinates: &loc, count:
1 )
    let region = MKCoordinateRegion(polyline.
boundingMapRect)
    mapSnapshotOptions.region = region
    mapSnapshotOptions.scale = UIScreen.main.scale
    mapSnapshotOptions.size = CGSize(width: 340,
height: 208)
    mapSnapshotOptions.showsBuildings = true
    mapSnapshotOptions.pointOfInterestFilter =
.includingAll
    let snapShotter = MKMapSnapshotter(options:
mapSnapshotOptions)
    snapShotter.start() { snapshot, error in
        guard let snapshot = snapshot else {
            return
        }
        UIGraphicsBeginImageContextWithOptions(
        mapSnapshotOptions.size, true, 0)
        snapshot.image.draw(at: .zero)
        let identifier = "custompin"
        let annotation = MKPointAnnotation()
        annotation.coordinate = location
        let pinView = MKPinAnnotationView(annotation:
```

```
        annotation, reuseIdentifier: identifier)
        pinView.image = UIImage(named: "custom-
annotation")!
        let pinImage = pinView.image
        var point = snapshot.point(for: location)
        let rect = self.locationMapImageView.bounds
        if rect.contains(point) {
            let pinCenterOffset = pinView.centerOffset
            point.x -= pinView.bounds.size.width / 2
            point.y -= pinView.bounds.size.height / 2
            point.x += pinCenterOffset.x
            point.y += pinCenterOffset.y
            pinImage?.draw(at: point)
        }

        if let image =
UIGraphicsGetImageFromCurrentImageContext() {
            UIGraphicsEndImageContext()
            DispatchQueue.main.async {
                self.locationMapImageView.image = image
            }
        }
    }
}
```

A full description of this method is beyond the scope of this book, but here's a simple explanation of what it does. Given a location, it takes a snapshot of the map at that location, adds the custom annotation you used earlier in the **Map** screen, converts it into an image, and assigns it to the `locationMapImageView` outlet in the `RestaurantDetailViewController` instance.

6. You have written all the methods that are required for the `RestaurantDetailViewController` class to display the desired `RestaurantItem` instance details in the **Restaurant Detail** screen. In the `private` extension before the `setupLabels()` method definition, add an `initialize()` method that calls the `setupLabels()` and `createMap()` methods:

```
func initialize() {
    setupLabels()
```

```
      createMap()
}
```

7. Modify the `viewDidLoad()` method to call the `initialize()` method when the `RestaurantDetailViewController` instance loads its view:

```
override func viewDidLoad() {
    super.viewDidLoad()
    initialize()
}
```

Recall that in *Chapter 16, Getting Started with MapKit,* you've already configured the `MapViewController` class to pass a `RestaurantItem` instance to the `RestaurantDetailViewController` instance. Build and run your app and go to the **Map** screen. Click on one of the restaurants to display a callout bubble. Click the button in the callout bubble, and you should see the restaurant details appear in the **Restaurant Detail** screen:

Figure 18.14: iOS Simulator showing Restaurant Detail screen

If you scroll down, you will see the map image in the last cell:

Figure 18.15: iOS Simulator showing map in Restaurant Detail screen

You have finished modifying the `RestaurantDetailViewController`
class, but you still need to pass the selected `RestaurantItem` instance
from the `RestaurantListViewController` instance to the
`RestaurantDetailViewController` instance. You'll do this in the next section.

Passing data to the RestaurantDetailViewController instance

You have added and connected the outlets for the **Restaurant Detail** screen inside
the `RestaurantDetailViewController` class. You've also added code to this
class to get restaurant data from a `RestaurantItem` instance and use it to populate
its outlets. The last thing you need to do is pass the selected `RestaurantItem`
instance from the `RestaurantListViewController` instance to the
`RestaurantDetailViewController` instance. Follow these steps:

1. Click the `RestaurantListViewController` file in the Project navigator.

2. Add the following code after `viewDidLoad():` to call
    a `showRestaurantDetail(segue:)` method if the segue identifier is
    `showDetail`:

```
override func prepare(for segue: UIStoryboardSegue,
sender: Any?) {
```

```
if let identifier = segue.identifier {
    switch identifier {
    case Segue.showDetail.rawValue:
        showRestaurantDetail(segue: segue)
    default:
        print("Segue not added")
    }
}
```

Recall that you added a segue between the **Restaurant List View Controller Scene** and the **Restaurant Detail View Controller Scene** in the storyboard. Before the RestaurantListViewController instance transitions to another view controller, the segue identifier is checked. If the segue identifier is showDetail, then the showRestaurantDetail method is executed. Only the segue between the **Restaurant List View Controller Scene** and the **Restaurant Detail View Controller Scene** has the showDetail identifier, so the destination view controller must be the RestaurantDetailViewController instance.

3. You'll see an error because the showRestaurantDetail(segue:) method hasn't been implemented. This method will pass the RestaurantItem instance from the RestaurantListViewController instance to the RestaurantDetailViewController instance. Add it after the opening curly brace of the private extension in the RestaurantListViewController class:

```
func showRestaurantDetail(segue: UIStoryboardSegue) {
    if let viewController = segue.destination as?
    RestaurantDetailViewController, let indexPath =
    collectionView.indexPathsForSelectedItems?.first {
        selectedRestaurant = manager.restaurantItem(at:
        indexPath.row)
        viewController.selectedRestaurant =
        selectedRestaurant
    }
}
```

This method first checks if the segue destination is an instance of `RestaurantDetailViewController`, and gets the index of the collection view cell that was tapped. Then, `manager` returns the `RestaurantItem` instance stored at that index, which is assigned to `selectedRestaurant`. The `RestaurantDetailViewController` instance's `selectedRestaurant` property is then set to this instance.

Now let's take a look at the **Restaurant List View Controller Scene** in the `Main` storyboard file. It is currently connected to a placeholder **View Controller Scene**. You'll update the `Main` storyboard file to remove the placeholder and connect the **Restaurant List View Controller Scene** to the **Restaurant Detail View Controller Scene** in the `RestaurantDetail` storyboard file. Follow these steps:

1. Click the `Main` storyboard file and locate the **Restaurant List View Controller Scene**. Click `restaurantCell` in the document outline. Then, *Ctrl + Drag* from `restaurantCell` to the `RestaurantDetail` storyboard reference (you added this storyboard reference in *Chapter 16, Getting Started with MapKit*) as shown:

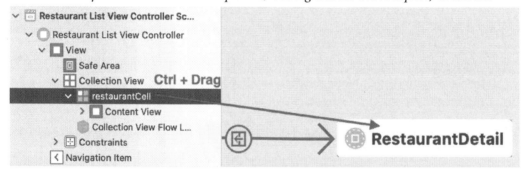

Figure 18.16: Editor area showing RestaurantDetail storyboard reference

2. Choose **Show** from the popup menu that appears:

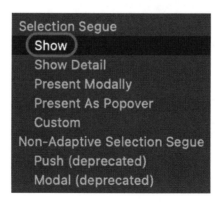

Figure 18.17: Segue pop-up menu with Show selected

3. Remove the placeholder scenes from the storyboard by selecting them and pressing *Delete* on your keyboard, as they are no longer needed:

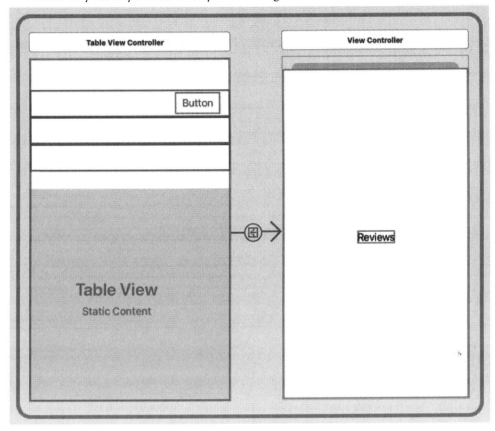

Figure 18.18: Editor area showing placeholder scenes to be removed

4. You will set the segue identifier to `showDetail`. As discussed earlier, this will set the `RestaurantDetailViewController` instance's `selectedRestaurant` property. Select the segue you just added:

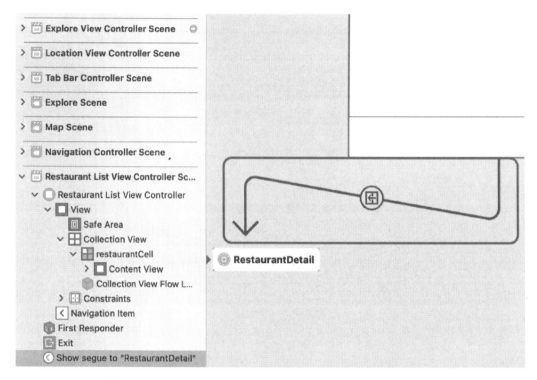

Figure 18.19: Segue between Restaurant List View Controller Scene
and RestaurantDetail storyboard reference

5. Click the Attributes inspector button. Under **Storyboard Segue**, set **Identifier** to `showDetail`:

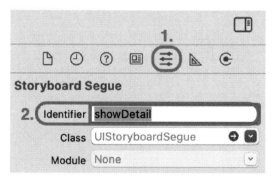

Figure 18.20: Attributes inspector setting for showDetail segue

Build and run your project. Select a city and a type of cuisine. Click on one of the restaurants in the **Restaurant List** screen. The details of that restaurant will appear in the **Restaurant Detail** screen:

Figure 18.21: iOS Simulator showing Restaurant Detail screen

The implementation for the **Restaurant Detail** screen is now complete. When you select a restaurant in the **Map** or **Restaurant List** screens, the details of that restaurant will be displayed in the **Restaurant Detail** screen. Awesome!

Summary

In this chapter, you connected outlets in the `RestaurantDetailViewController` class to the **Restaurant Detail** screen. Next, you added methods to `viewDidLoad()` to populate the table view when the **Restaurant Detail** screen is displayed. Finally, you passed the appropriate `RestaurantItem` instance from the `RestaurantListViewController` and `MapViewController` instances to the `RestaurantDetailViewController` instance, enabling it to display data from that `RestaurantItem` instance on the **Restaurant Detail** screen.

By doing this, you have learned how to make table views with static cells display data, as well as how to create a custom map image, which you can now implement in your own apps.

Congratulations! All the screens in your app now display data. However, if you look at the **Restaurant Detail** screen, there are no ratings, reviews, or photos for the restaurant, and no way to add them. You will implement this starting with the next chapter, where you'll create a custom control that allows you to add star ratings for a restaurant for the **Restaurant Detail** and **Review Form** screens.

19
Getting Started with Custom UIControls

At this point, your app has data in all of its screens, but the **Restaurant Detail** screen is incomplete. You can't set a star rating for a restaurant, and you can't add photos or reviews.

You have been using Apple's standard UI elements so far. In this chapter, you'll create a custom subclass of the `UIControl` class that displays restaurant ratings in the form of stars. You'll modify this subclass so users can set a rating for a restaurant by tapping it. After that, you'll implement a review form that allows users to submit restaurant reviews.

By the end of this chapter, you'll have learned how to create custom `UIControl` classes, handle touch events, and implement review forms for your own apps.

The following topics will be covered in this chapter:

- Creating a custom `UIControl` subclass
- Displaying stars in your custom `UIControl` subclass
- Adding support for touch events
- Implementing an unwind method for the **Cancel** button
- Creating the `ReviewFormViewController` class

Technical requirements

You will continue working on the `LetsEat` project that you modified in the previous chapter.

The completed Xcode project for this chapter is in the `Chapter19` folder of the code bundle for this book, which can be downloaded here:

`https://github.com/PacktPublishing/iOS-15-Programming-for-Beginners-Sixth-Edition`

Check out the following video to see the code in action:

`https://bit.ly/3cRFcXa`

Let's start by learning how to create a custom `UIControl` subclass that will display a star rating on the screen.

Creating a custom UIControl subclass

You've only used Apple's predefined UI elements so far, such as labels and buttons. All you had to do was click the Library button, search for the object you want, and drag it into the storyboard. However, there will be cases where the objects provided by Apple are either unsuitable or don't exist. In such cases, you will need to build your own. Let's review the **Restaurant Detail** screen that you saw in the app tour:

Figure 19.1: Restaurant Detail screen showing the star rating

You can see a group of five stars just above the **Add Review** button. Currently, the **Restaurant Detail View Controller Scene** in the `RestaurantDetail` storyboard file and the **Table View Controller Scene** in the `ReviewForm` storyboard file have blank view objects where the stars should be. You will create the `RatingsView` class, a custom subclass of the `UIControl` class, that you will use in both scenes. The `UIControl` class is a subclass of the `UIView` class, and it is used as the superclass for the `RatingsView` class because `RatingsView` instances have to respond when the user taps on them.

> **Important Information**
>
> You can learn more about `UIControl` at `https://developer.apple.com/documentation/uikit/uicontrol`.

A `RatingsView` instance will display ratings as stars. The user will also be able to select half-stars. Let's begin by creating a subclass of the `UIControl` class. Follow these steps:

1. Right-click the `Review Form` folder and select **New File**.

2. **iOS** should already be selected. Choose **Cocoa Touch Class** and then click **Next**.

3. Configure the file as follows:

   Class: `RatingsView`

   Subclass: `UIControl`

   Language: `Swift`

   Click **Next**.

4. Click **Create**. The `RatingsView` file will appear in the Project navigator.

Now you need to set the identity of the view object next to the **0.0** label in the **Restaurant Detail View Controller Scene** to `RatingsView`. Follow these steps:

1. Expand the `RestaurantDetail` folder in the Project navigator. Click the `RestaurantDetail` storyboard file and select the **View** object next to the **0.0 Label** as shown:

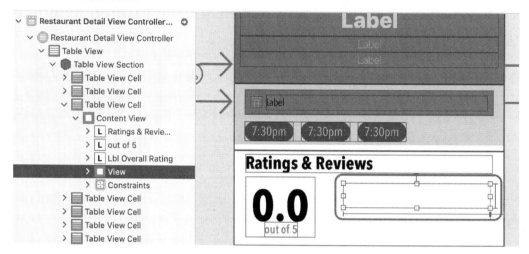

Figure 19.2: Editor area showing View object next to the 0.0 Label

2. Click the Identity inspector button. Under **Custom Class**, set **Class** to `RatingsView`:

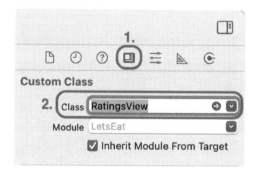

Figure 19.3: Identity inspector with Class set to RatingsView

Now let's modify the `RatingsView` class to make it display stars. You'll use the graphic assets inside the `Assets.xcassets` file to do this in the next section.

Displaying stars in your custom UIControl subclass

So far, you have created a new UIControl subclass named RatingsView in your project. You have also assigned the class of the view object next to the **0.0** label in the Restaurant Detail screen to the RatingsView class. For the rest of this chapter, an instance of the RatingsView class will be referred to as a ratings view (the same way an instance of the UIButton class is referred to as a button). In this section, you will add some code to the RatingsView class to make a ratings view display stars. Follow these steps:

1. Click the RatingsView file in the Project navigator and remove all the commented code.

2. Type the following after the RatingsView class declaration to declare the properties for the class:

```
private let filledStarImage = UIImage(named:
"filled-star")
private let halfStarImage = UIImage(named:
"half-star")
private let emptyStarImage = UIImage(named:
"empty-star")
private var totalStars = 5
var rating = 0.0
```

The first three properties, filledStarImage, halfStarImage, and emptyStarImage, are assigned the star images stored in the Assets.xcassets file.

The totalStars property determines the total number of stars to be drawn.

The rating property is used to store a restaurant rating. The types of stars drawn will be determined by the value of rating. For instance, if rating is 3.5, the ratings view will display three filled stars, one half-filled star, and one empty star.

Next, let's create the method that will draw the ratings view on the screen. All UIView subclasses have a draw(_:) method, which is responsible for drawing their views on the screen. You'll override the superclass implementation of this method for the RatingsView class. Follow these steps:

1. Add the following code in the class declaration after the property declarations:

```
override func draw(_ rect: CGRect) {
    let context = UIGraphicsGetCurrentContext()
    context!.setFillColor(UIColor.systemBackground.
    cgColor)
```

```
context!.fill(rect)
let ratingsViewWidth = rect.size.width
let availableWidthForStar = ratingsViewWidth /
Double(totalStars)
let starSidelength = (availableWidthForStar <=
rect.size.height) ? availableWidthForStar :
rect.size.height
for index in 0..<totalStars {
    let starOriginX = (availableWidthForStar *
    Double(index)) + ((availableWidthForStar -
    starSidelength) / 2)
    let starOriginY = ((rect.size.height -
    starSidelength) / 2)
    let frame = CGRect(x: starOriginX,
    y: starOriginY, width: starSidelength,
    height: starSidelength)
    var starToDraw: UIImage!
    if (Double(index + 1) <= self.rating) {
        starToDraw = filledStarImage
    } else if (Double(index + 1) <=
    self.rating.rounded()) {
        starToDraw = halfStarImage
    } else {
        starToDraw = emptyStarImage
    }
    starToDraw.draw(in: frame)
}
}
```

Let's break this down:

```
let context = UIGraphicsGetCurrentContext()
```

Creates an instance of `UIGraphicsGetCurrentContext` and assigns it to
`context`. You can think of it as a sketchpad, where you will compose UI
elements together.

```
context!.setFillColor(UIColor.systemBackground.
cgColor)
```

Sets the fill color of `context` to the default system background color.

```
context!.fill(rect)
```

Fills the rectangular area specified by `rect` with the fill color.

```
let ratingsViewWidth = rect.size.width
let availableWidthForStar = ratingsViewWidth /
Double(totalStars)
let starSidelength = (availableWidthForStar <=
rect.size.height) ? availableWidthForStar :
rect.size.height
```

These statements determine how big each star should be. The first statement gets the width of the ratings view and assigns it to `ratingsViewWidth`. The next statement gets the width available for each star by dividing the width of the ratings view by the number of stars that need to be drawn. This value is assigned to `availableWidthForStar`. For the third statement, imagine that each star is enclosed in a rectangle. This statement calculates how long each side of this rectangle should be in order to fit within the ratings view. If `availableWidthForStar` is less than or equal to the ratings view's height, `starSideLength` is set to `availableWidthForStar`; otherwise, it's set to be the same as the ratings view's height.

> **Important Information**
>
> The third statement makes use of a **ternary operator**. More information can be found at this link: `https://docs.swift.org/swift-book/LanguageGuide/BasicOperators.html`.

For example, let's assume the ratings view is 200 points wide and 50 points high. `availableWidthForStar` would be 200/5 = 40. Since 40 <= 50 evaluates to `true`, `starSideLength` will be set to `40`.

```
for index in 0..<totalStars {
```

Since `totalStars` is set to 5, this `for` loop repeats five times.

```
let starOriginX = (availableWidthForStar *
Double(index)) + ((availableWidthForStar -
starSidelength) / 2
let starOriginY = ((rect.size.height - starSidelength)
/ 2)
```

```
let frame = CGRect(x: starOriginX, y: starOriginY,
width: starSidelength, height: starSidelength)
```

These statements calculate the origin and size of the rectangle where each star should be drawn within the ratings view. This is then assigned to `frame`. The origin values are offset from the top-left corner of the ratings view, and the width and height are set to `starSidelength`.

For example, for the first star, `starOriginX` is (40*0.0) + (40-40)/2 = 0. `starOriginY` is (50 – 40)/2 = 5. `frame` would thus be a `CGRect` where x is 0, y is 5, `width` is 40, and `height` is 40.

```
var starToDraw: UIImage!
if (Double(index + 1) <= self.rating) {
    starToDraw = filledStarImage
} else if (Double(index + 1) <= self.rating.rounded())
{
    starToDraw = halfStarImage
} else {
    starToDraw = emptyStarImage
}
```

Depending on the value of the ratings view's `rating` property, these statements determine whether the star to be drawn is filled, half-filled, or empty.

For example, let's assume `rating` is 3.5.

The first star has an index of 0. This means `Double(0 + 1) <= 3.5` will be 1.0 <= 3.5, which evaluates to `true`. This means the first star that's drawn will be a filled star. The same is true for the second and third stars.

The fourth star has an index of 3. This means `Double(3 + 1) <= 3.5` will be 4.0 <= 3.5, which evaluates to `false`. The `else` clause evaluates `Double(3 + 1) <= 4.0`, which evaluates to `true`, so the fourth star drawn will be a half-filled star.

The fifth star has an index of 4. This means `Double(4 + 1) <= 3.5` will be 5.0 <= 3.5, which evaluates to `false`. The `else` clause evaluates `Double(4 + 1) <= 4.0`, which also evaluates to `false`, so the fifth star drawn will be an empty star.

```
starToDraw.draw(in: frame)
```

This statement draws the star in the specified `frame`.

That's all the code that's needed for the `RatingsView` class. Now, let's add an outlet to the `RestaurantDetailViewController` class so that it can manage what the ratings view displays. Follow these steps:

1. Click the `RestaurantDetailViewController` file in the Project navigator.

2. Type in the following code after the `overallRatingLabel` outlet:

```
@IBOutlet var ratingsView: RatingsView!
```

This creates an outlet in the `RestaurantDetailViewController` class for the ratings view. You now have an outlet named `ratingsView` of type `RatingsView` that you will connect to the ratings view in the storyboard later.

3. Add a method to assign `3.5` to a `ratingsView` instance's `rating` property. Type the following in your `private` extension after the `initialize()` method:

```
func createRating() {
    ratingsView.rating = 3.5
}
```

4. Modify the `initalize()` method to call the `createRating()` method:

```
func initialize() {
    setupLabels()
    createMap()
    createRating()
}
```

5. Open the `RestaurantDetail` storyboard file and select **Restaurant Detail View Controller** in the document outline. Click the Connections inspector button. Drag from the `ratingsView` outlet to the ratings view:

Figure 19.4: Connections inspector showing the ratingsView outlet

Build and run your project and go to the **Restaurant Detail** screen for any restaurant. The ratings view should display three and a half stars:

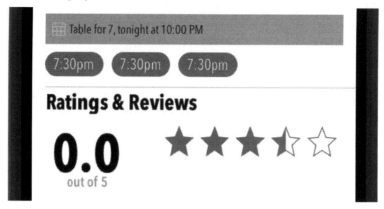

Figure 19.5: iOS Simulator showing ratings view displaying 3.5 stars

You have created and implemented the ratings view for the **Restaurant Detail** screen. It looks great, but at the moment, the ratings view does not respond when you tap on it. You will make it respond to touch events in the next section so the user can select a rating.

Adding support for touch events

At present, the `RestaurantDetailViewController` class has an outlet, `ratingsView`, connected to a ratings view in the **Restaurant Detail** screen. It displays a rating of three and a half stars, but you can't change the rating. You will need to support touch events to make the ratings view respond to taps.

> **Important Information**
>
> You can learn more about handling touches at `https://developer.apple.com/documentation/uikit/touches_presses_and_gestures/handling_touches_in_your_view`.

To support touch events, you'll modify the `RatingsView` class to track the user's touches on the screen and use them to determine the rating. Follow these steps:

1. Click the `RatingsView` file in the Project navigator and add the following property after the `draw(_:)` method:

```
override var canBecomeFirstResponder: Bool {
    true
}
```

canBecomeFirstResponder is a UIControl property that determines whether an object can become the first responder. The ratings view needs to become the first responder to respond to touch events. This method returns false by default, as not all user interface elements need to respond to touches. You override this method to make it return true so the ratings view can become the first responder.

2. To track the user's touches on the screen, add the following code after the canBecomeFirstResponder property you just added:

```swift
override func beginTracking(_ touch: UITouch, with
event: UIEvent?) -> Bool {
    guard self.isEnabled else {
        return false
    }
    super.beginTracking(touch, with: event)
    handle(with: touch)
    return true
}
```

Let's break this down:

```swift
override func beginTracking(_ touch: UITouch, with event:
UIEvent?) -> Bool {
```

This method is one of the methods declared in the UIControl class. It is called when the user's touch is within the bounds of a UIControl instance. The location, size, movement, and force of a touch on the screen are stored in a UITouch instance. This method needs to return true if you want to track the user's touches. You override this method so you can define custom behavior when the user touches the ratings view.

```swift
guard self.isEnabled else {
    return false
}
```

The isEnabled property is checked in this guard statement to see if the ratings view is enabled. If the ratings view is not enabled, the user's touches will not be tracked.

```swift
super.beginTracking(touch, with: event)
```

Calls the superclass implementation of this method. This will take care of any initialization required by the parent class.

```
handle(with: touch)
```

You'll pass the UITouch instance to this method, which will be executed for every touch. You'll declare and define this method in the next step.

```
return true
```

Tracks the user's touches when the ratings view is enabled.

3. You'll see an error because you haven't implemented handle(with:) yet, so create a private extension for RatingsView after all other code in the file and type the following code into it:

```
private extension RatingsView {
    func handle(with touch: UITouch) {
        let starRectWidth = self.bounds.size.width /
        Double(totalStars)
        let location = touch.location(in: self)
        var value = location.x / starRectWidth
        if (value + 0.5) < value.rounded(.up) {
            value = floor(value) + 0.5
        } else {
            value = value.rounded(.up)
        }
        updateRating(with: value)
    }
}
```

handle(with:) will calculate the rating value based on the location of the user's touch. It takes a UITouch instance as a parameter. First, starRectWidth is assigned the ratings view's width, divided by 5. Next, the UITouch instance's location within the ratings view is assigned to location. Then, value is assigned the x position of location divided by starRectWidth. This means value will contain a range of values between 0 and 5. Next, the if statement calculates the rating corresponding to the position of the touch and calls updateRating(with:), passing value to it. You'll implement updateRating(with:) in the next step.

To understand how the if statement works, let's say the ratings view's width is 200. starRectWidth would be set to 200/5 = 40. Let's assume the user touched the screen at position x = 130, y = 17, which corresponds to a point between the third and fourth stars. value would be assigned 130/40 = 3.25. So, the if statement would evaluate (3.25 + 0.5 < 3.25.rounded(.up)), which becomes (3.75 < 4.0), which returns true, thus value would be set to floor(3.25) + 0.5, which becomes 3.0 + 0.5, which is 3.5. So, updateRating(with:) would be passed a value of 3.5.

4. You'll see an error because you haven't implemented updateRating(with:) yet, so type the following code into the private extension after the handle(with:) method:

```
func updateRating(with newValue: Double) {
    if (self.rating != newValue && newValue >= 0 &&
    newValue <= Double(totalStars)) {
        self.rating = newValue
    }
}
```

updateRating(with:) checks to see if value is not equal to the current rating and between 0 and 5. If it is, value is assigned to rating.

Following on from the preceding example, since 3.5 is between 0 and 5, it will be assigned to rating if it's not equal to the current value of rating.

5. The ratings view will have to be redrawn once the rating has changed to display the correct state of the stars. Modify the rating property declaration as follows:

```
var rating = 0.0 {
    didSet {
        setNeedsDisplay()
    }
}
```

Here, you have defined a **property observer** to monitor changes in the rating property's value. Every time rating changes, setNeedsDisplay() is called and the ratings view is redrawn. Since the screen is redrawn only if the rating changes, there is a small performance benefit.

You've added all the code that's necessary for the ratings view to respond to touches. Now, you'll need to update the `RestaurantDetailViewController` class to set the `isEnabled` property for the ratings view. Click the `RestaurantDetailViewController` file in the Project navigator and modify the `createRating()` method, as follows:

```
func createRating() {
    ratingsView.rating = 3.5
    ratingsView.isEnabled = true
}
```

Setting the `isEnabled` property to `true` allows the ratings view to become the first responder and begin tracking touches, which will trigger `handle(with:)` to calculate the rating based on the position of the touch, which in turn calls `updateRating(with:)` to update the ratings view.

Build and run your project. Tapping on the ratings view now changes the rating, depending on where you tapped. Tap between the first and second stars, as shown:

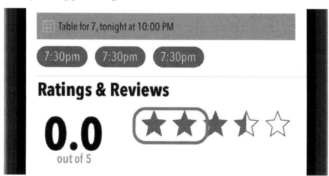

Figure 19.6: iOS Simulator showing ratings view tap location

The rating will change to one and a half stars.

Eventually, you'll calculate the overall rating by aggregating all the ratings submitted by users in the **Review Form** screen. If you tap the **Add Review** button, the **Review Form** screen is displayed but you can't dismiss it or set a rating. In the next section, you'll configure the **Cancel** button to dismiss the **Review Form** screen when tapped.

Implementing an unwind method for the Cancel button

Let's take a look at the **Review Form** screen. The segue between the **Add Review** button and the **Review Form** screen has already been made for you. Build and run your project, go to the **Restaurant Detail** screen, and tap the **Add Review** button:

Figure 19.7: iOS Simulator showing Add Review button

The **Review Form** screen is displayed (note that the top table view cell has a blank space where a ratings view should be, which you will add later):

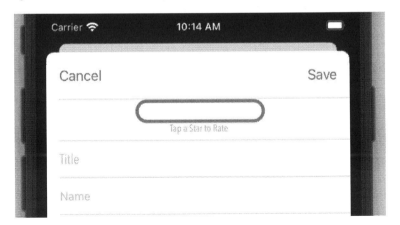

Figure 19.8: iOS Simulator showing Review Form screen

Once the **Review Form** screen appears on the screen, you can't dismiss it, as the button actions for the **Save** and **Cancel** buttons have not been configured. Just as you did with the **Locations** screen, you need to implement an unwind method to dismiss the **Review Form** screen. Follow these steps:

1. Click the `RestaurantDetailViewController` file in the Project navigator.

2. Implement the unwind method as follows in the `private` extension, before the `createRating()` method:

```
@IBAction func unwindReviewCancel(segue:
UIStoryboardSegue) {

}
```

This method will be called when the **Review Form** screen transitions to the **Restaurant Detail** screen.

3. Open the `ReviewForm` storyboard file and *Ctrl + Drag* from the **Cancel** button to the Exit icon in the Scene Dock, as shown:

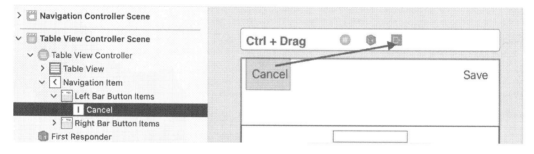

Figure 19.9: Table View Controller Scene showing Cancel button action being set

4. Choose `unwindReviewCancelWithSegue` in the popup menu:

Figure 19.10: Pop-up menu with unwindReviewCancelWithSegue: selected

Build and run your project. You can now dismiss the **Review Form** screen by tapping the **Cancel** button.

Next, let's look at the **Save** button. You'll create a view controller for the **Review Form** screen to process the data inside the **Review Form** screen's fields when the **Save** button is tapped. You'll do this in the next section.

Creating the ReviewFormViewController class

To process user input, you'll create the `ReviewFormViewController` class to be the view controller for the **Review Form** screen. For the time being, you'll configure this class to grab all the values from the **Review Form** screen's fields and print them in the Debug area. You will learn how to store reviews later in *Chapter 21, Understanding Core Data*. Follow these steps:

1. Right-click the `ReviewForm` folder and select **New File**.

2. **iOS** should already be selected. Choose **Cocoa Touch Class** and then click **Next**.

3. Configure the file as follows:

    Class: `ReviewFormViewController`

    Subclass: `UITableViewController`

    Also create XIB: Unchecked

    Language: `Swift`

    Click **Next**.

4. Click **Create**. The `ReviewFormViewController` file will appear in the Project navigator.

5. Delete everything after the `viewDidLoad()` method and all the commented code. Add the following outlets after the class declaration. They correspond to the fields inside the **Review Form** screen:

    ```
    @IBOutlet var ratingsView: RatingsView!
    @IBOutlet var titleTextField: UITextField!
    @IBOutlet var nameTextField: UITextField!
    @IBOutlet var reviewTextView: UITextView!
    ```

6. You also need to configure the action for the **Save** button. Add the following code after the `viewDidLoad()` method:

    ```
    @IBAction func onSaveTapped(_ sender: Any) {
        print(ratingsView.rating)
        print(titleTextField.text as Any)
        print(nameTextField.text as Any)
    ```

```
print(reviewTextView.text as Any)
dismiss(animated: true, completion: nil)
}
```

This method prints the contents of the **Review Form** screen's fields to the Debug area and dismisses it.

Now let's connect the outlets in the **ReviewFormViewController** class to the user interface elements in the **Table View Controller Scene** in the ReviewForm storyboard file, as follows:

1. Click the ReviewForm storyboard file in the Project navigator and click the **Table View Controller** icon inside the **Table View Controller Scene**. Click the Identity inspector button. Under **Custom Class**, set **Class** to ReviewFormViewController:

Figure 19.11: Identity inspector with Class set to ReviewFormViewController

Note that the name **Table View Controller Scene** will change to **Review Form View Controller Scene**.

2. Click the **View** inside the **Content View** of the first **Table View Cell** as shown, click the Identity inspector button, and under **Custom Class**, set **Class** to RatingsView. The view's name will change to **Ratings View**:

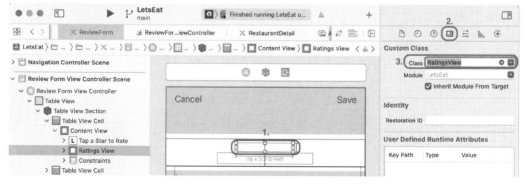

Figure 19.12: Identity inspector with Class set to RatingsView

3. Next, you will connect the outlets. Click the **Review Form View Controller** icon in the document outline and click the Connections inspector button:

Figure 19.13: Connections Inspector button

4. Connect the `ratingsView` outlet to the **Ratings View**:

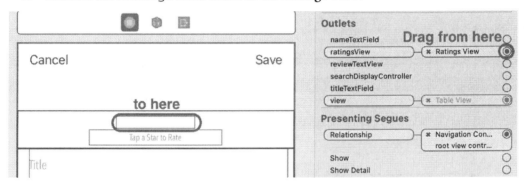

Figure 19.14: Connections inspector showing ratingsView outlet

5. Connect the `titleTextField` outlet to the first **Text Field**:

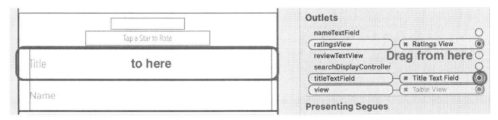

Figure 19.15: Connections inspector showing titleTextField outlet

6.   Connect the `nameTextField` outlet to the second **Text Field**:

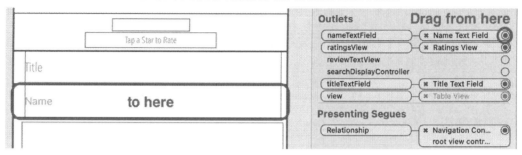

Figure 19.16: Connections inspector showing nameTextField outlet

7.   Connect the `reviewTextView` outlet to the **Text View**:

Figure 19.17: Connections inspector showing reviewTextView outlet

8.   Finally, connect the `onSaveTapped:` action to the **Save** button:

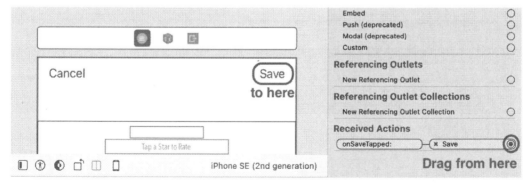

Figure 19.18: Connections inspector showing Save button action being set

Build and run your app. Go to the **Review Form** screen, set a rating, add some sample text to the fields, and tap the **Save** button:

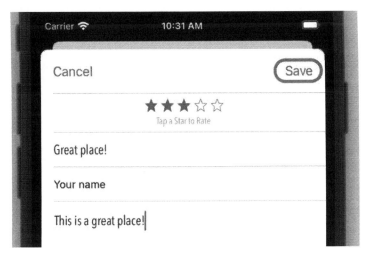

Figure 19.19: iOS Simulator showing Review Form screen

You'll see the data you entered appear in the Debug area:

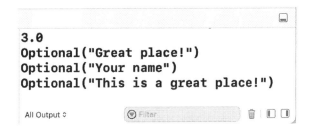

Figure 19.20: Debug area showing contents of Review Form screen text fields

Congratulations! The **Review Form** screen is now able to accept user input. You'll learn how to save and present the review data in *Chapter 21, Understanding Core Data.*

Summary

In this chapter, you created a new custom UIControl subclass, RatingsView, from scratch and added it to the **Restaurant Detail** and **Review Form** screens. You configured it to respond to touches so that a user can set a restaurant rating in the **Review Form** screen. Finally, you implemented the ReviewFormViewController class, a view controller for the **Review Form** screen, and configured the **Cancel** and **Save** button actions so that the user can dismiss the Review Form screen or submit a review.

You now have a good grasp of how to create custom `UIControl` classes, how to make them respond to user interaction, and how to implement a review form that can accept user input. This will be useful when you write your own apps.

In the next chapter, you'll learn how to work with photos from the camera or Photo Library, as well as how to apply photo filters to the photos that you have.

20
Getting Started with Cameras and Photo Libraries

In the previous chapter, you created the `RatingsView` class and added it to the **Restaurant Detail** and **Review Form** screens. You also enabled the user to submit a review using the **Review Form** screen, although the submitted review is only printed to the Debug area for now.

In this chapter, you will complete the implementation of the **Photo Filter** screen so you can get a photo from the camera or photo library, and apply a filter to it. You'll start by importing a `.plist` file containing the filters you want to use, then create a filter object class to store filter data, and create a data manager class to read the `.plist` file and populate an array of filter objects. Next, you'll create a protocol with a method to apply filters to images. After that, you'll create view controllers for the **Photo Filter** screen and the collection view in it, implement the `UIImagePickerDelegate` protocol, which allows you to get photos from the camera or the photo library, and implement methods to apply a selected filter to a photo. Note that the photo will not be saved. You will learn how to save reviews and photos in the next chapter.

By the end of this chapter, you'll have learned how to import photos into your own apps, and how to apply filters to them.

The following topics will be covered in this chapter:

- Understanding filters
- Creating model objects for the **Photo Filter** screen
- Creating the `ImageFiltering` protocol
- Creating classes for the **Photo Filter** screen
- Implementing the image picker delegate protocol
- Getting permission to use the camera or photo library

Technical requirements

You will continue working on the `LetsEat` project that you modified in the previous chapter.

The resource files and completed Xcode project for this chapter are in the `Chapter20` folder of the code bundle for this book, which can be downloaded here:

`https://github.com/PacktPublishing/iOS-15-Programming-for-Beginners-Sixth-Edition`

Check out the following video to see the code in action:

`https://bit.ly/3oZZ93P`

Let's start by learning about photo filters, and how to apply them to images.

Understanding filters

iOS has a range of built-in filters that you can use to enhance photos. These filters are available via the **Core Image** library. Core Image is an image processing and analysis technology that provides high-performance processing for still and video images. There are over 170 filters available in Core Image, giving you the ability to apply a wide range of cool effects to your photos.

> **Important Information**
> You can learn more about Core Image at `https://developer.apple.com/documentation/coreimage`.

For this app, you'll just be using 10 filters. The details of these filters are provided in a `.plist` file. Import this file into your app by following these steps:

1. If you have not yet done so, download and unzip the code bundle for this book at this link: `https://github.com/PacktPublishing/iOS-15-Programming-for-Beginners-Sixth-Edition`. You will find the `FilterData.plist` inside the `resources` folder in the `Chapter20` folder.

2. In the Project navigator, create a new group inside the `PhotoFilter` folder and name it `Model`.

3. Drag `FilterData.plist` to the `Model` folder. Make sure **Copy items if needed** is ticked and click **Finish**.

4. Click `FilterData.plist` in the Project navigator to see what it contains:

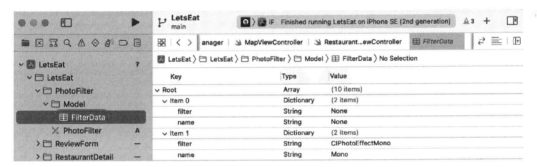

Figure 20.1: Editor area showing contents for FilterData.plist

As you can see, `FilterData.plist` is an array of dictionaries. Each dictionary contains the name of the filter and a descriptive label. In the next section, you'll see how you can use the information in `FilterData.plist` in your app.

Creating model objects for the Photo Filter screen

To get the information from `FilterData.plist` into your app, you'll create a structure, `FilterItem`, that can store details about a filter, and a data manager class, `FilterManager`, that will load `FilterData.plist` and create an array of `FilterItem` instances. This is similar to the method used to load cuisine and location information into your app. Let's start by creating the `FilterItem` structure. Follow these steps:

1. Right-click the `Model` folder in the `PhotoFilter` folder and select **New File**.

2. **iOS** should already be selected. Choose **Swift File** and click **Next**.

3. Name this file `FilterItem`. Click **Create**. The `FilterItem` file will appear in the Project navigator.

4. Inside the `FilterItem` file, type the following code after the `import` statement to declare and define the `FilterItem` structure:

```
struct FilterItem {
    let filter: String?
    let name: String?
    init(dict: [String: String]) {
        self.filter = dict["filter"]
        self.name = dict["name"]
    }
}
```

This structure has two properties and an initializer. The `filter` property will store filter names, and the `name` property will store the brief filter description. The initializer takes a dictionary as a parameter to set the `name` and `filter` properties when an instance of this class is created.

Now that you've created the `FilterItem` class, you'll create the data manager class, `FilterDataManager`. Follow these steps:

1. Right-click the `Model` folder in the `PhotoFilter` folder and select **New File**.

2. **iOS** should already be selected. Choose **Swift File** and click **Next**.

3. Name this file `FilterDataManager`. Click **Create**. The `FilterDataManager` file will appear in the Project navigator.

4. Inside the `FilterDataManager` file, type in the following code after the `import` statement to declare and define the `FilterDataManager` class:

```
class FilterDataManager: DataManager {
    func fetch() -> [FilterItem] {
        var filterItems: [FilterItem] = []
        for data in loadPlist(file: "FilterData") {
            filterItems.append(FilterItem(dict:
            data as! [String: String]))
        }
        return filterItems
    }
}
```

The `FilterDataManager` class adopts the `DataManager` protocol you created earlier in *Chapter 16, Getting Started with MapKit*. Calling the `fetch()` method loads data from `FilterData.plist`, creates an array of `FilterItem` instances, and returns it.

In the next section, you'll create a protocol with a method to apply a filter to an image.

Creating the ImageFiltering protocol

You need a way to apply a filter to an image. You will create a protocol, `ImageFiltering`, that implements a method, `apply(filter:to:)`, to do this. Any class that adopts this protocol will have access to this method, which applies a specified filter to an image. Follow these steps:

1. Right-click the `PhotoFilter` folder and select **New File**.

2. **iOS** should already be selected. Choose **Swift File** and click **Next**.

3. Name this file `ImageFiltering`. Click **Create**. The `ImageFiltering` file will appear in the Project navigator.

4. Modify the code in this file to declare and define the `ImageFiltering` protocol:

```swift
import UIKit
import CoreImage
protocol ImageFiltering {
    func apply(filter: String, originalImage:
    UIImage) -> UIImage
}
extension ImageFiltering {
    func apply(filter: String, originalImage:
    UIImage) -> UIImage {
        let initialCIImage = CIImage(image:
        originalImage, options: nil)
        let originalOrientation =
        originalImage.imageOrientation
        guard let ciFilter = CIFilter(name:
        filter) else {
            print("filter not found")
            return originalImage
        }
```

```
        ciFilter.setValue(initialCIImage, forKey:
    kCIInputImageKey)
    let context = CIContext()
    let filteredCIImage =
    (ciFilter.outputImage)!
    let filteredCGImage =
    context.createCGImage(filteredCIImage,
    from: filteredCIImage.extent)
    return UIImage(cgImage: filteredCGImage!,
    scale: 1.0, orientation:
    originalOrientation)
    }
}
```

Let's break this down:

```
import UIKit
```

The `UIKit` framework provides the required infrastructure for your iOS app. You import `UIKit` instead of `Foundation` because support for the `UIImage` class is not available in `Foundation`.

```
import CoreImage
```

Core Image is an image processing and analysis technology that provides high-performance processing for still and video images. You import `CoreImage` as it is required to access the built-in photo filters.

```
protocol ImageFiltering {
    func apply(filter: String, originalImage:
    UIImage) -> UIImage
}
```

Here, you declare a protocol named `ImageFiltering`. This protocol specifies a method, `apply(filter:originalImage:)`, that takes a filter name and an image as parameters.

```
extension ImageFiltering {
    func apply(filter: String, originalImage:
    UIImage) -> UIImage {
```

This extension of the `ImageFiltering` protocol contains the implementation of the `apply(filter:originalImage:)` method. This means that any class that adopts the `ImageFiltering` protocol will be able to execute this method.

```
let initialCIImage = CIImage(image:
originalImage, options: nil)
```

This statement converts the original image to a `CIImage` instance so that you can apply filters to it, and assigns it to `initialCIImage`.

```
let originalOrientation =
originalImage.imageOrientation
```

This statement stores the original image orientation in `originalOrientation`.

```
guard let ciFilter = CIFilter(name: filter)
else {
    print("filter not found")
    return originalImage
}
```

This `guard` statement gets the filter with the same name as `filter` and assigns it to `ciFilter`, and returns the original image if the filter is not found.

```
ciFilter.setValue(initialCIImage, forKey:
kCIInputImageKey)
let context = CIContext()
let filteredCIImage =
(ciFilter.outputImage)!
```

These statements apply the selected filter to `initialCIImage` and store the result in `filteredCIImage`.

```
let filteredCGImage =
context.createCGImage(filteredCIImage, from:
filteredCIImage.extent)
return UIImage(cgImage: filteredCGImage!,
scale: 1.0, orientation:
originalOrientation)
```

These statements convert the `CIImage` instance stored in `filteredCIImage` back into a `UIImage` instance and returns it.

This completes the implementation of the `ImageFiltering` protocol and the `apply(filter:originalImage:)` method. At this point, you have the following:

- `FilterData.plist`, which contains photo filter data inside your app.

- `FilterItem`, a class that can hold a filter and a filter description.

- `FilterDataManager`, a data manager class that loads data from `FilterData.plist` and generates an array of `FilterItem` instances.

- `ImageFiltering`, a protocol that contains a method, `apply(filter:originalImage:)`, which applies a filter to an image.

In the next section, you'll create classes for the UI elements in the **Photo Filter** screen, which allows you to manage this screen and the collection view inside it.

Creating classes for the Photo Filter screen

So far, you have imported `FilterData.plist` into your app, created the `FilterItem` and `FilterDataManager` classes, and created the `ImageFiltering` protocol. In this section, you'll set up the classes for the **Photo Filter** screen, which allows you to manage this screen and the collection view inside it.

Remember that you added the `PhotoFilter` storyboard file to your project in *Chapter 16, Getting Started with MapKit*. It contains a scene that consists of a large image view that will hold the user-selected photo and a collection view that will display filter previews. The following screenshot shows what this will look like when you have completed the implementation:

Figure 20.2: iOS Simulator showing the completed Photo Filter screen

This screen works as follows. When you tap on the **Add Photo** button in the **Restaurant Detail** screen and select a photo, the **Photo Filter** screen will appear, showing the selected photo with a scrolling list of filters just below it. Each filter in the scrolling list is displayed in a collection view cell. Tapping a filter in the scrolling list will apply the selected filter to the photo.

In the next section, you'll create and configure a class to manage the collection view cells. Each cell will display a thumbnail preview of what a photo looks like with the filter applied.

Creating a class for the collection view cells

The **Photo Filter** screen provides the user interface that allows the user to select a filter to be applied to a photo. The collection view will display thumbnail previews of what a photo looks like with the filter applied. If you click the PhotoFilter storyboard file in the Project navigator, you will see that the collection view is already present in the **View Controller Scene**, but there is no way to set the contents of the collection view cells. You will create a class to manage them now. Follow these steps:

1. Right-click the PhotoFilter folder and select **New File**.

2. **iOS** should already be selected. Choose **Cocoa Touch Class** and click **Next**.

3. Configure the file as follows:

   Class: FilterCell

   Subclass: UICollectionViewCell

   Also create XIB: Unchecked

   Language: Swift

   Click **Next**.

4. Click **Create**. The FilterCell file will appear in the Project navigator.

5. Add the following code to this file to declare and define the FilterCell class:

```swift
import UIKit
class FilterCell: UICollectionViewCell {
    @IBOutlet var nameLabel: UILabel!
    @IBOutlet var thumbnailImageView: UIImageView!
    override func awakeFromNib() {
        super.awakeFromNib()
        thumbnailImageView.layer.cornerRadius = 9
        thumbnailImageView.layer.masksToBounds = true
```

```swift
        }
    }

    extension FilterCell: ImageFiltering {
        func set(filterItem: FilterItem,
        imageForThumbnail: UIImage) {
            nameLabel.text = filterItem.name
            if let filter = filterItem.filter {
                if filter != "None" {
                    let filteredImage = apply(filter:
                    filter, originalImage:
                    imageForThumbnail)
                    thumbnailImageView.image =
                    filteredImage
                } else {
                    thumbnailImageView.image =
                    imageForThumbnail
                }
            }
        }
    }
```

The `FilterCell` class has two properties: a label, `nameLabel`, and an image view, `thumbnailImageView`. The label will display the filter name, while the image view will display a thumbnail preview of the filter.

This class also contains two methods, `awakeFromNib()` and `set(filterItem:imageForThumbnail:)`.

The `awakeFromNib()` method is called after the `FilterCell` instance has been loaded, and the two statements inside it round the corners of the image view.

The `set(filterItem:imageForThumbnail:)` method takes `UIImage` and `FilterItem` instances as parameters, assigns the `name` property of the `FilterItem` instance to `nameLabel`, applies the filter specified by the `filter` property to the `UIImage` instance, and assigns the image with the filter applied to `thumbnailImageView`.

> **Important Information**
>
> For more details about `awakeFromNib()`, see this link: `https://developer.apple.com/documentation/objectivec/nsobject/1402907-awakefromnib`.

6. Click the `PhotoFilter` storyboard file in the Project navigator.

7. In the document outline, select **Collection View Cell** in the **View Controller Scene**. Click the Identity inspector button. Under **Custom Class**, set **Class** to `FilterCell`:

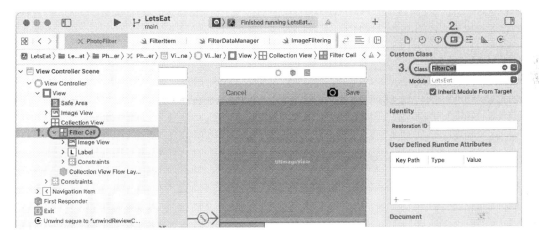

Figure 20.3: Identity inspector with Class set to FilterCell

8. Click the Attributes inspector button. Set **Identifier** to `filterCell`:

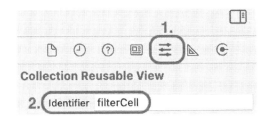

Figure 20.4: Attributes inspector with Identifier set to filterCell

9. Click the Connections inspector button. Connect the `nameLabel` and `thumbnailImageView` outlets to their corresponding UI elements as shown:

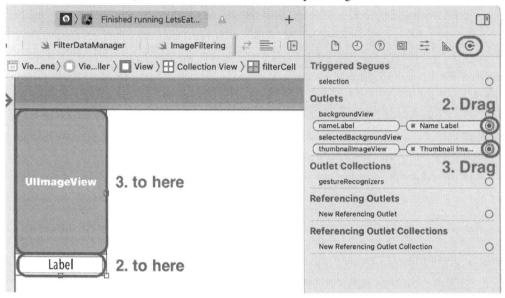

Figure 20.5: Connections inspector showing thumbnailImageView and nameLabel outlets

You have now completed setting up the collection view cells. In the next section, you'll create the view controller for the **Photo Filter** screen. This will allow you to select a photo and choose a filter to be applied to it.

Creating a view controller for the Photo Filter screen

So far, you have created the `FilterCell` class to manage the collection view cells in the **Photo Filter** screen. Now you'll create a view controller to manage this screen's contents. Follow these steps:

1. Right-click the `PhotoFilter` folder and select **New File**.

2. **iOS** should already be selected. Choose **Cocoa Touch Class** and click **Next**.

3. Configure the file, as follows:

    Class: `PhotoFilterViewController`

    Subclass: `UIViewController`

    Also create XIB: Unchecked

    Language: `Swift`

    Click Next.

4. Click **Create**. The `PhotoFilterViewController` file will appear in the Project navigator. Delete all the boilerplate code after the `viewDidLoad()` method.

5. Add the following code to the file to declare and define the `PhotoFilterViewController` class and its properties:

```
import UIKit
import AVFoundation
class PhotoFilterViewController: UIViewController {
    @IBOutlet var mainImageView: UIImageView!
    @IBOutlet var collectionView: UICollectionView!
    private let manager = FilterDataManager()
    var selectedRestaurantID: Int?
    private var mainImage: UIImage?
    private var thumbnail: UIImage?
    private var filters: [FilterItem] = []
    override func viewDidLoad() {
        super.viewDidLoad()
        initialize()
    }
}
```

Let's break this down:

```
import AVFoundation
```

This statement imports the `AVFoundation` framework. This framework contains methods for capturing, processing, synthesizing, controlling, importing, and exporting audiovisual media on Apple platforms.

> **Important Information**
>
> You can find out more about `AVFoundation` at this link:
>
> `https://developer.apple.com/av-foundation/`

```
class PhotoFilterViewController: UIViewController {
```

This statement declares the `PhotoFilterViewController` class, a subclass of the `UIViewController` class.

```
@IBOutlet var mainImageView: UIImageView!
```

This is an outlet for the image view that will display the user-selected photo with the filter applied.

```
@IBOutlet var collectionView: UICollectionView!
```

This is an outlet for the collection view that will display thumbnail previews of each filter.

```
private let manager = FilterDataManager()
```

This statement assigns an instance of the `FilterDataManager` class to the `manager` property.

```
var selectedRestaurantID:Int?
```

Each restaurant has a unique numeric identifier. This property is used to store that identifier. You'll see how it's used when storing photos using **Core Data** in the next chapter.

```
private var mainImage: UIImage?
```

This property stores the photo selected by the user.

```
private var thumbnail: UIImage?
```

This property stores the thumbnail for the user-selected photo.

```
private var filters: [FilterItem] = []
```

This property stores an array of `FilterItem` instances provided by `manager`.

```
override func viewDidLoad() {
    super.viewDidLoad()
    initialize()
}
```

This method calls an `initialize()` method when the `PhotoFilterViewController` instance loads its view. Note that this will generate an error, since `initialize()` hasn't been implemented yet.

6. As you did before, you will use extensions to organize your code. Add the following `private` extension containing the `initialize()` method after the closing curly brace:

```
// MARK: - Private Extension
private extension PhotoFilterViewController {
    func initialize() {
        setupCollectionView()
```

```
        checkSource()
    }
}
```

This extension contains the implementation of the `initialize()` method, which calls two other methods. `setupCollectionView()` sets up the collection view used to display the list of filters. `checkSource()` checks the user authorization status for the use of the camera. Note that these will generate errors since they haven't been implemented yet. You'll implement these methods in the next step.

7. Implement the `setupCollectionView()` and `checkSource()` methods in the `private` extension after the `initialize()` method:

```
func setupCollectionView() {
    let layout = UICollectionViewFlowLayout()
    layout.scrollDirection = .horizontal
    layout.sectionInset = UIEdgeInsets(top: 7,
    left: 7, bottom: 7, right: 7)
    layout.minimumInteritemSpacing = 0
    layout.minimumLineSpacing = 7
    collectionView.collectionViewLayout = layout
    collectionView.dataSource = self
    collectionView.delegate = self
}
func checkSource() {
    let cameraMediaType = AVMediaType.video
    let cameraAuthorizationStatus =
    AVCaptureDevice.authorizationStatus(for:
    cameraMediaType)
    switch cameraAuthorizationStatus {
    case .notDetermined:
        AVCaptureDevice.requestAccess(for:
        cameraMediaType) { granted in
            if granted {
                DispatchQueue.main.async {
                    self.showCameraUserInterface()
                }
            }
```

```
        }
    case .authorized:
        self.showCameraUserInterface()
    default:
        break
    }
}
```

Let's break this down:

```
setupCollectionView()
```

Sets up the collection view used to display thumbnail previews of the filters. Here, you create an instance of `UICollectionViewFlowLayout`, set the scroll direction, section insets, inter-item spacing, and line spacing properties, and assign it to the collection view. After that, you set the `PhotoFilterViewController` class as the delegate and data source for this collection view. Note that you're setting `delegate` and `dataSource` programmatically rather than using the storyboard; either approach is acceptable. Don't worry about the errors, they appear because you haven't adopted the `UICollectionViewDataSource` and `UICollectionViewDelegate` protocols for this class yet. You'll fix this later.

```
checkSource()
```

Checks the user authorization status for the use of the camera. Possible cases are as follows:

`.notDetermined` means the user hasn't been asked for access to the camera.

`.authorized` means the user has previously granted access to the camera.

`.restricted` means the user can't be granted access due to restrictions that have been set on the device.

`.denied` means the user has previously denied camera access to the app.

If the status is `.notDetermined`, the app will ask the user for permission and, if permission is given, the `showCameraUserInterface()` method is called. If the status is `.authorized`, the `showCameraUserInterface()` method is called. Note that this will generate an error because `showCameraUserInterface()` has not been implemented yet. If the status is `.restricted` or `.denied`, it falls under the `default:` case and the method exits.

8. There are a few more helper methods required. Add the following code to the private extension to implement them after the checkSource() method:

```
func showApplyFilterInterface() {
    filters = manager.fetch()
    if let mainImage = self.mainImage {
        mainImageView.image = mainImage
        collectionView.reloadData()
    }
}

@IBAction func onPhotoTapped(_ sender: Any) {
    checkSource()
}
```

Let's break this down:

```
showApplyFilterInterface()
```

This method will be called after the user selects a photo from the camera or photo library. It calls the FilterManager instance's fetch() method, which loads FilterData.plist and puts its contents into an array of FilterItem instances. This array is then assigned to the PhotoFilterViewController instance's filters property, which will later be used to populate the collection view with thumbnail previews of filters. The next statement assigns the PhotoFilterViewController instance's mainImage property to mainImageView, which is the outlet for the image view above the collection view, if mainImage has been set. The final statement tells the collection view to redraw itself.

```
onPhotoTapped()
```

This method calls the checkSource() method you implemented earlier, which calls the showCameraUserInterface() method if authorization has been granted. You'll assign this to the camera button in the **Photo Filter View Controller Scene** later.

> **Important Information**
>
> Apple stipulates that apps that use the camera or Photo Library must
> prompt the user accordingly. Later, you'll modify your app to display
> a dialog box asking for permission to use the camera or Photo Library
> by implementing the NSCameraUsageDescription and
> NSMicrophoneUsageDescription keys in Info.plist.
> To learn more about requesting permission to use the camera, go to
> https://developer.apple.com/documentation/
> avfoundation/cameras_and_media_capture/requesting_
> authorization_for_media_capture_on_ios.

9. You'll adopt the UICollectionViewDataSource protocol and implement the
    required methods to make the collection view display thumbnail previews of filters.
    Add a new extension after the private extension and implement them as follows:

```swift
extension PhotoFilterViewController:
UICollectionViewDataSource {
    func collectionView(_ collectionView:
    UICollectionView, numberOfItemsInSection
    section: Int) -> Int {
        filters.count
    }
    func collectionView(_ collectionView:
    UICollectionView, cellForItemAt indexPath:
    IndexPath) -> UICollectionViewCell {
        let cell = collectionView
        .dequeueReusableCell
        (withReuseIdentifier: "filterCell",
        for: indexPath) as! FilterCell
        let filterItem = filters[indexPath.row]
        if let thumbnail = thumbnail {
            cell.set(filterItem: filterItem,
            imageForThumbnail: thumbnail)
        }
        return cell
    }
}
```

> **Tip**
> Collection views are covered in *Chapter 13, Getting Started with MVC and Collection Views.*

The following should be familiar to you as you have done this before, but let's go over it again:

```
collectionView(_:numberOfItemsInSection:)
```

Determines the number of items the collection view is supposed to display, which is the same as the number of `FilterItems` inside the `PhotoFilterViewController` instance's `filters` array.

```
collectionView(_:cellForItemAt:)
```

Determines what to put in each cell. Here, you get the `FilterItem` instance corresponding to the cell's position in the collection view and pass it, along with the `PhotoFilterViewController` instance's `thumbnail` property, to the `set(filterItem:imageForThumbnail:)` method, which sets the image and label for the collection view cell.

10. You've set up the collection view using a `UICollectionViewFlowLayout` instance earlier. Now you'll set the size for the collection view cells. Add the following extension after the extension containing the data source methods:

```
extension PhotoFilterViewController:
UICollectionViewDelegateFlowLayout {
    func collectionView(_ collectionView:
    UICollectionView, layout
    collectionViewLayout:
    UICollectionViewLayout, sizeForItemAt
    indexPath: IndexPath) -> CGSize {
        let collectionViewHeight =
        collectionView.frame.size.height
        let topInset = 14.0
        let cellHeight = collectionViewHeight -
        topInset
        return CGSize(width: 150, height:
        cellHeight)
    }
}
```

`collectionView(_:layout:sizeForItemAt:)` returns the size each collection view cell should be. First, the height of the collection view is assigned to `collectionViewHeight`. Then, the value of `topInset` is set to `14.0` points. The height of the collection view cell is calculated by subtracting the `topInset` from the `collectionViewHeight`. This results in a 14-point gap between the top of the collection view cells and the top of the collection view. Finally, a `CGSize` instance with the width set to `150` points and the height set to `cellHeight` is returned as the size of the collection view cell. Previously, you did this using the Size inspector; now, you're doing it programmatically.

Now you'll connect the outlets and actions in this class to the UI elements in the `PhotoFilter` storyboard file. `collectionView` is the outlet for the collection view that displays the list of filters. `mainImageView` is for the image view just above it, which shows the image the user selected. `onPhotoTapped()` is for the camera button in the navigation bar. You'll also configure the **Cancel** button to dismiss the **Photo Filter** screen. Follow these steps:

1. Click the `PhotoFilter` storyboard file in the Project navigator. Select the **View Controller** icon of the **View Controller Scene** in the document outline. Click the Identity inspector button. Under **Custom Class**, set **Class** to `PhotoFilterViewController`:

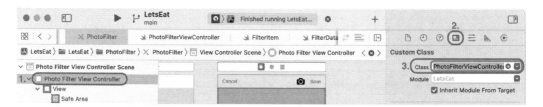

Figure 20.6: Identity inspector with Class set to PhotoFilterViewController

2. Select the Connections inspector. Click and drag from the `collectionView` outlet to the **Collection View** in the document outline:

Figure 20.7: Connections inspector showing the collectionView outlet

3. Click and drag from the `mainImageView` outlet to the **Image View** in the document outline:

Figure 20.8: Connections inspector showing the mainImageView outlet

4. Click and drag from the `onPhotoTapped:` action to the camera button:

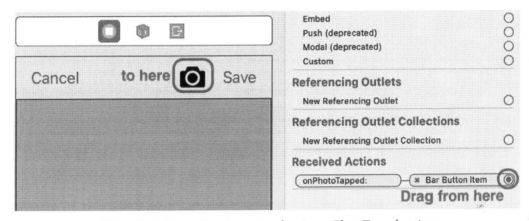

Figure 20.9: Connections inspector showing onPhotoTapped: action

5. The **Cancel** button is used to exit this screen if the user does not wish to make a selection. You'll connect the **Cancel** button to the unwind method you implemented in the previous chapter, which will dismiss this screen and return the user to the **Restaurant Detail** screen. *Ctrl + Drag* from the **Cancel** button to the Exit icon in the Scene Dock:

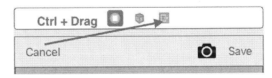

Figure 20.10: Photo Filter View Controller Scene showing Cancel button action being set

6. Select `unwindReviewCancelWithSegue:` in the pop-up menu:

Figure 20.11: Pop-up menu with unwindReviewCancelWithSegue: selected

All the outlets and actions for the `PhotoFilterViewController` class have been connected.

Next, you will implement the following methods:

*   `showCameraUserInterface()`, a method that will display either the view from the device camera or the photo library in an image picker interface.

*   Two `UIImagePickerControllerDelegate` protocol methods that will be called when you choose a picture in the image picker interface or click the **Cancel** button.

> **Important Information**
>
> To learn more about `UIImagePickerController`, go to `https://developer.apple.com/documentation/uikit/uiimagepickercontroller`.

> **Important Information**
>
> To learn more about `UIImagePickerControllerDelegate`, go to `https://developer.apple.com/documentation/uikit/uiimagepickercontrollerdelegate`.

To implement the `showCameraUserInterface()` and `UIImagePickerControllerDelegate` methods, click the `PhotoFilterViewController` file in the Project navigator and add the following extension after the `UICollectionViewDelegateFlowLayout` extension:

```
extension PhotoFilterViewController:
UIImagePickerControllerDelegate,
UINavigationControllerDelegate {
    func showCameraUserInterface() {
        let imagePicker = UIImagePickerController()
        imagePicker.delegate = self
```

```
#if targetEnvironment(simulator)
    imagePicker.sourceType =
    UIImagePickerController.SourceType.photoLibrary
#else
    imagePicker.sourceType =
    UIImagePickerController.SourceType.camera
    imagePicker.showsCameraControls = true
#endif
    imagePicker.mediaTypes = ["public.image"]
    imagePicker.allowsEditing = true
    self.present(imagePicker, animated: true,
    completion: nil)
}
func imagePickerControllerDidCancel(_ picker:
UIImagePickerController) {
    picker.dismiss(animated: true, completion: nil)
}
func imagePickerController(_ picker:
UIImagePickerController,
didFinishPickingMediaWithInfo info:
[UIImagePickerController.InfoKey : Any]) {
    if let selectedImage =
    info[UIImagePickerController.InfoKey
    .editedImage] as? UIImage {
        self.thumbnail =
        selectedImage.preparingThumbnail(of:
        CGSize(width: 100, height: 100))
        let mainImageViewSize =
        mainImageView.frame.size
        self.mainImage =
        selectedImage.preparingThumbnail(of:
        mainImageViewSize)
    }
    picker.dismiss(animated: true){
        self.showApplyFilterInterface()
    }
```

```
    }
}
```

Let's talk about `showCameraUserInterface()` first. This method is triggered when the camera button is tapped, displaying an image picker on the screen. This image picker is the standard iOS image picker that appears when you want to use an image—for instance, to add an image to a Facebook post or to a tweet.

Let's break this down:

```
let imagePicker = UIImagePickerController()
```

Creates an instance of the `UIImagePickerController` class and assigns it to `imagePicker`.

```
imagePicker.delegate = self
```

Sets the `imagePicker` instance's `delegate` property to the `PhotoFilterViewController` instance.

```
#if targetEnvironment(simulator)
    imagePicker.sourceType =
    UIImagePickerController.SourceType.photoLibrary
#else
    imagePicker.sourceType =
    UIImagePickerController.SourceType.camera
    imagePicker.showsCameraControls = true
#endif
```

This block of code is known as a conditional compilation block. It starts with an `#if` compilation directive and ends with an `#endif` compilation directive. If you're running on the simulator, only the statement setting the `imagePicker` instance's `sourceType` property to the photo library is compiled. If you're running on an actual device, the statements setting the `imagePicker` instance's `sourceType` property to camera and displaying the camera controls are compiled.

> **Important Information**
> You can learn more about conditional compilation blocks at this link:
> `https://docs.swift.org/swift-book/ReferenceManual/`
> `Statements.html#ID538`.

```
imagePicker.mediaTypes = ["public.image"]
```

Sets the camera interface to capture still images.

```
imagePicker.allowsEditing = true
```

Indicates the user is allowed to edit the selected image.

```
self.present(imagePicker, animated: true, completion: nil)
```

Presents `imagePicker` on the screen.

When the image picker appears onscreen, you have the option of selecting a photo or canceling. If you cancel, `imagePickerControllerDidCancel(_:)` is triggered and the image picker is dismissed.

If you select a photo, `imagePickerController(_:didFinishPickingMediaWithInfo:)` is triggered and a photo will be returned and assigned to `selectedImage`. Next, the `selectedImage` instance's `preparingThumbnail(of:)` method will be used to create a small image with a width and height of `100` points. This will then be assigned to the `thumbnail` property. After that, an image with the same size as `mainImageView` will be created from `selectedImage` using the `preparingThumbnail(of:)` method. This will be assigned to the `mainImage` property and the image picker will be dismissed.

> **Important Information**
> You can learn more about the `preparingThumbnail(of:)` method at this link: `https://developer.apple.com/documentation/`
> `uikit/uiimage/3750835-preparingthumbnail`.

Next, you'll implement `filterMainImage(filterItem:)`, a method to apply a filter to the image in the `mainImageView`. Add an extension containing this method after the `UIImagePickerControllerDelegate` extension:

```
extension PhotoFilterViewController: ImageFiltering {
    func filterMainImage(filterItem: FilterItem) {
```

```
        if let mainImage = mainImage, let filter =
    filterItem.filter {
        if filter != "None" {
            mainImageView.image =
            self.apply(filter: filter,
            originalImage: mainImage)
        } else {
            mainImageView.image = mainImage
        }
    }
    }
}
```

This makes the `PhotoFilterViewController` class adopt the `ImageFiltering` protocol. Remember that any class that adopts this protocol gets the `apply(filter:originalImage:)` method. The `filterMainImage(filterItem:)` method uses this method to apply the selected filter to the photo stored in the `PhotoFilterViewController` instance's `mainImage` property, and the result is assigned to the `mainImageView` outlet so that it is visible on the screen. If you selected the `None` filter, then `mainImage` is assigned to the `mainImageView` outlet.

You still need to know which filter the user picked, so you'll make the `PhotoFilterViewController` class adopt the `UICollectionViewDelegate` protocol and implement the method that identifies which cell in the collection view was tapped. Add the following extension containing this method after the `ImageFiltering` extension:

```
extension PhotoFilterViewController:
UICollectionViewDelegate {
    func collectionView(_ collectionView:
    UICollectionView, didSelectItemAt
    indexPath: IndexPath) {
        let filterItem = self.filters[indexPath.row]
        filterMainImage(filterItem: filterItem)
    }
}
```

The `collectionView(_:didSelectItemAt:)` method is called whenever the user taps a cell in the collection view. The `FilterItem` corresponding to the cell that was tapped is then passed to `filterMainImage(filterItem:)`.

The implementation of the `PhotoFilterViewController` class is now complete but remember that you have to ask for permission to use the camera or to access the photo library. You'll modify the `Info.plist` file in your project so that messages will be displayed to the user when your app attempts to access the camera or photo library.

Getting permission to use the camera or photo library

As mentioned earlier, Apple stipulates that your app must inform the user if it wishes to access the camera or photo library. If you don't do this, your app will be rejected and will not be allowed on the App Store.

You'll modify the `Info.plist` file in your project to make your app display messages when it tries to access the camera or photo library. Follow these steps:

1. Click the `Info.plist` file in the Project navigator to display a list of keys. Move your mouse pointer over any existing key and click the + button:

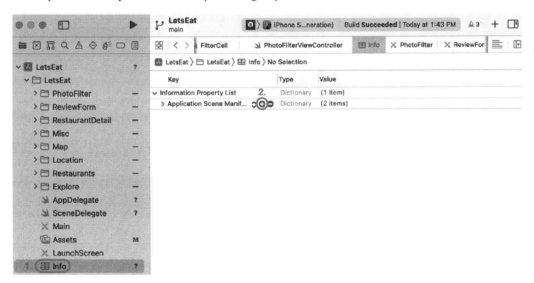

Figure 20.12: Editor area showing contents of Info.plist

2. A field should appear, allowing you to enter an additional key:

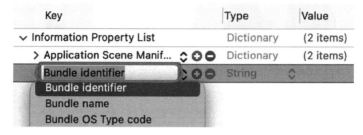

Figure 20.13: Editor area showing field used to enter keys

3. Enter the following keys:

```
NSPhotoLibraryUsageDescription
NSCameraUsageDescription
```

4. For each key's value, enter a string that explains to the user why you wish to use the camera or photo library:

Key	Type	Value
∨ Information Property List	Dictionary	(3 items)
> Application Scene Manifest	Dictionary	(2 items)
Privacy – Camera Usage Des...	String	This app uses your camera to take pictures
Privacy – Photo Library...	String	This app uses your Photo Library pictures

Figure 20.14: Info.plist with additional keys added

Build and run the project. Go to the **Restaurant Detail** screen and tap the **Add Photo** button. You should see the following alert:

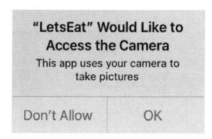

Figure 20.15: iOS Simulator showing camera access alert

Tap **OK**. The image picker will appear:

Figure 20.16: iOS Simulator showing image picker

Select a photo, and the **Photo Filter** screen will display the photo and a list of thumbnails with different filters applied to them. Tapping a filter will apply its effect to the photo:

Figure 20.17: iOS Simulator showing Photo Filter screen

You've modified the `info.plist` file in your project and your app now asks for permission before using the camera or the photo library. You can use the **Cancel** button to dismiss the **Photo Filter** screen and return to the **Restaurant Detail** screen. You can't use the **Save** button yet though, you'll implement its functionality in the next chapter.

Summary

In this chapter, you completed the implementation of the **Photo Filter** screen. You imported `FilterData.plist`, a `.plist` file containing the filters you want to use, created the `FilterItem` class to store filter data, and created the `FilterManager` data manager class to read the `.plist` file and populate an array of `FilterItem` instances. Next, you created a protocol, `ImageFiltering`, with a method to apply filters to images. Then, you created the `FilterCell` and `PhotoFilterViewController` classes in order to manage the collection view cells and the **Photo Filter** screen. After that you made the `PhotoFilterViewController` class adopt the `UIImagePickerDelegate` protocol, and added methods so that you can use photos from the camera or photo library in your app. Finally, you added code to `PhotoFilterViewController` to apply a selected filter to a picture.

You are now able to write your own apps that import photos from your camera or photo library, and apply filters to them.

Note that the selected picture cannot be saved. You will learn how to save reviews and pictures using Core Data in the next chapter so that they will reappear after you quit and relaunch the app.

21
Understanding Core Data

Your app is almost done! Every screen works as shown in the app tour that you went through in *Chapter 9, Setting Up the User Interface*. However, there is one last thing that you need to do. In *Chapter 19, Getting Started with Custom UIControls*, you implemented a **Review Form** screen, which lets you enter a review for a particular restaurant. In the previous chapter, you implemented a **Photo Filter** screen, which lets you get a photo from the camera or photo library and add a filter to it. But there is no way at present to save either reviews or photos, and they are lost when the app is closed.

In this chapter, you will use **Core Data** to save reviews and photos in your app. First, you'll learn about Core Data and its different components. Next, you'll create a data model for reviews and photos and create corresponding model objects for your app. After that, you'll set up Core Data components for your app.

You'll then learn about the mechanism used to save reviews and photos for a particular restaurant using the restaurant identifier. After that, you'll update the ReviewFormViewController and PhotoFilterViewController classes to save reviews and photos for a particular restaurant, and modify the RestaurantDetailViewController class to load and display reviews for a particular restaurant. You'll also calculate and display the overall rating for that restaurant.

Finally, on your own, you'll modify the `RestaurantDetailViewController` class to load and display photos for a particular restaurant.

By the end of this chapter, you'll understand how Core Data works. You'll also be able to set up Core Data components, and enable an interface between your app and Core Data components using a data manager class. You'll have also learned to save and load reviews and photos using Core Data, which you will then be able to implement in your own apps.

The following topics will be covered:

- Introducing Core Data

- Implementing Core Data components for your app

- Understanding how saving and loading works

- Updating the `ReviewFormViewController` class to save reviews

- Updating the `PhotoFilterViewController` class to save photos

- Displaying saved reviews and photos in the **Restaurant Detail** screen

- Calculating a restaurant's overall rating

Technical requirements

You will continue working on the `LetsEat` project that you modified in the previous chapter.

The completed Xcode project for this chapter is in the `Chapter21` folder of the code bundle for this book, which can be downloaded here:

`https://github.com/PacktPublishing/iOS-15-Programming-for-Beginners-Sixth-Edition`

Check out the following video to see the code in action:

`https://bit.ly/3o81yKK`

Let's start by learning about the components of Core Data and how it works.

Introducing Core Data

Core Data is Apple's mechanism for saving app data to your device. It provides persistence, undo/redo, background tasks, view synchronization, versioning, and migration. You can define your data types and relationships using Xcode's data model editor, and Core Data will generate class definitions for your data types automatically. Core Data can then create and manage object instances based on the class definitions.

> **Important Note**
>
> You can learn more about Core Data at this link: `https://developer.apple.com/documentation/coredata`.

Core Data provides a set of classes collectively known as the Core Data stack to manage and persist object instances, which are as follows:

- `NSManagedObjectModel`

  Describes your app's types, including their properties and relationships.

- `NSManagedObject`

  A class used to implement instances of your app's types based on data from the `NSManagedObjectModel`.

- `NSManagedObjectContext`

  Tracks changes to instances of your app's types.

- `NSPersistentStoreCoordinator`

  Saves and fetches instances of your app's types from stores.

- `NSPersistentContainer`

  Sets up the model, context, and store coordinator simultaneously.

> **Important Note**
>
> You can learn more about the Core Data stack at this link: `https://developer.apple.com/documentation/coredata/core_data_stack`.

In the next section, you'll implement Core Data components required for your app to save reviews or photos.

Implementing Core Data components for your app

Before you implement Core Data components for your app, let's think about what you need to do to save reviews or photos.

Imagine you're saving a review or photo using Microsoft Word. You first create a new Word document template with the relevant fields for a review or photo. You then create new Word documents based on the templates and fill in the data. You make whatever changes are necessary, perhaps changing the text of the review, or changing the effect you're applying to the photo. At this point, you have not saved the file yet. When you are happy with your document, you save it to the hard disk of your computer. The next time you want to view your review or photo, you search your hard disk for the relevant document and double-click it to open it in Word so you can see it once more.

Now that you have an idea of what you need to do, let's review the steps required to implement it. First, you need to create a data model for a review or photo. You do this by creating **entities** in Xcode's data model editor, which are like Microsoft Word templates. Entities can have **attributes**, which are like fields in the Microsoft Word templates.

Xcode can then create an `NSManagedObjectModel` class from this data model. Core Data will then use this `NSManagedObjectModel` class to create `NSManagedObject` instances, similar to Microsoft Word templates being used to create Microsoft Word files.

These `NSManagedObject` instances are placed in an `NSManagedObjectContext` instance, where your app has access to them, similar to opening Microsoft Word files in Microsoft Word. Then, when you bring up the **Review Form** screen or **Photo Filter** screen, the details of the review or the photo with the filter will be written to `NSManagedObject` instances, and you can modify them as much as you like, similar to Microsoft Word documents being edited in Microsoft Word.

When you're done with the review or photo, the `NSManagedObject` instances in the `NSManagedObjectContext` instance are saved to a file in your iOS device, called the **persistent store**. This is similar to saving Word documents to your hard disk when you're done with them.

The `NSPersistentStoreCoordinator` instance manages the flow of information between the persistent store and the `NSManagedObjectContext` instance.

You'll use the `NSPersistentContainer` class to create instances of `NSManagedObjectModel`, `NSManagedObjectContext`, and `NSPersistentStoreCoordinator` for your app.

> **Important Note**
>
> You can learn more about how to set up the Core Data stack at this link: `https://developer.apple.com/documentation/coredata/setting_up_a_core_data_stack`.

You'll create entities and attributes to represent a review or photo using Xcode's data model editor in the next section.

Creating a data model

Currently, when you tap **Save** in the **Review Form** screen, the data you entered in the fields is just printed to the Debug area, and tapping **Save** in the **Photo Filter** screen doesn't do anything. The first step is to create class definitions for objects to store data from the **Review Form** screen and the photo from the **Photo Filter** screen. You'll create entities for reviews and photos using Xcode's data model editor, and Xcode will automatically generate the class definitions. Let's create the entity for reviews first. Follow these steps:

1. Right-click the `Misc` folder in the Project navigator and choose **New Group**. Name this group `Core Data`.

2. Right-click the `Core Data` group and choose **New File**.

3. **iOS** should already be selected. Type `data` in the filter field, and select **Data Model**. Click **Next**:

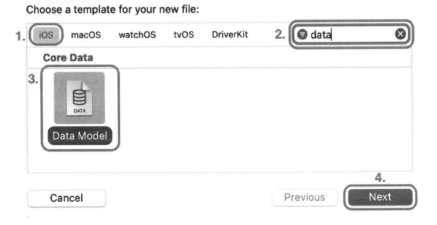

Figure 21.1: Data Model template selected

4. Name the file `LetsEatModel` and click **Create**. The data model editor appears in the Editor area:

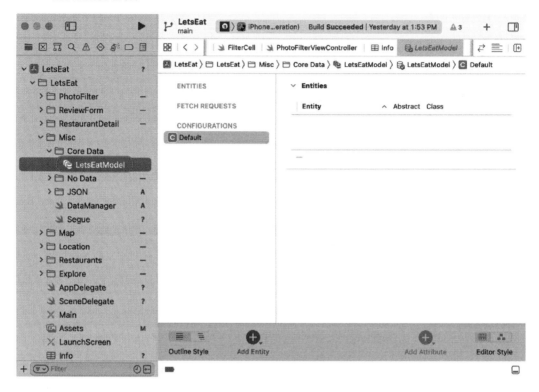

Figure 21.2: Editor area showing data model editor

5. Click the **Add Entity** button:

Figure 21.3: Add Entity button

6. An **Entity** appears under the **ENTITIES** section. The **Attributes** for this entity appear to the right of the entity:

Figure 21.4: Data model editor with Entity selected

7. Double-click **Entity** and rename it Review:

Figure 21.5: Data model editor with Entity renamed to Review

8. Click the + button in the **Attributes** section to create an attribute. Set the **Attribute** to name and the **Type** to String:

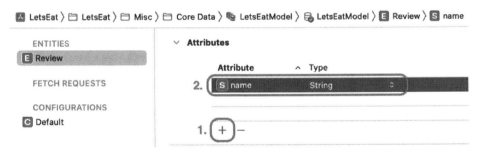

Figure 21.6: Data model editor showing the name attribute for the Review entity

9. You'll need to create an attribute for each field in the **Review Form** screen, and you'll store the restaurantID as well to associate the review with the restaurant. Add the following attributes and types:

Attribute	Type
customerReview	String
date	Date
rating	Double
restaurantID	Integer 64
title	String

Figure 21.7: Attributes to be added to the Review entity

date will be automatically set when the Review instance is created.

10. Check to see that your Review entity's attributes look like this when done:

Attribute	∧	Type	
S customerReview		String	↕
D date		Date	↕
S name		String	↕
N rating		Double	↕
N restaurantID		Integer 64	↕
S title		String	↕

Figure 21.8: The attributes for Review entity

11. Add one more attribute, uuid, of type UUID. This is used as a key value for each Review instance. Click the Data Model inspector, and under **Attribute**, untick **Optional**, as every Review instance must have a key value.

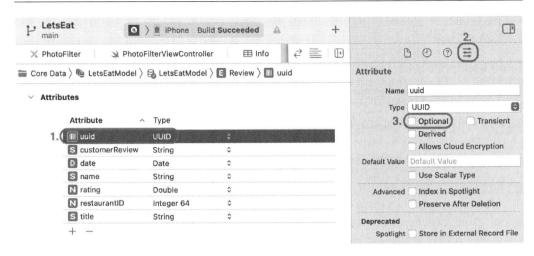

Figure 21.9: Data model inspector showing Optional unticked for the uuid attribute

12. Add a second entity, called `RestaurantPhoto`, with the following attributes. Core Data can't store `UIImage` objects, so the `photo` attribute's type is set to **Binary Data**. You will convert photos to binary data so that Core Data can store them, and convert them back to `UIImage` objects when you need them to be displayed in your app. `date` will be automatically set when the `RestaurantPhoto` instance is created. You'll use `restaurantID` to associate the photo with the restaurant, and `uuid` as the key value:

Attribute	Type
date	Date
photo	Binary Data
restaurantID	Integer 64
uuid	UUID

Figure 21.10: Attributes for the RestaurantPhoto entity

13. For `uuid`, don't forget to uncheck **Optional** in the Data Model inspector:

Figure 21.11: Data model inspector showing Optional unticked for the uuid attribute

You have finished creating the entities that you need for your app. Build your app. Class files for the `Review` and `RestaurantPhoto` entities will be automatically created by Xcode, but they will not be visible in the Project navigator. To make it easier to work with them, you will create a model object for each entity, starting with `ReviewItem` in the next section.

Creating ReviewItem

You have created two entities to store reviews and photo data using Xcode's data model editor. Xcode will then automatically generate two `NSManagedObject` class definitions from the data model, `Review` and `RestaurantPhoto`, but you can't see them in the Project navigator.

You will create two model objects, `ReviewItem` and `RestaurantPhotoItem`, that will work hand-in-hand with `Review` and `RestaurantPhoto` instances. Let's create `ReviewItem` now. Follow these steps:

1. Right-click the `ReviewForm` folder in the Project navigator and choose **New Group**. Name this group `Model`.

2. Right-click the `Model` folder inside the `ReviewForm` folder and select **New File**.

3. **iOS** should already be selected. Choose **Swift File** and then click **Next**.

4. Name this file `ReviewItem`. Click **Create**. The `ReviewItem` file appears in the Project navigator.

5. Modify the file as shown:

```
import UIKit
struct ReviewItem {
    var date: Date?
```

```
        var rating: Double?
        var title: String?
        var name: String?
        var customerReview: String?
        var restaurantID: Int64?
        var uuid = UUID()
    }
    extension ReviewItem {
        init(review: Review) {
            self.date = review.date
            self.rating = review.rating
            self.title = review.title
            self.name = review.name
            self.customerReview = review.customerReview
            self.restaurantID = review.restaurantID
            if let reviewUUID = review.uuid {
                self.uuid = reviewUUID
            }
        }
    }
```

As you can see, the `ReviewItem` structure's properties are the same as the `Review` entity's attributes. The initializer creates a `ReviewItem` instance and maps the attributes from `Review` to the properties of the `ReviewItem` instance.

In the next section, you'll create a second model object, `RestaurantPhotoItem`, which will be the model object for the `RestaurantPhoto` entity.

Creating RestaurantPhotoItem

The process for creating `RestaurantPhotoItem` is similar to creating `ReviewItem`. Follow these steps:

1. Right-click the `Model` folder inside the `PhotoFilter` folder and choose **New File**.

2. **iOS** should already be selected. Choose **Swift File** and then click **Next**.

3. Name this file `RestaurantPhotoItem`. Click **Create**.

4. Modify the file as shown:

```swift
import UIKit
struct RestaurantPhotoItem {
    var date: Date?
    var photo: UIImage?
    var photoData: Data {
        guard let photo = photo, let photoData =
        photo.pngData() else {
            return Data()
        }
        return photoData
    }
    var restaurantID: Int64?
    var uuid = UUID()
}
extension RestaurantPhotoItem {
    init(restaurantPhoto: RestaurantPhoto) {
        self.date = restaurantPhoto.date
        if let restPhoto = restaurantPhoto.photo {
            self.photo = UIImage(data: restPhoto,
            scale: 1.0)
        }
        self.restaurantID =
        restaurantPhoto.restaurantID
        if let restPhotoUUID = restaurantPhoto.uuid {
            self.uuid = restPhotoUUID
        }
    }
}
```

Similar to the ReviewItem structure, the properties of the
RestaurantPhotoItem structure are the same as the RestaurantPhoto
entity's attributes. There is one additional computed property, photoData, which
is used to store the representation of photo in binary data format, as Core Data
can't store UIImage instances.

The initializer creates a `RestaurantPhotoItem` instance and maps the attributes from the `RestaurantPhoto` entity to properties in `RestaurantPhotoItem` instance. Note the conversion from binary data to `UIImage` when setting the value for `photo`.

Now that you have declared and defined `ReviewItem` and `RestaurantPhotoItem`, let's create a Core Data manager, which will set up the Core Data components for your app, in the next section.

Creating a Core Data manager

At this point, Xcode has automatically generated the `Review` and `RestaurantData` class definitions from the data model, and you have declared and defined the corresponding model objects, `ReviewItem` and `RestaurantPhotoItem`. Now you'll create a `CoreDataManager` class that will set up the Core Data components for your app. Follow these steps:

1. Right-click the `Core Data` folder inside the `Misc` folder and choose **New File**.

2. **iOS** should already be selected. Choose **Swift File** and then click **Next**.

3. Name this file `CoreDataManager`. Click **Create**. The `CoreDataManager` file appears in the Project navigator.

4. Add the following code after the `import` statement:

```
import CoreData
```

This gives you access to the Core Data library.

5. Add the following code to declare and define the `CoreDataManager` structure:

```
struct CoreDataManager {
    let container: NSPersistentContainer
    init() {
        container = NSPersistentContainer(name:
        "LetsEatModel")
        container.loadPersistentStores {
            (storeDesc, error) in
            error.map {
                print($0)
            }
        }
    }
```

```
        }
    }
```

This creates and initializes instances of NSManagedObjectModel, NSPersistentStoreCoordinator, and NSManagedObjectContext.

6. To create an instance of the CoreDataManager structure that will be available throughout your app, click the AppDelegate file in the Project navigator and add the following code after the closing curly brace:

```
extension CoreDataManager {
    static var shared = CoreDataManager()
}
```

Next, you'll add methods to create Review and RestaurantPhoto instances, populate them using ReviewItem and RestaurantPhotoItem instances, and save them to the persistent store. Follow these steps:

1. Click the CoreDataManager file in the Project navigator. Add the following code after the initializer to implement the addReview(_:) method:

```
func addReview(_ reviewItem: ReviewItem) {
    let review = Review(context:
    container.viewContext)
    review.date = Date()
    if let reviewItemRating = reviewItem.rating {
        review.rating = reviewItemRating
    }
    review.title = reviewItem.title
    review.name = reviewItem.name
    review.customerReview =
    reviewItem.customerReview
    if let reviewItemRestID =
    reviewItem.restaurantID {
        review.restaurantID = reviewItemRestID
    }
    review.uuid = reviewItem.uuid
    save()
}
```

This method takes a `ReviewItem` instance as a parameter and gets an empty `Review` instance from the `NSManagedObjectContext` instance. The properties of the `ReviewItem` instance are assigned to the attributes of the `Review` instance, and the `save()` method is called to save the contents of the `NSManagedObjectContext` instance to the persistent store. Note that you will see an error as you have not yet implemented the `save()` method. Ignore this error for now.

2. Add the following code after the `addReview(_:)` method to implement the `addPhoto(_:)` method:

```
func addPhoto(_ restPhotoItem:
RestaurantPhotoItem) {
    let restPhoto = RestaurantPhoto(context:
    container.viewContext)
    restPhoto.date = Date()
    restPhoto.photo = restPhotoItem.photoData
    if let restPhotoID =
        restPhotoItem.restaurantID {
        restPhoto.restaurantID = restPhotoID
    }
    restPhoto.uuid = restPhotoItem.uuid
    save()
}
```

This method is similar to `addReview(_:)`. It takes a `RestaurantPhotoItem` instance as a parameter and gets an empty `RestaurantPhoto` instance from the `NSManagedObjectContext` instance. The properties of the `RestaurantPhotoItem` instance are assigned to the properties of the `RestaurantPhoto` instance, and the `save()` method is called to save the contents of the `NSManagedObjectContext` instance to the persistent store. Note that you will see an error as you have not yet implemented the `save()` method. Again, ignore this error for now.

3. Implement the `save()` method by adding the following code before the final curly brace:

```
private func save() {
    do {
        if container.viewContext.hasChanges {
```

```
            try container.viewContext.save()
        }
    } catch let error {
        print(error.localizedDescription)
    }
}
```

This `do-catch` block saves the contents of the `NSManagedObjectContext` instance to the persistent store. If the save was not successful, an error message is printed in the Debug area.

When you want to retrieve reviews and photos from the persistent store, you will use `restaurantID` as an identifier to get reviews and photos for a particular restaurant. Let's implement the methods required for this now. Add the following code after the `addPhoto(_:)` method to implement the `fetchReviews(by:)` and `fetchPhotos(by:)` methods:

```
func fetchReviews(by identifier: Int) ->
[ReviewItem] {
    let moc = container.viewContext
    let request = Review.fetchRequest()
    let predicate = NSPredicate(format:
    "restaurantID = %i", identifier)
    var reviewItems: [ReviewItem] = []
    request.sortDescriptors =
    [NSSortDescriptor(key: "date",
    ascending: false)]
    request.predicate = predicate
    do {
        for review in try moc.fetch(request) {
            reviewItems.append(ReviewItem(review:
            review))
        }
        return reviewItems
    } catch {
        fatalError("Failed to fetch reviews:
        \(error)")
    }
```

```
}

func fetchRestPhotos(by identifier: Int) ->
[RestaurantPhotoItem] {
    let moc = container.viewContext
    let request = RestaurantPhoto.fetchRequest()
    let predicate = NSPredicate(format:
    "restaurantID = %i", identifier)
    var restPhotoItems: [RestaurantPhotoItem] = []
    request.sortDescriptors =
    [NSSortDescriptor(key: "date",
    ascending: false)]
    request.predicate = predicate
    do {
        for restPhoto in try moc.fetch(request) {
            restPhotoItems.append(RestaurantPhotoItem
            (restaurantPhoto: restPhoto))
        }
        return restPhotoItems
    } catch {
        fatalError("Failed to fetch restaurant
        photos: \(error)")
    }
}
```

Let's break this down, starting with `fetchReviews(by:)`:

```
let moc = container.viewContext
```

This gets a reference to the `NSManagedObjectContext` instance.

```
let request = Review.fetchRequest()
```

This creates a **fetch request** that gets `Review` instances from the persistent store.

```
let predicate = NSPredicate(format: "restaurantID = %i",
identifier)
```

This creates a **fetch predicate** that only gets those `Review` instances with the specified `restaurantID`.

```
var reviewItems: [ReviewItem] = []
```

This creates an array, `reviewItems`, that you will use to store the results of the fetch request.

```
request.sortDescriptors = [NSSortDescriptor(key: "date",
ascending: false)]
```

This sorts the results of the fetch request by date, with the most recent items first.

```
request.predicate = predicate
```

This sets the predicate for the fetch request.

```
do {
    for review in try moc.fetch(request) {
        reviewItems.append(ReviewItem(review:
        review))
    }
    return reviewItems
} catch {
    fatalError("Failed to fetch reviews: \(error)")
}
```

This `do-catch` block performs the fetch request and places the results in the `items` array. If unsuccessful, your app will crash and an error message will be printed in the Debug area.

`fetchPhotos(by:)` works the same way as `fetchReview(by:)`, but returns an array of `RestaurantPhotoItems` instances instead.

You've created a `CoreDataManager` class that adds data to and retrieves data from the persistent store. Build and run your app to test for errors. It should work the same way as it did before.

You've implemented all the components of Core Data in your app. Next, you'll configure `RestaurantDetailViewController` to use Core Data to display reviews and photos in the **Restaurant Detail** screen. You'll start by learning how the **Restaurant Detail** screen will display reviews and photos for a particular restaurant.

> **Tip**
> Since this is a long chapter, you may wish to take a break here.

Understanding how saving and loading works

Let's review what you have done so far. You have created `Review` and `RestaurantPhoto` entities using the data model editor, and you have created the corresponding model objects for them, named `ReviewItem` and `RestaurantPhotoItem`. You created the `CoreDataManager` class to add and get `Review` and `RestaurantPhoto` instances from the persistent store. The `CoreDataManager` class uses the restaurant identifier to associate reviews and restaurant photos with a specific restaurant, but where does it come from?

Open the `Misc` folder in your project, and open the `JSON` folder. If you click on any one of the JSON files inside, you'll see that each restaurant has a unique numeric identifier. For example, the identifier for The Tap Trailhouse restaurant is `145237`, as shown in the screenshot below:

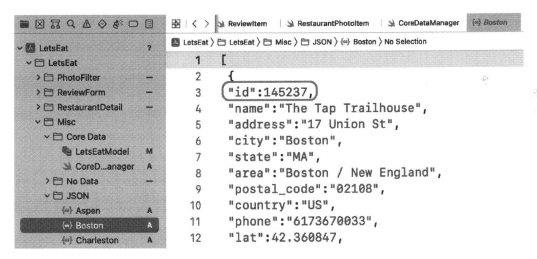

Figure 21.12: Editor area showing contents for Boston.json

When you save restaurant photos and reviews to the persistent store, you will save them together with this identifier. Then, when a particular restaurant is displayed in the **Restaurant Detail** screen, `RestaurantDetailViewController` will use a `ReviewDataManager` instance to retrieve reviews and restaurant photos of that restaurant and display them in collection views, as shown in the screenshot:

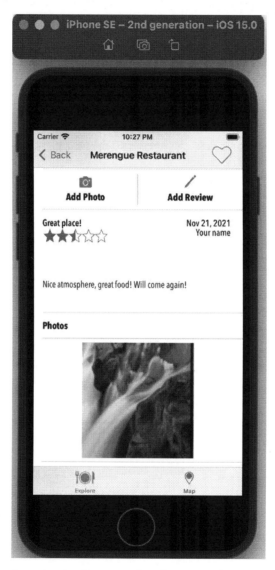

Figure 21.13: iOS Simulator showing Restaurant Detail screen with reviews and restaurant photos

If there are no reviews or photos, you'll use the `NoDataView` to inform the user there are no reviews or photos, as shown in the screenshot:

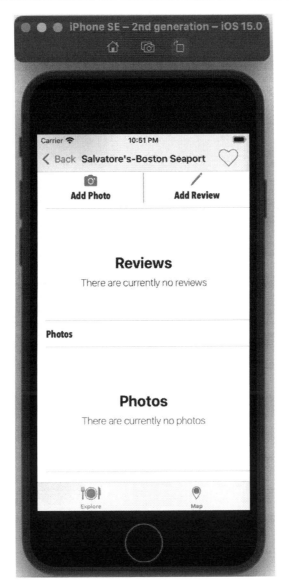

Figure 21.14: iOS Simulator showing Restaurant Detail screen without reviews or restaurant photos

`RestaurantItem` has a property, `restaurantID`, to store restaurant identifiers. When `RestaurantDataManager` loads a JSON file and creates an array of `RestaurantItem` instances, the identifier for each restaurant is obtained from the JSON file and stored in the `restaurantID` property.

In the next section, you'll update `ReviewFormViewController` to save a review with a restaurant identifier to the persistent store.

Updating the ReviewFormViewController class to save reviews

The **Save** button in the **Review Form** screen currently just prints the review to the Debug area when tapped. To save reviews, you'll need to modify the `onSaveTapped(_:)` method to save a review to the persistent store when the **Save** button is tapped. Follow these steps:

1. Click the `ReviewFormViewController` file in the Project navigator. Add the following property to the `ReviewFormViewController` class before the outlet declarations to store the restaurant identifier:

   ```
   var selectedRestaurantID: Int?
   ```

2. Create a `private` extension, move the `onSaveTapped(_:)` method into it, and modify it as follows:

   ```
   private extension ReviewFormViewController {
       @IBAction func onSaveTapped(_ sender: Any) {
           var reviewItem = ReviewItem()
           reviewItem.rating = ratingsView.rating
           reviewItem.title = titleTextField.text
           reviewItem.name = nameTextField.text
           reviewItem.customerReview =
           reviewTextView.text
           if let selRestID = selectedRestaurantID {
               reviewItem.restaurantID =
               Int64(selRestID)
           }
           CoreDataManager.shared.addReview(reviewItem)
           dismiss(animated: true, completion: nil)
       }
   }
   ```

Instead of printing the review details to the Debug area, `onSaveTapped(_:)` will now create a `ReviewItem` instance, assign data obtained from the **Review Form** screen to its properties, and call `CoreDataManager.shared.addReview(reviewItem)` to save the review to the persistent store.

Note that there is no mechanism to pass a restaurant identifier to
`ReviewFormViewController` at present. In the next section, you'll see how to get
the restaurant identifier from `RestaurantDetailViewController` and pass it to
`ReviewFormViewController`.

Passing RestaurantID to the ReviewFormViewController instance

The **Save** button in the **Review Form** screen can now save a review with a restaurant
identifier, but where does `ReviewFormViewController` get that identifier from?
You must pass the identifier value from `RestaurantDetailViewController` to
`ReviewFormViewController` so that it can save reviews with the restaurant identifier
for that restaurant. As you did before in *Chapter 17, Getting Started with JSONFiles*, you'll
use segue identifiers to determine which segue is occurring, and then implement methods
to pass the identifier value between the two view controllers. Follow these steps:

1. Open the `RestaurantDetail` storyboard file and select the segue used to go to
    the **ReviewForm** scene:

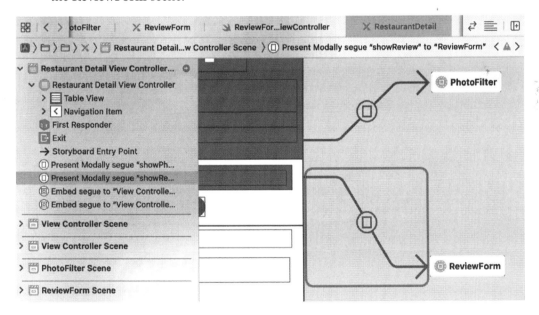

Figure 21.15: Editor area showing segue between Restaurant Detail and Review Form screens selected

2. In the Attributes inspector, set **Identifier** under **Storyboard Segue** to showReview and press *Return*:

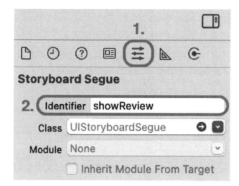

Figure 21.16: Attributes inspector with Identifier set to showReview

3. Click the RestaurantDetailViewController file in the Project navigator. Add the following code after viewDidLoad() to implement the prepare(for:sender:) method:

```
override func prepare(for segue:
UIStoryboardSegue, sender: Any?) {
    if let identifier = segue.identifier {
        switch identifier  {
        case Segue.showReview.rawValue:
            showReview(segue: segue)
        default:
            print("Segue not added")
        }
    }
}
```

The prepare(for:sender:) method checks to see if the segue has the showReview segue identifier. If it does, the showReview(segue:) method is executed prior to transitioning from the **Restaurant Detail** screen to the **Review Form** screen. There will be an error because showReview(segue:) has not been implemented yet. You'll add that next.

4. Add the showReview(segue:) method inside the private extension, before the createRating() method:

```
func showReview(segue: UIStoryboardSegue) {
    guard let navController = segue.destination as?
```

```
UINavigationController, let viewController =
navController.topViewController as?
ReviewFormViewController else {
    return
}
viewController.selectedRestaurantID =
selectedRestaurant?.restaurantID
}
```

This sets the `restaurantID` property of `ReviewFormViewController` to the identifier of the selected restaurant.

5. Click the `ReviewFormViewController` file in the Project navigator. Add the following code inside the `viewDidLoad()` method to print the restaurant identifier to the Debug area:

```
super.viewDidLoad()
print(selectedRestaurantID as Any)
```

This will let you know you have successfully passed the identifier value to `ReviewFormViewController`.

Build and run your project, set a location, and tap **All**. Tap a restaurant, and tap the **Add Review** button. In the **Review Form** screen, enter a review and tap **Save**:

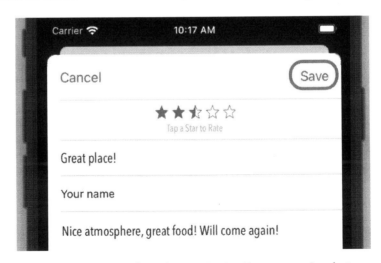

Figure 21.17: iOS Simulator showing Review Form screen Save button

The restaurant identifier will appear in the Debug area:

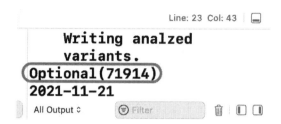

Figure 21.18: Debug area showing the restaurant identifier

You've successfully passed the restaurant identifier from
`RestaurantDetailViewController` to `ReviewFormViewController`. Now,
let's do the same for photos. You'll update `PhotoFilterViewController` to save
photos with a restaurant identifier to the persistent store when the **Save** button is tapped
in the next section.

Updating the PhotoFilterViewController class to save photos

The code that enables the `PhotoFilterViewController` class to save
photos to the persistent store is similar to the code you implemented in the
`ReviewFormViewController` class for saving reviews. You will now update the
`PhotoFilterViewController` class to save photos when the **Save** button is tapped.
Follow these steps:

1. Click the `PhotoFilterViewController` file in the Project navigator.
    Add the following method inside the `private` extension after the
    `initialize()` method:

```
func saveSelectedPhoto() {
    if let mainImage = self.mainImageView.image {
        var restPhotoItem =
        RestaurantPhotoItem()
        restPhotoItem.date = Date()
        restPhotoItem.photo =
        mainImage.preparingThumbnail(of:
```

```
            CGSize(width: 100, height: 100))
        if let selRestID = selectedRestaurantID
        {
            restPhotoItem.restaurantID =
            Int64(selRestID)
        }
        CoreDataManager.shared
        .addPhoto(restPhotoItem)
    }
    dismiss(animated: true, completion: nil)
}
```

Remember that `mainImageView` is the outlet for the large image view in the **Photo Filter** screen. The `saveSelectedPhoto()` method first checks to see if the `image` property of `mainImageView` is set. If it is, the image is assigned to `mainImage`. Next, a `RestaurantPhotoItem` instance is created and assigned to `restPhotoItem`, and the current date is assigned to the `restPhotoItem` instance's `date` property. The `mainImage` instance's `preparingThumbnail(of:)` method is used to create a smaller version of the image, which is assigned to the `restPhotoItem` instance's `photo` property. After that, the `restPhotoItem` instance's `restaurantID` property is set to the selected restaurant's identifier. Finally, the `CoreDataManager.shared.addPhoto(_:)` method is called to save the photo to the persistent store, and the **Photo Filter** screen is dismissed.

2. You need to trigger this method when the **Save** button is tapped. Add the following method inside the `private` extension after the `onPhotoTapped(_:)` method:

```
@IBAction func onSaveTapped(_ sender: Any) {
    saveSelectedPhoto()
}
```

This method will be connected to the **Save** button later.

3. To assign the `onSaveTapped(_:)` method to the **Save** button, open the
    `PhotoFilter` storyboard file and click the **Photo Filter View Controller** icon in
    the **Photo Filter View Controller Scene**. Open the Connections inspector. Drag
    from the **onSaveTapped** action to the **Save** button:

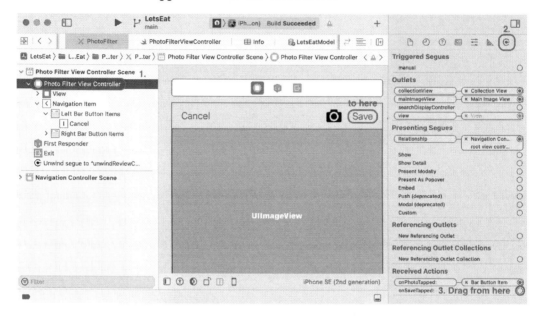

Figure 21.19: Connections inspector showing onSaveTapped: being assigned to the Save button

Before you can save, you need to pass the restaurant identifier to
`PhotoFilterViewController`. As you did before, you'll use segue identifiers to
determine which segue is occurring, and then implement methods to pass the identifier
value between the two view controllers. Follow these steps:

1. Click the `RestaurantDetail` storyboard file in the Project navigator and select
    the segue used to go to the **Photo Filter** screen:

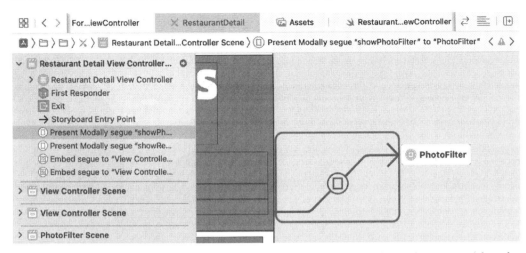

Figure 21.20: Editor area showing segue between Restaurant Detail and Photo Filter screens selected

2. In the Attributes inspector, set **Identifier** under **Storyboard Segue** to
    showPhotoFilter and press *Return*:

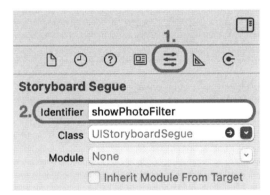

Figure 21.21: Attributes inspector with Identifier set to showPhotoFilter

3. Click the RestaurantDetailViewController file in the Project navigator.
    Update the prepare(for:sender:) method, as follows:

```
override func prepare(for segue: UIStoryboardSegue,
sender: Any?){
    if let identifier = segue.identifier {
        switch identifier {
        case Segue.showReview.rawValue:
            showReview(segue: segue)
        case Segue.showPhotoFilter.rawValue:
            showPhotoFilter(segue: segue)
```

```
        default:
            print("Segue not added")
        }
    }
}
```

This makes the prepare(for:sender:) method check to see if
the segue has the showPhotoFilter segue identifier. If it does, the
showPhotoFilter(segue:) method is executed prior to transitioning from the
Restaurant Detail screen to the **Photo Filter** screen. There will be an error because
showPhotoFilter(segue:) has not been implemented yet.

4. Add the showPhotoFilter(segue:) method after the showReview()
    method inside your private extension:

```
func showPhotoFilter(segue: UIStoryboardSegue) {
    guard let navController = segue.destination as?
    UINavigationController, let viewController =
    navController.topViewController as?
    PhotoFilterViewController else {
        return
    }
    viewController.selectedRestaurantID =
    selectedRestaurant?.restaurantID
}
```

This sets PhotoFilterViewController's restaurantID property to the
identifier of the selected restaurant.

Build and run your project, set a location, and tap **All**. Tap a restaurant, and tap the **Add
Photo** button. Select a photo, apply a filter, and tap **Save**:

Figure 21.22: iOS Simulator showing Photo Filter screen with Save button selected

The photo will be saved to the persistent store, and you will be returned to the **Restaurant Detail** screen.

At this point, you can save reviews and photos. Fantastic! In the next section, you will add code to load the reviews and photos from the persistent store to be displayed on the **Restaurant Detail** screen.

Displaying saved reviews and photos on the Restaurant Detail screen

The **Save** buttons inside the **Review Form** and **Photo Filter** screens now save reviews and photos with a restaurant identifier. Now you need to configure the **Restaurant Detail** screen to display them. If you look in `RestaurantDetail.storyboard`, you'll see that collection views have already been set up to display photos and reviews in the static table view cells. All you need to do is to implement the respective view controllers for the view and collection view cells. You'll start with the view and collection view cells used to display reviews. Follow these steps:

1. Right-click the `LetsEat` folder in the Project navigator and choose **New Group**. Name this group `Reviews`.

2. Right-click the folder and select **New File**.

3. **iOS** should already be selected. Choose **Cocoa Touch Class**, and then click **Next**.

4. Configure the file as follows:

   Class: `ReviewCell`

   Subclass: `UICollectionViewCell`

   Also create XIB: Unchecked

   Language: `Swift`

   Click **Next**.

5. Click **Create**. The `ReviewCell` file appears in the Project navigator. Enter the following code between the curly braces:

```swift
import UIKit
class ReviewCell: UICollectionViewCell {
    @IBOutlet var titleLabel: UILabel!
    @IBOutlet var dateLabel: UILabel!
    @IBOutlet var nameLabel: UILabel!
    @IBOutlet var reviewLabel: UILabel!
    @IBOutlet var ratingsView: RatingsView!
}
```

`ReviewCell` now has the properties for all the outlets in the collection view cell. Let's create `ReviewsViewController` next. Follow these steps:

1. Right-click the `Reviews` folder, and select **New File**.

2. **iOS** should already be selected. Choose **Cocoa Touch Class**, and then click **Next**.

3. Configure the file as follows:

   Class: `ReviewsViewController`

   Subclass: `UIViewController`

   Also create XIB: Unchecked

   Language: `Swift`

   Click **Next**.

4. Click **Create**. The `ReviewsViewController` file appears in the Project navigator. Modify this file as follows:

```swift
import UIKit
class ReviewsViewController: UIViewController {
    @IBOutlet var collectionView: UICollectionView!
    var selectedRestaurantID: Int?
    private var reviewItems: [ReviewItem] = []
    private var dateFormatter: DateFormatter = {
        let formatter = DateFormatter()
        formatter.dateFormat = "MMM dd, yyyy"
        return formatter
    }()
    override func viewDidLoad() {
        super.viewDidLoad()
        initialize()
    }
    override func viewDidAppear(_ animated: Bool) {
        super.viewDidAppear(animated)
        checkReviews()
    }
}
```

As you can see, the implementation of ReviewsViewController is straightforward. You have an outlet for a collection view, collectionView. selectedRestaurantID stores the restaurant identifier. reviewItems contains an array of ReviewItem instances. dateFormatter is an instance of the DateFormatter class that will be used to format the date for display. Don't worry about the errors, as you'll be typing in the implementation of the initialize() and setupDefaults() methods in the next step.

> **Important Information**
>
> To learn more about the DateFormatter class, visit this link: https://developer.apple.com/documentation/foundation/dateformatter.

5. Add a private extension with the following code, as shown:

```
private extension ReviewsViewController {
    func initialize() {
        setupCollectionView()
    }

    func setupCollectionView() {
        let flow = UICollectionViewFlowLayout()
        flow.sectionInset = UIEdgeInsets(top: 7, left: 7,
        bottom: 7, right: 7)
        flow.minimumInteritemSpacing = 0
        flow.minimumLineSpacing = 7
        flow.scrollDirection = .horizontal
        collectionView.collectionViewLayout = flow
    }
}
```

The private extension contains the implementation for initialize() and setupCollectionView() methods. initialize() just calls setupCollectionView(). setupCollectionView() is used to configure the flow and spacing of the collection views and is similar to code you've written before.

6. Add the following method after setupCollectionView() to implement checkReviews():

```
func checkReviews() {
    let viewController = self.parent as?
```

```
            RestaurantDetailViewController
        if let restaurantID =
    viewController?.selectedRestaurant?
        .restaurantID {
            reviewItems =
            CoreDataManager.shared
            .fetchReviews(by: restaurantID)
            if !reviewItems.isEmpty {
                collectionView.backgroundView = nil
            } else {
                let view = NoDataView(frame:
                CGRect(x: 0, y: 0, width:
                collectionView.frame.width,
                height:
                collectionView.frame.height))
            view.set(title: "Reviews", desc:
            "There are currently no reviews")
            collectionView.backgroundView = view
            }
        }
        collectionView.reloadData()
    }
```

This method will retrieve all restaurant reviews for the specified restaurant identifier. Let's break this down:

```
let viewController = self.parent as?
RestaurantDetailViewController
```

This statement assigns `RestaurantDetailViewController` to a temporary constant, `viewController`.

```
if let restaurantID =
viewController?.selectedRestaurant?.restaurantID {
```

This statement assigns the restaurant identifier of the restaurant shown in the **Restaurant Detail** screen to `restaurantID`.

```
reviewItems = CoreDataManager.shared
.fetchReviews(by: restaurantID)
```

This statement gets an array of reviews matching the given `restaurantID` from the persistent store and assigns it to `reviewItems`.

```
if !reviewItems.isEmpty {
    collectionView.backgroundView = nil
} else {
    let view = NoDataView(frame:
    CGRect(x: 0, y: 0, width:
    collectionView.frame.width,
    height:
    collectionView.frame.height))
    view.set(title: "Reviews", desc:
    "There are currently no reviews")
    collectionView.backgroundView = view
}
```

If there are reviews for this restaurant, the collection view's background view is set to `nil`; otherwise, you create a `NoDataView` instance, set the `title` and `desc` properties to `"Reviews"` and `"There are currently no reviews"` respectively, and assign it to the collection view's background view.

```
collectionView.reloadData()
```

This code tells the collection view to redraw itself onscreen.

7. Implement the data source methods for the collection view by adding the following extension:

```
extension ReviewsViewController:
UICollectionViewDataSource {
    func collectionView(_ collectionView:
    UICollectionView, numberOfItemsInSection
    section: Int) -> Int {
        reviewItems.count
    }
    func collectionView(_ collectionView:
    UICollectionView, cellForItemAt indexPath:
    IndexPath) -> UICollectionViewCell {
        let cell = collectionView
        .dequeueReusableCell
        (withReuseIdentifier: "reviewCell",
```

```
            for: indexPath) as! ReviewCell
        let reviewItem = reviewItems[indexPath.item]
        cell.nameLabel.text = reviewItem.name
        cell.titleLabel.text = reviewItem.title
        cell.reviewLabel.text =
        reviewItem.customerReview
        if let reviewItemDate = reviewItem.date {
            cell.dateLabel.text =
            dateFormatter.string(from:
            reviewItemDate)
        }
        if let reviewItemRating = reviewItem.rating
        {
            cell.ratingsView.rating =
            reviewItemRating
        }
        return cell
    }
}
```

This is similar to what you've done before. The number of cells to be displayed in the collection view is the same as the number of items in the reviewItems array. You set each cell's contents using the properties of the corresponding ReviewItem instance.

8. Add the flow layout delegate methods for the collection view by adding the following extension:

```
extension ReviewsViewController:
UICollectionViewDelegateFlowLayout {
    func collectionView(_ collectionView:
    UICollectionView, layout collectionViewLayout:
    UICollectionViewLayout, sizeForItemAt
    indexPath: IndexPath) -> CGSize {
        let edgeInset = 7.0
        if reviewItems.count == 1 {
            let cellWidth =
            collectionView.frame.size.width -
            (edgeInset * 2)
```

```
                return CGSize(width: cellWidth, height:
        200)
    } else {
        let cellWidth =
        collectionView.frame.size.width -
        (edgeInset * 3)
        return CGSize(width: cellWidth, height:
        200)
        }
    }
}
```

This method returns the size of the collection view cell to be displayed. If there is only one item in the `reviewItems` array, the cell's width is set to the width of the collection view—14 points; otherwise, it is set to the width of the collection view—21 points. The height is set to `200` points.

`ReviewsViewController` is now complete. Now, you'll finish the implementation of the `RestaurantDetail` storyboard file. Follow these steps:

1. Click the `RestaurantDetail` storyboard file in the Project navigator. Select the **View Controller Scene** containing the collection view for reviews. Click the Identity inspector button, set **Class** to `ReviewsViewController`, and press *Return*:

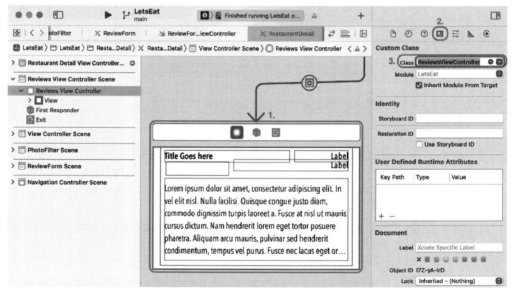

Figure 21.23: Identity inspector with Class set to ReviewsViewController

The scene name will change to **Reviews View Controller Scene**.

2. Select the **Collection View Cell** in the document outline. Click the Identity inspector button, set **Class** to `ReviewCell`, and press *Return*:

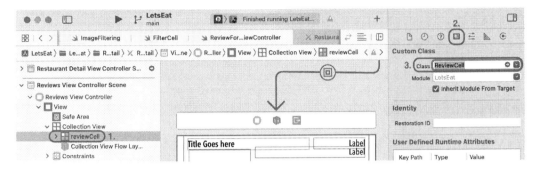

Figure 21.24: Identity inspector with Class set to ReviewCell

3. Select the view in the document outline. Click the Identity inspector button, set **Class** to `RatingsView`, and press *Return*:

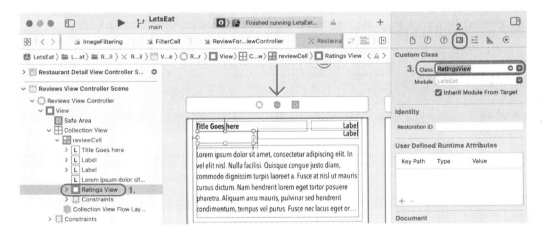

Figure 21.25: Identity inspector with Class set to RatingsView

4. Select **reviewCell** in the document outline. Click the Attributes inspector button. Set **Identifier** to `reviewCell` if it's not already set:

Figure 21.26: Attributes inspector with Identifier set to reviewCell

5. Click the Connections inspector. Drag from the `dateLabel` outlet to the **Label** shown, if it's not already set:

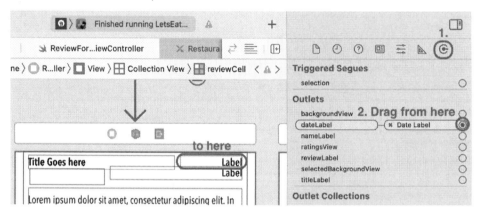

Figure 21.27: Connections inspector showing dateLabel outlet

6. Drag from the `nameLabel` outlet to the **Label** shown, if it's not already set:

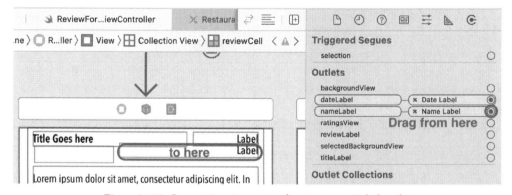

Figure 21.28: Connections inspector showing nameLabel outlet

7. Drag from the `reviewLabel` outlet to the **Label** shown, if it's not already set:

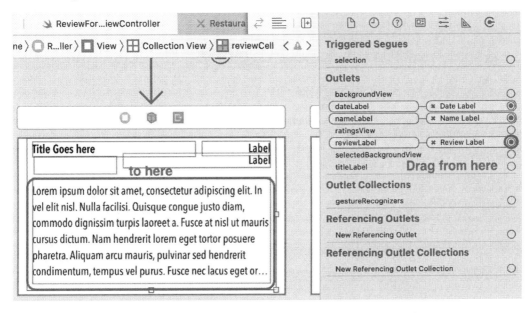

Figure 21.29: Connections inspector showing reviewLabel outlet

8. Drag from the `titleLabel` outlet to the **Label** shown, if it's not already set:

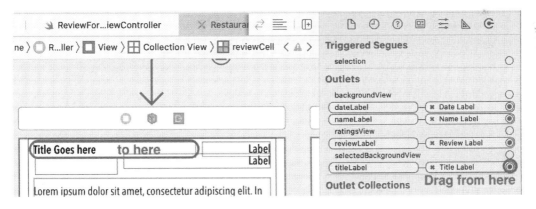

Figure 21.30: Connections inspector shown titleLabel outlet

9. Drag from the `ratingsView` outlet to the ratings view shown, if it's not already set:

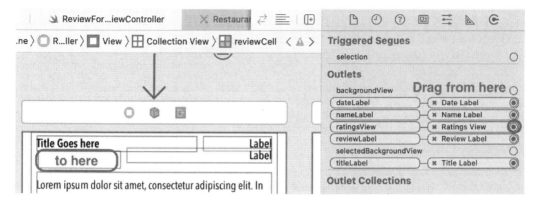

Figure 21.31: Connections inspector showing the ratingsView outlet

10. Select the **Reviews View Controller** icon for the **Reviews View Controller Scene** in the document outline. Drag from the `collectionView` outlet to the **Collection View** as shown, if it's not already set:

Figure 21.32: Connections inspector showing the collectionView outlet

11. Select **Collection View** in the document outline. Drag from the `delegate` and `dataSource` outlets to the **Reviews View Controller** icon:

Figure 21.33: Connections inspector showing the dataSource and delegate outlets

Build and run your app. You should see the reviews you added earlier appear:

Figure 21.34: iOS Simulator showing Restaurant Detail screen containing reviews

The implementation of view controllers for the collection view and collection view cells used to display reviews is now complete, and your app now can display reviews that were entered using the **Review Form** screen earlier. If you have more than one review, you can swipe left and right to see each review. Since each review has a rating, you can use them to calculate and add an overall rating for a restaurant. Let's modify the app to do this next.

Calculating a restaurant's overall rating

The **Restaurant Detail** screen's overall rating label displays **0.0**, and the ratings view displays 3.5 stars, regardless of the actual rating. To add an overall rating, you need to get the ratings from all the reviews and average them. Let's add a new method to `CoreDataManager` to do this. Follow these steps:

1. Click the `CoreDataManager` file inside the Project navigator (inside the Core Data folder in the `Misc` folder). Add the following method before the `addReview(_:)` method:

```
func fetchRestaurantRating(by identifier: Int) ->
Double {
    let reviewItems = fetchReviews(by: identifier)
    let sum = reviewItems.reduce(0, {$0 +
    ($1.rating ?? 0)})
    return sum / Double(reviewItems.count)
}
```

In this method, all reviews for a particular restaurant are fetched from the persistent store and assigned to `reviews`. The `reduce()` method takes a closure, which is used to add all the review ratings together. Finally, the average rating value is calculated and returned.

> **Important Information**
>
> You can learn more about the `reduce()` method at this link: `https://developer.apple.com/documentation/swift/array/2298686-reduce`.

2. Click the `RestaurantDetailViewController` file in the Project navigator (inside the `RestaurantDetail` folder). Update the `createRating()` method, as follows:

```
func createRating() {
    ratingsView.isEnabled = false
    if let restaurantID =
    selectedRestaurant?.restaurantID {
        let ratingValue =
        CoreDataManager.shared.
        fetchRestaurantRating(by:
        restaurantID)
        ratingsView.rating = ratingValue
        if ratingValue.isNaN {
            overallRatingLabel.text = "0.0"
        } else {
            let roundedValue = ((ratingValue *
            10).rounded() / 10)
            overallRatingLabel.text =
            "\(roundedValue)"
        }
    }
}
```

The method first assigns the `selectedRestaurant` instance's `restaurantID` property to `restaurantID`. If successful, the `CoreDataManager.shared.fetchRestaurantRating()` method is called, which gets all the reviews with `restaurantID`'s restaurant identifier value, and calculates the average rating. `ratingValue` is then set to the average rating and used to update the ratings view's `rating` property, which determines the number of stars displayed in the **Restaurant Detail** screen. `roundedValue` is then calculated from `ratingValue` to return a number with 1 decimal point, and is used to set the `text` property for `overallRatingLabel`.

3. The overall rating will also need to be updated whenever the user adds a new review in the **Review Form** screen. Add the following code after the `viewDidLoad()` method:

```
override func viewDidAppear(_ animated: Bool) {
    super.viewDidAppear(animated)
    createRating()
}
```

This will recalculate the rating when the **Review Form** screen is dismissed and the **Restaurant Detail** screen reappears.

Build and run your project, and you should now see an overall rating for restaurants that have reviews, as well as a corresponding star rating as shown:

Figure 21.35: iOS Simulator showing Restaurant Detail screen with overall ratings

There's still one thing left to do, and that's adding photo reviews. Your challenge is to add photo reviews and to display them in the collection view just under the collection view used for reviews. The way to do this is very similar to the way you used to add reviews. This chapter covers all you need to know, and if you get stuck, feel free to use the completed project files for this chapter, which you will find in the `Chapter21` folder of the code bundle of this book, downloadable from `https://github.com/PacktPublishing/iOS-15-Programming-for-Beginners-Sixth-Edition`. You can also watch the CiA video for this chapter, located at `https://bit.ly/3o81yKK`.

Summary

In this chapter, you learned about Core Data and its different components. You created data models for your app named `Review` and `RestaurantPhoto`, and you created the corresponding model objects for your app named `ReviewItem` and `RestaurantPhotoItem`. After that, you implemented `CoreDataManager` to set up Core Data components for your app.

You updated `ReviewFormViewController` and `PhotoFilterViewController` to save reviews and photos together with a restaurant identifier to the persistent store. You modified `RestaurantDetailViewController` to load reviews for a particular restaurant based on the restaurant identifier, and displayed them in a collection view. You also calculated and displayed the overall rating for that restaurant.

Finally, on your own, you modified `RestaurantDetailViewController` to load photos for a particular restaurant based on the restaurant identifier, and displayed them in a collection view.

You now have a basic understanding of how Core Data works. You're also able to set up Core Data components and enable an interface between your app and Core Data components using a data manager class. You also know how to save and load reviews and photos using Core Data, which you will now be able to implement in your own apps.

You have come to the end of a long journey, and have now finished building your app's primary functionality. All the screens work, and reviews and photos are persistent. Fantastic job!

This concludes *Part 3* of this book. In the next part, you'll find out about the cool new features Apple has introduced in iOS 15 and how to add them to your app, starting with getting your app ready for Apple Macs in the next chapter.

Part 4: Features

Welcome to *Part 4* of this book. In this part, you will implement the latest iOS 15 features. First, you will modify your app to work on both an iPhone and an iPad, and make it work on Macs. Next, you will learn how to develop SwiftUI apps, a great new way of developing apps for all Apple platforms. After that, you'll learn how to implement asynchronous and parallel programming using Swift Concurrency, and how to implement shared experiences using SharePlay. Finally, you'll see how to test your app with internal and external testers, and upload it into the App Store.

This part comprises the following chapters:

- *Chapter 22, Getting Started with Mac Catalyst*

- *Chapter 23, Getting Started with SwiftUI*

- *Chapter 24, Getting Started with Swift Concurrency*

- *Chapter 25, Getting Started with SharePlay*

- *Chapter 26, Testing and Submitting Your App to the App Store*

By the end of this part, you'll be able to implement cool iOS 15 features in your own apps. You'll also be able to test and publish your own apps to the App Store. Let's get started!

22
Getting Started with Mac Catalyst

Apple's Mac Catalyst feature allows you to make a Mac version of an iPad app. This allows you to share the same project and source code for both platforms, making it easier to maintain. During WWDC2021, Apple announced updates to Mac Catalyst that allow you to add more features just for Mac, such as keyboard navigation and printing using *Command + P*. This chapter will focus on how to make your existing iPhone app run on iPad, so you can make a Mac version of it. By doing so, you will be able to reach an audience of over 100 million active Mac users.

In this chapter, you'll modify your app to make it run on iPads and Macs. First, you'll fix some user interface issues in your app. Next, you'll learn how to make your app's user interface work on the iPad, taking advantage of the iPad's larger screen size. After that, you'll use the iPad version of your app to create the Mac version.

By the end of this chapter, you'll be able to make your existing iOS apps run well on all iOS devices, and also be able to make Mac apps from your iPad apps.

The following topics will be covered:

- Fixing user interface issues
- Making your app run on all iOS devices
- Making your app run on the Mac

Technical requirements

You will continue working on the `LetsEat` project that you modified in the previous chapter.

The completed Xcode project for this chapter is in the `Chapter22` folder of the code bundle for this book, which can be downloaded here:

`https://github.com/PacktPublishing/iOS-15-Programming-for-Beginners-Sixth-Edition`

Check out the following video to see the code in action:

`https://bit.ly/3IbY41R`

Let's start by making some changes to the user interface to make it look better.

Fixing user interface issues

One of the things that you will find is that an iOS app is never really done. You'll always find ways to improve and refine your app. Build and run your app, and compare it with the design shown in the app tour (in *Chapter 9, Setting Up the User Interface*). You will notice upon close inspection that your app's screens have minor differences when compared to the screens shown in the app tour, and require changes. Let's start with the **Explore** screen for your app:

Figure 22.1: iOS Simulator showing Explore screen

The changes required for the **Explore** screen are as follows. Refer to the numbers to see the part that needs to be changed:

- The navigation bar (**1**) is not present on the app tour and will have to be removed.

- The collection view cells (**2**) have sharp edges. You'll implement rounded corners for the cells to match the cells shown in the app tour.

- The tab bar buttons are blue (**3**). You'll change the tab bar button color to red to match the app tour.

Now let's see the **Locations** screen for your app:

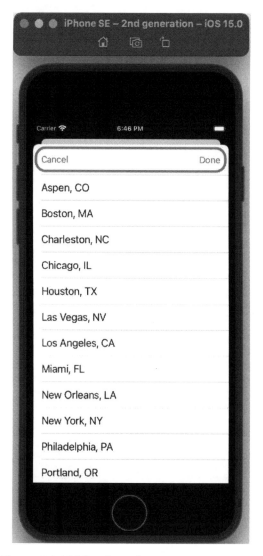

Figure 22.2: iOS Simulator showing Locations screen

The large title at the top of the **Locations** screen shown in the app tour is missing, and you will have to add it.

As you can see, there are only four minor changes that need to be made, and these changes are easy to implement. You'll start by modifying the **Explore** screen. Follow these steps:

1. Click the `ExploreViewController` file inside the `Explore` folder in the Project navigator.

2. Add a `viewWillAppear()` method after the `viewDidLoad()` method, and add code inside this method to hide the navigation controller's navigation bar:

```
override func viewWillAppear(_ animated: Bool) {
    super.viewWillAppear(animated)
    navigationController?.setNavigationBarHidden(true,
    animated: false)
}
```

Note that if you add this code to `viewDidLoad()`, the navigation bar will be hidden only when the **Explore** screen first appears, and will reappear when you transition from either the **Locations** screen or the **Restaurant List** screen back to the **Explore** screen.

3. To round the corners of the collection view cells on the **Explore** screen, click the `ExploreCell` file (inside the `View` folder in the `Explore` folder) in the Project navigator, and add the following method after the outlet declarations:

```
override func awakeFromNib() {
    super.awakeFromNib()
    exploreImageView.layer.cornerRadius = 9
    exploreImageView.layer.masksToBounds = true
}
```

4. To change the colors of the tab bar buttons, click the `AppDelegate` file in the Project navigator and add a `private` extension containing the following methods after the last curly brace:

```
private extension AppDelegate {
    func initialize() {
        setupDefaultColors()
    }
    func setupDefaultColors() {
        UITabBar.appearance().tintColor = .systemRed
        UITabBarItem.appearance().
        setTitleTextAttributes(
```

```
        [NSAttributedString.Key.foregroundColor:
        UIColor.systemRed], for:
        UIControl.State.selected)
        UINavigationBar.appearance().tintColor =
        .systemRed


    }
}
```

The `AppDelegate` file contains the declaration and the definition of the `AppDelegate` class. This class handles application events, for example, what happens when an application is launched, sent to the background, terminated, and so on. You can add code here to configure your app as it is starting up.

As you have done before, you'll use an `initialize()` method to call all other setup methods. In this case, the `initialize()` method calls the `setupDefaultColors()` method.

The `setupDefaultColors()` method will change the tint colors for items in the tab bar and navigation bar to red. It makes use of the `appearance()` method, which sets attributes globally for every tab and nav bar that has been or will be created.

> **Important Information**
>
> More information about the `appearance()` method can be found here: `https://developer.apple.com/documentation/uikit/uiappearance`.

5. You have to call the `initialize()` method as the app is starting up, so modify the `application(_:didFinishLaunchingWithOptions:)` method as follows:

```
func application(_ application:
UIApplication, didFinishLaunchingWithOptions
launchOptions: [UIApplication.LaunchOptionsKey: Any]?) ->
Bool {
    initialize()
    return true
}
```

6.   Click the Main storyboard file in the Project navigator. Under the **Explore View Controller Scene**, click **Explore Image View**. Select the Attributes inspector and under **View**, change the **Content Mode** to **Aspect Fill**:

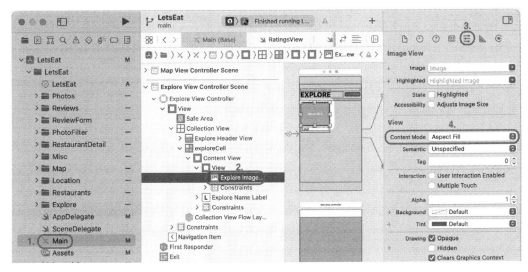

Figure 22.3: Main storyboard file showing Explore Image View set to Aspect Fill

This allows images to take up the full image view frame and display the rounded corners you coded in *Step 3*.

Build and run your app. The **Explore** screen should look like this:

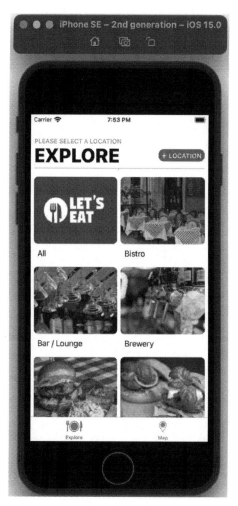

Figure 22.4: iOS Simulator showing updated Explore screen

You'll see that the navigation bar is gone, the corners of each cell are rounded, and the **Explore** and **Map** button icons and titles are now red when selected.

7. Next, you'll update the `LocationViewController` class. Click the `LocationViewController` file inside the `Location` folder in the Project navigator and modify the `initialize()` method to set a title for the **Locations** screen:

```
func initialize() {
    manager.fetch()
```

```
title = "Select a location"
navigationController?.navigationBar.
prefersLargeTitles = true
}
```

Each view controller has a `title` property that can be displayed in the navigation bar. This code sets the title to `Select a location` and displays it in large letters at the top of the screen.

Build and run your app, and tap the **LOCATION** button. The **Locations** screen should look like this:

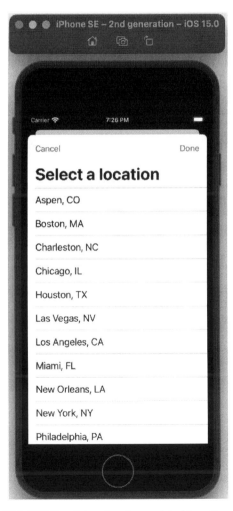

Figure 22.5: iOS Simulator showing updated Locations screen

You'll see **Select a location** in large letters at the top of the screen, and the **Cancel** and **Done** buttons are now red.

Great! You've finished cleaning up the design for the app on the iPhone. The four issues mentioned earlier have been addressed, and your app's screens now look exactly like the screens shown in the app tour. As you can see, even minor changes can make your app more visually appealing.

So far, you've been running your app in the iPhone simulator. In the next section, you'll run your app in the iPad simulator to see what changes are required. You'll then modify your app so that the user interface will take advantage of the iPad's larger screen.

Making your app run on all iOS devices

Before you can make a Mac app from your existing iOS app, you need to modify the user interface to work with iPad. To see what changes you will need to make, you'll build and run your app on the iPad simulator. Follow these steps:

1. Close the simulator if it is running. Choose **iPad Pro (9.7-inch)** from the list of simulators in the **Scheme** menu and run your app:

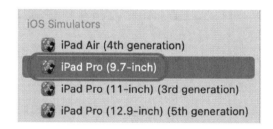

Figure 22.6: Scheme menu with iPad Pro (9.7-inch) selected

2. The iPad simulator will launch and appear as shown in the following screenshot:

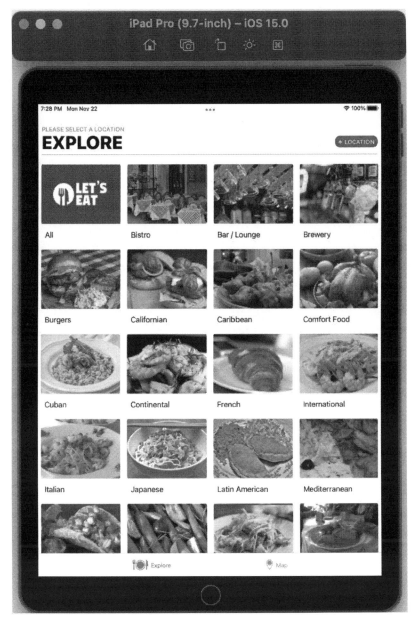

Figure 22.7: iPad simulator showing Explore screen

As you can see, the collection view on the **Explore** screen automatically takes up the whole width of the screen, and the collection view cells are the same size that they were on the iPhone. Even though you can use exactly the same user interface for both iPhone and iPad, it would be better if you could customize it to suit each device.

To do this, you'll add some code so your app can identify the type of device it's running on. Next, you'll update your app's user interface to suit the iPad's larger screen and make your app automatically switch the user interface based on the device type.

Let's see how to make your app detect the type of device it is running on in the next section.

Identifying device type

You need to add some code to your app so that it knows the device it is running on. Follow these steps:

1. Right-click the `Misc` folder and select **New File**.

2. **iOS** should already be selected. Choose **Swift File** and then click **Next**.

3. Name this file `Device`. Click **Create**. The `Device` file appears in the Project navigator.

4. Modify the file as shown to create a `Device` enumeration:

```
import UIKit
enum Device {
    static var isPhone: Bool {
        UIDevice.current.userInterfaceIdiom ==
        .phone
    }
    static var isPad: Bool {
        UIDevice.current.userInterfaceIdiom ==
        .pad
    }
}
```

Here, an enumeration is used instead of a class or structure because you can't accidentally make an instance of it. The `UIDevice` class represents the device the app is running on. `UIDevice.current.userInterfaceIdiom` returns `.phone` if the app is running on an iPhone, and returns `.pad` if the app is running on an iPad. So `isPhone` returns `true` when the app is running on the iPhone, and `isPad` returns `true` when the app is running on the iPad.

In addition to device type, you also have to consider device orientation. For example, an iPhone in landscape orientation is wider than an iPhone in portrait orientation even though it is the same iPhone. Let's learn how to handle device orientation using **size classes** in the next section.

Understanding size classes

Although you can now identify what kind of device your app is running on, you also have to consider the effects of device orientation on your user interface. It can be challenging to do this as there is a wide variety of screen sizes, in both portrait and landscape orientation. To make this easier, instead of using the physical resolution of the device, you will use size classes.

> **Important Information**
>
> For more information on size classes, see this link: `https://developer.apple.com/design/human-interface-guidelines/ios/visual-design/adaptivity-and-layout/`.

Size classes are traits which are automatically assigned to a view. Two classes are defined which describe the height and width of a view; regular (expansive space) and compact (constrained space). Let's look at size classes for a full-screen view on different devices:

Device	Portrait	Landscape
iPad	Regular width Regular height	Regular width Regular height
iPhone 11 Pro Max	Compact width Regular height	Regular width Compact height
iPhone SE (2nd generation)	Compact width Regular height	Compact width Compact height

Figure 22.8: Size classes for different iOS devices

You'll have to consider not only the device type, but also the size class when you're designing the user interface. In the next section, you'll learn how to set the collection view cell size based on device and size class.

Updating the Explore screen

For the **Explore** screen, let's say you have decided to display three columns on the iPad, two columns for the compact width size class and three columns for the regular width size class. You'll add methods to set the size of the collection view cell depending on the device and orientation. Follow these steps:

1. Click the `ExploreViewController` file in the Project navigator and modify the `initialize()` method inside the `private` extension as follows:

```
func initialize() {
    manager.fetch()
    setupCollectionView()
}
```

You'll see an error because `setupCollectionView()` is not declared or defined yet. You'll do that next.

2. The `setupCollectionView()` method will be used to add a `UICollectionViewFlowLayout` instance to the collection view in the **Explore** screen. Declare and define this method after the `initialize()` method:

```
func setupCollectionView() {
    let flow = UICollectionViewFlowLayout()
    flow.sectionInset = UIEdgeInsets(top: 7, left: 7,
    bottom: 7, right: 7)
    flow.minimumInteritemSpacing = 0
    flow.minimumLineSpacing = 7
    collectionView.collectionViewLayout = flow
}
```

This method creates an instance of the `UICollectionViewFlowLayout` class, sets all the edge insets for the collection view to 7 points, sets the minimum interitem spacing to 0 points, sets the minimum line spacing to 7 points, and assigns it to the collection view. Remember that you initially set these values for the collection view using the Size inspector in *Chapter 10, Building Your User Interface*.

3. Add an extension containing the methods that will set the size of the collection view cells and the collection view section header after the closing curly brace:

```
extension ExploreViewController:
UICollectionViewDelegateFlowLayout {
    func collectionView(_ collectionView:
```

```
    UICollectionView, layout collectionViewLayout:
    UICollectionViewLayout, sizeForItemAt indexPath:
    IndexPath) -> CGSize {
        var columns: CGFloat = 2
        if Device.isPad ||
        (traitCollection.horizontalSizeClass !=
        .compact) {
            columns = 3
        }
        let viewWidth = collectionView.frame.size.width
        let inset = 7.0
        let contentWidth = viewWidth - inset *
        (columns + 1)
        let cellWidth = contentWidth / columns
        let cellHeight = cellWidth
        return CGSize(width: cellWidth, height:
        cellHeight)
    }
    func collectionView(_ collectionView:
    UICollectionView, layout collectionViewLayout:
    UICollectionViewLayout,
    referenceSizeForHeaderInSection section: Int) ->
    CGSize {
        return CGSize(width: collectionView.frame.width,
        height: 100)
    }
}
```

These methods are declared in the `UICollectionViewDelegateFlowLayout` protocol, and they define item size and spacing in the collection view. They will override the settings in the Size inspector. Let's break them down:

```
func collectionView(_ collectionView: UICollectionView,
layout collectionViewLayout: UICollectionViewLayout,
sizeForItemAt indexPath: IndexPath) -> CGSize {
```

This method returns a `CGSize` instance that the collection view cell size should be set to.

```
var columns: CGFloat = 2
```

The `columns` variable determines how many columns appear on screen, and is initially set to 2.

```
if Device.isPad || (traitCollection.horizontalSizeClass
!= .compact) {
```

Checks to see whether the app is running on an iPad or the `horizontalSizeClass` property is not `.compact`.

```
columns = 3
```

If the app is running on an iPad or the horizontal size class is not `.compact`, set `columns` to 3.

```
let viewWidth = collectionView.frame.size.width
```

Gets the width of the screen and assigns it to `viewWidth`.

```
let inset = 7.0
```

```
let contentWidth = viewWidth - inset * (columns + 1)
```

Subtracts the space used for the edge insets so the cell size can be determined.

```
let cellWidth = contentWidth / columns
```

Gets the width of the cell by dividing `contentWidth` by `columns`, and assigns it to `cellWidth`.

```
let cellHeight = cellWidth
```

Sets the height of the cell to be the same as the width of the cell.

```
return CGSize(width: cellWidth, height: cellHeight)
}
```

Returns the cell size.

Assume you're running on iPhone 13 Pro Max in portrait mode. `columns` is set to 2. `viewWidth` would be assigned the width of the iPhone screen, which is 414 points. `contentWidth` is set to 414 - (7 x 3) = 393. `cellWidth` is set to `contentWidth` / `columns` = 196.5, and `cellHeight` is set to `cellWidth`, so the `CGSize` returned would be (196.5, 196.5), enabling two cells to fit in a row.

When you rotate the same iPhone to landscape mode, `columns` is set to 3. `viewWidth` would be assigned the height of the iPhone screen, which is 896 points. `contentWidth` is set to 896 - (7 x 4) = 868. `cellWidth` is set to `contentWidth` / `columns` = 289.3, and `cellHeight` is set to `cellWidth`, so the `CGSize` returned would be (289.3, 289.3), enabling three cells to fit in a row.

```
func collectionView(_ collectionView: UICollectionView,
  layout collectionViewLayout: UICollectionViewLayout,
  referenceSizeForHeaderInSection section: Int) -> CGSize {
```

This method returns the size the collection view section header should be set to.

```
return CGSize(width: collectionView.frame.width, height: 100)
```

The width of the collection view section header will depend on device orientation but the height will always be `100`.

Build and run your app on the iPad simulator. You should see three columns displayed:

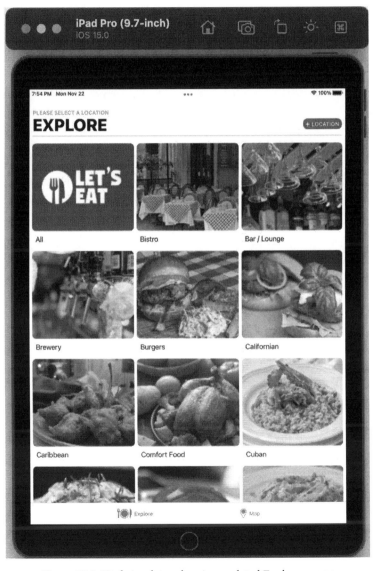

Figure 22.9: iPad simulator showing updated Explore screen

Build and run your app on the iPhone 13 Pro Max simulator, you should see two columns displayed:

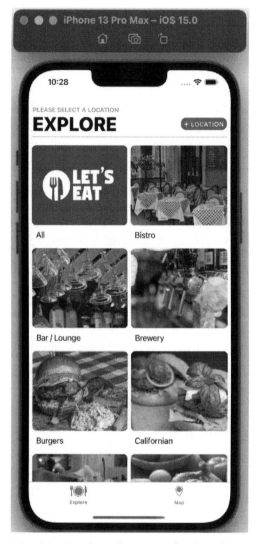

Figure 22.10: iPhone 13 Pro Max Simulator showing updated Explore screen in portrait mode

Choose **Device | Rotate Left** in the simulator menu, you will see three columns displayed:

Figure 22.11: iPhone 13 Pro Max Simulator showing updated Explore screen in landscape mode

Choose **Device | Rotate Right** in the simulator menu to return to a vertical orientation.

You have completed modifying the **Explore** screen. Now, let's see how to make the **Restaurant List** screen adapt to different device types and orientations as well. You'll modify the `RestaurantListViewController` class in the next section.

Updating the Restaurant List screen

You have already modified the **Explore** screen to automatically adapt to the device your app is running on. You'll now do the same for the **Restaurant List** screen. If you build and run on the iPad simulator, this is what the **Restaurant List** screen looks like:

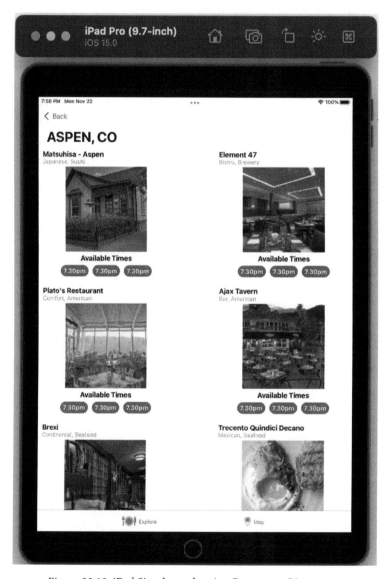

Figure 22.12: iPad Simulator showing Restaurant List screen

As you can see, there are only two columns, and there is a large white space between them. Let's say you want three columns on the iPad, one column for the compact width size class and two columns for the regular width size class. Follow these steps:

1. Click the `RestaurantListViewController` file inside the `Restaurants` folder in the Project navigator. Create an `initialize()` method inside the `private` extension before all other code already in the extension:

```
func initialize() {
    createData()
    setupTitle()
    setupCollectionView()
}
```

The `createData()` and `setupTitle()` methods are both called in `viewDidAppear()`, but you'll modify `viewDidAppear()` to call `initialize()` instead later. You'll see an error because the `setupCollectionView()` method is not declared or defined yet.

2. Declare and define the `setupCollectionView()` method in the `private` extension after the `initialize()` method:

```
func setupCollectionView() {
    let flow = UICollectionViewFlowLayout()
    flow.sectionInset = UIEdgeInsets(top: 7, left: 7,
    bottom: 7, right: 7)
    flow.minimumInteritemSpacing = 0
    flow.minimumLineSpacing = 7
    collectionView.collectionViewLayout = flow
}
```

Just like before, `setupCollectionView()` creates an instance of the `UICollectionViewFlowLayout` class, configures it, and assigns it to the collection view.

3. Add an extension containing `UICollectionViewDelegateFlowLayout` methods after the closing curly brace:

```
extension RestaurantListViewController:
UICollectionViewDelegateFlowLayout {
    func collectionView(_ collectionView:
    UICollectionView, layout collectionViewLayout:
```

```
        UICollectionViewLayout, sizeForItemAt indexPath:
    IndexPath) -> CGSize {
        var columns: CGFloat = 0
        if Device.isPad {
            columns = 3
        } else {
            columns =
            traitCollection.horizontalSizeClass
            == .compact ? 1 : 2
        }
        let viewWidth = collectionView.frame.size.width
        let inset = 7.0
        let contentWidth = viewWidth - inset *
        (columns + 1)
        let cellWidth = contentWidth / columns
        let cellHeight = 312.0
        return CGSize(width: cellWidth, height:
        cellHeight)
    }
}
```

The collectionView(_:layout:sizeForItemAt:) method
implemented here works almost exactly the same as the implementation in the
ExploreViewController class, but cellHeight is set to 312 points instead
of being set to cellWidth. Note that if you're not running your app on an iPad,
columns will be set to 1 for the compact width size class and to 2 for the regular
width size class.

4. Update viewDidAppear() by removing calls to the createData() and
setupTitle() methods and adding a call for the initialize() method:

```
override func viewDidAppear(_ animated: Bool) {
    super.viewDidAppear(animated)
    initialize()
}
```

Build and run your app on the iPad simulator, and go to the **Restaurant List** screen, as shown:

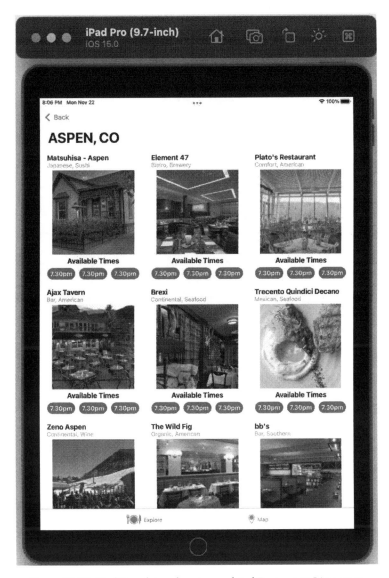

Figure 22.13: iPad Simulator showing updated Restaurant List screen

There are three columns now, and the wide white gap is gone. Now build and run your app on the iPhone 13 Pro Max simulator. The **Restaurant List** screen should display a single column:

Figure 22.14: iPhone 13 Pro Max Simulator showing updated Restaurant List screen in portrait mode

Choose **Device | Rotate Left** in the simulator menu, and you should see two columns:

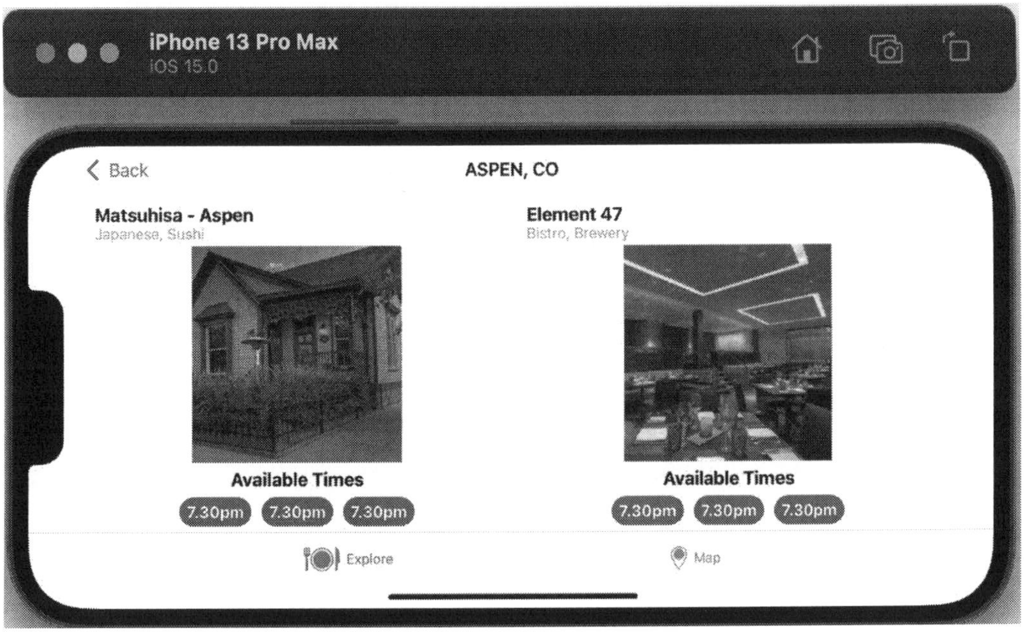

Figure 22.15: iPhone 13 Pro Max Simulator showing updated
Restaurant List screen in landscape mode

Choose **Device | Rotate Right** in the simulator menu, and quit the simulator.

The **Explore** screen and the **Restaurant List** screen have been updated and now your app looks good on the iPad. It's now a perfect candidate to be made into a Mac app. Let's see how you can build a Mac app from your existing iPad app in the next section.

Updating the app to work on macOS

You have modified your app's screens to work well on all iOS devices. Now you'll learn how to make your app run on a Mac.

Apple have updated Mac Catalyst during WWDC2021, which makes it possible to build a Mac app from an existing iPad app with Mac-specific optimizations. As you will see, both apps will share the same project and source code.

> **Important Information**
>
> Watch the video at the following link to see the latest updates to Mac Catalyst announced by Apple during WWDC2021: `https://developer.apple.com/videos/play/wwdc2021/10052/`.
>
> More information about Mac Catalyst is available at `https://developer.apple.com/mac-catalyst/`.

Before you begin, note that this only works if have a free or paid Apple developer account. If you use the project files in the `Chapter24` folder downloaded from GitHub at `https://github.com/PacktPublishing/iOS-15-Programming-for-Beginners-Sixth-Edition`, you have to set the development team for your app to make it run on your Mac. Follow these steps:

1. Select your project in the Project navigator:

Figure 22.16: Project navigator showing LetsEat project selected

2. In the **General** tab, tick the **Mac** checkbox:

Figure 22.17: Editor area showing Mac checkbox in General pane

3. In the **Enable Mac support?** dialog box, click **Enable**:

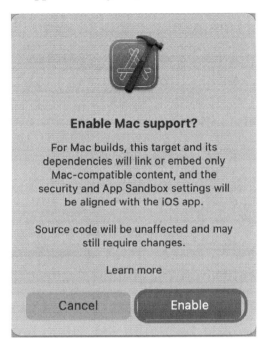

Figure 22.18: Enable Mac support? dialog box

4. Note the **Mac** checkbox is now ticked:

Figure 22.19: Editor area showing Mac checkbox ticked

Your app will be recompiled to run on your Mac. Note the **Show "Designed for iPad" Run Destination** checkbox. If you have an Apple Silicon Mac, you can select this destination to run your unmodified iPad apps natively on your Mac.

5. Your Mac has been set as the run destination. Build and run your app.

6. If your project fails to build, click the Issue navigator button and check the error message:

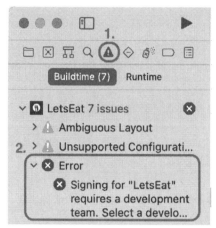

Figure 22.20: Issue navigator showing error message

If you see the error shown here, this is because you need a free or paid developer account to run your app on actual hardware.

7. Check to see that your developer account has been added to Xcode in **Xcode | Preferences | Accounts**.

> **Tip**
>
> Adding your developer account to Xcode is covered in *Chapter 1, Getting Familiar with Xcode*.

8. Click the **Signing & Capabilities** tab. Select your paid or free developer account in the **Team** drop-down menu:

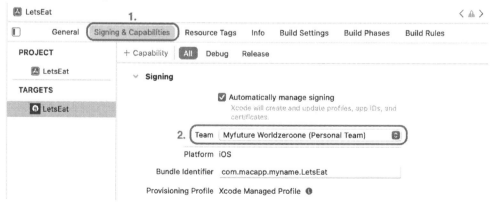

Figure 22.21: Editor area showing Team drop-down menu in Signing & Capabilities tab

9. Build and run again, and you should see your app running on your Mac:

Figure 22.22: LetsEat Mac app

Your app is now running on your Mac! Awesome!

If you still see errors, try changing the **Bundle Identifier** value to a unique value, and try running your app on your iOS device first.

You'll need to do some more work to make it a really nice Mac app, but that is beyond the scope of this book. Apple has a great tutorial on how to do so at this link: `https://developer.apple.com/tutorials/mac-catalyst`.

Summary

In this chapter, you learned how to build a Mac app from an existing iOS app.

You started by refining your app's user interface when running on the iPhone. Next, you added some code to make your app detect the device that it's running on, and modified your app's screens to work on all iOS devices. Finally, you used Mac Catalyst to build a Mac app from your iPad app. Your app now works great on iPhone, iPad, and Mac.

You're now able to make your existing iPhone apps run well on iPad, and also to make Mac apps from your iPad apps. As you have seen, once you have an iPhone app, you can make it work on iPad and Mac with relatively little effort.

In the next chapter, you'll learn a completely new way to build apps using **SwiftUI**, a modern way to write apps for any Apple platform.

23
Getting Started with SwiftUI

In previous chapters, you created the **user interface** (**UI**) for the *Let's Eat* app using storyboards. The process involved dragging objects representing views to a storyboard, creating outlets in view controller files, and connecting the two together.

This chapter will focus on **SwiftUI**, an easy and innovative way to create apps across all Apple platforms. Instead of specifying the user interface using storyboards, SwiftUI uses a declarative Swift syntax, and works with new Xcode design tools to keep your code and design in sync. Features such as Dynamic Type, Dark Mode, localization, and accessibility are automatically supported.

In this chapter, you will build a simplified version of the *Let's Eat* app using SwiftUI. This app will just contain the **Restaurant List** and **Restaurant Detail** screens. Since writing apps with SwiftUI is very different from what you have already done, you will not be modifying the `LetsEat` project you have been working on. You will create a new SwiftUI Xcode project instead.

You'll start by adding and configuring SwiftUI views to create the **Restaurant List** screen. Next, you'll add the model objects to your app, and configure the navigation between the **Restaurant List** and **Restaurant Detail** screens. After that, you'll learn how to use `UIKit` and SwiftUI views together by adding and configuring a map view for the **Restaurant Detail** screen. Finally, you'll create the **Restaurant Detail** screen.

By the end of this chapter, you'll have learned how to build a SwiftUI app that reads model objects, presents them in a list, and allows navigation to a second screen containing a map view. You can then implement this for your own projects.

The following topics will be covered:

- Creating a SwiftUI Xcode project

- Creating the **Restaurant List** screen

- Adding model objects and configuring navigation

- Using UIKit and SwiftUI views together

- Creating the Restaurant Detail screen

Technical requirements

You will create a new SwiftUI Xcode project for this chapter.

The resource files and completed Xcode project for this chapter are in the `Chapter23` folder of the code bundle for this book, which can be downloaded here:

`https://github.com/PacktPublishing/iOS-15-Programming-for-Beginners-Sixth-Edition`

Check out the following video to see the code in action:

`https://bit.ly/3DnHuIN`

Let's start by creating a new SwiftUI Xcode project for your SwiftUI app in the next section.

Creating a SwiftUI Xcode project

A SwiftUI Xcode project is created in the same way as a regular Xcode project, but you configure it to use SwiftUI instead of storyboards. As you will see, the user interface is generated entirely in code, and you'll be able to see changes in the user interface immediately as you modify your code.

> **Important Information**
>
> You can watch a video of Apple's SwiftUI presentation from WWDC 2020 at `https://developer.apple.com/videos/play/wwdc2020/10119`.
>
> You can watch a video showing what's new in SwiftUI from WWDC 2021 at `https://developer.apple.com/videos/play/wwdc2021/10018/`.
>
> Apple's official SwiftUI documentation can be found online at `https://developer.apple.com/xcode/swiftui/`.

Let's begin by creating a new SwiftUI Xcode project. Follow these steps:

1. Create a new Xcode project.

2. Click **iOS**. Select the **App** template, and then click **Next**:

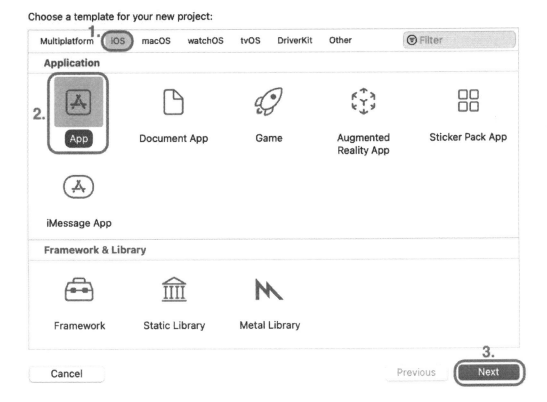

Figure 23.1: Project template screen with iOS App template selected

3.   The **Choose options for your new project:** screen appears:

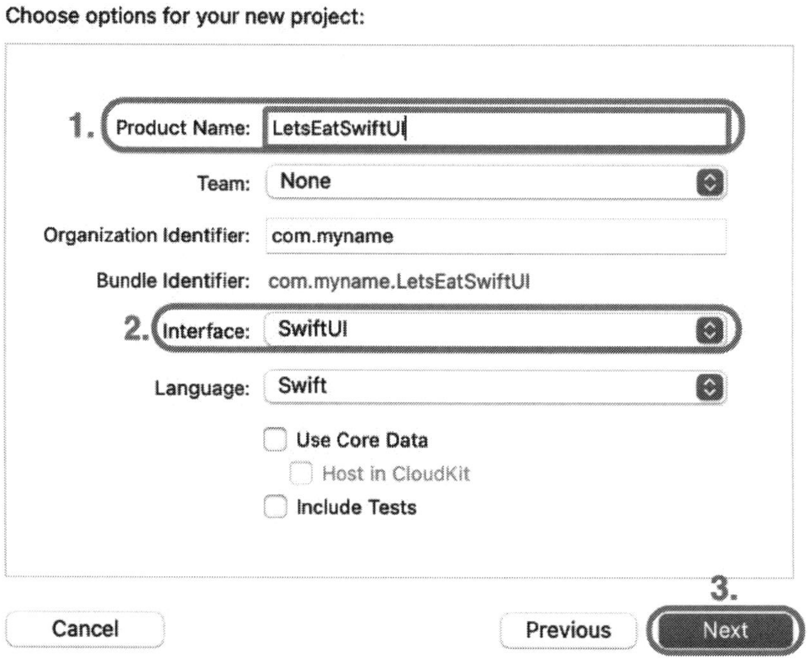

Choose options for your new project:

Figure 23.2: Project options screen

Configure this screen as follows:

- **Product Name:** `LetsEatSwiftUI`

- **Interface: SwiftUI**

The other settings should already be set. Make sure all the checkboxes are unticked. Click **Next** when done.

4.   Choose a location to save the `LetsEatSwiftUI` project and click **Create**.

5.   Your project appears on the screen, with the `ContentView` file selected in the Project navigator. You'll see the content of this file on the left side of the Editor area, and a canvas containing a preview on the right side:

Figure 23.3: Xcode showing LetsEatSwiftUI project

6. The `ContentView` file contains code that will generate the initial view for your app. Click the Scheme menu and choose **iPhone SE (2nd generation)** so the view will be previewed using an **iPhone SE (2nd generation)**'s screen:

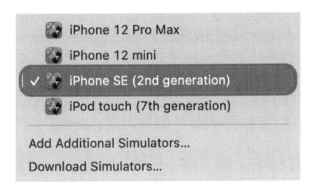

Figure 23.4: Scheme menu with iPhone SE (2nd generation) selected

7. Click the **Resume** button in the canvas to generate the preview:

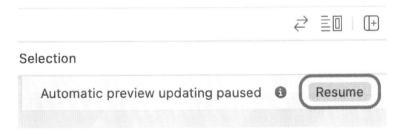

Figure 23.5: Canvas showing Resume button

8.   Verify that a preview of your app is displayed in the canvas:

Figure 23.6: Canvas showing app preview

If the canvas isn't visible, select **Canvas** from the **Adjust Editor Options** menu to show it. If you are using a MacBook, you can use the pinch gesture on your trackpad to resize the simulated image.

9.   If you need more room to work, click the Navigator and Editor buttons to hide the Navigator and Editor areas, and drag the border in the Editor area to resize the canvas:

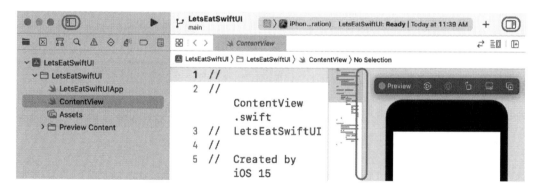

Figure 23.7: Xcode interface showing Navigator button, Editor button, and border

Now let's look at the `ContentView` file. This file contains two structures, `ContentView` and `ContentView_Previews`. The `ContentView` structure describes the view's content and layout, and conforms to the `View` protocol. The `ContentView_Previews` structure declares a preview for the `ContentView` structure. The preview is displayed in the canvas.

To see this in action, change the `Hello, World!` text to `Lets Eat` as shown:

```
struct ContentView: View {
    var body: some View {
        Text("Lets Eat").padding()
    }
}
```

The preview in the canvas updates to reflect your changes:

Figure 23.8: Canvas showing app preview with text view

You have successfully created your first SwiftUI project! Now let's create the **Restaurant List** screen, starting with a view that will display the data of a particular restaurant.

Creating the Restaurant List screen

When using storyboards, you modify attributes of a view using the Attributes inspector. In SwiftUI, you can modify either your code or the preview in the canvas. As you have seen, changing the code in the `ContentView` file will immediately update the preview, and modifying the preview will update the code.

Let's customize the `ContentView` structure to display the data of a particular restaurant. Follow these steps:

1. Click the Library button. Type `tex` in the filter field, and drag a **Text** view to the canvas and drop it under the `Lets Eat` text:

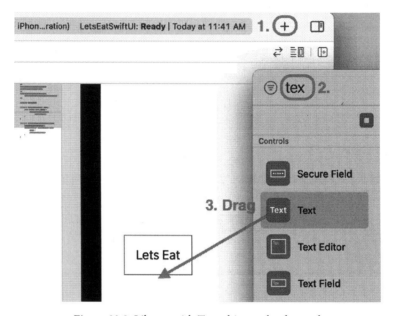

Figure 23.9: Library with Text object to be dragged

2. Xcode has automatically added code to the `ContentView` file for this text view. Verify that your code looks like this:

```
struct ContentView: View {
    var body: some View {
        VStack {
            Text("Lets Eat").padding()
            Text("Placeholder")
        }
    }
}
```

As you can see, a second text view has been added after the text view containing the `"Lets Eat"` string, and both text views are enclosed in a `VStack` view. A `VStack` view contains subviews that are arranged vertically, and it is similar to a vertically oriented stack view.

3. You will use details for The Tap Trailhouse, a restaurant in Boston, as sample data. Modify the text views in the VStack view to show the name and cuisines offered by The Tap Trailhouse restaurant:

```
struct ContentView: View {
    var body: some View {
        VStack {
            Text("The Tap Trailhouse").padding()
            Text("Brewery, Burgers, American")
        }
    }
}
```

4. Verify that the changes are reflected in the preview:

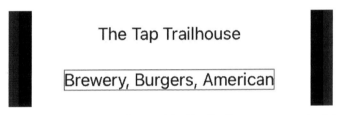

The Tap Trailhouse

Brewery, Burgers, American

Figure 23.10: App preview showing The Tap Trailhouse name and cuisines

5. You'll use a SwiftUI image view to display a photo of the restaurant. Modify your code as shown to add an image view to your VStack view:

```
struct ContentView: View {
    var body: some View {
        VStack {
            Text("The Tap Trailhouse").padding()
            Text("Brewery, Burgers, American")
            Image(systemName: "photo")
        }
    }
}
```

Note that the image view has one parameter, systemName. This parameter allows you to choose one of the images in Apple's **SF Symbols** library. You'll replace this SF Symbols image with a photo later.

> **Important Information**
>
> You can learn more about the SF Symbols library here: `https://developer.apple.com/sf-symbols/`.

6. Verify that your canvas now displays two text views and one image view as shown:

Figure 23.11: App preview showing two text views and one image view

7. To change the way your text looks, you use **modifiers** instead of the Attributes inspector. These are methods that change how your objects look or behave. Update your code as shown to set the style and color of your text views:

```
struct ContentView: View {
    var body: some View {
        VStack {
            Text("The Tap Trailhouse")
                .font(.headline)
            Text("Brewery, Burgers, American")
                .font(.subheadline)
                .foregroundColor(.secondary)
            Image(systemName: "photo")
        }
    }
}
```

Note the changes to the text in the preview.

8. To make sure your view stays in the middle of the screen, you'll embed it in an `HStack` view and add `Spacer` objects to both sides. An `HStack` view contains subviews that are arranged horizontally, and it is similar to a horizontally oriented stack view. A `Spacer` object is a flexible space that expands horizontally in an `HStack` view. *Command + click* on your `VStack` view and choose **Embed in HStack** from the pop-up menu:

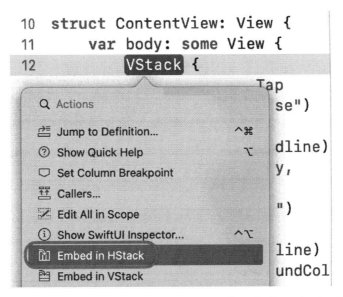

Figure 23.12: Editor area showing pop-up menu with Embed in HStack selected

9. Verify that your code looks like this:

```
struct ContentView: View {
    var body: some View {
        HStack {
            VStack {
                Text("The Tap Trailhouse")
                    .font(.headline)
                Text("Brewery, Burgers, American")
                    .font(.subheadline)
                    .foregroundColor(.secondary)
                Image(systemName: "photo")
            }
        }
    }
}
```

10. Add two `Spacer` objects to the `HStack` view as shown to center the view horizontally on your screen:

```
HStack {
    Spacer()
    VStack {
        Text("The Tap Trailhouse")
            .font(.headline)
        Text("Brewery, Burgers, American")
            .font(.subheadline)
            .foregroundColor(.secondary)
        Image(systemName: "photo")
    }
    Spacer()
}
```

Your view is now complete. You will use this view as a cell in the **Restaurant List** screen in the next section.

Adding model objects and configuring navigation

You now have a view that can be used to display the details of a restaurant. You'll use this view as a cell in a SwiftUI list, which is a container that presents data in a single column. You'll also configure model objects to populate this list. Follow these step:.

1. *Command + click* on the `HStack` view and choose **Embed in List** to display a list containing five cells in the canvas:

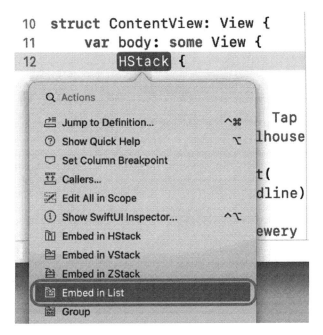

Figure 23.13: Editor area showing pop-up menu with Embed in List selected

2. Verify that your code looks like this:

```
struct ContentView: View {
    var body: some View {
        List(0 ..<5) { item in
            Spacer()
            VStack {
                Text("The Tap Trailhouse")
                    .font(.headline)
                Text("Brewery, Burgers, American")
                    .font(.subheadline)
                    .foregroundColor(.secondary)
                Image(systemName: "photo")
            }
            Spacer()
        }
    }
}
```

As you can see, the view you created in the previous section is now enclosed in a list configured to display five items, and the `HStack` view is no longer needed. Note that no delegates and data sources are required to display data in the list.

3. Open the `resources` folder contained in the `Chapter23` folder of the code bundle you downloaded from `https://github.com/PacktPublishing/iOS-15-Programming-for-Beginners-Sixth-Edition`. Drag the `RestaurantItem.swift` file to the Project navigator and click **Finish** when prompted to add them to your project.

4. Click the `RestaurantItem` file in the Project navigator and you should see the following code inside it:

```swift
import Foundation
import MapKit
struct RestaurantItem: Identifiable {
    var id = UUID()
    var name: String
    var address: String
    var city: String
    var cuisines: [String] = []
    var lat: CLLocationDegrees
    var long: CLLocationDegrees
    var imageURLString: String
    var title: String {
        return name
    }
    var subtitle: String {
        if cuisines.isEmpty { return "" }
        else if cuisines.count == 1 { return
        cuisines.first! }
        else { return cuisines.joined(
        separator: ", ")}
    }
}
let testData = [
RestaurantItem(name: "The Tap Trailhouse",
address: "17 Union St", city: "Boston", cuisines:
["Brewery","Burgers","American"], lat: 42.360847, long:
-71.056819, imageURLString: "https://resizer.otstatic.
```

```
com/v2/profiles/legacy/145237.jpg"),
RestaurantItem(name: "o ya", address: "9 East Street",
city: "Boston", cuisines: ["Japanese","Sushi","Int'l"],
lat: 42.351353, long: -71.056941, imageURLString:
"https://resizer.otstatic.com/v2/profiles/legacy/28066"),
RestaurantItem(name: "Skipjack's Boston", address: "199
Clarendon St.", city: "Boston", cuisines: ["American",
"Burgers","Brewery"], lat: 42.349887, long: -71.07484,
imageURLString: "https://resizer.otstatic.com/v2/
profiles/legacy/11656"),
RestaurantItem(name: "The Elephant Walk", address: "900
Beacon Street", city: "Boston", cuisines: ["Panasian",
"Vietnamese","Int'l"], lat: 42.346541, long: -71.105827,
imageURLString: "https://resizer.otstatic.com/v2/
profiles/legacy/1635"),
RestaurantItem(name: "Metropolis Cafe", address:
"584 Tremont Street", city: "Boston", cuisines:
["Mediterranean", "Int'l","Tapas"], lat: 42.3432, long:
-71.0727, imageURLString: "https://resizer.otstatic.com/
v2/profiles/legacy/2829")
]
```

The `RestaurantItem` file contains a structure, `RestaurantItem`, and an array, `testData`.

The `RestaurantItem` structure is similar to the `RestaurantItem` class that you used in your `LetsEat` project. To use this structure in a list, you have to make it conform to the `Identifiable` protocol. This protocol specifies that a list item must have an `id` property that can identify a particular item. A `UUID` instance is assigned to each `RestaurantItem` instance upon creation to ensure each `id` is unique.

> **Important Information**
>
> You can learn more about the `Identifiable` protocol at this link:
> https://developer.apple.com/documentation/swift/
> identifiable.

`testData` is an array containing five `RestaurantItem` instances representing five restaurants in the Boston area. It fulfills the same function as the JSON files you used in the earlier chapters of this book.

5. Click the `ContentView` file in the Project navigator. Add a `restaurantItems` property to your view to hold data for the list after the opening curly brace of the `ContentView` structure:

```
struct ContentView: View {
    var restaurantItems: [RestaurantItem] = []
    var body: some View {
```

6. Modify your code as shown to populate your list with your test data, and display a restaurant's data in each cell:

```
struct ContentView: View {
    var restaurantItems: [RestaurantItem] = []
    var body: some View {
        List(restaurantItems) { restaurantItem in
            Spacer()
            VStack {
                Text(restaurantItem.title)
                    .font(.headline)
                Text(restaurantItem.subtitle)
                    .font(.subheadline)
                    .foregroundColor(.secondary)
                AsyncImage(url: URL(string:
                restaurantItem.imageURLString))
                    .mask(RoundedRectangle
                    (cornerRadius: 9))
            }
            Spacer()
        }
    }
}
struct ContentView_Previews: PreviewProvider {
    static var previews: some View {
        ContentView(restaurantItems: testData)
    }
}
```

Let's see how this works.

The ContentView structure stores an array of RestaurantItem instances in the restaurantItems property. This array is passed to the list. For every item in the restaurantItems array, a view is created and assigned with data from the item's properties. The image for each restaurant is downloaded from the URL stored in the item's imageURLString property, and displayed using the new AsyncImage view introduced in iOS 15. Since there are five items in the array, five views appear in the canvas.

> **Important Information**
>
> You can learn more about the AsyncImage view at this link:
>
> https://developer.apple.com/documentation/swiftui/
> asyncimage

The ContentView_Previews structure passes in the testData array (stored in the RestaurantItem file) to the ContentView structure, which is then used to populate the view.

7. When you make major changes to your code, the automatic updating of the canvas is paused. Click the **Resume** button to resume if required. Note that the cell size has changed to suit the restaurant image's size.

Next, you'll implement navigation so that when a cell is tapped, a second screen is presented that will show details of a particular restaurant. Follow these steps:

1. Modify your code as shown to wrap your list in a **navigation view**:

```
var body: some View {
    NavigationView {
        List(restaurantItems) { restaurantItem in
            Spacer()
            VStack {
                Text(restaurantItem.title)
                    .font(.headline)
                Text(restaurantItem.subtitle)
                    .font(.subheadline)
                    .foregroundColor(.secondary)
                AsyncImage(url: URL(string:
                restaurantItem.imageURLString)
                .mask(RoundedRectangle
                (cornerRadius: 9))
```

```
            }
        Spacer()
        }
    }
}
```

> **Tip**
>
> To re-indent your code, select all code by typing *Command + A* and type *Control + I*.

A navigation view is similar to the `UINavigation` class that you've used before in your app.

2. Add a modifier to set the list's `title` property to show `Boston, MA` at the top of the screen:

```
        .mask(RoundedRectangle(cornerRadius: 9))
    }
    Spacer()
}.navigationTitle("Boston, MA")
```

3. Wrap the cell in a **navigation link view** as shown:

```
List(restaurantItems) { restaurantItem in
    NavigationLink(destination:
    Text(restaurantItem.title)) {
        Spacer()
        VStack {
            Text(restaurantItem.title)
                .font(.headline)
                .fixedSize()
            Text(restaurantItem.subtitle)
                .font(.subheadline)
                .foregroundColor(.secondary)
                .fixedSize()
            AsyncImage(url: URL(string:
            restaurantItem.imageURLString)
                .mask(RoundedRectangle
                (cornerRadius: 9))
```

```
        }
    Spacer()
    }
}.navigationTitle("Boston, MA"
```

A navigation link view has a `destination` property, which specifies the view to be presented when a cell is tapped. Currently the specified view is a text view showing the name of the restaurant.

The `.fixedSize()` modifier is used to ensure the text is not truncated.

4. Note that the list in the canvas has automatically displayed disclosure arrows:

Figure 23.14: App preview showing disclosure arrow

5. To see this working as it should in an app, click the **Live Preview** button in the canvas:

Figure 23.15: Canvas showing Live Preview button

6. Click any cell in the preview to display text containing the name of the tapped restaurant:

Figure 23.16: App preview showing a selected cell

This is a great way of ensuring your list works as expected.

7. The view code is starting to look cluttered, so you'll extract the cell into its own separate view. *Command + click* the `NavigationLink` view and choose **Extract Subview**:

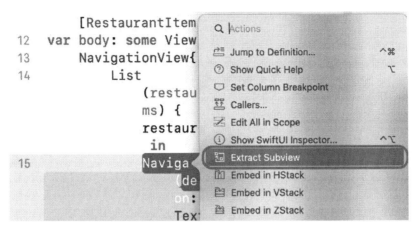

Figure 23.17: Editor area showing pop-up menu with Extract Subview selected

8. All the view code for the cell has been moved into a separate view named
    `ExtractedView`:

```
12      var body: some View {
13          NavigationView{
14              List(restaurantItems) { restaurantItem in
15                  ExtractedView()
16              }.navigationTitle("Boston, MA")
17          }
18      }
19  }
20
21  struct ContentView_Previews: PreviewProvider {
22      static var previews: some View {
23          ContentView(restaurantItems: testData)
24      }
25  }
26
27  struct ExtractedView: View {
28      var body: some View {
29          NavigationLink(destination: Text(restaurantItem.title)){
```

Figure 23.18: Editor area showing name of extracted view highlighted

9. Change the name of the method call and the extracted view to `RestaurantCell`.
    Your code should look like this:

```
var body: some View {
    NavigationView {
        List(restaurantItems) { restaurantItem in
            RestaurantCell()
        }.navigationTitle("Boston, MA")
```

```
            }
        }
    }
struct ContentView_Previews: PreviewProvider {
    static var previews: some View {
        ContentView(restaurantItems: testData)
    }
}
struct RestaurantCell: View {
    var body: some View {
        NavigationLink(destination:
```

Don't worry about the error, you'll fix it in the next step.

10. Add a property to the RestaurantCell view to hold a RestaurantItem instance:

```
struct RestaurantCell: View {
    var restaurantItem: RestaurantItem
```

11. Add code to the ContentView structure to pass the RestaurantItem instance to the RestaurantCell view as shown:

```
struct ContentView: View {
    var restaurantItems: [RestaurantItem] = []
    var body: some View {
        NavigationView {
            List(restaurantItems) { restaurantItem in
                RestaurantCell(restaurantItem:
                restaurantItem)
            }.navigationTitle("Boston, MA"
        }
    }
}
```

12. Verify that the preview still works the way it did before.

You've completed the implementation of the **Restaurant List** screen. Next, you'll see how you can use UIKit and SwiftUI views together to create a map view that you'll use in the **Restaurant Detail** screen.

Using UIKit and SwiftUI Views together

At this point, you have created the **Restaurant List** screen, and tapping each cell in this screen displays the restaurant's name on a second screen. You'll modify your app to display a **Restaurant Detail** screen when a cell on the **Restaurant List** screen is tapped, but before that, you'll create a SwiftUI view that displays a map.

When using storyboards, all you needed to do was to drag in a map view from the Library to a view in the storyboard. SwiftUI does not have a native map view but you can use the same map view that you used in the storyboard to render the map. In fact, you can use any view subclass in SwiftUI by wrapping them in a SwiftUI view that conforms to the `UIViewRepresentable` protocol. Let's create a custom view that can present a map view now. Follow these steps:

1. Choose **File | New | File** to open the template selector.

2. **iOS** should already be selected. In the **User Interface** section, click **SwiftUI View** and click **Next**:

Figure 23.19: File template screen with SwiftUI View selected

3. Name the new file `MapView` and click **Create**. The `MapView` file will appear in the Project navigator.

4. In the `MapView` file, import `MapKit`, and make the `MapView` structure conform to the `UIViewRepresentable` protocol as shown. Don't worry about the error that appears, you'll fix that in the next few steps:

```
import SwiftUI
import MapKit
struct MapView: UIViewRepresentable {
    var body: some View {
        Text("Hello World")
    }
}
```

The `UIViewRepresentable` protocol is a wrapper that allows you to use any `UIKit` view in your SwiftUI view hierarchy.

> **Important Information**
>
> To learn more about the `UIViewRepresentable` protocol, visit this link:
> `https://developer.apple.com/documentation/swiftui/uiviewrepresentable`.

5. You need two methods to conform to the `UIViewRepresentable` protocol: a `makeUIView(context:)` method that creates an `MKMapView` and an `updateUIView(_:context:)` method that configures it and responds to any changes. Modify your code as shown to replace the `body` property with a `makeUIView(context:)` method that creates and returns an empty `MKMapView` instance:

```
struct MapView: UIViewRepresentable {
    func makeUIView(context: Context) -> MKMapView {
        MKMapView(frame: .zero)
    }
}
```

6. Modify your code as shown to add an `updateUIView(_:context:)` method just after the `makeUIView(context:)` method. This sets the map view's region to center the map on The Tap Trailhouse's location:

```
func updateUIView(_ uiView: MKMapView, context:
Context) {
    let coordinate = CLLocationCoordinate2D
    (latitude: 42.360847, longitude: -71.056819)
```

```
    let span = MKCoordinateSpan(latitudeDelta:
    0.001, longitudeDelta: 0.001)
    let region = MKCoordinateRegion(center:
    coordinate, span: span)
    uiView.setRegion(region, animated: true)
  }
```

Note that this is the same method you used to make a region for the **Map** screen in the *Let's Eat* app.

7. The error is now gone, and a blank map view appears in the canvas. This is because the preview is in static mode and only renders SwiftUI views. You'll need to turn on live preview to see the map. Click the **Live Preview** button and you should see a map of Boston centered on The Tap Trailhouse's location in a moment:

Figure 23.20: App preview showing map

If it doesn't work, check your internet connection, and click the **Try Again** or **Resume** buttons above your preview.

8. The latitude and longitude values are currently hardcoded. Declare two properties to hold the latitude and longitude values as shown after the `MapView` structure declaration:

```
struct MapView: UIViewRepresentable {
    var lat: CLLocationDegrees
    var long: CLLocationDegrees
```

9. Modify the `updateUI(_:context:)` method to use these properties instead of the hardcoded values:

```
func updateUIView(_ view: MKMapView, context: Context) {
    let coordinate = CLLocationCoordinate2D(
    latitude: lat, longitude: long)
```

10. Update the `MapView_Previews` structure to pass in sample latitude and longitude values as shown. This will generate the same map you saw earlier in the preview:

```
struct MapView_Previews: PreviewProvider {
    static var previews: some View {
        MapView(lat: 42.360847, long: -71.056819)
    }
}
```

11. In the canvas, check to see that the map is still displayed (You may need to click **Resume**).

You've created a SwiftUI map view that shows the restaurant's location. Now, let's see how to make the complete **Restaurant Detail** screen in the next section.

Completing the Restaurant Detail screen

You now have a SwiftUI map view displaying a map. Now, you'll create a new SwiftUI view to represent the **Restaurant Detail** screen and add the map view to it. Follow these steps:

1. Choose **File | New | File** to open the template selector.

2. **iOS** should already be selected. In the **User Interface** section, click **SwiftUI View** and click **Next**.

3. Name the new file `RestaurantDetail` and click **Create**. The `RestaurantDetail` file appears in the Project navigator.

4. Declare and define the `RestaurantDetail` and `RestaurantDetail_Previews` structures as shown:

```swift
import SwiftUI
struct RestaurantDetail: View {
    var selectedRestaurant: RestaurantItem
    var body: some View {
        VStack {
            MapView(lat: selectedRestaurant.lat,
            long: selectedRestaurant.long)
            .frame(height: 250)
            VStack(alignment: .leading) {
                Text(selectedRestaurant.title)
                    .font(.largeTitle)
                    .fontWeight(.bold)
                Text(selectedRestaurant.subtitle)
                    .font(.headline)
                    .foregroundColor(.secondary)
                Text(selectedRestaurant.address)
                    .font(.headline)
                Text(selectedRestaurant.city)
                    .font(.headline)
            }.padding()
            Spacer()
        }
    }
}

struct RestaurantDetail_Previews: PreviewProvider {
    static var previews: some View {
        NavigationView {
            RestaurantDetail(selectedRestaurant:
            testData[0])
        }
    }
}
```

The `RestaurantDetail` structure contains a `Vstack` view enclosing a map view and a second `Vstack` view. The map view displays a map showing the restaurant's location. The second `Vstack` view encloses four text views. These display the restaurant's name, cuisines, address, and city. A `Spacer` object pushes the first `Vstack` view to the top of the screen. A `RestaurantItem` instance is assigned to the `selectedRestaurant` property, and data from this instance is used to populate the `RestaurantDetail` structure's views.

To create the preview in the canvas, the `RestaurantDetail_Previews` structure passes in the first `RestaurantItem` instance in the `testData` array. Note that the `RestaurantDetail` instance is enclosed in a `NavigationView` instance to make the navigation bar appear in the preview.

5. The preview displays a map view above the restaurant text views, but does not render the map. As before, click the **Live Preview** button.

6. The canvas now displays the **Restaurant Detail** screen with a rendered map:

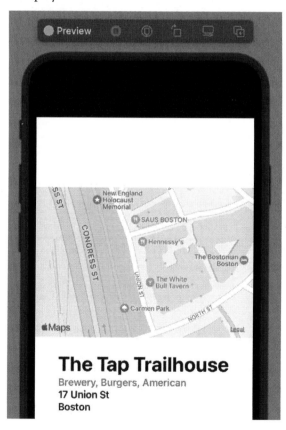

Figure 23.21: App preview showing Restaurant Detail screen

You've completed the implementation of the **Restaurant Detail** screen using SwiftUI. Now you'll modify the list in the **Restaurant List** screen so that the **Restaurant Detail** screen will be displayed when a cell is tapped.

7. Click the `ContentView` file in the Project navigator and modify the `RestaurantCell` structure's code to use the `RestaurantDetail` structure as the destination when a cell is tapped:

```
var body: some View {
    NavigationLink(destination:
    RestaurantDetail(selectedRestaurant:
    restaurantItem )){
        Spacer()
```

8. Click the **Live Preview** button in the canvas. Tap a row in the **Restaurant List** screen. You'll see the **Restaurant Detail** screen for that restaurant appear:

Figure 23.22: App preview showing Restaurant Detail screen

As you can see, the app preview works fine in the canvas. If you want to run in the simulator, you'll need to make one small change in the `ContentView` structure. Click the `ContentView` file in the Project navigator and assign the `testdata` array to the `restaurantItems` property as shown:

```
struct ContentView: View {
    var restaurantItems: [RestaurantItem] = testData
    var body: some View {
```

Build and run your app, and it will appear in the simulator:

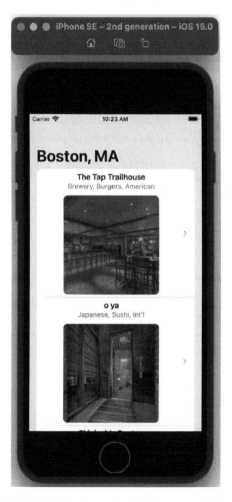

Figure 23.23: iOS Simulator showing Restaurant List screen

You have completed building a simple SwiftUI app! Awesome!

Summary

In this brief introduction to SwiftUI, you've seen how to build a simplified version of the *Let's Eat* app using SwiftUI.

You started by adding and configuring SwiftUI views to create the **Restaurant List** screen. You then added the model objects to your app, and configured the navigation between the **Restaurant List** and **Restaurant Detail** screens. After that, you used UIKit and SwiftUI views together by adding and configuring a map view for the **Restaurant Detail** screen. Finally, you created the **Restaurant Detail** screen and added the map view you created earlier to it.

You now know how to use SwiftUI to create an app that reads model objects, presents them in a list, and allows navigation to a second screen containing a map view. You can then implement this for your own projects.

In the next chapter, you will learn about **Swift concurrency**, a new way to handle asynchronous operations in Swift.

24
Getting Started with Swift Concurrency

Apple introduced **Swift Concurrency** during WWDC2021, which adds support for structured asynchronous and parallel programming to Swift 5.5. This allows you to write concurrent code which is more readable and easier to understand.

In this chapter, you will learn the basic concepts of Swift Concurrency. Next, you will examine an app without concurrency and explore its issues. After that, you will use **async/await** to implement concurrency in the app. Next, you'll make your app more efficient by using **async-let**. Finally, you'll modify the `RestaurantListViewController` class in your *Let's Eat* app to use `async/await` for loading restaurant images.

By the end of this chapter, you'll have learned the basics on how Swift Concurrency works, and how to update your own apps to use it.

The following topics will be covered:

- Understanding Swift Concurrency
- Examining an app without concurrency
- Updating the app using `async/await`
- Improving efficiency using `async-let`
- Updating `RestaurantListViewController` to use async/await

Technical requirements

You will use a sample app, *BreakfastMaker*, to help you understand the concepts of Swift Concurrency. Later in the chapter, you will continue working on the `LetsEat` project that you modified in *Chapter 22, Getting Started with Mac Catalyst*.

The completed Xcode project for this chapter is in the `Chapter24` folder of the code bundle for this book, which can be downloaded here:

`https://github.com/PacktPublishing/iOS-15-Programming-for-Beginners-Sixth-Edition`

Check out the following video to see the code in action:

`https://bit.ly/3d4YWH5`

Let's start by learning about Swift Concurrency in the next section.

Understanding Swift Concurrency

In Swift 5.5, Apple has added support for writing asynchronous and parallel code in a structured way.

Asynchronous code allows your app to suspend and resume code. This allows your app to do things like update the user interface while still performing operations like downloading data from the internet.

Parallel code allows your app to run multiple pieces of code simultaneously.

> **Important Information**
>
> You can find links to all of Apple's Swift Concurrency videos during WWDC2021 at `https://developer.apple.com/news/?id=2o3euotz`.
>
> You can read Apple's Swift Concurrency documentation at `https://docs.swift.org/swift-book/LanguageGuide/Concurrency.html`.

To give you an idea of how Swift Concurrency works, imagine that you are making a poached egg sandwich for breakfast. Here is one way of doing it:

1. Put two slices of bread into the toaster.
2. Wait two minutes until the bread is toasted.

3. Put an egg in a bowl with some water and put the bowl into the microwave.

4. Wait six minutes until the egg is cooked.

5. Make your sandwich.

This takes eight minutes in total. Now think about this sequence of events. Do you spend that time just staring at the toaster and the microwave? You'll probably be using your phone while the bread is in the toaster and the egg is in the microwave. In other words, you can do other things while the bread and egg are being prepared. So, the sequence of events would be more accurately described as follows:

1. Put two slices of bread into the toaster.

2. Use your phone for two minutes until the bread is toasted.

3. Put an egg in a bowl with some water and put the bowl into the microwave.

4. Use your phone for six minutes until the egg is cooked.

5. Make your sandwich.

Here, you can see that your interaction with the toaster and microwave can be suspended, then resumed, which means these operations are asynchronous. The operation still takes eight minutes, but you were able to do other things during that time.

There is another factor to consider. You don't need to wait for the bread to finish toasting before you put the egg in the microwave. This means you could modify the sequence of steps as follows:

1. Put two slices of bread into the toaster.

2. While the bread is toasting, put an egg in a bowl with some water, and put the bowl into the microwave.

3. Use your phone for six minutes until the egg is cooked.

4. Make your sandwich.

Toasting the bread and poaching the egg are now carried out in parallel, which saves you two minutes. Great! Do note however that you have more things to keep track of.

Now that you understand the concepts of asynchronous and parallel operations, let's study the issues an app that does not have concurrency has in the next section.

Examining an app without concurrency

You've seen how asynchronous and parallel operations can help you prepare breakfast faster and allow you to use your phone while you're doing it. Now let's look at a sample app that simulates the process of preparing breakfast. Initially, this app does not have concurrency implemented, so you can see how that affects the app. Follow these steps:

1. If you have not already done so, download the `Chapter24` folder of the code bundle for this book at this link: `https://github.com/PacktPublishing/iOS-15-Programming-for-Beginners-Sixth-Edition`.

2. Open the `resources` folder in the `Chapter24` folder, and you'll see two folders, `BreakfastMaker-start` and `BreakfastMaker-complete`. The first folder contains the app that you will be modifying in this chapter, and the second contains the completed app.

3. Open the `BreakfastMaker-start` folder and open the `BreakfastMaker` Xcode project. Click on the `Main` storyboard file in the Project navigator. You should see four labels and a button in the **View Controller Scene** as shown:

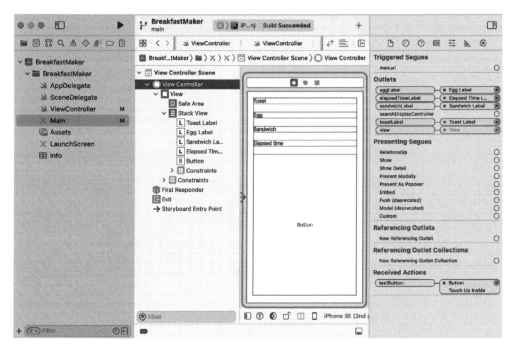

Figure 24.1: Main storyboard file showing the View Controller Scene

The app will display a screen which shows the status of the toast, egg, and sandwich, and the time taken to prepare the sandwich. The app will also display a button you can use to test the responsiveness of the user interface.

4. Click the `ViewController` file in the Project navigator. You should see the following code in the Editor area:

```swift
import UIKit
class ViewController: UIViewController {
    @IBOutlet var toastLabel: UILabel!
    @IBOutlet var eggLabel: UILabel!
    @IBOutlet var sandwichLabel: UILabel!
    @IBOutlet var elapsedTimeLabel: UILabel!
    override func viewDidAppear(_ animated: Bool) {
        super.viewDidAppear(animated)
        let startTime = Date().timeIntervalSince1970
        toastLabel.text = "Making toast..."
        toastLabel.text = makeToast()
        eggLabel.text = "Poaching egg..."
        eggLabel.text = poachEgg()
        sandwichLabel.text = makeSandwich()
        let endTime = Date().timeIntervalSince1970
        elapsedTimeLabel.text = "Elapsed time is
        \(((endTime - startTime) * 100).rounded()
        / 100) seconds"
    }
    func makeToast() -> String {
        sleep(2)
        return "Toast done"
    }
    func poachEgg() -> String {
        sleep(6)
        return "Egg done"
    }
    func makeSandwich() -> String {
        return "Sandwich done"
    }
    @IBAction func testButton(_ sender: UIButton) {
        print("Button tapped")
    }
}
```

As you can see, this code simulates the process of making breakfast that was described in the previous section. Let's break it down:

```
@IBOutlet var toastLabel: UILabel!
```

```
@IBOutlet var eggLabel: UILabel!
```

```
@IBOutlet var sandwichLabel: UILabel!
```

```
@IBOutlet var elapsedTimeLabel: UILabel!
```

These outlets are linked to four labels in the `Main` storyboard file. When you run the app, these labels will display the status of the toast, egg, and sandwich, and also show the time taken to complete the process.

```
override func viewDidAppear(_ animated: Bool) {
```

This method is called when the view controller's view appears on screen.

```
let startTime = Date().timeIntervalSince1970
```

This sets `startTime` to the current time, so the app can later calculate how long it takes to make the sandwich.

```
toastLabel.text = "Making toast..."
```

This makes `toastLabel` display the text `Making toast...`.

```
toastLabel.text = makeToast()
```

This calls the `makeToast()` method, which waits for two seconds to simulate the time taken to make toast, then returns the text `Toast done`, which will be displayed by `toastLabel`.

```
eggLabel.text = "Poaching egg..."
```

This makes `eggLabel` display the text `Poaching egg...`.

```
eggLabel.text = poachEgg()
```

This calls the `poachEgg()` method, which waits for six seconds to simulate the time taken to poach an egg, then returns the text `Egg done`, which will be displayed by `eggLabel`.

```
sandwichLabel.text = makeSandwich()
```

This calls the `makeSandwich()` method, which returns the text `Sandwich done`, which will be displayed by `sandwichLabel`.

```
let endTime = Date().timeIntervalSince1970
```

This sets `endTime` to the current time.

```
elapsedTimeLabel.text = "Elapsed time is
\(((endTime - startTime) * 100).rounded()
/ 100) seconds"
```

This calculates the elapsed time (approximately eight seconds), which will be displayed by `elapsedTimeLabel`.

```
@IBAction func testButton(_ sender: UIButton) {
    print("Button tapped")
}
```

This displays `Button tapped` in the Debug area each time the button on screen is tapped.

Build and run the app, and tap the button the moment the user interface appears:

Figure 24.2: iOS Simulator running the BreakfastMaker app showing the button to be tapped

You should notice the following issues:

- Tapping the button has no effect initially, and you'll only see `Button tapped` in the Debug area after approximately eight seconds.

- `Making toast...` and `Poaching egg...` are never displayed, and `Toast done` and `Egg done` only appear after approximately eight seconds.

The reason why this happens is because your app's code did not update the user interface while the `makeToast()` and `poachEgg()` methods are running. Your app did register the button taps, but was only able to process them and update the labels after `makeToast()` and `poachEgg()` have completed execution. These issues do not give the user a good experience with your app.

You have now experienced the issues presented by an app that does not have concurrency implemented. In the next section, you'll modify the app using async/await so that it is able to update the user interface while the `makeToast()` and `poachEgg()` methods are running.

Updating the app using async/await

As you have seen previously, the app is unresponsive when the `makeToast()` and `poachEgg()` methods are running. To resolve this, you will use async/await in the app.

Writing the `async` keyword in the method declaration indicates that the method is asynchronous. This is what it looks like:

```
func methodName() async -> returnType {
```

Writing the `await` keyword in front of a method call marks a point where execution may be suspended, thus allowing other operations to run. This is what it looks like:

```
await methodName()
```

> **Important Information**
>
> You can watch Apple's WWDC2021 video discussing async/await at https://developer.apple.com/videos/play/wwdc2021/10132/.

You will modify your app to use `async/await`. This will enable it to suspend the `makeToast()` and `poachEgg()` methods to process button taps and update the user interface, then resume execution of both methods afterward. Follow these steps:

1. Modify the `makeToast()` and `poachEgg()` methods as shown to make the code in their bodies asynchronous:

```
func makeToast() -> String {
    try! await Task.sleep(nanoseconds: 2 * 1_000_000_000)
    return "Toast done"
}
func poachEgg() -> String {
    try! await Task.sleep(nanoseconds: 6 * 1_000_000_000)
    return "Egg done"
}
```

`Task` represents a unit of asynchronous work. `Task` has a static method, `sleep(nanoseconds:)`, which pauses execution for a specified duration, measured in nanoseconds. Multiplying by 1,000,000,000 converts the duration to seconds. The `await` keyword indicates this code can be suspended to allow other code to run.

2. Errors will appear for both `makeToast()` and `poachEgg()`. Click either error icon to display the error message:

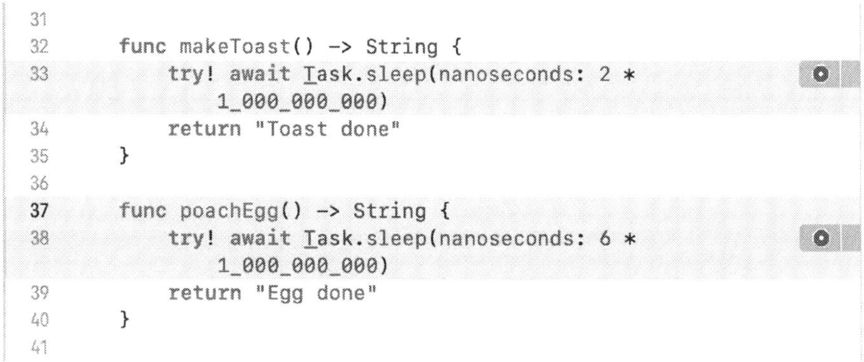

```
31
32      func makeToast() -> String {
33          try! await Task.sleep(nanoseconds: 2 *         ⊙
                1_000_000_000)
34          return "Toast done"
35      }
36
37      func poachEgg() -> String {
38          try! await Task.sleep(nanoseconds: 6 *         ⊙
                1_000_000_000)
39          return "Egg done"
40      }
41
```

Figure 24.3: Errors with error icons highlighted

The error is displayed because you're calling an asynchronous method inside a method that does not support concurrency. You will need to add the `async` keyword to the method declaration to indicate it is asynchronous.

3. For each method, click the **Fix** button to add the `async` keyword to the method declaration.

4. Verify that your code looks like this after you're done:

```
func makeToast() async -> String {
    try! await Task.sleep(nanoseconds: 2 * 1_000_000_000)
    return "Toast done"
}
func poachEgg() async -> String {
    try! await Task.sleep(nanoseconds: 6 * 1_000_000_000)
    return "Egg done"
}
```

5. The errors in the `makeToast()` and `poachEgg()` methods should be gone, but new errors will appear in the `viewDidAppear()` method. Click one of the error icons to see the error message, which will be the same as the message you saw earlier. This is because you're calling an asynchronous method inside a method that does not support concurrency.

6. Click the **Fix** button, and more errors will appear.

7. Ignore the one in the method declaration for now and click the one next to the `makeToast()` method call to see the error message:

```
override func viewDidAppear(_ animated: Bool)   ⊗
    async {
    super.viewDidAppear(animated)
    let startTime = Date().timeIntervalSince1970
    toastLabel.text = "Making toast..."
    toastLabel.text = makeToast()  ⊙ Expression is 'as...
    eggLabel.text = "Poaching eggs..."
    eggLabel.text = poachEgg()  ⊙ Expression is 'async'...
    sandwichLabel.text = makeSandwich()
    let endTime = Date().timeIntervalSince1970
```

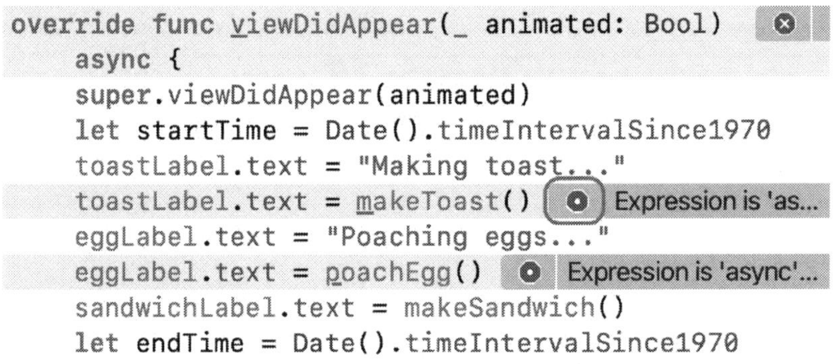

Figure 24.4: Errors with error icon for makeToast() highlighted

This error message is displayed because you did not use `await` when calling an asynchronous function.

8. Click the **Fix** button to insert the `await` keyword before the method call.

9. Repeat *step 7* and *step 8* for the error next to the `poachEgg()` method call. The `await` keyword will be inserted for the `poachEgg()` method call as well.

10. Click the error icon in the `viewDidLoad()` method declaration to see the error message:

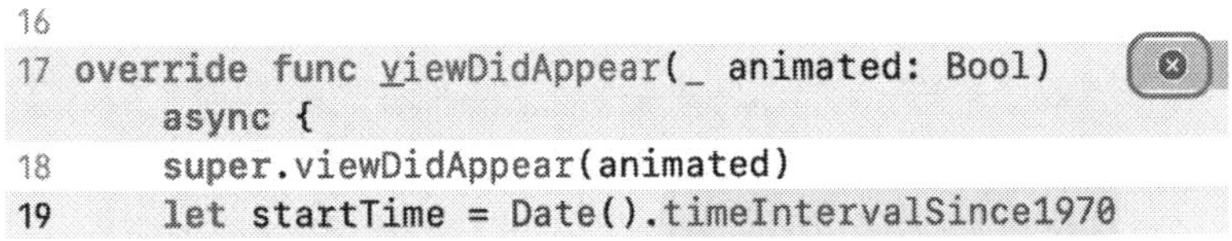

```
16
17 override func viewDidAppear(_ animated: Bool)     ⊗
       async {
18     super.viewDidAppear(animated)
19     let startTime = Date().timeIntervalSince1970
```

Figure 24.5: Error with error icon highlighted

This error is displayed because you can't use the `async` keyword to make the `viewDidAppear()` method asynchronous, as this capability is not present in the superclass.

11. To resolve this issue, you'll remove the `async` keyword and enclose all the code after `super.viewDidAppear()` in a `Task` block, which will allow it to execute asynchronously in a synchronous method. Modify your code as follows:

```
override  func viewDidAppear(_ animated: Bool) {
    super.viewDidAppear(animated)
    Task {
        let startTime = Date().timeIntervalSince1970
        toastLabel.text = "Making toast..."
        toastLabel.text = await makeToast()
        eggLabel.text = "Poaching egg..."
        eggLabel.text = await poachEgg()
        sandwichLabel.text = makeSandwich()
        let endTime = Date().timeIntervalSince1970
        elapsedTimeLabel.text = "Elapsed time is
        \(((endTime - startTime) * 100).rounded()
        / 100) seconds"
    }
}
```

Build and run the app, and tap the button as soon as you see the user interface. Note that `Button tapped` now appears immediately in the Debug area, and the labels update as they should. This is because the app is now able to suspend the `makeToast()` and `poachEgg()` methods to respond to taps and update the user interface, and resume them later. Awesome!

However, if you look at the elapsed time, you'll see that the app takes slightly longer to prepare breakfast than it did before:

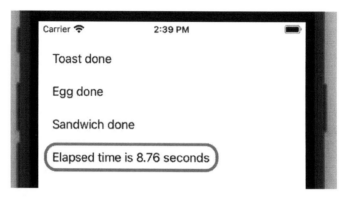

Figure 24.6: iOS Simulator running the BreakfastMaker app showing elapsed time

This is partly due to the overhead required for suspending and resuming methods, but there is another factor involved. Even though the `makeToast()` and `poachEgg()` methods are now asynchronous, the `poachEgg()` method only starts execution after the `makeToast()` method has finished execution. In the next section, you'll see how you can use `async-let` to run the `makeToast()` and `poachEgg()` methods in parallel.

Improving efficiency using async-let

Even though your app is now responsive to button taps and is able to update the user interface while the `makeToast()` and `poachEgg()` methods are running, both methods still execute sequentially. The solution here is to use `async-let`. Writing `async` in front of a `let` statement when you define a constant, and then writing `await` when you access the constant, allows parallel execution of asynchronous methods:

```
async let temporaryConstant1 = methodName1()
async let temporaryConstant2 = methodName2()
await variable1 = temporaryConstant1
await variable2 = temporaryConstant1
```

Here, methodName1() and methodName2() will run in parallel.

You will modify your app to use async-let to enable the makeToast() and poachEgg() methods run in parallel. In the ViewController file, modify the code in the Task block as follows:

```
Task {
    let startTime = Date().timeIntervalSince1970
    toastLabel.text = "Making toast..."
    async let tempToast = makeToast()
    eggLabel.text = "Poaching egg..."
    async let tempEgg = poachEgg()
    await toastLabel.text = tempToast
    await eggLabel.text = tempEgg
    sandwichLabel.text = makeSandwich()
    let endTime = Date().timeIntervalSince1970
    elapsedTimeLabel.text = "Elapsed time is
    \(((endTime - startTime) * 100).rounded()
    / 100) seconds"
}
```

Build and run the app. You'll see that the elapsed time is now less than what it was before:

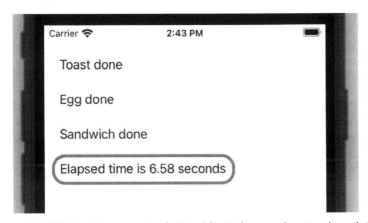

Figure 24.7: iOS Simulator running the BreakfastMaker app showing elapsed time

This is because using async-let allows both the makeToast() and poachEgg() methods to run in parallel, and the poachEgg() method no longer waits for the makeToast() method to complete before starting execution. Cool!

> **Important Information**
>
> There is still lots more to learn about Swift Concurrency, such as structured concurrency and actors, but that is beyond the scope of this chapter. You can learn more about structured concurrency at `https://developer.apple.com/wwdc21/10134`, and you can learn more about actors at `https://developer.apple.com/wwdc21/10133`.

In the next section, you'll update the `RestaurantListViewController` class in the *Let's Eat* app to use `async/await` when getting restaurant images.

Updating RestaurantListViewController to use async/await

When you run your *Let's Eat* app, you may notice a delay when the **Restaurant List** screen is displaying a list of restaurants. This is because the code used to download restaurant images is not asynchronous, and the app is not able to do other work while restaurant images are being downloaded.

The code that downloads the restaurant image data and converts it into an image is inside the `collectionView(_:cellForItemAt:)` method in the `RestaurantListViewController` class definition. You'll modify this code so that it is performed asynchronously.

Open your `LetsEat` project that you modified in *Chapter 22, Getting Started with Mac Catalyst*, and open the `RestaurantListViewController` file (inside the `Restaurants` folder) in the Project navigator. Update the `collectionView(_:cellForItemAt:)` method as shown below:

```
if let imageURL = restaurantItem.imageURL {
    Task {
        guard let url = URL(string: imageURL)
        else {
            return
        }
        let (imageData, response) = try await
        URLSession.shared.data(from: url)
        guard let httpResponse = response as?
        HTTPURLResponse, httpResponse.statusCode
        == 200 else {
            return
```

```
            }
            guard let cellImage = UIImage(data:
            imageData) else {
                return
            }
            cell.restaurantImageView.image = cellImage
            }
        }
    return cell
}
```

Let's break this down:

```
Task {
```

This creates a unit of asynchronous work.

```
guard let url = URL(string: imageURL)
else {
    return
}
```

This guard statement creates a URL from the RestaurantItem instance's imageURL property and assigns it to url, and returns if it is not able to do so.

```
let (imageData, response) = try await
URLSession.shared.data(from: url)
```

This asynchronously downloads the data from the URL stored in url, and assigns it to imageData. The response from the server is assigned to response.

```
guard let httpResponse = response as? HTTPURLResponse,
httpResponse.statusCode == 200 else {
    return
}
```

This guard statement checks to see if the server response code is 200 (which means that the download was successful) and returns if it is not.

```
guard let cellImage = UIImage(data: imageData) else {
    return
}
```

This `guard` statement creates a `UIImage` instance from the data stored in `imageData` and assigns to `cellImage`, and returns if it is not able to do so.

```
cell.restaurantImageView.image = cellImage
```

This assigns the `UIImage` stored in `cellImage` to the `restaurantCell` instance's `restaurantImageView` property, which will be displayed in the **Restaurant List** screen's collection view. Otherwise, the default image set for the `restaurantImageView` property will be displayed.

```
return cell
```

This returns the `restaurantCell` instance.

Build and run your app. You'll notice that the **Restaurant List** screen will be more responsive and scroll more smoothly than before:

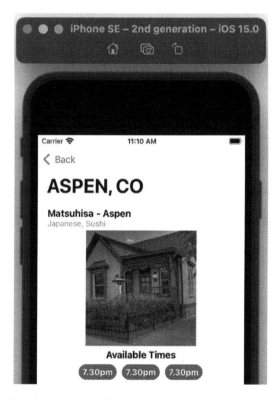

Figure 24.8: iOS Simulator showing the Restaurant List screen with downloaded images

If you disable your internet connection, the **Restaurant List** screen will still work but it will display the default placeholder images instead:

Figure 24.9: iOS Simulator showing the Restaurant List screen with default images

---

Important Information

You can find more information on how to use async/await with `URLSession` at `https://developer.apple.com/wwdc21/10095`.

You have successfully implemented asynchronous code in your app's `RestaurantListViewController` class. Fantastic! There are still a lot of things to learn about Swift Concurrency, such as structured concurrency and actors, but that is beyond the scope of this chapter.

Summary

In this chapter, you learned about Swift Concurrency, and how to implement it in both the *BreakfastMaker* and *Let's Eat* apps.

You started by learning the basic concepts of Swift Concurrency. Next, you examined an app without concurrency and explored its issues. After that, you implemented concurrency in the app using `async`/`await`. Next, you made your app more efficient by using `async-let`. Finally, you updated the `RestaurantListViewController` class in your *Let's Eat* app to use `async`/`await` for loading restaurant images.

You now understand the basics of Swift Concurrency and will now be able to use `async`/`await` and `async-let` in your own apps.

In the next chapter, you will learn about **SharePlay**, a great way to share group experiences for users of your app.

25
Getting Started with SharePlay

Apple introduced **SharePlay** during WWDC 2021, which allows users to share experiences by integrating your apps into FaceTime using the **Group Activities** framework.

In this chapter, you'll implement SharePlay for a sample app by adding Group Activities support to it. You'll begin by learning how SharePlay works. Next, you'll explore the app you'll be adding SharePlay support to using the Group Activities framework. After that, you'll learn how to create a custom group activity for this app, and how to manage a group activity session. Finally, you will test the SharePlay experience in the app using two iOS devices.

By the end of this chapter, you'll have learned how SharePlay works, and how to update your own apps to use it.

The following topics will be covered:

- Understanding SharePlay
- Exploring the *ShareOrder* app
- Creating a custom Group Activity
- Managing a group activity session
- Testing SharePlay in the *ShareOrder* app

Technical requirements

You will implement and test the Group Activities framework in a sample app named *ShareOrder*. A paid Apple developer account and at least two iOS devices running iOS 15.1 or later with the *ShareOrder* app installed will be required. You can also use one Mac with macOS 12.1 or later installed and one iOS device with iOS 15.1 or later installed.

The completed Xcode project for this chapter is in the `Chapter25` folder of the code bundle for this book, which can be downloaded here:

`https://github.com/PacktPublishing/iOS-15-Programming-for-Beginners-Sixth-Edition`

Check out the following video to see the code in action:

`https://bit.ly/3I9zb6Y`

Let's start by learning about SharePlay in the next section.

Understanding SharePlay

SharePlay was introduced by Apple during WWDC 2021. It enables shared user experiences for participants in a FaceTime session. For example, a user may wish to watch a video together with another user. All the user needs to do is to FaceTime with the other user, launch the video app, and initiate SharePlay. The same app will launch for the other user and play the same video, and SharePlay ensures that the video stays in sync between both users.

You can also create custom SharePlay experiences. An example of this is the *DrawTogether* app demonstrated during WWDC 2021. In the demonstration, three users initially joined a FaceTime session. One user launched the *DrawTogether* app, and initiated the SharePlay session in the app. The other users were presented with a SharePlay prompt containing a **Join** button. When the **Join** button was tapped, the *DrawTogether* app was launched for the other users, and whatever a user drew on their screen appeared on the screens of the other users.

> **Important Information**
>
> You can see how the *DrawTogether* app works and how it is implemented here: `https://developer.apple.com/videos/play/wwdc2021/10187`.
>
> You can download the *DrawTogether* app here: `https://developer.apple.com/documentation/groupactivities/drawing_content_in_a_group_session`.

SharePlay is powered by the Group Activities framework. This framework uses FaceTime to synchronize your app's activities and to invite other participants to join those activities. Objects representing shared activities must conform to the `GroupActivity` protocol. After a group activity has started, a `GroupSession` object is used to synchronize app behavior between all participants.

> **Important Information**
>
> You can find links to all of Apple's Group Activities-related videos during WWDC 2021 here:
>
> ```
> https://developer.apple.com/videos/
> wwdc2021/?q=group%20activities
> ```
>
> You can read Apple's Group Activities documentation here:
>
> ```
> https://developer.apple.com/documentation/
> GroupActivities
> ```

In this chapter, you will implement the Group Activities framework in a sample app named *ShareOrder* by following these steps:

1. Add the Group Activities capability to the *ShareOrder* app.

2. Create and configure a *ShareOrder* structure conforming to the `GroupActivity` protocol. This structure will contain metadata that describes the group activity.

3. Configure the *ShareOrder* app's user interface with a button to activate the group activity.

4. Implement a `GroupSession` object that allows your app to join a group activity session.

5. Implement a `GroupSessionMessenger` object that allows your app to send and receive messages. These messages are used to synchronize what the users do in the app.

Before you do so, let's see how the *ShareOrder* app works in the next section.

Exploring the ShareOrder app

The app you will be working on, *ShareOrder*, is a simple app that records and displays what you want to order at a restaurant. Let's build and run this app to see how it works. Follow these steps:

1. If you have not already done so, download the `Chapter25` folder of the code bundle for this book at this link: `https://github.com/PacktPublishing/ iOS-15-Programming-for-Beginners-Sixth-Edition`.

2. Open the `Chapter25` folder, and you'll see two folders, `ShareOrder-start` and `ShareOrder-complete`. The first folder contains the app that you will be modifying for this lesson, and the second contains the completed app.

3. Open the `ShareOrder-start` folder and open the `ShareOrder` Xcode project. Click on the `Main` storyboard file in the Project navigator. You should see a + button in the navigation bar and a table view filling the rest of the screen.

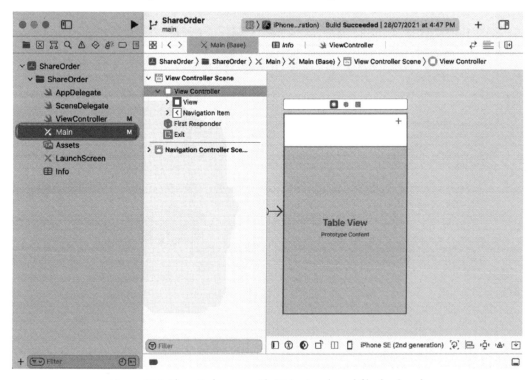

Figure 25.1: ShareOrder app with Main storyboard file displayed

The app will display a screen showing an empty table view upon launch. Tapping on the + button will present a dialog box, which allows you to enter an order, which will then appear in the table view.

4. Click the `ViewController` file in the Project navigator. You should see the following code in the Editor area:

```swift
import UIKit
class ViewController: UIViewController {
    var orders: [String] = []
    @IBOutlet var tableView: UITableView!
    override func viewDidLoad() {
        super.viewDidLoad()
        title = "ShareOrder"
        tableView.register(UITableViewCell.self,
        forCellReuseIdentifier: "orderCell")
    }
    @IBAction func addOrder(_ sender: UIBarButtonItem)
    {
        let alert = UIAlertController(title: "New
        Order", message: "Add a new order",
        preferredStyle: .alert)
        let saveAction = UIAlertAction(title: "Save",
        style: .default) {
            [unowned self] action in
            guard let textField =
            alert.textFields?.first,
            let orderToSave = textField.text else {
                return
            }
            self.orders.append(orderToSave)
            self.tableView.reloadData()
        }
        let cancelAction = UIAlertAction(title:
        "Cancel", style: .cancel)
        alert.addTextField()
        alert.addAction(saveAction)
        alert.addAction(cancelAction)
```

```
            present(alert, animated: true)
        }
    }
}
extension ViewController: UITableViewDataSource {
    func tableView(_ tableView: UITableView,
    numberOfRowsInSection section: Int) -> Int {
        orders.count
    }
    func tableView(_ tableView: UITableView,
    cellForRowAt indexPath: IndexPath) ->
    UITableViewCell {
        let cell = tableView.dequeueReusableCell
        (withIdentifier: "orderCell", for: indexPath)
        cell.textLabel?.text = orders[indexPath.row]
        return cell
    }
}
```

Let's break this down:

```
var orders: [String] = []
```

This property holds an array of orders, which are of type `String`. This array will be the data source for the table view in the app.

```
@IBOutlet var tableView: UITableView!
```

This outlet is connected to the table view in the view controller scene inside the Main storyboard file.

`viewDidLoad()` method:

The code in this method sets the title in the navigation bar to `ShareOrder`, and registers the reuse identifier `orderCell` for the table view cells.

`addOrder(_:)` method:

This method is connected to the + button in the navigation bar. It creates an alert with a text field and two buttons, **Save** and **Cancel**. Tapping the + button will display the alert. You can then enter your order in the text field. Tapping **Save** will add the order to the `orders` array and reload the table view. Tapping **Cancel** will dismiss the alert.

> **Tip**
>
> You may wish to review *Chapter 17, Getting Started with JSON Files*, where you used an alert to ensure that a location has been selected before you choose a cuisine.

```
extension ViewController: UITableViewDataSource { ...
}
```

This extension contains the data source methods for the table view. The number of rows to be displayed is the same as the number of orders in the `orders` array. Each cell in the table view will display the corresponding string in the `orders` array.

> **Tip**
>
> You may wish to review *Chapter 15, Getting Started with Table Views*, which covers the table view data source methods in more detail.

Build and run the app. Tap the + button, enter some text in the alert's text field, and tap **Save**. It will appear in the table view, as shown below:

Figure 25.2: iOS Simulator running the ShareOrder app

Now that you are familiar with the *ShareOrder* app and how it works, you will add Group Activities support for it. After you have done so, adding an order during a SharePlay session will make the order appear on the screen of all participants. You'll start by creating a custom Group Activity for the *ShareOrder* app in the next section.

Creating a custom Group Activity

You have seen that the *ShareOrder* app lets you add orders which will be displayed on the screen. You will add a group activity for this app that lets participants add orders during a SharePlay session which will appear on every participant's screen. A custom object is required to represent this activity. The steps required to implement this are as follows:

- Add the Group Activities entitlement to the *ShareOrder* app.

- Create a new structure named `ShareOrder` that conforms to the `GroupActivity` protocol, and configure the group activity metadata.

- Add a button to the *ShareOrder* app's user interface and add an action for this button to activate the group activity.

> **Important Information**
> You can learn more about creating a custom Group Activity at this link:
> `https://developer.apple.com/documentation/`
> `groupactivities/inviting-participants-to-share-an-`
> `activity`.

Let's start by adding the Group Activities entitlement to the *ShareOrder* app in the next section.

Adding the Group Activities entitlement

Because your app will have interactions between different devices, it must have the `com.apple.developer.group-session` entitlement. You'll use Xcode to add this entitlement to your app. Note that you need a paid Apple developer account for this. Follow these steps:

1. Click the `ShareOrder` project (the topmost item in the Project navigator) and click the `ShareOrder` target. Select the **Signing & Capabilities** pane in the Editor area. Verify that **Team** has been set to a paid Apple developer account.

Figure 25.3: Xcode Signing & Capabilities pane with account set

> **Tip**
>
> Instructions on how to set a development team and how to run your app on an iOS device are provided in *Chapter 1, Getting Familiar with Xcode*.
>
> Instructions on how to get a paid Apple Developer account are provided in *Chapter 26, Testing and Submitting Your App to the App Store*.

2. Plug in one of your iOS devices running iOS 15 and verify that the *ShareOrder* app can run on your device.

3. In the **Signing and Capabilities** pane, click the + button to add a capability to the *ShareOrder* app.

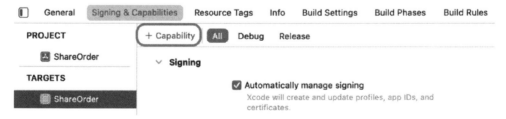

Figure 25.4: Xcode Signing and Capabilities pane with + button highlighted

4.   In the window that appears, search for and double-click the Group Activities capability to add it to the *ShareOrder* app:

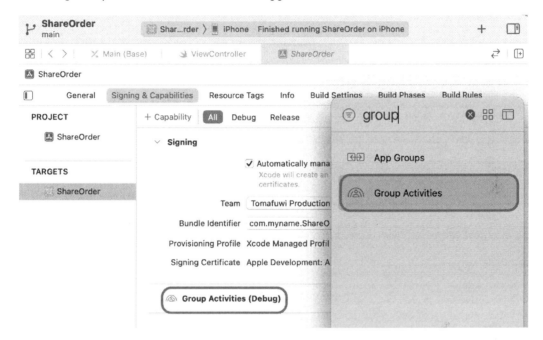

Figure 25.5: Group Activities capability added to ShareOrder app

You have added the Group Activities entitlement to the *ShareOrder* app. Next, you will create a `ShareOrder` structure to represent a group activity in the next section.

Creating the ShareOrder structure

The activity that you will implement for the *ShareOrder* app will let orders added during a SharePlay session appear on the screen of all participants. You need an object to represent this activity. You will implement this object by creating a `ShareOrder` structure. This structure will conform the `GroupActivity` protocol, and will contain metadata describing the activity. To create and configure the `ShareOrder` structure, follow these steps:

1.   Click the `ViewController` file in the Project navigator and import the `GroupActivities` framework as shown:

```
import UIKit
import GroupActivities
```

2. Add the following extension after the last curly brace to create and configure the ShareOrder structure:

```
extension ViewController {
    struct ShareOrder: GroupActivity {
        var metadata: GroupActivityMetadata {
            var metadata = GroupActivityMetadata()
            metadata.title = NSLocalizedString("Share
            Order", comment: "Title of group activity")
            metadata.type = .generic
            return metadata
        }
    }
}
```

This structure represents the *ShareOrder* app's shareable experience. It conforms to the GroupActivity protocol, which provides context and metadata to start an activity-related session. Here, you use a computed property named metadata to set the metadata title and the comment. For custom activities, the metadata type is set to .generic.

You have created and configured the ShareOrder structure. In the next section, you will add a button to the *ShareOrder* app's user interface and configure this button to activate the group activity during a FaceTime session.

Activating a custom group activity

You have created and configured the ShareOrder structure used to represent a custom group activity for the *ShareOrder* app. Now you will add a button to the *ShareOrder* app's navigation bar to activate this group activity while you are in a FaceTime session with other participants. Follow these steps:

1. Click the Main storyboard file in the Project navigator and click the Library button.

2. In the Library's filter field, search for a **Bar Button Item** object and drag it to the navigation bar next to the + button:

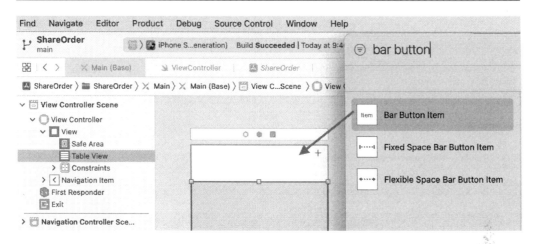

Figure 25.6: Library with Bar Button Item selected

3. With the bar button item selected, click the Attributes inspector button. Under **Bar Item**, set **Image** to `person.2.fill`:

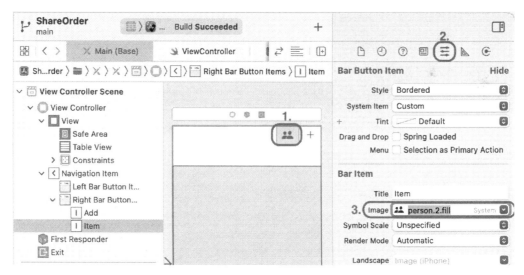

Figure 25.7: Attributes inspector showing bar button item with Image set to person.2.fill

This sets the icon for the bar button item.

4. Click the Adjust Editor Options button and choose **Assistant** to display the assistant editor.

    The contents of the `ViewController` file will appear in the assistant editor.

5. *Control + Drag* from the bar button item you just added to just before the `addOrder(_:)` method in the assistant editor.

    A pop-up dialog box will appear.

6. In the **Name** field, enter the name `activateGroupActivity` and click **Connect**:

Figure 25.8: Pop-up dialog box with Name set to activateGroupActivity

7. Add the following code to the `activateGroupActivity(_:)` method to activate the group activity when the bar button item is tapped:

```
@IBAction func activateGroupActivity(_ sender: Any) {
    Task {
        do {
            try await ShareOrder().activate()
        } catch {
            print("Unable to activate")
        }
    }
}
```

This will display a SharePlay prompt with a **Join** button to all participants in the FaceTime session.

8. Click the **x** button to close the assistant editor.

You have just added a button that will activate your group activity when tapped. In the next section, you'll learn how to manage a group activity session in the *ShareOrder* app.

Managing a group activity session

You have created the `ShareOrder` structure to represent a group activity for the *ShareOrder* app, and you have added a button to the app's navigation bar to activate the group activity during a FaceTime session. Now you need to add code to allow participants to join this group activity session and keep all participants in sync with one another. The steps required to implement this are as follows:

- Create a `GroupSession` object that lets the app join a group activity session.

- Create a `GroupSessionMessenger` object that lets the app send and receive messages to synchronize content.

> **Important Information**
>
> You can learn more about session management at this link: `https://developer.apple.com/documentation/groupactivities/joining-your-app-to-a-shared-activity`.

Let's see how to implement and configure a `GroupSession` object for the *ShareOrder* app in the next section.

Implementing a GroupSession object

The *ShareOrder* app currently has an object to represent the group activity, and a button that is used to activate the group activity during a FaceTime session. You'll add code to your app to implement a `GroupSession` object, which will allow participants to join the group activity session. To implement and configure the `GroupSession` object for the *ShareOrder* app, follow these steps:

1. Click the `ViewController` file in the Project navigator. Add an optional property after the `orders` property to hold an instance of the group activity session:

   ```
   var orders: [String] = []
   var groupSession: GroupSession<ShareOrder>?
   ```

2. Add the following code to `viewDidLoad()` to create an asynchronous task to receive a group session:

   ```
   override func viewDidLoad() {
       super.viewDidLoad()
       title = "ShareOrder"
       tableView.register(UITableViewCell.self,
       forCellReuseIdentifier: "orderCell")
   ```

```
Task {
    for await session in ShareOrder.sessions() {
        configureGroupSession(session)
    }
}
```

> **Tip**
>
> Task is a unit of asynchronous work, and is covered in *Chapter 24, Getting Started with Swift Concurrency.*

You'll see an error because configureGroupSession(_:) has not yet been implemented.

3. Add the following code to the extension after the ShareOrder structure definition to implement the configureGroupSession(_:) method:

```
func configureGroupSession(_ groupSession:
GroupSession<ShareOrder>) {
    orders.removeAll()
    self.groupSession = groupSession
}
```

This method removes all the orders in the orders array, then assigns the received group activity session to the groupSession property.

4. Modify the configureGroupSession(_:) method by adding code to join the group activity session:

```
func configureGroupSession(_ groupSession:
GroupSession<ShareOrder>) {
    orders.removeAll()
    self.groupSession = groupSession
    groupSession.join()
}
```

You can choose **Product | Build** from the Xcode menu bar to verify there are no errors in the ShareOrder project at this point.

Now that you've implemented and configured the GroupSession object, you'll implement and configure a GroupSessionMessenger object for the *ShareOrder* app in the next section.

Implementing a GroupSessionMessenger object

Once the users of the *ShareOrder* app have joined the SharePlay session, any orders they add to the app will appear on everyone's screen. This synchronization is handled by a `GroupSessionMessenger` object, which can send messages to and receive messages from other devices in the group activity session. Do note that it is important to keep the size of the messages small, as large message sizes may cause apps to crash. For this app, the messages will just hold the strings containing the orders submitted, which will be quite small. To implement the `GroupSessionMessenger` object for the *ShareOrder* app, follow these steps:

1. In the `ViewController` file, add a new optional property after the `groupSession` property to hold an instance of `GroupSessionMessenger`:

    ```
    var groupSession: GroupSession<ShareOrder>?
    var messenger: GroupSessionMessenger?
    ```

2. Modify the `configureGroupSession(_:)` method to create an instance of `GroupSessionMessenger` and assign it to the `messenger` property:

    ```
    func configureGroupSession(_ groupSession:
    GroupSession<ShareOrder>) {
        orders.removeAll()
        self.groupSession = groupSession
        let messenger = GroupSessionMessenger(session:
        groupSession)
        self.messenger = messenger
        groupSession.join()
    }
    ```

3. Add an asynchronous task to receive `GroupSessionMessenger` messages after the `messenger` property assignment:

    ```
        let messenger = GroupSessionMessenger(session:
        groupSession)
        self.messenger = messenger
        Task.detached { [weak self] in
            for await (message, _) in messenger.messages(of:
            String.self) {
                await self?.handle(message)
            }
        }
    ```

The received `GroupSessionMessenger` message contains a string representing an order. You will implement a `handle(_:)` method and pass the message to this method to be processed. You'll see an error because the `handle(_:)` method has not yet been implemented.

4. Implement the `handle(_:)` method after the `configureGroupSession(_:)` method as shown:

```
func handle(_ message: String) {
    self.orders.append(message)
    self.tableView.reloadData()
}
```

This method appends the string from the message to the `orders` array, and reloads the table view.

5. Modify the `addOrder(_:)` method as follows to send a `GroupSessionMessenger` message when a participant taps the + button:

```
self.orders.append(orderToSave)
if let messenger = messenger {
    Task {
        do {
            try await messenger.send(orderToSave)
        } catch {
            print("Failed to send")
        }
    }
}
self.tableView.reloadData()
```

The code you added to the `addOrder(_:)` method creates an asynchronous task that sends the message containing the order to all other participants in the FaceTime session. When the message is received, it will be processed by the `handle(_:)` method, which adds the order to the `orders` array and reloads the table view.

Build and run the *ShareOrder* app on your iOS 15 device. It should work as it did before. In the next section, you'll test SharePlay in the *ShareOrder* app by using two iOS devices in a FaceTime session.

Testing SharePlay in the ShareOrder app

You have added all the code required to implement SharePlay in the *ShareOrder* app. In order to test it, you'll need two iOS devices running iOS 15.1 or later with the *ShareOrder* app installed. You could also use a Mac running macOS 12.1 Monterey or later as one of the devices. You'll initiate a FaceTime session between both devices and initiate a SharePlay session. You should be able to add orders from either device, and any orders you add will appear on both screens. Follow these steps:

1. Install the *ShareOrder* app on your second iOS device.

2. Start a FaceTime call between the two devices and launch the *ShareOrder* app on the first device.

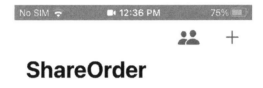

Figure 25.9: ShareOrder running on first device during FaceTime call

3. Tap the button to activate the group activity. You should see a SharePlay prompt on the second device.

Figure 25.10: Tapping button on first device triggers SharePlay prompt on second device

4. Tap the **Join** button in the SharePlay prompt, and the *ShareOrder* app will launch on the second device. Add an order using the + button, and it will appear on the screen of both devices.

Figure 25.11: Same orders appear on both devices

Congratulations! You've just implemented SharePlay in the *ShareOrder* app!

Summary

In this chapter, you implemented SharePlay for the *ShareOrder* app by adding Group Activities support to it.

You started by learning how SharePlay works. Next, you explored the *ShareOrder* app to see how it works. After that, you created a custom group activity for this app, and added code to manage a group activity session. Finally, you tested the SharePlay experience in the app using two iOS devices.

You now understand the basics of SharePlay and will now be able to add custom group activities into your own apps.

In the next chapter, you will learn how to test and submit your app to the App Store.

26

Testing and Submitting Your App to the App Store

Congratulations! You have reached the final chapter of this book!

Over the course of this book, you have learned about the Swift programming language and how to build an entire app using Xcode. However, you've only been running your app in the iOS Simulator or on your own device using a free Apple Developer account.

In this chapter, you will start by learning how to obtain a paid Apple Developer account. Next, you'll learn about certificates, identifiers, test device registration, and provisioning profiles. After that, you'll learn how to create an App Store listing and submit your app to the App Store. Finally, you'll learn how to conduct testing for your app using internal and external testers.

By the end of this chapter, you'll have learned how to build and submit apps to the App Store and how to conduct internal and external testing for your app.

The following topics will be covered:

- Getting an Apple Developer account

- Exploring your Apple Developer account

- Submitting your app to the App Store

- Conducting internal and external testing

Technical requirements

You will need an Apple ID and a paid Apple Developer account to complete this chapter.

There are no project files for this chapter as it is meant to be a reference on how to submit apps and is not specific to any particular app.

> **Important Information**
>
> To see the latest updates to the App Store, visit `https://developer.apple.com/app-store/whats-new/`.
>
> Apple has introduced a new continuous integration and delivery service built into Xcode 13 named **Xcode Cloud**. To learn more, visit this link: `https://developer.apple.com/xcode-cloud/`.
>
> To see more information on how to submit your apps, visit `https://developer.apple.com/app-store/submissions/`.

Let's start by learning how to get a paid Apple Developer account, which is required for App Store submission, in the next section.

Getting an Apple Developer account

As you have seen in earlier chapters, all you need to test your app on a device is a free Apple ID. But the apps will only work for a few days, and you will not be able to add advanced features such as Sign in with Apple or upload your app to the App Store. For that, you need a paid Apple Developer account. Follow these steps to purchase an Individual/Sole Proprietorship Apple Developer account:

1. Go to `https://developer.apple.com/programs/` and click on the **Enroll** button.

2. Scroll to the bottom of the screen and click **Start Your Enrollment**.

3. Enter your Apple ID and password when prompted.

4. On the **Trust this browser?** screen, click **Not Now**.

5. Click **Continue enrollment on the web >**.

6. On the **Confirm your personal information** screen, enter your personal information and click **Continue** when done.

7. On the **Select your entity type** screen, choose **Individual/Sole Proprietor**. Click **Continue**.

8. On the **Review and Accept** screen, tick the checkbox at the bottom of the page and click **Continue**.

9. On the **Complete your purchase** screen, click **Purchase**.

10. Follow the onscreen directions to complete your purchase. Once you have purchased your account, go to `https://developer.apple.com/account/` and sign in with the same Apple ID that you used to purchase your developer account. You should see something similar to the following:

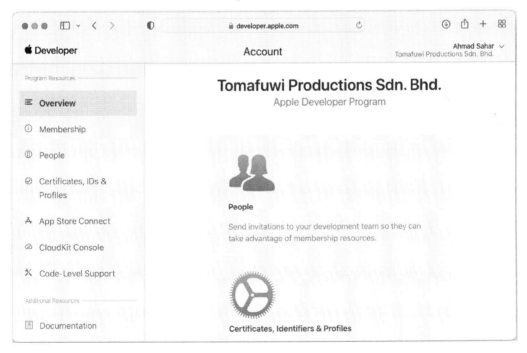

Figure 26.1: Apple Developer website with paid Apple Developer account logged in

Now that you have a paid Apple Developer account, let's learn how to configure the various settings required for your app in the next section.

Exploring your Apple Developer account

Your Apple Developer account has everything you need to develop and submit apps. You can view your membership status, add and organize members of your development team, access developer documentation, download beta software, and more. All these features are beyond the scope of this book, though, and this section will only cover what you need to do to get your app on the App Store.

First, you'll get Apple Developer certificates that you'll install on your Mac. These certificates will be used to digitally sign your app. Next, you'll need to register your app's App ID and the devices that you'll be testing your app on. After that, you'll be able to generate provisioning profiles that allow your apps to run on your test devices, and allow you to submit apps to the App Store. Let's start by learning about **certificate signing requests**, which are required to obtain Apple Developer certificates that you will install on your Mac, in the next section.

Generating a certificate signing request

Before you write apps that will be submitted to the App Store, you need to install a developer certificate on the Mac that you're running Xcode on. Certificates identify the author of an app. To get this certificate, you'll need to create a **certificate signing request** (**CSR**). Here's how to create a CSR:

1. Open the `Utilities` folder on your Mac and launch **Keychain Access**.

2. Choose **Certificate Assistant | Request a Certificate From a Certificate Authority...** from the **Keychain Access** menu:

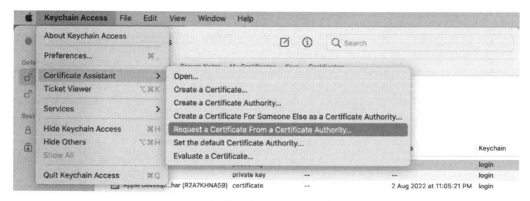

Figure 26.2: Keychain Access application

3. For the **User Email Address** field, enter the email address of the Apple ID that you used to register your Apple Developer account. In the **Common Name** field, enter your name. Select **Saved to disk** under **Request is:** and click **Continue**:

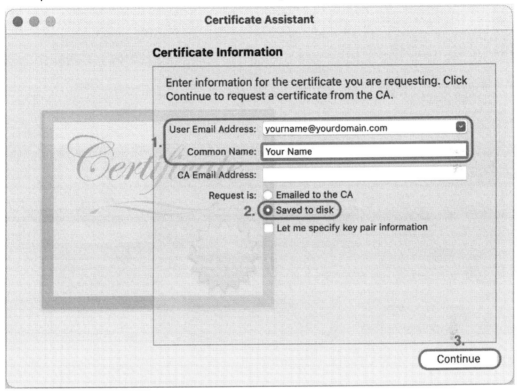

Figure 26.3: Certificate Assistant screen

4. Save the CSR to your hard disk.

5. Click **Done**.

Now that you have a CSR, let's look at how you will use it to get **development certificates** (for testing on your own device) and **distribution certificates** (for App Store submission) in the next section.

Creating development and distribution certificates

Once you have a certificate signing request, you can use it to create development and distribution certificates. Development certificates are used when you want to test your app on your test devices, and distribution certificates are used when you want to upload your app to the App Store. Here's how to create development and distribution certificates:

1. Log in to your Apple Developer account and click **Certificates, IDs & Profiles**:

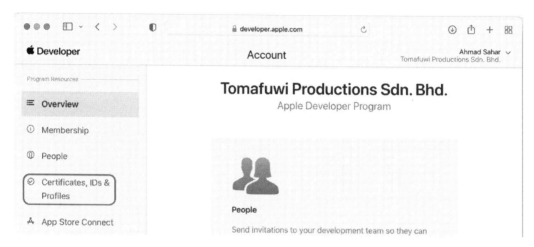

Figure 26.4: Apple Developer website with paid Apple Developer account logged in

2. You'll see the **Certificates** screen. Click the + button:

Figure 26.5: Certificates screen showing + button

3. Click the **Apple Development** radio button, and click **Continue**:

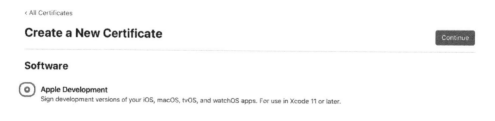

Figure 26.6: Create a New Certificate screen showing Apple Development radio button

4. Click **Choose File**:

Figure 26.7: Upload a Certificate Signing Request screen

5. Upload your CSR by selecting **Choose File** under **Upload a Certificate Signing Request**, selecting the CSR file you saved earlier to your hard disk, and clicking **Choose**.

6. Click **Continue**:

Figure 26.8: Upload a Certificate Signing Request screen with certificate uploaded

7. Your certificate will be generated automatically. Click **Download** to download the generated certificate onto your Mac:

Figure 26.9: Download Your Certificate screen

8. Double-click the downloaded certificate to install it on your Mac.

9. Repeat *Steps 3-8* again, but this time, choose **Apple Distribution** in *Step 3*:

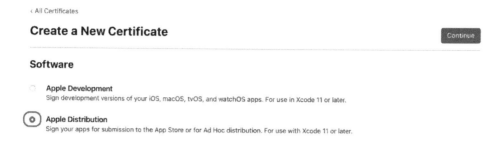

Figure 26.10: Create a New Certificate screen showing Apple Distribution radio button

Great! You now have development and distribution certificates. The next step is to register the **App ID** for your app to identify it on the App Store. You will learn how in the next section.

Registering an App ID

When you created your project in *Chapter 1, Getting Familiar with Xcode*, you created a bundle identifier for it (also known as an App ID). An App ID is used to identify your app on the App Store. You'll need to register this App ID in your developer account prior to uploading your app to the App Store. Here's how to register your App ID:

1. Log in to your Apple Developer account, and click **Certificates, IDs & Profiles**.

2. Click **Identifiers**.

3. Click the + button:

Figure 26.11: Identifiers screen

4. Click **App IDs** and click **Continue**:

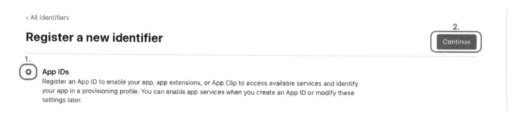

Figure 26.12: Register a new identifier screen

5.   Click **App** and click **Continue**:

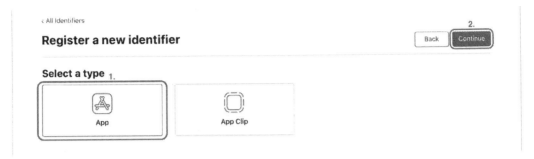

Figure 26.13: Identifier type screen

6.   **iOS** should already be selected. Enter a description for this App ID, such as `Lets Eat Packt Publishing App ID`. Tick the **Explicit** button and enter your app's **Bundle ID** in the field. Make sure that this value is the same as the bundle identifier you used when you created the project. Click the **Continue** button when you're done:

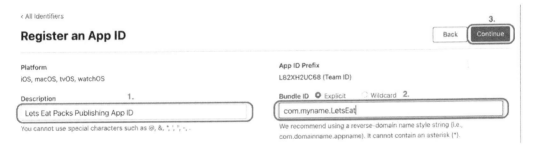

Figure 26.14: Description and Bundle ID screen

7.   Click **Register**:

Figure 26.15: Register screen

Your App ID has now been registered. Cool! Next, you'll register the devices you'll be testing your app on in the next section.

Registering your devices

To run your apps on your personal devices for testing, you will need to register them in your developer account. Here's how to register your devices:

1. Log in to your Apple Developer account, and click **Certificates, IDs & Profiles**.

2. Click **Devices**.

3. Click the + button:

Figure 26.16: Device registration screen

4. The **Register a New Device** screen appears:

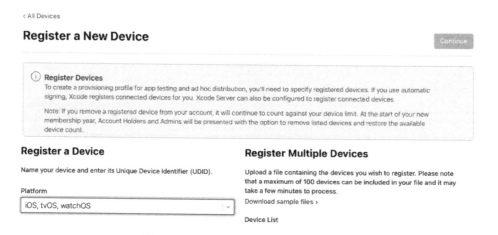

Figure 26.17: Register a New Device screen

You'll need a **Device Name** and a **Device ID** to register your device.

5. Connect your device to your Mac. Launch Xcode and choose **Devices and Simulators** from the **Window** menu. Choose the device in the left pane and copy the **Identifier** value:

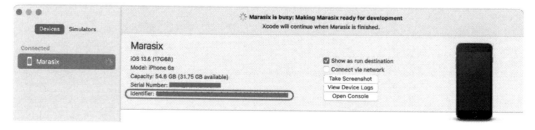

Figure 26.18: Devices and Simulators window

6. Type a name for the device in the **Device Name** field and paste the identifier value into the **Device ID (UDID)** field. Click **Continue**:

Figure 26.19: Register a New Device screen

You have successfully registered your test devices. Great! The next step is to create **provisioning profiles**. An **iOS App Development profile** is required so that your apps will be allowed to run on your test devices, and an **iOS App Store Distribution profile** is required for apps that will be uploaded to the App Store. You will create development and distribution profiles in the next section.

Creating provisioning profiles

You will need to create two provisioning profiles. An iOS app development profile is required for apps to run on test devices. An iOS App Store distribution profile is used to submit your app to the App Store. Here's how to create the development profile:

1. Log in to your Apple Developer account, and click **Certificates, IDs & Profiles**.

2. Click **Profiles**.

3. Click the + button:

Figure 26.20: Profiles screen

4.   Click **iOS App Development** and click **Continue**:

Figure 26.21: Register a New Provisioning Profile screen

5.   Select the **App ID** for the app you want to test and click **Continue**:

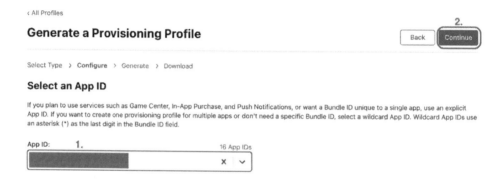

Figure 26.22: Selecting an App ID screen

6.   Select a **Development** certificate and click **Continue**:

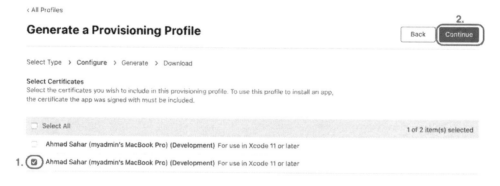

Figure 26.23: Selecting development certificate screen

7. Tick all of the devices you will be testing this app on and click **Continue**:

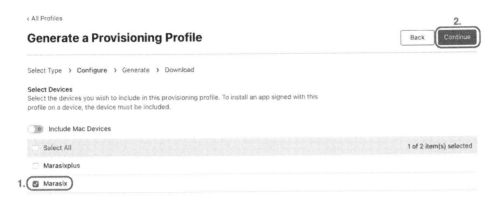

Figure 26.24: Selecting device screen

8. Enter a name for the profile and click **Generate**:

Figure 26.25: Generating development profile screen

9. Click the **Download** button to download the profile.

10. Double-click the profile to install it.

Next, you'll create a distribution profile:

1. Click the **All Profiles** link to go back to the previous page:

Figure 26.26: All Profiles link

2. Click the + button:

Figure 26.27: Profiles screen

3. Click **App Store** and click **Continue**:

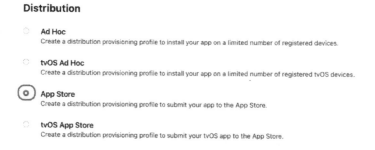

Figure 26.28: Register a New Provisioning Profile screen

4. Select the **App ID** for the app you want to publish to the App Store and click **Continue**:

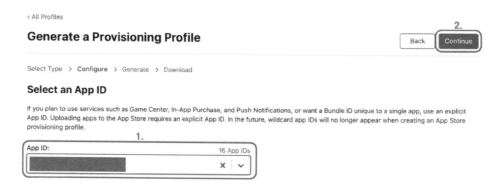

Figure 26.29: Selecting an AppID screen

5. Select a **Distribution** certificate and click **Continue**:

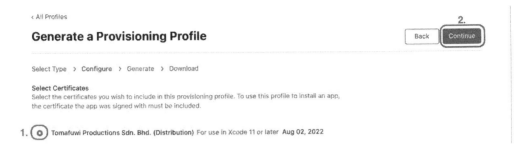

Figure 26.30: Selecting distribution certificate screen

6. Enter a name for the profile and click **Generate**:

Figure 26.31: Generating distribution profile screen

7. Click the **Download** button to download the profile.

8. Double-click the profile to install it.

You've completed all of the steps necessary prior to submitting your app to the App Store. Let's learn more about the submission process in the next section, using the *ShareOrder* app as an example.

Submitting your app to the App Store

You are now ready to submit your app to the App Store! In this section, the *ShareOrder* app will be used as an example. Let's recap what you've done up to this point. You've created development and distribution certificates, registered your App ID and test devices, and generated development and distribution profiles.

To test your app on your test devices, you'll use the development certificate, App ID, registered test devices, and development profile. To submit your app to the App Store, you'll use the distribution certificate, App ID, and distribution profile. You'll configure Xcode to manage this automatically for you.

Before you submit your app, you have to create your app's icons and get screenshots of your app. Then you can create an App Store listing, generate an archive build to be uploaded, and complete the App Store Connect information. Apple will then review your app, and if all goes well, it will appear on the App Store.

In the next section, let's see how to create icons for your app, which will appear on the device screen when the app is installed.

Creating icons for your app

Before you upload your app to the App Store, you have to create an icon set for it. Here's how to create an icon set for your app:

1. Create an icon for your app that is 1,024 x 1,024 pixels.

2. Use a website such as `https://appicon.co` to generate all the different icon sizes and download the icon set.

3. Click `Assets.xcassets` in the Project navigator and replace the `AppIcon` image set with the one you downloaded:

Figure 26.32: Assets.xcassets file showing AppIcon image set

When you run your app in the simulator or device and quit your app, you should be able to see the app's icon on the Home screen. Neat!

Let's look at how to create screenshots next. You'll need them for your App Store submission, so customers can see what your app looks like. You'll do this in the next section.

Creating screenshots for your app

You'll need screenshots of your app, which will be used in your App Store listing. To create them, run your app in the simulator and click the screenshot button. It will be saved to the desktop:

Figure 26.33: Simulator showing screenshot button

Use the **iPhone 13 Pro Max, iPhone 8 Plus, iPad Pro (12.9-inch) (2nd generation),** and **iPad Pro (12.9-inch) (5th generation)** simulators, and get a few screenshots on each showing all of the different features of your app. The reason why you have to use all these simulators is that you will need screenshots of your app running on different screen sizes, which will be discussed in more detail in the next section, where you will learn how to create an App Store listing. The App Store listing contains all of the information about your app that will be displayed in the App Store, so customers can make an informed decision about downloading or purchasing your app.

Creating an App Store listing

Now that you have icons and screenshots of your app, you'll create the App Store listing. This allows customers to see information about your app before they download it. Follow these steps:

1. Go to http://appstoreconnect.apple.com and select **My Apps**:

Figure 26.34: App Store Connect website

2. Click the + button at the top-left of the screen and select **New App**:

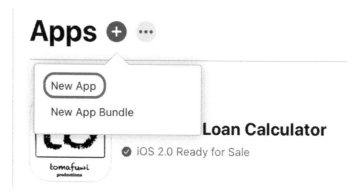

Figure 26.35: New App button and menu

3. A **New App** screen displaying a list of fields will appear:

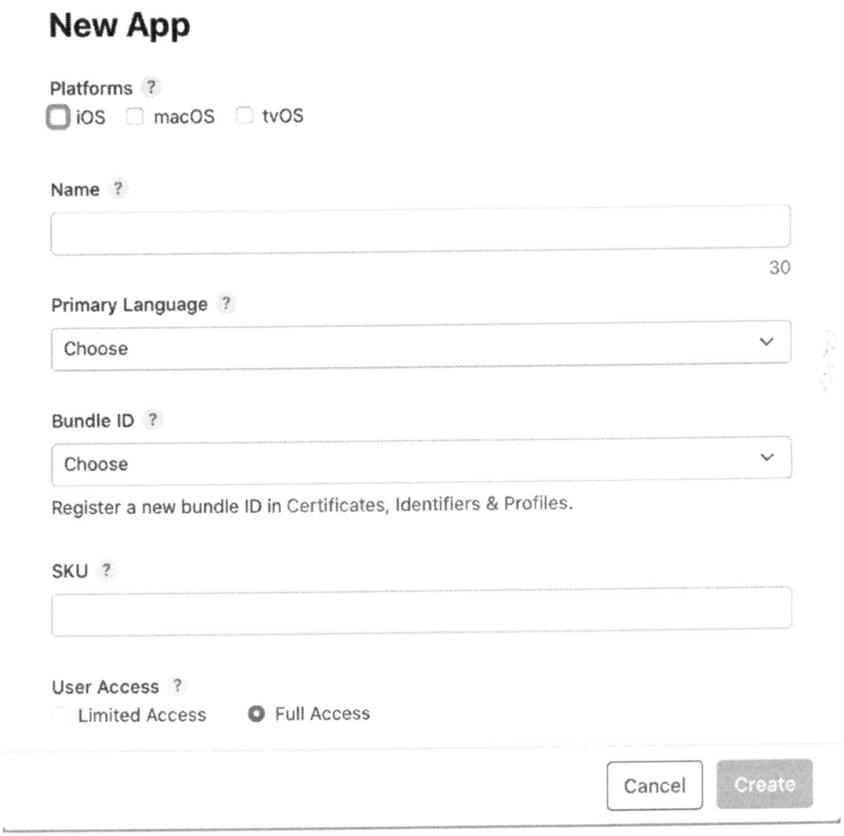

New App

Platforms ?

☐ iOS   ☐ macOS   ☐ tvOS

Name ?

```
                                                              30
```

Primary Language ?

Choose   ⌄

Bundle ID ?

Choose   ⌄

Register a new bundle ID in Certificates, Identifiers & Profiles.

SKU ?

User Access ?

Limited Access   ● Full Access

Cancel   Create

Figure 26.36: App details screen

Enter your app details:

Platforms: All the platforms your app supports (iOS, macOS, and/or tvOS).

Name: The name of your app.

Primary Language: The language your app uses.

BundleID: The bundleID you created earlier.

SKU: Any reference number or string that you use to refer to your app.

User Access: Manages who in your developer account team can see this app in App Store Connect. If you're the only one in your team, just set it to **Full Access**.

Click **Create** when you're done.

The app will now be listed in your account, but you still need to upload the app and all of the information about it. To upload the app, you need to create an archive build, and you will learn how to do that in the next section.

Creating an archive build

You'll create an archive build that will be submitted to Apple for placement on the App Store. This will also be used for your internal and external testing. Here are the steps to create an archive build:

1. Open Xcode, select the project name in the Project navigator, and select the **General** pane. In the **Identity** section, you can change the **Version** and **Build** number as you see fit. For instance, if this is the first version of your app and the first time you have built it, you can set **Version** to 1.0 and **Build** to 1:

Figure 26.37: Editor area showing General pane

2. Select the **Signing & Capabilities** pane. Make sure **Automatically manage signing** is ticked. This will allow Xcode to create certificates, app IDs, and profiles, and register devices that are connected to your Mac. Select your paid developer account in the **Team** menu:

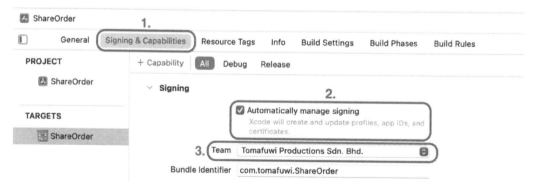

Figure 26.38: Editor area showing Signing & Capabilities pane

3. Select **Any iOS Device** as the build destination:

Figure 26.39: Scheme menu with Any iOS Device selected

4. If your app does not use encryption, update your `Info.plist` file by adding `ITSAppUsesNonExemptEncryption`, making its type `Boolean`, and setting its value to `NO`:

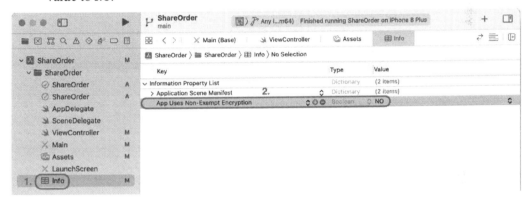

Figure 26.40: Project navigator with Info.plist selected

5. Select **Archive** from the **Product** menu:

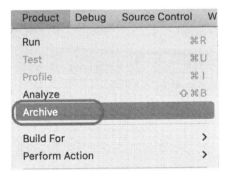

Figure 26.41: Product menu with Archive selected

6. The **Organizer** window appears with the **Archives** tab selected. Your app will appear on this screen. Select it and click the **Distribute App** button:

Figure 26.42: Organizer window with Distribute App button selected

7. Select **App Store Connect** and click **Next**:

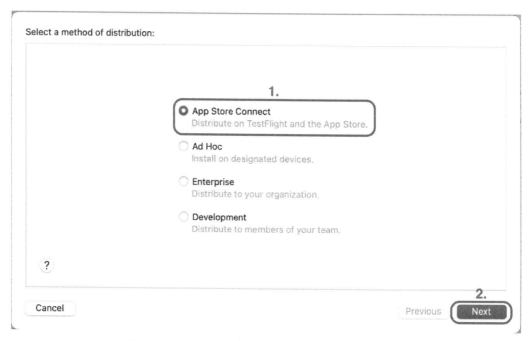

Figure 26.43: Method of the distribution selection screen

8. Select **Upload** and click **Next**:

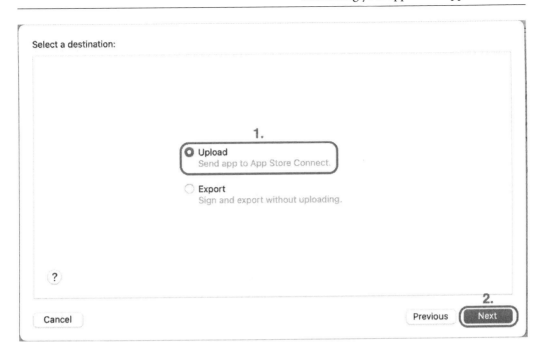

Figure 26.44: Destination selection screen

9. Leave the defaults as they are and click **Next**:

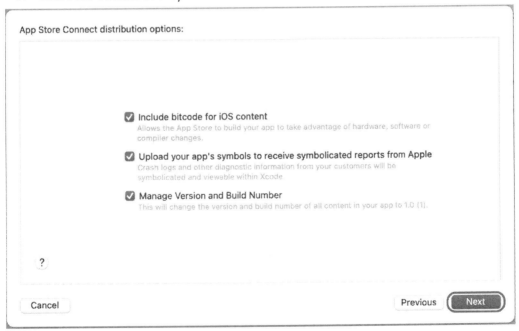

Figure 26.45: Distribution options selection screen

10. Select **Automatically Manage Signing** and click **Next**:

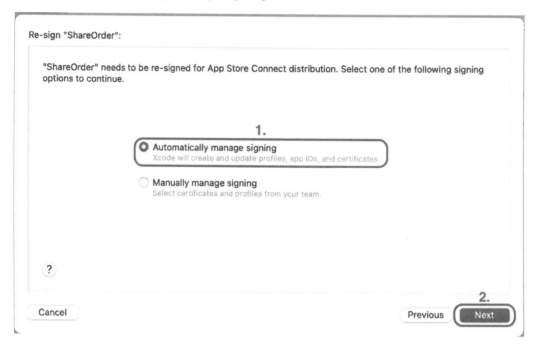

Figure 26.46: Signing screen

11. If you're prompted for a password, enter the Mac account password and click **Always Allow**.

12. Click **Upload**:

Figure 26.47: Content review screen

13. Wait for the upload to complete.

14. Click **Done**:

Figure 26.48: Archive upload complete screen

At this point, the build of the app that will be distributed by the App Store has been uploaded. In the next section, you'll learn how to upload screenshots and complete the information about your app that will appear on the App Store along with the app.

Completing the information in App Store Connect

Your app has been uploaded, but you will still need to complete the information about your app in App Store Connect. Here are the steps:

1. Go to `http://appstoreconnect.apple.com` and select **My Apps**.

2. Select the app that you just created:

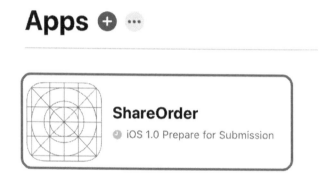

Figure 26.49: Apps screen with your app selected

3. Select **App Information** on the left side of the screen, and make sure all of the information is correct:

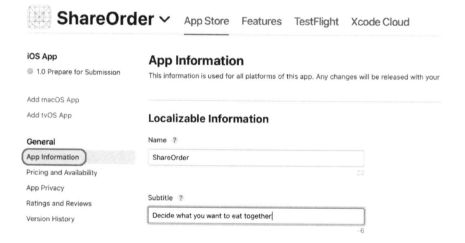

Figure 26.50: App Information screen

4. Do the same for the **Pricing and Availability** and **App Privacy** sections:

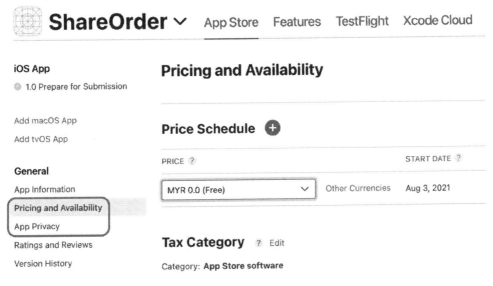

Figure 26.51: App Pricing and Availability screen

5. Select **Prepare for Submission** on the left side of the screen. In the **App Preview and Screenshots** section, drag in the screenshots that you took earlier. Use the iPhone 13 Pro Max screenshots in the **iPhone 6.5" Display** section, the iPhone 8 Plus screenshots in the **iPhone 5.5" Display** section, and the iPad screenshots in their respective sections:

Figure 26.52: Prepare for Submission screen showing App Preview and Screenshots section

6. Scroll down and fill in the **Promotional Text**, **Description**, **Keywords**, **Support URL**, and **Marketing URL** fields:

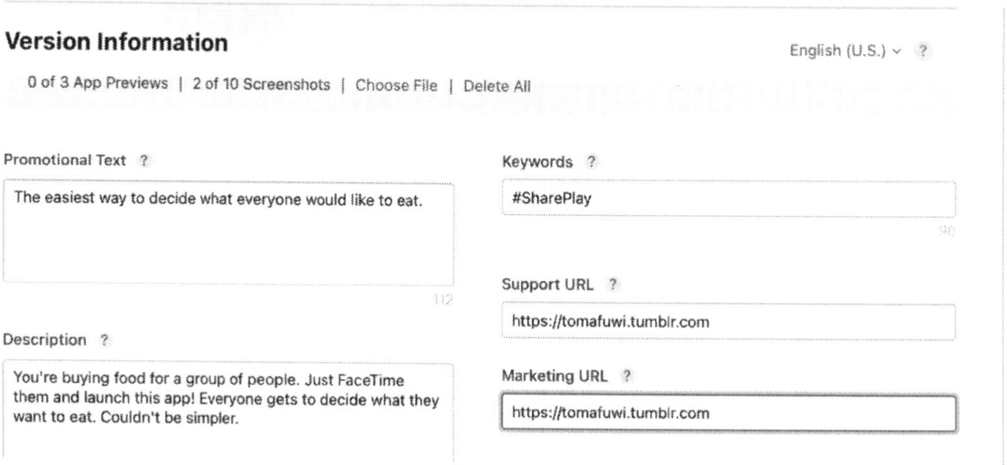

Version Information
English (U.S.)
0 of 3 App Previews | 2 of 10 Screenshots | Choose File | Delete All
Promotional Text
The easiest way to decide what everyone would like to eat.
112
Description
You're buying food for a group of people. Just FaceTime them and launch this app! Everyone gets to decide what they want to eat. Couldn't be simpler.
Keywords
#SharePlay
90
Support URL
https://tomafuwi.tumblr.com
Marketing URL
https://tomafuwi.tumblr.com

Figure 26.53: Version Information section

7. Scroll down to the **Build** section and you'll see the archive build you uploaded earlier. If you don't see it, click the + button, select a build, and click **Done**:

Build
Upload your builds using one of several tools. See Upload Tools
Select a build before you submit your app

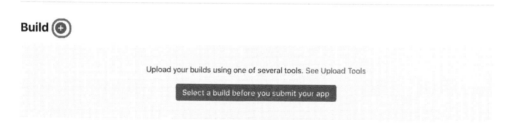

Figure 26.54: Build selection screen

8. Verify that your build is in the **Build** section:

Build

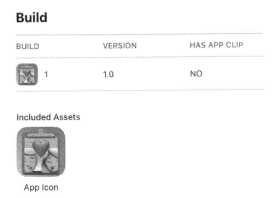

BUILD	VERSION	HAS APP CLIP
1	1.0	NO

Included Assets

App Icon

Figure 26.55: Build section

9. Scroll down to the **General App Information** section and fill in all the required details:

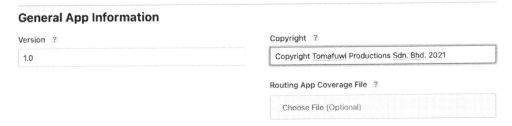

General App Information

Version ?

1.0

Copyright ?

Copyright Tomafuwi Productions Sdn. Bhd. 2021

Routing App Coverage File ?

Choose File (Optional)

Figure 26.56: General App Information section with Edit button shown

10. Scroll down to the **App Review Information** section. If you would like to provide any additional information to the app reviewer, put it here:

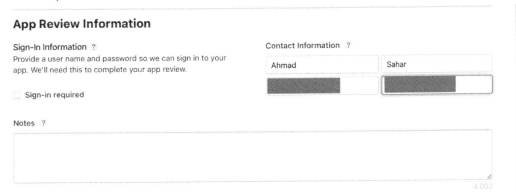

App Review Information

Sign-In Information ?
Provide a user name and password so we can sign in to your app. We'll need this to complete your app review.

☐ Sign-in required

Contact Information ?

Ahmad   Sahar

Notes ?

Figure 26.57: App Review Information section

11. Scroll down to the **Version Release** section and maintain the default settings:

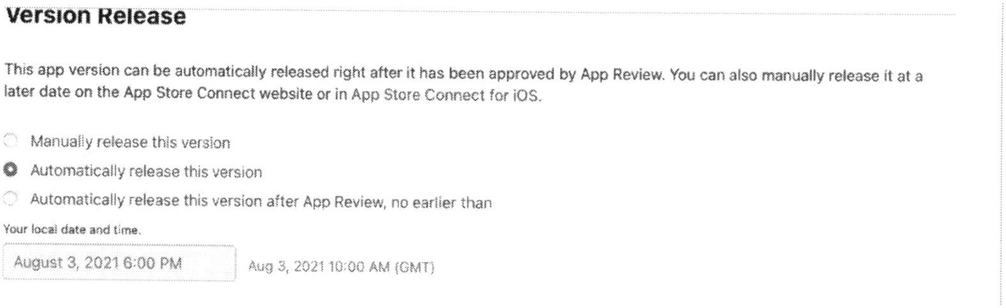

Figure 26.58: Version Release section

12. Scroll back up to the top of the screen and click the **Submit for Review** button:

iOS App 1.0

Save   Submit for Review

Figure 26.59: Submit for Review button

13. Verify that the app status has changed to **Waiting for Review**:

Figure 26.60: App status showing Waiting for Review

You will need to wait for Apple to review the app, and you will receive an email if your app is approved or rejected. If your app is rejected, there will be a link that takes you to the Apple Resolution Center page, which describes why your app was rejected. After you have fixed the issues, you can then update the archive and resubmit.

You now know how to submit your app to the App Store! Awesome!

In the next section, you'll learn how to conduct internal and external testing for your app, which is important in ensuring that the app is high quality and bug-free.

Testing your app

Apple has a facility named **TestFlight** that allows you to distribute your apps to testers prior to releasing it to the App Store. You'll need to download the TestFlight app, available from `https://developer.apple.com/testflight/`, to test your app. Your testers can be members of your internal team (internal testers) or the general public (external testers). Let's see how to allow internal team members to test your app first in the next section.

Testing your app internally

Internal testing is good when the app is in an early stage of development. It only involves members of your internal team. Apple does not review apps for internal testers. You can send builds to up to 100 testers for internal testing. Follow these steps.

1. Go to `http://appstoreconnect.apple.com` and select **My Apps**.

2. Select the app that you want to test.

3. Click the **TestFlight** tab:

Figure 26.61: TestFlight tab

4. Click the + button next to **Internal Testing** to create a new internal test group:

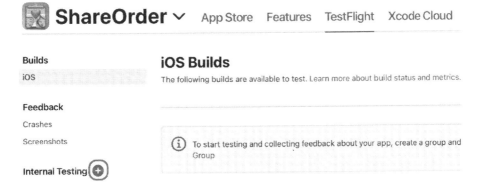

Figure 26.62: TestFlight screen showing + button

5. The **Create New Internal Group** dialog box will appear. Name your internal test group and click **Create**:

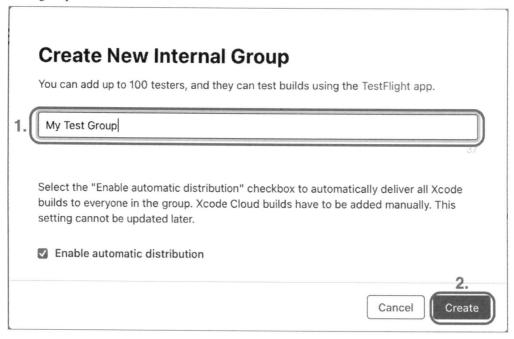

Figure 26.63: Create New Internal Group dialog box

6. After your test group has been created, click the + button to add users to your group:

Figure 26.64: Test group screen showing + button

7. Tick all of the users that you want to send test builds to and click **Add**. They'll be invited to test all available builds:

Add Testers to the Group "My Test Group"

Select up to 100 testers, and they'll be invited to test all available builds in the TestFlight app. They'll also be notified when new builds are added. If you'd like to add a tester you don't see, add them in Users and Roles.

Testers (1 Selected)   🔍   1 of 100 Total Testers

EMAIL ∧	NAME	ROLE
☑ ▆▆▆▆▆▆▆	Ahmad Sahar	Admin, Account Holder

                                    Cancel   Add

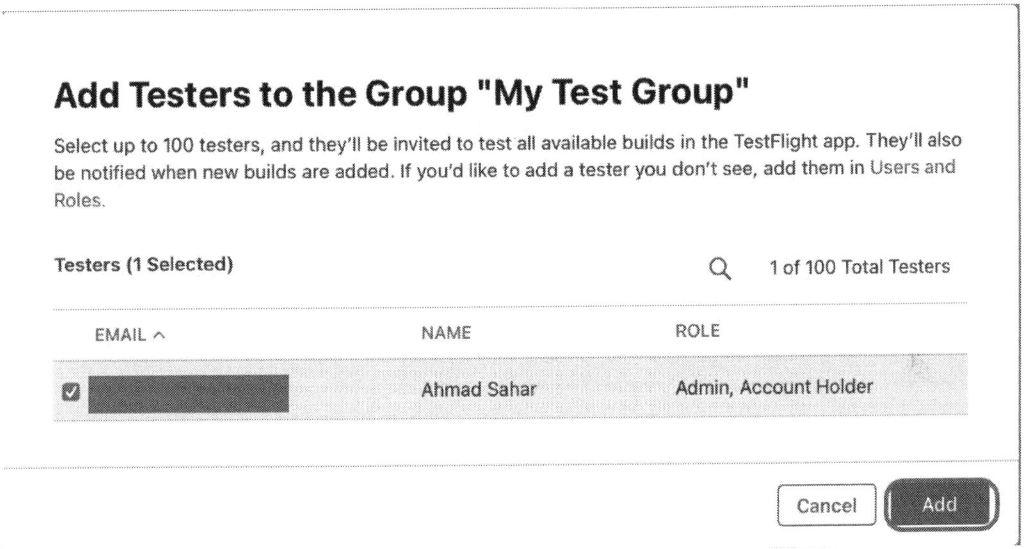

Figure 26.65: Add Testers screen

8. Verify your testers have been added:

Tester (1) ⊕   🔍 ⬆ [Edit]

EMAIL	NAME	STATUS ∧	SESSIONS	CRASHES	FEEDBACK
▆▆▆▆▆▆	Ahmad Sahar	◎ Invited Rese... Aug 3, 2021			

Figure 26.66: TestFlight screen showing Tester section

Internal testing will only involve members of your team. If you want to conduct testing with a large number of testers, you will need to do external testing, which is described in the next section.

Testing your app externally

External testing is good when the app is in the final stages of development. You can select anyone to be an external tester, and you can send builds to up to 10,000 testers. Apple may review apps for external testers. Here are the steps:

1. Go to `http://appstoreconnect.apple.com` and select **My Apps**.

2. Select the app that you want to test.

3.   Click the **TestFlight** tab:

4.   Click the + button next to **External Testing**:

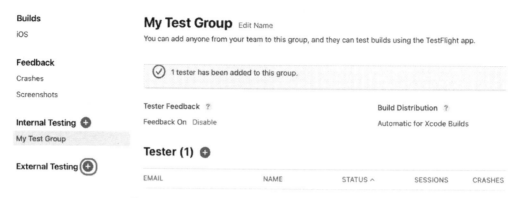

Figure 26.67: TestFlight screen showing + button

5.   Type in a name for the test group and click **Create**:

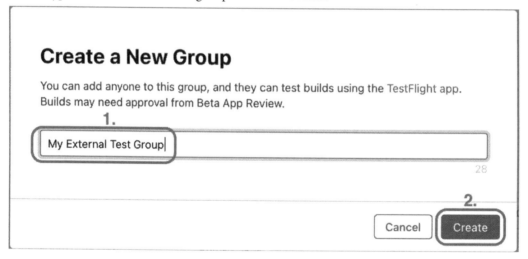

Figure 26.68: Create a New Group screen

6.   Click the + button next to **Testers** and choose **Add New Testers**:

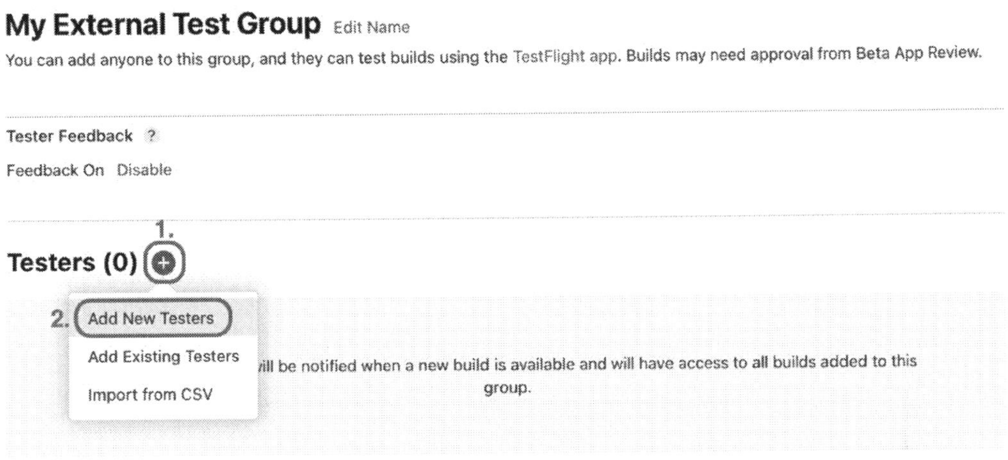

My External Test Group Edit Name

You can add anyone to this group, and they can test builds using the TestFlight app. Builds may need approval from Beta App Review.

Tester Feedback ?

Feedback On Disable

Testers (0) ⊕ *1.*

2. Add New Testers

Add Existing Testers   ill be notified when a new build is available and will have access to all builds added to this

Import from CSV   group.

Figure 26.69: Add New Testers button and menu

7. Enter the names and email addresses of your testers, and Apple will notify them automatically when a build is ready to be tested:

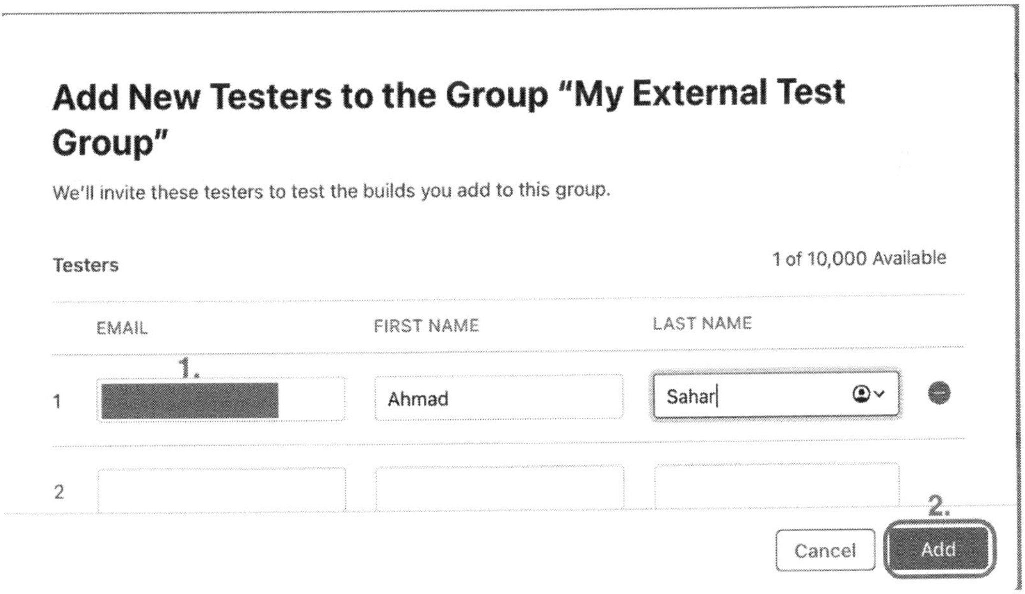

Add New Testers to the Group "My External Test Group"

We'll invite these testers to test the builds you add to this group.

Testers   1 of 10,000 Available

	EMAIL	FIRST NAME	LAST NAME	
1	*1.*	Ahmad	Sahar ⊕˅	⊖
2				

Cancel   **Add** *2.*

Figure 26.70: Add New Testers to the Group screen

8.   In the **Builds** section, click the +:

Builds (0)

No builds have been added to this group.

Figure 26.71: Builds section

9.   Choose one of your builds and click **Next**:

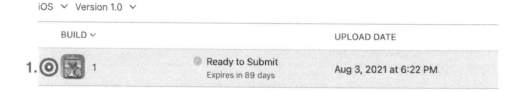

Select a Build to Test

Select a build, and we'll invite the group "My External Test Group" to start testing. Before your build can be tested, it may have to be approved by Beta App Review.

iOS ∨   Version 1.0 ∨

BUILD ∨	UPLOAD DATE
1.⊚ 🗋 1 ● Ready to Submit Expires in 89 days	Aug 3, 2021 at 6:22 PM

2.

Cancel   Next

Figure 26.72: Select a Build screen

10. Enter **Test Information** and click **Next**:

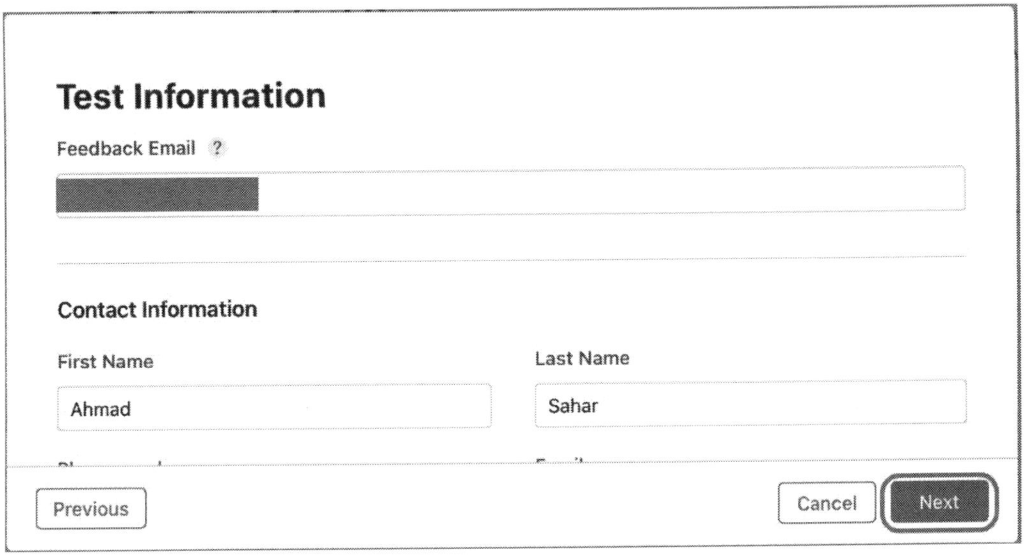

Test Information

Feedback Email ?

▬▬▬▬▬▬▬▬

Contact Information

First Name

Ahmad

Last Name

Sahar

Previous

Cancel

Next

Figure 26.73: Test Information screen

11. Enter **What to Test** and click **Submit for Review**:

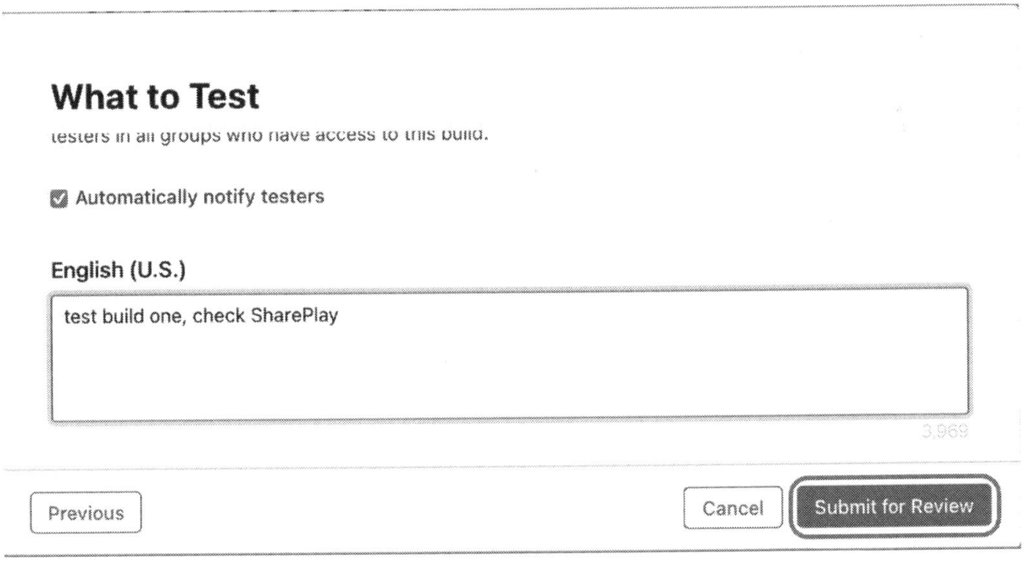

What to Test

testers in all groups who have access to this build.

☑ Automatically notify testers

English (U.S.)

test build one, check SharePlay

3,969

Previous

Cancel

Submit for Review

Figure 26.74: What to Test screen

As with app submissions to the App Store, you will need to wait for Apple to review the app, and if your app is rejected, Apple's Resolution Center page will have the details on why your app was rejected. You can then fix the issues and resubmit.

Great! You now know how to test your apps internally and externally, and you have reached the end of this book!

Summary

You have now completed the entire process of building an app and submitting it to the App Store. Congratulations!

You started by learning how to obtain an Apple Developer account. Next, you learned how to generate a certificate signing request to create certificates that allow you to test apps on your own devices and publish them on the App Store. You learned how to create a bundle identifier to uniquely identify your app on the App Store, and register your test devices. After that, you learned how to create development and production provisioning profiles, to allow apps to run on your test devices and be uploaded to the App Store. Next, you learned how to create an App Store listing and submit your release build to the App Store. Finally, you learned how to conduct testing for your app using internal and external testers.

You now know how to build and submit apps to the App Store and conduct internal and external testing for your app.

Once an app has been submitted for review, all you can do is wait for Apple to review your app. Don't worry if the app gets rejected—it happens to all developers. Work with Apple to resolve issues via the Resolution Center, and do your research to know what is and what is not acceptable to Apple.

After your apps are on the App Store, feel free to reach out to me (@shah_apple) and Craig Clayton (@thedevme) on Twitter to let us know—we would love to see what you have built.

Index

W

X

JOIN THE DISCUSSION!

The author of this book, Ahmad Sahar, will soon be hosting a Webinar for readers, and wants to hear from you.

We've set up a **Discord** server where you can get updates about the **Webinar**, as well as connect directly with Ahmad and meet other members of the iOS community.

Discuss this book, iOS development in general, and prepare for the conference!

Everyone is welcome to join, and we'd love for you to be a part of our new community.

To join, you can visit the below link or scan the QR code:

https://packt.link/iOSProgrammingforBeginners

Packt.com

Subscribe to our online digital library for full access to over 7,000 books and videos, as well as industry leading tools to help you plan your personal development and advance your career. For more information, please visit our website.

Why subscribe?

- Spend less time learning and more time coding with practical eBooks and Videos from over 4,000 industry professionals

- Improve your learning with Skill Plans built especially for you

- Get a free eBook or video every month

- Fully searchable for easy access to vital information

- Copy and paste, print, and bookmark content

Did you know that Packt offers eBook versions of every book published, with PDF and ePub files available? You can upgrade to the eBook version at packt.com and as a print book customer, you are entitled to a discount on the eBook copy. Get in touch with us at customercare@packtpub.com for more details.

At www.packt.com, you can also read a collection of free technical articles, sign up for a range of free newsletters, and receive exclusive discounts and offers on Packt books and eBooks.

Other Books You May Enjoy

If you enjoyed this book, you may be interested in these other books by Packt:

Mastering iOS 14 Programming - Fourth Edition

Mario Eguiluz Alebicto , Chris Barker , Donny Wals

ISBN: 978-1-83882-284-2

- Build a professional iOS application using Xcode 12.4 and Swift 5.3

- Create impressive new widgets for your apps with iOS 14

- Extend the audience of your app by creating an App Clip

- Improve the flow of your code with the Combine framework

- Enhance your app by using Core Location

SwiftUI Cookbook

Giordano Scalzo , Edgar Nzokwe

ISBN: 978-1-83898-186-0

- Explore various layout presentations in SwiftUI such as HStack, VStack, LazyHStack, and LazyVGrid

- Discover features that allow you to manipulate and transform objects

- Create a cross-platform app for iOS, macOS, and watchOS

- Get up to speed with drawings in SwiftUI using built-in shapes, custom paths, and polygons

- Discover modern animation and transition techniques in SwiftUI

- Add user authentication using Firebase and Sign in with Apple

- Handle data requests in your app using Core Data

Packt is searching for authors like you

If you're interested in becoming an author for Packt, please visit `authors.packtpub.com` and apply today. We have worked with thousands of developers and tech professionals, just like you, to help them share their insight with the global tech community. You can make a general application, apply for a specific hot topic that we are recruiting an author for, or submit your own idea.

Made in the USA
Columbia, SC
26 August 2022

66069678R00428